PENGUIN BOOKS

ENGLISH SOCIETY IN THE EIC

After taking his first degree in Cambridge, Roy Porter became a Fellow first of Christ's College and then of Churchill College, Cambridge, and University Lecturer in History. In 1979 he moved to the Wellcome Institute for the History of Medicine, London, where he is now Senior Lecturer in the Social History of Medicine; his current work in this field focuses upon quackery, psychiatry and popular health care. He has also worked on the history of geology. Dr Porter has edited *Patients and Practitioners* and co-edited the *Dictionary of the History of Science* and *The Anatomy of Madness* (3 vols.). He is the author of *Mind Forg'd Manacles* (Penguin 1989), which was awarded the Leo Gershoy Prize for 1988 by the American Historical Association, and co-author, with Dorothy Porter, of *In Sickness and in Health: the British Experience 1650–1850*.

THE PENGUIN SOCIAL HISTORY OF BRITAIN

General Editor: J. H. Plumb

Maurice Keen: *English Society in the Later Middle Ages 1348–1500*
Joyce Youings: *Sixteenth-Century England*
Roy Porter: *English Society in the Eighteenth Century*
Jose Harris: *Private Lives, Public Spirit: Britain 1870–1914*
John Stevenson: *British Society 1914–45*
Arthur Marwick: *British Society Since 1945*

Roy Porter

English Society in the Eighteenth Century

Revised edition

Penguin Books

PENGUIN BOOKS

Published by the Penguin Group
Penguin Books Ltd, 27 Wrights Lane, London W8 5TZ, England
Penguin Books USA Inc., 375 Hudson Street, New York, New York 10014, USA
Penguin Books Australia Ltd, Ringwood, Victoria, Australia
Penguin Books Canada Ltd, 10 Alcorn Avenue, Toronto, Ontario, Canada M4V 3B2
Penguin Books (NZ) Ltd, 182–190 Wairau Road, Auckland 10, New Zealand

Penguin Books Ltd, Registered Offices: Harmondsworth, Middlesex, England

First published in Pelican Books 1982
Published simultaneously by Allen Lane
Revised editon published in Penguin Books 1990
10 9 8 7 6

Printed in England by Clays Ltd, St Ives plc
Filmset in Monophoto Bembo

Contents

To Jack Plumb

Editorial Foreword

Historians respond to the problems of their time almost without being conscious of the process, and the focus of their study changes with the changing times. In the nineteenth century all countries of Europe and America were preoccupied with the origins of national identity, with the need to forge a living past that would give meaning not only to the present but also to the future: Ranke, Macaulay, Michelet, Bancroft and other great historians of the nineteenth century were so preoccupied. As Britain's national identity seemed to be inexorably involved with the evolution of constitutional rights, with liberty, freedom and, particularly, democracy, it is not surprising that an ever growing number of professional historians should devote all their skills and interest to constitutional, legal and political history and that these subjects should dominate university syllabuses when they were first designed in the late nineteenth century.

The First World War, the Great Depression and the economic disasters which followed gave great impetus to the study both of diplomatic and economic history, one generally attracting the conservative, the other the radical historians in the 1920s and 1930s. After the Second World War interest in diplomatic history faded first or, rather, transmogrified itself into International Relations and Strategic Studies. Economic history drifted into a professional morass and developed a confused identity — the quantifiers and the econometricians moved in and so did the sociologists, especially American sociologists, hoping to establish an ideology which would refute the Marxist interpretation which had flourished within the realm of economic history.

But the problems of Western industrial society have become much more complex since the Second World War. Fantastic economic growth, and it has been fantastic this last thirty years, has created its own social tensions and, even more important, the very nature of highly industrialized society, apart from its

growth has created new conflicts. Institutions which have lasted
for ten thousand years, not only in the West but also in the East,
have suddenly seemed to be in jeopardy. In the last two decades
there has been a mushrooming of interest among historians in
the problems of demography, of the nature of the family, of the
position of women, children, slaves and servants, of the uses of
leisure, of the influence of printing, of the expansion of the arts,
of the importance of the images society creates for itself, and of
the interpretation of class not in economic but in social terms. A
new panorama of social history has spread before the eyes of
scholars and led them to subjects which historians of previous
generations would have thought of interest only to antiquarians.

Naturally, other forms of history are not dead, even though
some of them are corpse-like, but there can be little doubt that
the historical imagination, for better or worse, has become
intoxicated with social history: for example, the volume of work
on death in the last ten years is prodigious and it is matched by
the quantity of studies on childhood or marriage.

The danger of social history, which in spite of its present
explosion has, in some of its aspects, long roots reaching back
through G. M. Trevelyan to Macaulay and Sir Walter Scott, has
been the tendency to drift into descriptive history, of how
people lived and spent their days with little or no attempt to
analyse why their lives, their beliefs, their activities were what
they were. Also, the evidence social historians, even very good
ones, used in the past, was impressionistic – diaries, letters,
personal memories, together with material collected from folk-
lorists and antiquarians. Naturally, most of this evidence related to
the literate class, until very recent times a modest segment of the
nation.

In order to give this material greater rigour, sociological
theory, either of Marxist or capitalist bent, has been used and,
often, in discussion of death, birth, education of children or the
position of women, it has been infused with modern psychological
analysis. Although this has given rise to some nonsense, particularly in the history of childhood, it has given the subject, on
the whole, greater intellectual weight.

As with economic history, there has also been a powerful
movement which has attempted to quantify the evidence of the
past in order to give a statistical basis for some of the fundamental

questions of social history — average size and nature of the family, whether nuclear or extended; the age of marriage for men and women; death rates and ages at death; an attempt has even been made to quantify literacy. Huge mountains of data have been assembled and computers have hummed away merrily at great expense, but the results remain extremely tentative. Before the nineteenth century record-keeping was erratic and its reliability was not easy to test. There is, too, one unknown factor of great importance — how many of the population were never recorded at all, neither their births, marriages nor deaths? Indeed, most of the results obtained are easy to criticize and must be treated with considerable scepticism. Even so, generalizations about the family and about its size, about marriage, about bastardy, about age of death, all are firmer than they were and, because they are, help us to understand the life of the country in greater depth.

Although statistics may give shadow and depth to the picture, they cannot paint it, and social history still depends upon a great range of records. Formerly it depended most of all on letters, diaries and imaginative literature but, although these are still of the greatest value, more attention has now been given to artefacts: to the study of houses and gardens, to newspapers, bills and trade cards, to carriages, instruments, games and toys, indeed to everything that may throw a light on the way life was lived or the way it hurried towards its future or clung to its past. By extending its range and its depth, by encompassing a multiplicity of scenes, social history has become a far more complex and intellectually exciting discipline than it was.

Over the last ten years the flow of monographs and articles on the social history of England has increased, mushroomed like an atomic explosion, and the time is more than ripe for an attempt at synthesis.

J. H. Plumb

Acknowledgements

A work of this kind must inevitably be largely a distillation of the research and interpretations of others, and a dialogue with them. I cannot acknowledge all their work here (though I list some of it in the 'Further Reading' section). I hope I haven't anywhere used their work in vain. The following scholars and friends have read this book at various stages (some more than once): John Brewer, Robert Brown, W. F. Bynum, David Cannadine, Estelle Cohen, Linda Colley, Mark Goldie, Joanna Innes, Chris Lawrence, Sue Limb, Gillian Morris, Michael Neve, Jacqueline Rainfray, Keith Snell, David Souden, John Styles, Sylvana Tomaselli and Christopher Wright. I have benefited immensely from their help, though I am of course entirely responsible for the outcome. Jack Plumb has given me every encouragement with the project; I hope the result will not seem a travesty of 'Plumb's century'. The first part of this book was written in the peaceful surroundings of Churchill College, Cambridge, and during the latter stages I have basked in the time for research and the facilities offered by the Wellcome Institute for the History of Medicine. I should like to express deep gratitude to Verna Cole and Frieda Houser for ever-cheery help with typing; to Tim Harris and Chris Husband for help with references; to Mrs Jean Runciman, who has read the proofs; and to Nick Collins, who has compiled the index.

Roy Porter, February 1981

Preface to the Revised Edition

It is highly flattering, but far more daunting, to be called upon to revise a book completed eight years previously. One must correct errors. Inevitably one wishes one had said this, and had not said that. One wishes to add qualifications and nuances. One hopes to incorporate the findings of fresh research from a score of fields. The danger is that, before one realizes it, one succumbs to the fate of the unfortunate person who pulled on a loose thread on a pullover and quickly ended up with nothing but a heap of used wool. At times, in the thick of revisions, I have suspected that it would be easier to start all over again from scratch, or to move over and let someone else have a try.

Not least, the last half-decade has seen a spirited attack from the academic 'new right' upon the very perception of social history animating this series as a whole and certainly this individual volume. The works of J. C. D. Clark in particular have offered a very different agenda, and alternative priorities, for the social history of the eighteenth century. I radically disagree with Clark on innumerable points. Above all, his is a vision of English society which finds almost no room for discussion of so many of the topics which seem to me of cardinal importance: family formation, the domestic economy, gender hierarchies, sexuality, wealth and property distribution, crime, work and labour relations, the interplay between elite and popular culture, town and country, and so forth.

But, unlike certain of his critics, I do not believe that such readings of the eighteenth century can be dismissed out of hand as either merely cranky, nostalgic or ideologically biased. I believe Clark has been right to argue that Georgian England was an 'old order', dominated by title, land and church, and also to insist that such an order had not significantly been undermined by 1800 – though he is myopic in his apparent lack of interest in, even distaste for, so many of the areas in which the ways of life of ordinary English people changed dramatically during the eighteenth century.

Confronting the challenge of such revisionist accounts, I find myself applauding their stress upon the sheer strength of the English state and those who governed it, while, against them, wishing to draw attention to massive social and economic, intellectual and cultural change. But it was that precise mixture of resilience among the powerful, and ferment from below, which I sought to highlight in the first edition eight years ago. For this reason, I have decided not to undertake a radical restructuring or reinterpretation of this book, but rather to make alterations to details and to rewrite particular discussions where major new research has appeared, changing emphasis here and there, and arguing certain points more fully. I have above all attempted to draw attention in the 'Further Reading' section to the more important new works of research and interpretation that have appeared over the last eight years.

Finally I would like to convey deep thanks to all those readers of the first edition – many of them hitherto unknown to me – who have been so kind as to contact me with their comments and criticisms. Writing books can be a melancholy and solitary business; in that process, nothing is more inspiriting to an author than to feel that he is actually being read, even if, occasionally, by those he outrages and disappoints. Nearly twenty-five years ago, my first and best teacher, Jack Plumb, taught me that it was up to scholars to write history that would satisfy people's desire to understand their own past. It was the wisest advice I have had; I hope I have been able, in some measure, to live up to it. The dedication of this book is an acknowledgement of my profound debt to the scholar who fired me with this vision of the historian's business.

Roy Porter
January 1989

Conversion Tables

1 inch = 2.54 centimetres
1 yard = 0.914 metres
1 mile = 1.609 kilometres

1 pound weight = 0.454 kilograms

1 gallon = 4.546 litres

1 acre = 0.405 hectares

12 pennies (d.) = 1 shilling (s.)
20 shillings = 1 pound (£1)
21 shillings = 1 guinea

Given the rate of inflation over the last generation, it makes little sense to try to give modern real-worth equivalents of eighteenth-century monetary units. Multiplying eighteenth-century sums, however, by a factor of perhaps 60 or 80 will give a rough-and-ready 1990 equivalent. In the Georgian age, rock-bottom wages for males were about a shilling a day, but a man fully employed all the weeks of the year – and most were not – would not have been able to support a family on such a sum. For that, earnings in the region of some £30–£40 a year would be required. A careful artisan family could hope to keep itself from hunger and out of debt on a pound a week, and members of the petty bourgeoisie would commonly have incomes of between £50 and £100 a year. About £300 was the least that would keep a gentleman in any style.

As to outgoings, for much of the century a full loaf of bread cost about 4d. and a pot of ale 1d.; a meal could be bought in a London tavern for about 1s. 6d. A new two-up and two-down brick cottage would cost about £150.

Introduction

Interpretations of eighteenth-century English society have varied mightily. Many Victorians were repelled by its 'soullessness', seeing it as rationalist, cynical, and materialist. Old-school literary historians admired it as an age of wise traditionalism, of elegance and wit, or of Squire Western rumbustiousness; today's 'new tory' historians equally admire it as a stable church-and-kind order, with affinities to the *anciens régimes* of the Continent. The effect of such characterizations has been to portray Georgian England as a golden age, and to emphasize the great divide between past and present. This side of the watershed of the French Revolution or the First Reform Bill lie modern times: our world of the masses, democracy, progress, opportunity, alienation – or whatever; on the far side, there is the world we have lost, utterly lost, best evoked by George Eliot in *Adam Bede* over a century ago, recalling even then the irrecoverable times of the early 1800s. 'Leisure is gone', reflected the novelist,

– gone where the spinning wheels are gone, and the pack-horses, and the slow waggons, and the pedlars, who brought bargains to the door on sunny afternoons. Ingenious philosophers tell you, perhaps, that the great work of the steam-engine is to create leisure for mankind. Do not believe them; it only creates a vacuum for eager thoughts to rush in. Even idleness is eager now, eager for amusement: prone to excursion-trains, art-museums, periodical literature, and exciting novels: prone even to scientific theorizing, and cursory peeps through microscopes. Old Leisure was quite a different personage; he only read one newspaper, innocent of leaders, and was free from that periodicity of sensations which we call post-time. He was a contemplative, rather stout gentle-man, of excellent digestion – of quiet perception, undiseased by hypoth-esis: happy in his inability to know the causes of things, preferring the things themselves. He lived chiefly in the country, among pleasant seats and homesteads, and was fond of sauntering by the fruit-tree wall, and scenting the apricots when they were warmed by the morning sunshine, or of sheltering himself under the orchard boughs at noon, when the summer pears were falling. He knew nothing of weekday services, and thought none the worse of the Sunday sermon if it allowed him to sleep from the text to the blessing — liking the afternoon service best because the prayers were the shortest, and not ashamed to say so; for he had an easy, jolly conscience, broadbacked like himself, and able to carry a great deal of beer and port-wine — not being made squeamish by doubts and qualms and lofty aspirations. Life was not a task to him, but a sinecure; he fingered the guineas in his pocket, and ate his dinners, and slept the sleep of the irresponsible; for had he not kept his charter by going to church on the Sunday afternoons! Fine old Leisure! Do not be severe on him, and judge him by our modern standard; he never went to Exeter Hall, or heard a popular preacher, or read *Tracts for the Times*, or *Sartor Resartus*.

For excellent reasons, mainstream social historians have long been out of sympathy with such evocations of the magic of the past; they have rightly emphasized the 'modernity' of so much of Georgian life. Eminent Georgians were not, after all, lovable paternalist eccentrics; not all squires were bucolic Squire Westerns, who loved a good dog and a good wench, and in that order: many were profit-hungry capitalists. Labourers were not all forelock-touching and deferential, but as tenacious of their rights as any modern trade-unionist.

It is salutary to resist the urge to turn the Georgian century into prelapsarian 'olden times'. Yet it would equally be a mistake to assimilate the eighteenth century by denying its differences. Rather, the eighteenth century marked a distinctive moment in the making of modern England. Its society was capitalist, materialist, market-oriented; its temper worldly, pragmatic, responsive to economic forces. Yet its political institutions and its distributions of wealth and power were unashamedly inegalitarian, hierarchical, hereditary and privileged. Economic activity took place on a human scale (though often it did not bear a human face); change generally occurred at a pace people could adapt to; custom still enjoyed great authority; and deep-rooted localism, grounded on community loyalties, shaped what remained a 'face-to-face society'. All this was possible because people were not breathing down each other's necks, for by our standards England was — in 1700 and still, though less so, in 1800 — empty. Competition for space, natural resources and livelihoods was not so cutthroat or so ferociously dictated by impersonal economic iron laws as it was to become in the heyday of the Victorian trade-cycle. Runaway population growth and tumultuous industrial transformation were to change all that. But though these can be discerned in the last third of the eighteenth century, they did not peak until the nineteenth.

The following chapters interweave themes and chronology. In Chapter 1, I offer a flavour of Georgian society by highlighting its particularity and diversity: the poles of experience between rich and poor, young and old, male and female, town and country, North and South; between England and other places where English-speaking people lived; between England and Continental Europe. Regions became more integrated and mutually interdependent during the century, owing largely to the spread of market relations, yet England also remained a patchwork of distinctive local communities – a fact that must silently temper all the generalizations I venture. In Chapters 2 and 3, I review the social ranks and their interrelations, stressing hierarchical inequalities and friction, but also the fundamental tenacity of the overall structure. The ascendancy of the propertied was reinforced by their effective monopoly over the inflexions of power: landed estates, status, patronage, office and political and legal authority within the state. In Chapter 4, I further emphasize how the stability of society was reinforced down the generations by the reproduction of particular habits of living: the dovetailing of family life with economic life, home with workplace; the parts played by household, workplace and community in integrating individuals into their social position; the conditioning effects of education and religion.

In Chapters 5 and 6, I turn to explore forces working for change, and their socio-economic impact. Overcoming possible traditional scruples about gentility, the titled, rich and powerful increasingly gave a lead in the pursuit of wealth and the production of a new consumer culture. Acquisitiveness and opportunism found a new respectability; this in turn had certain socially accommodating and integrative consequences, helping to mould consensus among the affluent and the aspirant. Yet new wealth (with its poor relation, new poverty) also proved a social solvent. Gaps were widening between successful capitalists and those they proletarianized, between patrician and plebeian cultures. These connected processes of cultural consensus and cultural atomization are further explored in Chapter 7, which examines the attempts of polite and educated society to validate more individualistic lifestyles, in conformity with ideals of liberty, progress and refinement. 'Civilization' could be held as both a carrot and a stick before the lower orders. Chapter 8 then examines industrialization as the upshot of the earlier unhindered development of a market-relations and commercial culture.

Pioneered by the *nouveaux riches* and their development of new manufacturing towns, rapid industrialization challenged the old ways. It threatened traditional work-practices, and with that, the integration of living and labouring based upon the traditional family working unit. It also threatened to replace the 'moral economy' with political economy, and to substitute marginal utility for traditional values such as 'politeness', 'tradition' and 'deference'. In the concluding chapter, I therefore pose the question as to whether, by embracing capitalism, the scions of Georgian society were digging their own graves by helping or allowing to come into existence a self-confident manufacturing bourgeoisie, a desperate proletariat and political disaffection. I conclude that what the challenge of these new forces – fanned by the French Revolution – chiefly reveals is the elasticity and tenacity of the *status quo*.

The Georgian century teetered on 'modernity' in various ways. Not least, it tried to weigh and measure itself. This primitive auto-analysis opens up the tantalizing prospect of quantified history. Yet most attempts by Georgian political arithmeticians at 'painting by numbers' are unreliable (sometimes their enumerations mainly reveal their compilers' assumptions). Highly sophisticated profiles of social trends are now being drawn, on the basis of raw eighteenth-century data – particularly pioneering has been the work of the Cambridge Group for the History of Population and Social Structure in using parochial documents to trace literacy, demographical change and family patterns. Such 'number-crunching' is immensely valuable. Yet it cannot wholly escape the irremediably defective foundations upon which it is built. In their registers, parish clerks were required to record Anglican baptisms, marriages and burials. We can only guess (and some guesses are better informed than others) what proportion of all births got registered as baptisms, of unions as marriages, of deaths as burials; or indeed what proportion of the population was Anglican, or how many clerks were conscientious. In any case, such proportions doubtless varied from place to place and from time to time. We have official returns for trade imports and exports, but smugglers kept no books. We can enumerate criminal prosecutions but not lawlessness. Moreover, the cult of quantification in the age of the computer runs the risk of creating mists of mythical 'averages' which veil the significant contours. Placing faith, for example, in measures of 'average wages' would be misguided. Not only was there no average person, but for few did the recorded money wages alone represent total income or livelihood. The Georgian equivalent of what we call the 'black economy' was vast. Even assessing wage differentials from region to region, or decade to decade, makes sense only if we can be confident (and usually we cannot) that we are comparing like with like. I offer figures in this book, but usually for graphical purposes rather than as trustworthy indices. For similar reasons I have tried to avoid technical jargon when discussing matters such as social structure. English society was disparate, fluid, and spangled with contrasts and anomalies. No single social scientific terminology captures that complexity in its entirety.

I have quoted a lot from eighteenth-century writers. I do not offer these voices from the past as 'proof' of my points; contemporary observers had their own axes to grind, and in any case were often simply wrong. However, what people experienced, believed and uttered is of no less importance than what they ate. Furthermore, the comments of foreign visitors (again, often biased: Anglomania was rife) at least indicate what seemed special about England to continental eyes.

This is a book essentially about England. Better would have been a social history of the British Isles and of the British Empire, but that would have been completely beyond my powers.

I have kept money values in Georgian units, but added a conversion table. The period discussed extends roughly from the Glorious Revolution (1688) to the Peace of Amiens (1802), and I have somewhat cavalierly applied the epithets 'Georgian' and 'Hanoverian' to it. I have modernized punctuation in some quotations, but retained original spellings.

Last, a word about gender and gender terminology. It is very easy for a male historian to write as if only adult males existed, or, at least, made history. I have tried to avoid this. I have, however, kept to the conventional use of 'he' and 'his' when people of both sexes are being referred to. Current circumlocutions and neologisms such as 'he/she', 's/he' or 'his or her' are clumsy. Phrases such as 'Englishmen' and 'the common man' are too evocative of the language of the time to be lightly jettisoned.

1. *Contrasts*

England is a rich sea, but strewn with many reefs, and those who voyage there would do well to take precautions. [Casanova]

England 'is different in every respect from the rest of Europe', thought Casanova, and all foreign commentators agreed that in many ways England was unique. *Vive la différence* was most Englishmen's toast. Theirs was a breezy, bigoted chauvinism which embarrasses us now. 'I do not think there is a people more prejudiced in its own favour than the British people,' judged the Swiss visitor César de Saussure in the 1720s; 'they look on foreigners in general with contempt, and think nothing is as well done elsewhere as in their own country.' The body politic puffed itself up with patriotism: 'I glory in the name of Briton,' George III was to boast. Foreigners – 'French dogs' above all – were jostled in the streets: 'Before they learn there is a God to be worshipped,' wrote Fougeret de Montbron, 'they learn there are Frenchmen to be detested.' Even the cosmopolitan expatriate Edward Gibbon thanked 'the bounty of Nature, which cast my birth in a free and civilized country, in an age of science and philosophy, in a family of honourable rank, and decently endowed with the gifts of fortune'.

Confidence was bred of success. Britain's *arriviste* pride was swelled by her glorious and lucrative triumphs in the War of the Spanish Succession (1702–13), the Seven Years' War (1756–63), and from 1793 in the Revolutionary and Napoleonic wars (even if, as Admiral Vernon warned, 'our fleets are defrauded with injustice, marred by violence and maintained by cruelty'). 'No nation,' judged the Sussex shopkeeper Thomas Turner in that *annus mirabilis* of victories, 1759, 'had ever greater occasion to adore the Almighty Disposer of all events than Albion, whose forces meet with success in all quarters of the world.'

Success turned plain-dealing, choleric, insular John Bull from a

blundering butt of ridicule into a swaggerer. Victory made Jolly
Jack Tars national heroes, however much critics abused successive
ministries. English boys – Samuel Johnson was an exception –
ached to go to sea. In 1782 the yeoman's son William Cobbett
saw the ocean for the first time and the Channel squadron riding
at anchor at Spithead. 'No sooner did I see it than I wished to be
a sailor' (he enlisted, but by mistake ended up in a marching
regiment). The great English patriotic songs – 'God Save the
King', 'Rule Britannia', 'Heart of Oak' and 'The Roast Beef of
Old England' – were all penned during this century, and sung
lustily in public. Choruses of 'God Save the King' greeted
George III at the theatre – more out of a swelling patriotism than
any love for the Hanoverians. The great caricaturist William
Hogarth, who signed himself 'Britophil', caught the mood with
flattering – if double-edged – national stereotypes. People loved
his beer-swilling, roast-beef-guzzling, four-square Englishmen,
the 'dread and envy' of starveling, bare-foot, onion-nibbling
French peasants, oppressed by lecherous Jesuits and mincing
courtiers. The English abroad saw the Continent through such
prejudices: all was poverty and superstition, vainglory and
tyranny. 'I think nothing so terrible as objects of misery,'
confided Lady Mary Wortley Montagu, travelling through northern France in 1718, 'and all the country villages of France shew
nothing else.'

The English postured as plucky David battling the Bourbon
or Habsburg Goliath. Through much of the seventeenth century,
Albion's island had been marginal to the European power map.
Eclipsed by the Sun King, Charles II had been a client, James II a
tool. Even under the Georges, England's native resources and
manpower remained puny compared to those of Bourbon France,
Habsburg Austria or Romanov Russia. In 1700 there were well
over three Frenchmen to every Englishman, and even in 1800
the ratio was still over two and a half to one. There were twice
as many Italians as English, and the English remained outnumbered by Spaniards.

But spirit counted more than numbers for a people who
prided themselves upon being a free, civilian, industrious race –
not slaves to military despots – yet a nation who, if forced, could
roll up their sleeves, beat ploughshares into swords, and fight.
England's peacetime standing army was pygmy by continental

standards: in war in 1794 its strength was 45,000, compared to Prussia's 190,000. Certain opposition backwoodsmen, fearing tyranny, wanted to abolish it altogether, devolving arms-bearing on to citizen militias, such as Edward Gibbon was a captain in. Unlike sailors, soldiers were rarely popular, and the armed forces were recruited in a hand-to-mouth way. In war, the Royal Navy requisitioned ships and sailors from the merchant marine, and press-ganged men in ports. British warships long remained inferior in design to the French or Spanish, some disintegrating at sea, making 'Gravesend voyages'. Yet these rather off-hand ways did not stop Britannia ruling the waves in a century of scarcely checked global imperial expansion.

Englishmen excused their vices as virtues and indulged them with brio. They liked being thought bloody-minded roughnecks. 'Anything that looks like a fight,' observed the Frenchman Henri Misson, 'is delicious to an Englishman' – something even a lord could confirm. 'I love a mob,' explained the Duke of Newcastle; 'I headed one once myself.' Duelling remained common among top people. In 1712 the Duke of Hamilton and Lord Mohun met; both died. In 1789 the Duke of York fought Colonel Lennox. In 1798 none other than Prime Minister William Pitt and George Tierney, a leading Whig, exchanged shots. Violence was endemic. In 1770, following a pupil rebellion, the Riot Act had to be read at Winchester School. At Rugby, the young gentlemen mined the head's study with gunpowder. Yet fighting was rated manly, and pugnacity (*alias* 'love of liberty') preferred to servility. Better 'governed by a mob, than a standing army', judged Charles James Fox.

The English – so foreigners saw them – ate to excess, drank like lords, and swore like troopers (among 'cunning women' cursing was still a fine art). Henry Herbert, ninth Earl of Pembroke, was 'so blasphemous at tennis that the primate of Ireland was forced to leave off playing with him'. Dr Johnson 'could not bear anything like swearing', yet he was in a minority, since in his day even fashionable ladies habitually made the air blue. A traveller arriving in London, quipped the German pastor Karl Moritz, might jump to the conclusion that everyone was called 'Damme'. The vernacular had not yet been disinfected by delicacy. Househunting early in married life, the Newcastle businessman Henry Carr told a friend that his wife 'wanted a canny hole of her own to fart in, to use a Northern expression'. And, to complete the roster of vices, every gallant had his gal: 'where is male chastity to be found?' bemoaned John Wesley, himself no stranger to the lusts of the flesh.

Few cared in what by earlier and later standards was a very easy-going society – tolerant of abuse as well as diversity. Tourists hacked bits off 'Shakespeare's chair' in Stratford (the German philosopher Lichtenberg paid 1s. for a sliver) and chiselled souvenir flakes off Stonehenge. Cathedral walls are scrawled with eighteenth-century graffiti. The helpless were fair game. The fifth Earl of Berkeley seduced the seventeen-year-old daughter of a Gloucester tradesman – but then had seven children by her and eventually married her. And such devil-take-the-hindemost behaviour was admired for its gusto, pluck, and 'bottom'. In the countryside the same Earl, waylaid by a highwayman, unhesitatingly shot him. In the Commons, Prime Minister Sir Robert Walpole reputedly munched Norfolk apples to show he was at heart just a plain-dealing squire; he was proud to be thought 'no saint, no Spartan, no reformer'.

And when they could not be passed off as virtues, the peculiarities of the English – their cantankerousness or hypochondria – was put down to the island's unsettled climate, which was obviously responsible for those other treasured character traits, eccentricity and contrariness. 'We are precarious, uncertain, wild, enduring mortals,' rhapsodized that normally crusty gentleman, John Byng, 'and may we so endowed continue, the wonder and balance of the universe.' In the guise of a Spanish tourist, the poet Southey commented in 1807:

The English love to be at war, but do not love to pay for their amusement; and now that they are at peace, they begin to complain that the newspapers are not worth reading, and rail at the French as if they really wished to begin again. There is not a people upon the earth who have a truer love for their Royal family than the English, yet they caricature them in the most open and insolent manner. They boast of the freedom of the press, yet as surely and systematically punish the author who publishes anything obnoxious, and the book-seller who sells it, as we in our country should prevent the publication. They cry out against intolerance and burn down the houses of those whom they regard as heretics. They love liberty; go to war with their neighbours, because they choose to become republicans, and insist upon the right of enslaving the negroes. They hate the French and ape all their fashions, ridicule their neologisms and then naturalize them, laugh at their inventions and then adopt them, cry out against their political measures and then imitate them; the levy in mass, the telegraph, and the income tax are all from France. And the common people, not to be behind hand with their betters in absurdities, boast as heartily of the roast beef of Old England, as if they were not obliged to be content themselves with bread and potatoes. Well may punch be the favourite liquor of the English – it is a truly emblematic compound of contrarieties.

The English thus fell in love with themselves in the eighteenth century. But did they really have anything to be proud about? In 1700 theirs was still a second-rate rustic nation of hamlets and villages. Outside London it had no town to match even Bologna, Liége or Rouen in size. Nearly 80 per cent of the population lived in the countryside, and almost 90 per cent were employed either in agriculture or in processing rural produce. By later standards, England was empty: its 1700 population of barely 5 million is about the same as the present-day population of Surrey, Kent and Essex. Millions of acres were waste, heath, marsh or fen. Roads were perhaps worse than the Romans had left them:

> Cleveland in the clay
> Bring two shoes and carry one away

ran the jingle.

In 1700 the harvest was still the heartbeat of the economy. Would there be enough bread? And who could afford it? Lives depended on these questions, and the weather alone held the answer. And, depending on sun or rain, the country reposed or rioted, business boomed or went bust, interest rates and investment levels see-sawed. Industry still fed off the soil: timber, hides, hops, flax, madder, saffron, horn for knife-handles, bones for glue – these were essential raw materials. And most industry was cottage industry: spinning, lace-making, stocking-knitting, tanning, smithying and coopering thrived in villages more than in large towns. Family life and work danced in step to the phases of nature. Ploughing, harvesting, fruit-picking, fishing and chimney-sweeping – all such work was seasonal. Social life – with its feasts, fasts and fairs, its post-harvest bonfires and enforced winter unemployment – syncopated with the rural rhythms of toil and tribulation, abundance and idleness.

Few got fat off the land, and many scratched Lenten livings off hungry soil. All-weather outdoor toil took its toll: the working masses grew old prematurely through immeasurable fatigue. Gregory King, the pioneer statistician, estimated near the end of the seventeenth century that about half the families in England were not commanding a subsistence.

Yet one critical watershed *had* been passed. English husbandry undoubtedly under-used its resources, for Gregory King thought a quarter of the land was unproductive in 1688, and Arthur Young, touring the North nearly a century later, could still comment, 'It is extremely melancholy to view such tracts of land as are indisputably capable of yielding many beneficial crops, lie totally waste.' But – as everybody noted – the rural economy was far better capitalized, and more businesslike and productive, than almost any on the Continent, where east of the Elbe serfs were still legally yoked to the soil, and debt-ridden, share-cropping peasants starved on subdivided holdings in France, Spain and Italy. Famine had still brought mortality in parts of Stuart England, and subsistence crises traumatized many regions of Europe (including Ireland) through the eighteenth century. Between 1696 and 1697 famine killed a third of the population of Finland, and close on a million people starved to death in France in 1769. The rural economies of most of *ancien régime* Europe were trapped in cycles of over-population and under-production: chronic indebtedness, exhausted soil, paltry grain yields, uneconomic fragmentation of holdings and population pressure spelt mass misery and periodic disasters. But the English had earned their pardon from this death sentence. People no longer starved to death *en masse* in Georgian England. Bad harvests gave local short-falls, but not absolute dearth. Indeed, grain was exported on an increasing scale in the first half of the century. Shortages were brief, regional and confined to particular crops, and their effects were cushioned by the capitalization of the grain trade and better marketing circuits. English grain rioters protested not against the absence of corn, but against its dearness and maldistribution, and against profiteering, or about being forced to eat rye bread instead of wheaten.

By 1700 England had in this one respect escaped the 'biological *ancien régime*', the remorseless pressure of population upon inelastic land and food supply, which had blighted Europe since the Middle Ages. Agricultural productivity was improving, thanks to the spread of convertible husbandry, new rotations, fodder crops and fen drainage. Yet micro-organisms still tyrannized over English bodies. Medicine was not yet winning the battle against disease and death. In twentieth-century England death visits the aged; in 1700 almost the reverse was true. Far more people died in infancy or their teens than in their seventies and eighties. Maybe a fifth of all babies died in their first year; perhaps one in three died – of gastro-enteric disorders and fevers – before the age of five. In the 1740s, in certain London parishes, up to three in four children died before the age of six. The deaths of children had to be accepted. Hester Thrale, wife of the great London brewer Henry Thrale, 'regarded the death of various daughters at school with great equanimity'. Despite appalling childhood mortality, England had a very youthful population profile – over half the nation in 1700 was under twenty-one – yet it was a population ever vulnerable. Average life expectancy was about thirty-seven years.

The Grim Reaper harvested the poor. Pauper children died like flies, especially during the 1720s and 1730s, decades of severe epidemics and the Gin Craze. But the gentry had no immunity. All Edward Gibbon's six brothers and sisters died in infancy (the historian barely survived a sickly youth – 'I swallowed more physick than food'), and none of Queen Anne's children lived to grow up. Tens of thousands of mothers died in childbed. Plague had mercifully quit England before the century began (no thanks to doctors; possibly rats had become immune to the disease), and medicine disarmed smallpox through inoculation and vaccination before the Georgian era was out. But fevers – typhus, dysentery, measles, influenza, those 'panzer divisions of death' – invaded in repeated epidemics that left doctors helpless. Death was ever-present and struck out of the blue. 'Last Thursday sennight a most Melancholy Accident happened,' reported the *Northampton Mercury* in 1771:

two farmers went to a Neighbour's House to view a sick Calf, the Weather was then most intensely cold; while they were handling the Calf it went mad, and slaver'd on each of them; alarmed at this, they, by Advice of Friends, set off to bathe in the Sea; but on the Tuesday following they were brought back dead in a Cart, to the Terror of the whole neighbourhood.

Death was a mystery of Providence. No less awful, however, were the endemic evils a rather hard-bitten society accepted as the inevitable fate of particular trades or groups. Industrial diseases were rife: silicosis destroyed potters, chimney-sweeps got cancer, lead-poisoning killed paint-makers. Farm-labourers were crippled with rheumatism, the poor suffered from rickets and scurvy, while gout and dropsy crippled hard-drinking squires, whose tight-laced, wasp-waisted daughters often paid for elegance with ill-health. Cosmetic poisoning defaced the fashionable – Lady Coventry reputedly died poisoned by lead-based make-up.

It was the powerful who sliced up the nation's wealth cake. Around 1688, Gregory King thought that the least a family (say, a man, his wife, and three children) could live on, without getting into debt or receiving poor relief or charity, was about £40 a year. He believed peers' families netted about £2,800 (an underestimate: their purses were perhaps twice as big), but most of the working population lived below the breadline. For instance, 364,000 'labouring people and servants' had family incomes of just £15 a year; 400,000 'cottagers and paupers' were on £6 10s. a year; 50,000 seamen on £20; and 35,000 soldiers on £14. Together they made up over half the families in the country. His calculations suggest that the top 1.2 per cent of the population possessed 14.1 per cent of the national income; the bottom 67.1 per cent a mere 29.9 per cent of it.*

King's pioneer enumerations are not gospel: his sources were limited and he had biases of his own. But his general profile stands. King thought that family units in the labouring classes were typically trapped in poverty because they could not earn sufficient for subsistence. With unintentional irony, King labelled these people – the country's labour force – 'persons decreasing the wealth of the country'. 'Suppose the rich grind the face of the poor, what remedy against such oppression can be found in a Christian country?' No adequate answer came to John Wesley's question.

* In 1980 the top 1 per cent owned 25 per cent of all personal wealth in England.

Poverty spelt lives of deprivation and dependence: a tasteless, unsatisfying diet of bread; freezing in shacks and cellars, with farm animals occasionally living under the same roof (at least they gave off warmth); enduring the petty tyranny of poor-law overseers; engaging in back-breaking toil for pittances under often brutal masters, and the prospect ahead only of pinching old age or the poor-house. Everyone below the income commanded by skilled craftsmen was undernourished. This biological fact had social causes – it was a consequence of the way the powerful, aided by the law, carved up the national wealth. Indeed, the differential politics of property and poverty became more explicit during the century. Take taxation: as governments sought greater revenue, they chose 'socially retrogressive' policies, increasing not the land tax (paid by landowners) but indirect taxation, levied on consumables (such as salt and beer) which hit everyone. Thus, more of the ordinary person's money got syphoned off into the Exchequer, where it largely financed war and paid the interest due to wealthy investors in the National Debt.

The poor were a festering problem to Georgian government, especially local government. Yet hardly anyone – not even most reformers and radicals – doubted that there always would, or indeed *should*, be rich and poor: it was a dependent relationship that seemed as natural as that between husband and wife or master and servant:

> God bless the squire and his relations
> And keep us in our proper stations

was the prayer not just of squires. 'Mankind are happier,' the petty-bourgeois Samuel Johnson was sure, 'in a state of inequality and subordination.' Parsons such as Archdeacon William Paley even attempted the Herculean labour of convincing the poor that it was really they who were the lucky ones: 'Some of the necessities which poverty imposes ... are not hardships but pleasures.' Admittedly, the horrors of grinding toil and chill penury were expunged for a very few by meteoric ascent: John Taylor began work as a journeyman, rose to become a button manufacturer and founder of Lloyds Bank, and left a fortune of £200,000. But to the bulk of the population, toil, deprivation, uncertainty and suffering were the constant daily facts of life.

The social hierarchy was another basic fact. Few questioned

that there was some natural order of high and low – that there should be aristocrats and 'shopocrats', nobility and 'mobility' ('nobs' and 'mobs'), lords, esquires, plain Mr and Mrs, not to mention plain Hodge. It followed that, at the theatre, polite society sat in the stalls while the commonalty made pandemonium in the gallery and fribbles catcalled in the pit. Likewise in town, Quality resided in squares and rows, while the middling sort dwelt in courts, and the poor festered in alleys and warrens. Within one large house, the better-off basked on the first floor, while servants and the down-at-heel shivered in tiny garrets and dingy cellars. Differentiation was the key to society, and it was endlessly echoed by accent and idiom, dress, address, and addresses. 'Upside-down world' satires, such as *The Beggar's Opera*, which implicity caricatured Walpole and the great as gangsters, or the radicalism which challenged King George in the name of 'King David' (a Yorkshire counterfeiter), 'Captain Ludd' or 'King Mob', exposed the hollowness of titles while ironically perpetuating them.

The ruling class was not a caste rigidly distinguished by ancient pedigrees. Unlike the Habsburgs, English grandees did not make a fetish of blue blood. But being a grandee had its biological consequences. The wealthy were healthier and lived longer; they came earlier to sexual maturity; being better fed and hence taller, they literally looked down on the poor. They regulated their lives by a different clock. Labourers rose, ate and went to bed by the sun (lighting was costly). The rich, bathed in candlelight, did everything at a more civilized hour. And throughout society, differentiation required a show of superiority and deference paraded in the rituals of bowing and scraping, headbaring, standing, curtseying and knuckling foreheads for one's betters.

Yet suffering was *everyone's* lot sooner or later, low- or highborn. Physical pain, the great leveller, was always waiting its cue. In sickness, there were no anaesthetics, and alcohol was the best pain-killer. People had to cope philosophically, and religiously, with disease (though the English were also notorious for suicide). In 1776 Parson Woodforde had John Reeves, the local farrier, draw a tooth, 'but shockingly bad indeed, he broke . . . one of the fangs of the tooth and it gave me exquisite pain all the day after, and my face was swelled prodigiously . . . Gave the old man that drew it however 0–2–6. He is too old, I think to draw teeth, can't see very well.'

Pain's partners were discomfort and danger. The unfortunate traveller shared his bed at the inn with strangers and fleas, and his roads with gibbeted corpses and highwaymen. 'I was robbed last night as I expected,' wrote Lord North in 1774, in a tone of resignation perhaps ill-becoming a Prime Minister. 'Our loss was not great, but as the postillion did not stop immediately one of the two highwaymen fired at him – It was at the end of Gunnersbury Lane.' Horace Walpole, fired at in Hyde Park, wryly observed, 'One is forced to travel, even at noon, as if one was going to battle.' Yet people travelled more and more.

Life was raw. Practically all youngsters were thrashed at home, at school, at work – and child labour was universal. Blood sports such as cock-fighting were hailed as manly trials of skill and courage. Felons were publicly whipped, pilloried and hanged, traitors were drawn and quartered. Jacobites' heads were spiked on Temple Bar till 1777. Work-animals were driven relentlessly: England was notoriously 'hell for horses', and cruelty to animals worsened with industrialization and the craving for speed.

People were not squeamish about inflicting or bearing physical pain. Cudgelling remained a favourite West Country pastime, and village sports sometimes led to deaths (football hooliganism is nothing new). Sailors boasted of the countless lashes they had endured. Turbulence simmered and often boiled over. Benjamin Franklin, writing in 1769, was staggered:

I have seen, within a year, riots in the country, about corn; riots about elections; riots about workhouses; riots of colliers, riots of weavers, riots of coal-heavers; riots of sawyers; riots of Wilkesites; riots of government chairmen; riots of smugglers, in which custom house officers and excisemen have been murdered, the King's armed vessels and troops fired at.

Life was cheap, and people had to have strong stomachs. In 1764 two drunken bricklayers were lobbing bricks at each other for fun in Gray's Inn Lane. One was struck on the right temple and killed. In the same year a Tooley Street porter drank three pints of gin for a half-crown wager, won his bet and promptly dropped dead. Until 1789 women were occasionally burned alive at the stake for murdering their husbands (the crime of petty treason), though a kindly hangman might strangle them before the flames reached them. When a seven-year-old girl was hanged in Norwich for stealing a petticoat, no one protested. Condemned felons at the gallows often seemed more concerned to be 'launched into eternity' in style than to try to escape: what man would deny the crowd the brave end they expected? Indeed, mobs often took the law into their own hands. In Bristol in 1735 James Newth, condemned to hang for murdering his wife, poisoned himself, and the disappointed crowd saw him buried instead of strung up. Incensed at being cheated of their entertainment, they dug up the suicide's body and, as the *Gentleman's Magazine* put it, 'dragged his guts about the highway, poked his eyes out, and broke almost all his bones'.

No doubt gentlemen enjoyed reading that report, for executions were not just pleasures for plebs. George Selwyn, the necrophiliac rake and poet, notoriously got his kicks from hangings. Permanent wooden grandstands were erected round Tyburn Tree, called Mother Proctor's Pews, and their owner had good congregations. When Earl Ferrers was hanged in 1760, Mother Proctor took a collection of £500: Englishmen loved a lord, even unto death. Crowds also flocked to see convicted whores stripped to the waist and whipped. Papists and witches equally remained the targets of mass fear and reprisals. In 1700 a mob at St Albans did a reputed witch to death. Outsiders often were targets of appalling cruelties. 'Last Saturday,' a newspaper reported in 1751:

a ragged beggar came to a Public House in Puckle-Church in Gloucestershire, to ask Charity of some countrymen who were drinking there, who told him, in a joking manner, they used to hang all Beggars and would hang him; he told them he was not fit to die; but they taking hold of him, he begg'd they would do him no harm; however they got a Rope, put it about his Neck, and drew him up to a Bacon Rack, and bid him cry Bacon; to which they hung him so long, that he seem'd without Life, his tongue extending from his Mouth, so let him fall again, and perceiving they had carried their Folly too far, and being frightened with the Apprehension of what might ensue, carried the Beggar to a neighbouring Field, and laid him under a Hay-Rick for dead. He recovered his senses, and making mournful groans, a Woman heard him, and upon approaching the Hay-Rick, the poor Man gave her instruction by signs, how he came in that Condition, and pointed to the House where he receiv'd the Injury, and died soon after.

The House of Hanover inherited a hard-working, hard-living, plain-speaking nation, which only gradually became more pre-occupied with refinement. The Duchess of Northumberland entered in her diary for 6 May 1760: 'Went home; voided a large stone. Tired to death. Went to ball; tired to death. A Bad Supper. Miss Townshend drunk.' Hardly any houses boasted a bath. Before cottons became cheap, clothes were difficult to wash; children were sometimes sewn into theirs for the winter. Vermin were not just metaphorical; rat-catchers royal and flea-catchers royal made good livings. In the 1770s Andrew Cooke advertised himself as 'Bug Destroyer to His Majesty'. Chamber-pots were provided in dining-room sideboards, to save breaking up post-prandial conversation among the men. Back in the 1660s Pepys nonchalantly defecated into a fireplace (servants cleaned up the mess), and on one occasion he caught Lady Sandwich 'doing something upon the pot' in the dining-room. Food hygiene was no better than personal hygiene. The omnipresence of animals meant streets were awash with dung. What we have lost above all from the world we have lost in the stench. Small consola-tion that eyes may have been less offended than noses, for much was invisible in a world lit by candlelight, rushlight, and moonlight.

People had an ingrained tolerance of such inconvenience and squalor, and compensated by aggressive pursuit of pleasures and passions. Emotion was near the surface. The English leapt to cheer and jeer, and – for all Lord Chesterfield's strictures – they laughed and cried out loud. In social gatherings, people jested and capered, sang and shouted a lot; they threw themselves into the hurly-burly of fun-making, love-making, noise-making. They joined in rough sports, liked horse-play, and rode hard. The national institution of the stiff upper lip came later (though many, Dissenters in particular, already esteemed the importance of being earnest).

Alcohol gave stimulus, release, oblivion. The *Gentleman's Maga-zine* listed ninety-nine ways of calling a man drunk, from the genteel 'sipping the spirit of Adonis' to the vulgar 'stripping me naked'. To gain a reputation as a blade one had to be at least a three-bottle man. Sheridan, Pitt the Younger, and the Greek scholar Porson were all said to be six-bottle men, and Sir William Blackstone wrote his *Commentaries on the Laws of England* with a glass of port as his boon companion – though Oxford dons were notorious for what Gibbon dubbed 'their dull and deep potations', and the third Cambridge professor of history died after a drunken fall.

Drinking was competitive. 'I was always ambitious,' confessed man-about-town William Hickey, 'of sitting out every man at the table when I presided.' Eminent gentlemen, from Addison and Bolingbroke to Charles James Fox and Lord Eldon, bore out the aptness of the simile, 'drunk as a lord'. Yet hard drinking was not the privilege of peers. In his youth, Samuel Johnson remembered, 'all the decent people in Lichfield got drunk every night, and were not the worse thought of'. The shopkeeper Thomas Turner's diary shows the tradespeople of rural Sussex no less befuddled in the 1750s. After one head-splitting revel, Turner remorsefully recorded, 'we continued drinking like horses, as the vulgar phrase is, and singing till many of us were very drunk, and then we went to dancing, and pulling wigs, caps and hats; and thus we continued in this frantic manner, behaving more like mad people than they that profess the name of Christians.' Above all, the intoxication of the London poor in the Gin Craze was lethal: 'Drunk for a penny, dead drunk for tuppence; straw free,' advertised the gin-shops.

As a solace of the flesh, gluttony shared the honours with drinking. In an agrarian society, handsome eating was a token of success; generous hospitality was expected and admired. Englishmen tucked in and took pride in their boards and bellies. Until the elongated fashions of the Regency dandies and the Romantics, for whom consumptive thinness was *à la mode*, men and women were pleased to be corpulent and resigned to gout. 'Sir,' declared Dr Johnson, 'I mind my belly very well, for I look upon it that he who will not mind his belly will scarcely mind anything else.' 'He lived in a strange voluptuous manner, caring for nothing but his guts,' was Thomas Wilson's verdict on Bishop Hildersley. 'The goose is a silly bird,' groused Samuel Ogden, Dr Johnson's favourite sermon-writer, 'too much for one, and not enough for two.' Wiser Cambridge dons, however, clearly found fowl medicinal: Thomas Gray recorded how, dying of dropsy, Dr Ridlington, a fellow of Trinity Hall, 'prescribed himself a boiled chicken entire and five quarts of small beer', and recovered. But it was roast beef which was the Englishman's sacramental meal, immortalized in Hogarth's prints (Hogarth expired soon after finishing a steak), Fielding's song 'The Roast Beef of Old England', and the Sublime Society of Beefsteaks. Parson Woodforde, whose diary is a meticulous record of his belly, scratched this last entry the day he died: 'Very weak this morning, scarce able to put on my clothes and with great difficulty get downstairs with help. Dinner today, roast beef etc.' Life's pains were people's fate. But, from the splenetic don to the bent-backed hedger and ditcher, at daily Hall or annual harvest-home they could hope to forget.

The geography of social relations was as imposing and established as the hills, partly because it was – in Laslett's phrase – a 'face-to-face society'. Subjects were set into the social strata not primarily by choice, or by 'faceless' bureaucracy and paper qualifications (except for baptism, marriage and burial records in parish registers, people did not automatically figure in official files), but rather by their personal connections with others, especially authority figures: fathers, masters, husbands, parsons, patrons. People had to shift for themselves. There was no all-encompassing welfare state, no comprehensive system of social services, guaranteeing care from cradle to grave. How one made out depended on skills in the games of deference and condescension, patronage and favour, protection and obedience, seizing opportunities and making the most of them. In J. H. Plumb's words, in Georgian society, 'without protection, the poor and the weak and the sick went under; the rich and the strong prospered'.

The rawness, the pain, but also perhaps the humane mercies, of this pre-bureaucratic society are all revealed in a harrowing report in the *Gentleman's Magazine* for 1748:

At a Christening at Beddington in Surrey the nurse was so intoxicated that after she had undressed the child, instead of laying it in the cradle she put it behind a large fire, which burnt it to death in a few minutes. She was examined before a magistrate, and said she was quite stupid and senseless, so that she took the child for a log of wood; on which she was discharged.

Slightly over half the nation was female. Yet, compared with men, we know little about what women felt, thought and did. It was men who left most records behind – a fact that speaks all too eloquently of how muted women had to be. Millions of women earned their keep by toiling in light industry, in workshops, in taverns, in eating places, in the fields and in domestic service. Except among the upper bourgeoisie and gentry, they were expected to be money earners as well as bearing children and running the home. Yet very few women achieved prominence, or fortune, in the world of work, and we have very little record of their experiences. Till now, historians of women have focused attention more on 'bluestockings' than the seamstresses who sewed them.

Public life on a grand scale was a men-only club (as were almost all clubs themselves). There were no female parliamentarians, explorers, lawyers, magistrates or factory entrepreneurs, and almost no women voters. For Dr Johnson, the idea of a woman preacher was 'like a dog walking on his hind legs'. A woman hoping to be accepted as an intellectual had to run the gauntlet. Catherine Macaulay was sneered at for her ambitions to be a serious historian and political writer (she had also committed the abomination of marrying a man half her age). Public opinion (largely male but echoed by conformist women) tight-laced women into constrictive roles: wives, mothers, housekeepers, subordinate workers, domestic servants, maiden aunts. Few escaped. Such stereotyping created a kind of invisibility: women were to be men's shadows.

Much of our evidence about what women were like and thought – or were expected to think – comes from men, from sermons and courtesy manuals, from male diarists, writers, painters and doctors. We know little about 'Tetty' Johnson or Margaret Boswell except through their husbands. Women who wrote about themselves – such as Lady Mary Wortley Montagu, or the 'bluestockings' in the salon 'petticoateries' run by Mrs Delaney, Mrs Chapone, Mrs Vesey and others – lamented their circumstances: the pains of pregnancy, the odiousness of suitors, the vapid tedium of polite society. But at bottom many also broadly shared men's views about women's place and the relations between the sexes. With high-minded propriety, 'bluestockings' no less than men expected female chastity and submission. When she became pregnant out of wedlock, Mary Wollstonecraft was cold-shouldered by erstwhile female friends, such as the author Mrs Inchbald and the actress Mrs Siddons (were they genuinely shocked, or did they have their own reputations to think about?). 'Wit in women is apt to have bad consequences,' judged Elizabeth Montagu icily in 1750; 'like a sword without a scabbard, it wounds the wearer and provokes assailants. I am sorry to say the generality of women who have excelled in wit have failed in chastity.' Mrs Chapone, a fellow bluestocking, could defend a husband's 'divine right to obedience', while paradoxically asserting 'the general truth, that women as rational and accountable beings, are free agents, as well as men'. Sometimes, however, women accepted their place with resignation: self-censorship became second nature. Thus Lady Mary Wortley Montagu advised her daughter to 'conceal whatever learning she attains, with as much solicitude as she would hide crookedness or lameness'. Evidently men liked dumb broads. 'If you happen to have any learning,' Dr Gregory advised young ladies, 'keep it a profound secret, especially from the men.' In Samuel Richardson's influential novel, it was virtue (crudely, her virginity) that won the servant Pamela her upper-class husband.

In a man's world it is not surprising that a lady parroted her master's voice. Most found that if they acquiesced and worked the system, they could exercise considerable power within their own allotted spheres. A few rejected their fate: thus Mary Astell, the Greek scholar, dreamed of college retreats ('nunneries') where spinster academics could pursue religion and scholarship. But there was no organized 'feminist' movement campaigning for equality for women in public life – just brave individuals, misfits, victims and rebels, from the satirical playwright Mrs Mary Manley at the beginning of the century to Mary Wollstonecraft at the end.

The basic assumption governing relations between the sexes, underpinning attitudes and institutions, and backed ultimately by law, was that men and women were naturally different in capacity, and so ought to play distinct social roles. Anatomy determined destiny, and men were destined to be on top. Men were intended (so men claimed) to excel in reason, business, action; women's forte lay in being submissive, modest, docile, virtuous, maternal and domestic (reality, however, was not so simple: men were terrified of 'shrewishness'; husbands who capitulated to 'petticoat government' were laughing-stocks). High public office, the professions, the universities and the Church were closed to women (though many, such as Sarah Churchill and the Duchess of Devonshire, exercised immense behind-the-scenes power, because of rank, breeding, force of personality and sexual charms).

Received opinion was that they should permanently depend on men – as daughters on their fathers, and, once wives, on the 'masculine dominion' of their husbands. At the beginning of the century it was still common among the Quality for a father to arrange his daughter's marriage: she would at best have a veto over his choice. In common law, wives had no rights over their children or to matrimonial property (though land could be held in trust for wives). This was because 'in marriage husband and wife are one person, and that person is the husband', as Sir William Blackstone deftly explained, glossing 'the very being, or legal existence, of the woman is suspended during marriage.' 'Women in England,' an early eighteenth-century book put it, 'with all their moveable goods so soon as they are married are wholly *in potestate viri*, at will and disposition of the husband'; even a woman's 'very necessary apparel, by the law, is not hers, in property'. A husband had the right to beat his wife, ruled a judge, provided the stick was no thicker than a man's thumb. A married woman could make a will only with her husband's consent, and after her death he could have it set aside. Whereas men could be themselves, women had to conform to men's expectations of them: for instance, in Samuel Richardson's novel *Pamela*, Mr B. set out some forty rules for what he required in a wife.

Many men judged women to be simply inferior, the weaker vessel. 'There is inequality in the sexes,' judged Lord Halifax. For Lord Chesterfield, 'women are children of a larger growth' – 'a man of sense only trifles with them'. And so in polite society the sexes were segregated – more than, say, in France. Frenchwomen presided over the salons of the *philosophes*: English ladies were encouraged to conserve their strength by indulging only in tea-table gossip and ornamental pastimes such as embroidery. As for talk, a lady's was assumed to be small, tittle-tattle in fact: society ladies withdrew after dinner, leaving their heroic husbands to settle the destiny of nations, toast their mistresses with bumpers, and drink themselves under the table. 'Imbecility in females is a great enhancement of their personal charms,' tartly observed Jane Austen.

Good women were typecast as obedient guardian angels of family and virtue, as James Thomson's unctuous verses show:

> Well-ordered Home Man's best delight to make;
> And by submissive wisdom, modest skill,
> With every gentle care-eluding art,
> To raise the virtues, animate the bliss,
> And sweeten all the toils of human life:
> This be the female dignity and praise.

In polite society a lady's chastity before marriage, and reputation after, were thought crucial by gentlemen. Men generously conceded that they themselves could not vie with such paragons of sexual purity, but as Dr Johnson explained, 'If we require more perfection from women than from ourselves it is doing them honour.' Aside from the yellow-eyed monster of male jealousy, this double standard expressed practical fears. A husband would not contemplate a cuckoo in the nest, nor would he wish to bequeath his property to a son unless he was sure of paternity. Dr Johnson did not beat about the bush: 'The chastity of women is of importance, as all property depends on it.' By contrast, 'between man and wife, a husband's infidelity is nothing ... Wise married women don't trouble themselves about infidelity in their husbands ... The man imposes no bastards upon his wife.' (The fates of serving-wenches, milliners and mistresses did not even enter into that Christian's reckoning.) A wife's adultery was ground enough in law for divorce, but not vice versa (although divorces were very rare, since they required a private Act of Parliament).

In reality, however, society ladies – especially in London – were much less submissive than these idealizations suggest, and many happily colluded in men's games of clandestine flirtation and conquest. Moreover, force of character, charm, inherited wealth or family name gave heiresses or matriarchs enormous bargaining strength and a chance to influence family destinies.

In affluent society, boys and girls, even small ones, were educated separately. Girls were less frequently sent away to school, being consigned to servants and aunts, becoming thus 'nurs'd upon ignorance and vanity'. Lady Mary Wortley

Montagu complained of her nurse, 'She took so much pains, from my infancy, to fill my head with superstitious tales and false notions, it was none of her fault I am not at this day afraid of witches and hobgoblins or turned methodist.' Young ladies were groomed for matrimony, and with reason. If a daughter failed to trap a husband, she might become an 'old maid', a burden on her family, forced into a frustrating post as lady's companion or governess, with no independence and existing in an impoverished no-man's land between family and servants.

When a gentleman was casting round for a husband for his daughter in the early Georgian matrimonial market, his first considerations were security, family, title and land. Matrimony was not narrowly about love and bliss, but involved wider matters of family policy, securing honour, lineage and fortune – and families were patrilineal. Sir William Temple was not being outrageously cynical in observing, 'Our marriages are made, just like other common bargains and sales, by the mere consideration of interest or gain, without any love or esteem.' Fathers had to dangle handsome dowries as bait to catch well-connected, landed, titled husbands for their daughters. Up to £25,000 might be needed to hook a peer. Newspaper announcements revelled in the horse-trading:

MARRIAGES

25 March 1735, John Parry, Esq. of Carmarthenshire, to a daughter of Walter Lloyd, Esq. member for that county, a fortune of £8,000. The Lord Bishop of St Asaph to Miss Orell, with £30,000. Married, the Rev Mr Roger Waind, of York, about twenty six years of age, to a Lincolnshire lady, upwards of eighty, with whom he is to have £8,000 in money, £300 per annum and a coach-and-four during life only.

In society, marriage was recommended as an alliance of sense. Too much sensibility – still more, sensuality – was suspect; giddy romance would wither on stony soil. A circumspect settlement might allow respect and regard to take deep root between husband and wife; but it was the successful aggrandizement of name and acres which probably mattered most to hard-headed families, marriageable daughters (and sons) being strategic pawns (though as pawns they had some power). Cheapened by market-place haggling, small wonder holy matrimony was cynically viewed. As Jarrett has written, 'The world of the popular prints was one in which the marriages of labourers disintegrated into violence, while those of noblemen degenerated into vice.' Daughters loathed being sacrificed to strangers. 'People in my way are sold like slaves, and I cannot tell what price my masters will put on me,' complained Mary Wortley Montagu, who, detesting her father's choice of mate, eloped (hers was a case of out of the frying pan . . .). Yet if matrimony had many pains, spinsterhood had no pleasures – and, in any case, as the witticism went, it was worth enduring marriage for the benefits of widowhood; and, unlike men, few women remained single by choice. A wife at least had the run of a house and financial security.

Once married, a lady in polite society had four cardinal functions. The first duty was to obey her husband. Second, she had to produce heirs. Women's letters harrowingly chronicle the fatigue, ill-health and premature ageing they suffered as they repeatedly grew full-bellied. Lady Bristol, who married at the age of nineteen in 1695, bore a son in 1696, a daughter in 1697, a son in January 1699, another in December in the same year and yet another in 1701. She miscarried of triplets in the same year, produced a son and a daughter in April 1703 and a stillborn son in 1704. Between 1706 and 1710 she bore three more sons and two daughters, and she had sons in 1712 and 1713, and daughters in 1715 and 1716. At thirty-nine she had had her last pregnancy, having produced twenty children, few of whom lived to grow up. Lady Bristol's fertility was exceptional, but many dreaded the childbirth treadmill. 'I am in a great fright,' wrote Lady Caroline Fox to her husband on first indications of pregnancy, 'and if my fears prove true, I shall be vastly angry with you,' for 'twould be very hard for me as I have not yet recovered my strength from the last lying-in.' Many tried to space their confinements, by delaying weaning a previous infant, by *coitus interruptus*, or simply by denying their husband access to bed, perhaps pleading illness. Patent abortifacients were advertised in newspapers, but there is little sign that women used mechanical contraceptive appliances (though French ladies had sponges and douches). Condoms (called by Casanova 'English overcoats' and by Boswell 'armour') were on sale in London, but were used by men dallying with whores as prophylactics against venereal disease rather than as contraceptives.

Having brought an infant into the world, the early-eighteenth-century lady's duty to it was largely discharged, for affluent families hired attendants, wet-nurses and nurse-maids, and later governesses, tutors, singing teachers and dancing masters. Women of quality traditionally had little to do with day-to-day child-rearing, for adults were not meant to be interested in childish things. Relations between parents and children were expected to be formal – we would find them distant. Even in happy families respect was more visible than affection. With child mortality high, avoiding excessive attachment to one's offspring may have served as an emotional defence mechanism.

The third duty of the married lady was to run the household. This involved providing food, drink and comforts; commanding domestic servants, especially personal maids and kitchen staff; supervising accounts; and arranging entertainment. Her fourth duty was to be ladylike, an ambassadress of grace. Ladies' polite ac-complishments included the arts of dressing, conversing agree-ably (though avoiding fishing in male ponds such as politics or religion), singing or playing a genteel instrument (spinets were ideal), and cultivating taste in decoration, furnishing and the arts – sewing, lace-making, drawing.

Within the professional and landed classes, the roles of wife and mother began to evolve during the century. Not that the ultimate male–female power imbalance was redressed: in 1800 women were still as disadvantaged as ever in law and locked out of public office. But attitudes towards marriage were changing in ways which curbed the power of parents over their offspring's choice and gave more positive roles to wives as mothers within the domestic family. Moralists and preachers had always deplored the *mariage de convenance*, and gradually more people began to accept the superior claims of personal choice of mate, affection, and even love. Increasingly, prospective partners were allowed to explore romantic feelings (though, in polite society, not sex) before marriage. Daughters were granted greater say in picking a husband (parents settled for the right of veto, while of course continuing to command the power of the purse). A season of balls, family parties and visits to resorts such as Bath was invented, to give Miss more chance to meet eligible suitors. The *quid pro quo* for this curtailment of parent power was Hardwicke's Marriage Act (1753), which forbade the marriage of those under the age of twenty-one without parental consent, and required the publishing of banns. This aimed to close the lovers' loophole of eloping and contracting an instant, legally binding marriage performed by sympathetic or mercenary parsons (though romantic runaways could still gallop off to the matrimonial paradise of Scotland). Marrying for love became respectable. 'Anything is to be preferred or endured,' advised Jane Austen, early in the next century, 'rather than marrying without affection ... Nothing can be compared to the misery of being bound without love.'

Warmth, and even tenderness, came to characterize the public face of upper-class conjugality. 'Husband and wife are always together,' wrote the Duc de La Rochefoucauld of English polite society in the 1780s (he exaggerated, but hit upon the essential change), 'and share the same society ... They pay all their visits together. It would be more ridiculous to do otherwise in England than it would be to go everywhere with your wife in Paris.' Spouses began treating each other with less formality. Couples whose parents or grandparents had 'Sir'd or 'Madam'd each other adopted familiar terms of endearment. Children were now allowed to 'mama' and 'papa' their parents.

Above all, the woman's domestic situation changed. As living grew more gracious, and refined emotions were cultivated, the lady's role as domestic quartermistress, as commissar of the laundry and purveyor of pickles, preserves and poultices, devolved upon the shoulders of the proverbially fierce, key-jangling housekeeper. (In any case, it became more common to purchase items such as soap and starch rather than make them at home.) The fashionable lady was freed to cultivate the more 'feminine' graces: her toilet, tea-table conversation, shopping, spending pin-money, paying and receiving calls, philanthropy, the vapours, scents and sensibility, all encouraged and mirrored by that recent narcissistic invention, the novel. Chic learning, including Newtonian science, was presented palatably predigested in books specially written for ladies, and women's magazines such as the *Ladies' Diary* appeared, containing short stories, the latest fashions, and items on history and geography. Lavishing too much time on household management, a magazine ambiguously warned in the 1740s, might win a lady 'the reputation of a notable housewife, but not of a woman of fine taste'.

Ladies were beginning to make more time for their children, too. From about mid-century it became the done thing for well-bred ladies to interest themselves with nursing their babies and training toddlers – more with the exquisite delight of discovering a new pet under one's nose than with the dutifulness of the Victorian matriarch – though Queen Charlotte proved a foretaste of Queen Victoria. Many ladies abandoned the wet-nurse and experimented with breast-feeding; swaddling disappeared, partly in response to mothers' new-found desire to fondle, dandle and dress their infants. Mothers began to take their children out of servants' hands, fearing lest (as William Darrell wrote) 'peasantry is a disease (like the plague) easily caught'. Joseph Addison planted the nursery seed early in the century: 'Female virtues are of a domestic turn.' The bluestocking Mrs Chapone watered it: 'The principal virtues ... of a woman must be of a private and domestic kind.' And mothering and domesticity came into vogue, as is faithfully mirrored in the novels of Jane Austen.

The role of angel in the house promised fulfilment to many ladies whose talents and emotions otherwise had few outlets. Greater maternal affection probably provided valuable attention and warmth for the children too (possibly one factor in checking infant mortality, thus explaining the increasing size of grandee families). But ultimately the cult of the family merely created dolls' houses for women to live in within a man's world, reaffirming men's grip on the rest of society. And ladies grew doll-like: ornamental, flirtatious, delicate, helpless. 'Ladies spend many of the first years of their lives,' Mary Wollstonecraft remarked,

in acquiring a smattering of accomplishments; meanwhile strength of body and mind are sacrificed to libertine notions of beauty, to the desire of establishing themselves – the only way women can rise in the world – by marriage. And this desire making mere animals of them, when they marry they act as such children may be expected to act, they dress, they paint, and nickname God's creatures. Surely these weak beings are only fit for a seraglio. Can they be expected to govern a family with judgement, or take care of the poor babes whom they bring into the world?

Lower down the social scale, women had no option of retreating into mere domesticity, 'separate spheres'. Among working people, marriage had always meant – alongside affection – an astute bargain to set up mutually beneficial household partnerships. For most, marriage alone established independence as a producer or proprietor. Through marriage, women gained the strength, protection, status and earning-power of husbands; men got the domestic management and labour of a wife (and the savings nest-egg she might bring). Together, men and women needed the labour of children around farmyards, in domestic industries such as textiles, and in running shops. Independent women with some property (for example, widows) sometimes avoided a church wedding, however, for if they married their property would pass in law to their spouse. They might prefer a 'common law' community ceremony, sanctified by such symbolic actions as jumping backwards over a broom.

We know little about what working women felt about their lives and their mates. Once married, women might easily be reduced to the status of drudges and chattels. Indeed, highly ritualized wife sales were sometimes set up by working men – occasionally with the wife's consent – seeking to escape the 'wed-lock'. A wife would fetch a few guineas, or might be traded in for an ox. These sales were the only practical – though not legally binding – form of divorce available to any but the very rich. Yet, through controlling the household, the children, the farmyard or kitchen garden, working women must often, in fact, have ruled the roost, especially those whose husbands were away as migrant workers, soldiers or seamen. Men, however, avenged themselves on women who too openly wore the breeches by stigmatizing them as scolds.

Women had always worked alongside men, performing heavy tasks in the fields or in industry (for example, humping baskets of coal on their backs up mineshafts). Girls had commonly been apprenticed to 'men's' trades (there were, for instance, female barbers and surgeons). And though most women worked in subordinate positions, as domestic servants, or alongside their husbands on the family smallholding or in a cottage industry, there were independent women who grazed their own flocks, or ran millinery shops, chop-houses, taverns, brothels or even lunatic asylums. Many such small business women were daughters inheriting a concern from their fathers, or widows keeping a family business going after their husband's death (as for instance, the widow of John Baskerville, the noted Birmingham typefounder). Such a situation arose quite commonly as women tended to outlive men, and businessmen generally took younger wives. Occasionally, a very exceptional woman smuggled herself, disguised, into the army, as did Hannah Snell, or followed a profession (Mrs Lydia Walliss became a valuer).

The coming of factories offered certain new openings for female labour, while closing others, above all dramatically curtailing domestic spinning. The textile factories of the late eighteenth century (though as yet few in number) generated a hungry demand for concentrated female labour outside the face-to-face world of the farm, domestic service and cottage industry. Factory work reduced the operative to the slave of a machine, and the hours were extremely taxing, but it was better paid than domestic service (though women got less than men), and not living under a master's roof gave single women a whiff of independence. Factory girls began to marry younger: they were freer than domestic servants, they reached their earnings peak early, and their cash savings attracted husbands.

Where available, factory work perhaps extended the options open to young working women; but these options contracted in a numerically far more telling field: agriculture. In the fields, women had traditionally performed largely similar tasks to men. But gradually they were made more marginal, and reduced to poorly paid tasks such as weeding, especially in the great corn belt of central and southern England. This was partly due to the spread of heavier tools, such as the scythe, but it was mainly because of the growing surplus of male labourers. As population outstripped jobs on the land, men commandeered the work and kept their womenfolk at home. Farmers preferred to employ men, rather than pay them poor relief. Similar pressures affected trades, where apprenticeship for women became a rarity. Squeezed out of the labour market, women looked to early matrimony as their safest career bet. In all classes, the eighteenth century reinforced the pattern of the man at work and the woman at home.

As critics pointed out at the time, women were confronted with 'Hobson's choice'. Many openings for them contracted, as men moved into traditional female vocations such as midwifery and hairdressing, and witches were hounded. As married lady or spinster, domestic servant or factory girl, mother or 'old maid' – with, in all cases, what Mrs Chapone called devotion to 'religion

... discretion, good sense ... good temper' expected of them –
virtuous women had been set on a pedestal which gave them
little room to move, except to fall. Such expectations led to
miniatured lives of dependence, frustrations and waste – which
an exceptional pen such as Fanny Burney's or Jane Austen's
might turn to great art. Of course, one option *was* to fall. In a
man's world, women could always earn a living by selling
themselves. Most prostitutes led wretched lives; though by the
standards of other centuries, top-notch coquettes, courtesans and
demi-mondaines – women such as Kitty Fisher and Kitty Kennedy – were respected and even socially fêted. Lavinia Fenton, an
ale-house keeper's daughter, went on the stage, became mistress of
the Duke of Bolton on '£400 during pleasure and £200 p.a. for
life', gave him three sons, and married him on the death of his
Duchess. It was certainly easier for a woman to achieve notoriety
than power.

But the great majority of women who obediently and honour-
ably did what they were told were condemned to a second-class
life hedged with briars. The autobiography of Elizabeth Ham is a
rare record of such a bleak existence. Born in 1783 of a Dorset
yeoman family which gave her cold baths but denied her affection, Elizabeth was brought up by a cousin, offered a cheap,
broken schooling in petty accomplishments, and driven by parental hardship into a spinster existence governessing. Trapped
between the servants and family, her work was humiliating,
empty and bitterly lonely. Religion alone gave her solace (though
her Unitarianism itself lost her jobs). Such was the pathetic life of
a 'career girl'. Yet the cult of motherhood, sensibility and the
home could also be a cage. Every door opened on to a blank
wall.

The life and death of Mary Wollstonecraft form a tragic coda
to these dilemmas. She was one of very few women who
attempted to walk clean out of the male-allotted range of female
parts, asserting in 1792 *The Rights of Woman*, in a book which
complemented but subtly challenged Tom Paine's *Rights of Man*.
She wanted women to be free to carve out careers, and proclaimed
free love to end the sexual double standard, denouncing marriage
as 'legalized prostitution'. She envisaged women as independent
and whole, uniting the qualities traditionally parcelled out between
Adam and Eve: rationality *and* feeling, career *and* motherhood.

Reality proved more difficult. Even in her ideas, she could not escape her times, her autobiographical novels *Mary* and *Maria* succumbing to modish, morbid sensibility, her concept of female fulfilment glorying in the domestic mother, her vision of women idealizing them as born victims. And her life acted out these contradictions but did not resolve them: high-minded and cerebral radicalism in London gave way to passionate sexual involvement with an American in Paris during the French Revolution, followed by suicide attempts when he asserted *his* freedom.

She remained utterly ambivalent about marriage and monogamy. Her liaison with the philosopher William Godwin, and marriage to him on becoming pregnant (both had denounced matrimony as legalized prostitution), were tragically followed by death in childbed. She showed great courage in the face of vilification – Horace Walpole dubbed her a 'hyena'. But her truncated life echoed her fictions with novelettish doom, as she failed successively to transcend contrarieties. Biology and society baulked escape.

Great Britain was not the least important eighteenth-century invention. The Act of Union (1707) abolished the Scottish Parliament by agreement, united the governments of England and Scotland at Westminster, and established the Union Jack. In Georgian parliamentary politics, Caledonia was to lead the field in corruption. The century closed with the end of short-lived Irish parliamentary self-government, by the inclusion of Ireland in the Union in 1801. Great Britain, however, was a euphemism for greater England. No eighteenth-century monarch visited Wales, Scotland or Ireland (though George I and George II frequently went home to Hanover).

Though some regions (Dublin and the midland valley of Scotland, for example) became anglicized, the Celtic fringes retained their distinctive identity, as did off-shore islands such as Guernsey and Man, both in effect smugglers' lairs. They stayed distinct partly because they were increasingly made to serve as primary producers for England's economic needs. In their contrasting ways, the Scottish and Irish economies were drastically reshaped by Westminster. John Bull's other island, anglicized Ireland, was the most colonial part of Britain, being bullied and bled by a frequently absentee Protestant landlord class. Landlords' incomes trebled during the century, largely at the expense of the indigenous Catholic peasantry, and by 1750 three quarters of a million pounds in rent was leaving Ireland annually. Bishop Berkeley thought London was the Irish metropolis, though Dublin itself was English enough. In peacetime the largest concentration of the British army had to be stationed in Ireland. Catholics, though the vast majority, suffered legal disabilities, including disfranchisement. Furthermore, Irish industry was sacrificed to English manufacturers, from 1698 the export of Irish wool and cloth being banned, except to England. By mid-century, Ulster was already establishing its industrial edge over the pastoral South, which was suffering worsening subsistence crises. Famine struck, particularly in 1726–9 and 1739–41, the latter killing 400,000. Even so, aided by potatoes and the parcellization of holdings, population grew ominously, outpacing the English. There were over two Irish mouths to feed in 1800 for every one in 1700.

Scotland lacerated itself, becoming increasingly torn between the Jacobite-sympathizing, Gaelic-speaking Highland clans, which were proscribed after the bloody culmination at Culloden of the Young Pretender's 1745 rebellion (40,000 Highlanders were soon to emigrate to America), and the Edinburgh–Glasgow axis of capitalist landlords, merchants, lawyers, clergy and professors (Adam Smith among them), who believed that the Scots' economic, cultural and even religious future lay in throwing in their lot with England. Realistically, they were right. Under post-Union free-trade, Scottish cattle-droving, linens, mining and metal trades thrived. Agriculture and industry were modernized. Yet the sacrifice was great. Ambitious Scots anglicized their voices (the Irishman Thomas Sheridan gave them elocution lessons), disguised their names (the founder of Almack's London club was baptized John McCall), and took the high road south: 'Macs' not 'Micks' were the most resented immigrants in Hanoverian England – because of their success: they were the top educators, engineers, surgeons and philandering biographers.

Wales remained a backwater lacking even a capital; with fewer than 400,000 people in 1700 – not many more than Devon – it was a pastoral economy, freckled with sleepy market towns (Wrexham, the largest, had a bare 4,000 inhabitants, Cardiff just over a thousand) and mining, smelting and quarrying villages.

The province was left to itself: some of its Anglican bishops never set foot within the principality. It was dominated by a small-time squirarchy, which in a few regions only, such as Glamorgan, caught the improvement bug. Not until the 1770s did tourists swarm to the mountains, though the London-based Society for the Propagation of Christian Knowledge inspired a circulating school movement from the 1730s, printing Welsh Bibles. And the development of industry depended upon English enterprise. The South Wales copper, iron and coal industries, centred upon Swansea and Neath and big business by 1800, were primed with Bristol and West Midlands capital.

Obviously, English possessions overseas also had lives of their own, aided by 'salutary neglect' (a licence to merchants to pillage as they chose). The Thirteen Colonies of North America were an Arcadian, open-society version of England, free of the encumbrances of king and nobility, prelates and paupers, but blessed with unlimited land, Indians to expropriate, black slaves and indentured servants; or perhaps less 'England' than Britain, as waves of dispossessed Scots and Irish flooded in. The North American colonies expanded rapidly, their 1700 population of 340,000 rising to 1,200,000 by 1760. By contrast, the Caribbean colonies and, in the latter part of the century, British India presented an exaggerated version of the hierarchies of the homeland. Nabobs – officials of the East India Company – enacted their plundering fantasies before a captive audience of natives: young William Hickey, in London a ne'er-do-well, had sixty-three underlings as an East India Company clerk in Calcutta. Successful nabobs could hope to bring back a couple of hundred thousand pounds (though up to two thirds of them succumbed to tropical diseases).

When Edmund Burke indicted Warren Hastings for misrule in India in 1783, he complained: 'England has erected no churches, no hospitals, no palaces, no schools, England has built no bridges, made no highways, cut no navigations, dug out no reservoirs.' But native society was not spared the civilizing itch much longer. By the early nineteenth century it was falling to the white man's mission, to Evangelicals and Utilitarians. 'Europeans lord it over the natives with a high hand,' commented Byron's friend, Edward Trelawney; 'every outrage may be committed with impunity.'

Imperial domination spread. Slaves were the precious life-blood of the West Indian economy, where King Sugar reigned and in which £70 million had been invested by 1790. Under the *asiento*, British slave-traders transported a million and a half Africans to the Caribbean during the century: 'All this great increase in our treasure,' wrote Joshua Gee in 1729, 'proceeds chiefly from the labour of negroes in the plantations.' West African gold gave England the guinea. In 1787, Sierra Leone in West Africa was set up as a trial settlement of free blacks, as was New South Wales from 1788 for transported criminal whites. The future of English society was irreversibly being skewed by empire.

What was the anatomy of England itself? England was quilted out of myriad particularist, insular, chauvinistic communities. Everywhere there were hidden local economies and secret pockets of people. Fenland settlements and mining encampments seemed forbidding to travellers, like tribal no-go areas, and wayfarers and 'foreigners' were widely treated with suspicion. Yet by continental standards, it was truly a united kingdom. Unlike France, Poland or Spain, not to mention such patchwork fantasies as the Habsburg empire, only one national group owned the land, the writ of one law ran into all corners, and just one tongue was spoken and written (Cornish became extinct about 1780). English-speakers from places as far-flung as Truro and Berwick would certainly have had difficulties with each other's intonation and idiom, but contemporary Frenchmen were speaking languages as distinct as Basque and German, and numberless patois besides. Unlike their English counterparts, the noblemen of many other nations disdained even to speak the native tongue of their peasants. Russian counts spoke French, Danish lords spoke German. Georgian England had no such linguistic barriers.

The England of 1700 was, of course, a society whose communications were sluggish and often arduous. By road the haul from Newcastle to London was ('God willing', as advertisements said) nine days; from Chester, six days. Defoe thought a tree-trunk might take three years to be dragged from Sussex to its dockyard destination in Chatham (it seasoned itself *en route*). Ox-waggons were common. Celia Fiennes, riding side-saddle along the Great North Road, simply lost it. The mail was costly. All such age-old obstacles reinforced insularity and a geography of cultural difference. Northerners – so report had it – tucked in to potatoes and oatcakes, and made their own clothes; southerners did none of these. Catholic recusancy was encrusted in old enclaves such as South Lancashire. Weights, measures, prices, wage-rates, the length of a mile, and even the time of day, varied regionally.

Yet despite all this England was highly integrated even in 1700. There were no provincial assemblies in the style of the French *parlements*. Even before newspapers became widespread, country people were remarkably *au courant* with St James and Westminster politics – partly through handwritten 'intelligences' which rattled down with stage-coaches. Already people were travelling not just on business or health but for pleasure; and the brisk seasonal labour market ensured a high circulation of working people, townsfolk for example flocking out into the country for the harvest. Nostalgia's picture of a stable village England where the rude forefathers of the hamlet slept, where time stood still, and generations of Hodges ploughed the same furrows as their ancestors, is – at least outside the proprietorial classes – a myth. Turnover was rapid: 'movers' outnumbered 'stayers'. Between 1676 and 1688, no fewer than 40 per cent of the inhabitants of Clayworth in Nottinghamshire changed parish. In the late eighteenth century, 70 per cent of the population of Cardington in rural Bedfordshire had been born elsewhere. Boys and, though less so, girls were routinely apprenticed to tradesmen and farmers or sent into service in neighbouring villages. Most migration was local, creeping caterpillar-like towards the larger towns. But the brave ventured over the hills and far away, to London, to sea, into the army, or off to the colonies (though fewer English families emigrated than in the seventeenth or nineteenth centuries). Unmarried farm servants and many journeymen expected to change jobs each year, offering themselves at district hiring fairs ('mops'), held in pastoral areas after lambing and in cornlands after harvest. Seasonal migratory labour (for harvesting, for instance) was vital to the economy and was not impeded by the Laws of Settlement. From the 1760s armies of navvies appeared like ants on the landscape, digging canals. And London proved an irresistible honeypot for the young, offering work, money and excitement, or anonymity and escape. England's roads were trudged by men, sometimes families, tramping for work, their money sewn into their coat linings as protection against footpads. 'We daily see manufacturers [artisans] leaving the places where wages are low and removing to others where they can get more money,' observed one writer in 1752.

Above all, as roads and transport improved, mobility and integration accelerated in proportion. Louis Simond, a Swiss-American visitor during the Regency, hit on a truth when he wrote:

Nobody is provincial in this country. You meet nowhere with those persons who never were out of their native place, and whose habits are wholly local – nobody above poverty who has not visited London once in his life; and most of those who can, visit it once a year. To go up to town from 100 or 200 miles distance, is a thing done on a sudden, and without any previous deliberation. In France the people of the provinces used to make their will before they undertook such an expedition.

England was a close-knit country above all because its economy was strikingly interlocking, and at the centre London was a bottomless pit of consumption. London was England's one conurbation (even if sturgeon could still be caught at Stepney). It was the powerhouse of politics, law, the Court, fashion and the arts and sciences (the Royal Society of London dated from 1660); the forge of luxury industry; the capital of finance (the Bank of England had been founded in 1694); the greatest port for overseas trade. The metropolis rubbed people up differently. Dr Johnson believed that 'When a man is tired of London, he is tired of life.' For the bucolic William Cobbett, by contrast, it was 'the Great Wen', the epitome of mere wastefulness. Yet all agreed that by its sheer size and wealth, London dominated England. In 1770 London had approaching 700,000 inhabitants – about one in eight Englishmen, or close on half the town dwellers in the kingdom. The next largest – toytown by contrast – was Norwich, with nearly 30,000 souls. Of the rest, only Bristol, Exeter, (probably) York, Newcastle, Colchester and Yarmouth topped 10,000. Most of the other 800 market towns had just a thousand or two.

London reached out all over the kingdom, primarily through its economic tentacles. Foodstuffs trundled in from all quarters.

'The neighbourhood of London sucks the vitals of trade in this island to itself,' punned Defoe. Corn floated down the Thames valley in barges from Oxfordshire; vegetables came up from Kentish market gardens; cheese and salt were sent from Cheshire, fish from Devon and Sussex coasts, poultry from Suffolk, potted chars from Lake Windermere; cattle and sheep were driven on the hoof from Wales, Scotland and the East Midlands for fattening on the Thames marshes. Early in the century some 80,000 cattle and 610,000 sheep reached Smithfield every year. And non-edibles were drawn in too, above all coal, brought by coaster from Newcastle (70 per cent of Tyneside coal was destined for London). London's insatiable demands spurred competitive, go-ahead market agriculture and advanced commercial practices throughout the nation – long-distance credit, bills of exchange, and a commissariat of middle men: corn-badgers, chapmen, wholesale butchers, graziers and drovers, cattle-fatteners, and the like. The purveyance of London ran smoothly: unlike Parisians, Londoners did not fear the provinces would cause them to starve.

London lorded it over the kingdom in other ways as well. It became the cynosure for all other cities. Provincial towns had felt the pinch in Tudor and Stuart times, in some cases suffering economic decline (itself largely due to metropolitan competition), in others a loss of political autonomy to grafting grandees and to the Court. Partly because of the Reformation, civic life had become comatose. As late as 1700 Birmingham had no bookshop or assembly rooms. Tourists went to view country seats, not provincial towns.

But from the late seventeenth century, an 'urban renaissance' took place. Population grew, outports (especially those on the west coast, such as Bristol, Liverpool and Whitehaven) flourished. And, not least, provincial towns gained stature as foci of polite society, consumption, communications and the arts. In search of cultural identity, burghers did not trumpet their 'provinciality' (contrast the Victorians, who boasted of grassroots honesty and homespun values). Rather they mimicked the capital. London town set the tone. Provincial fashion impresarios cloned London's pleasure gardens, walks, assembly rooms, theatres and concert halls, and tradesmen flocked to hear London actors, such as James Quin, Kitty Clive and Mrs Siddons, and scientific lecturers, such as Benjamin Martin. They bought London newspapers, patent medicines and couture. Bath and rival resorts tempted London visitors for the season. William Wilberforce disparaged Brighton as 'Piccadilly by the sea-side'.

Yet England was a mosaic in which regional contrasts remained ineradicable. These were partly because the heterogeneous demands of London food consumption and, more generally, market forces encouraged each region to specialize in particular commodities. Differences were also environmental responses to variations of latitude, altitude, soil and climate. Local economies formed epicycles in the orbit of the national (partly because some were illicit – for instance the underground distributive networks that poaching, coining and smuggling generated).

To some, there was a world of difference between London's madding crowd and the immemorial litany of rural life, a contrast evoked by Alexander Pope's pastoral lines on Martha Blount leaving Town:

> She went, to plain-work and to purling brooks,
> Old-fashion'd halls, dull aunts, and croaking rooks,
> She went from op'ra, park, assembly, play,
> To morning walks, and pray'rs three hours a day;
> To pass her time 'twixt reading and Bohea,
> To muse, and spill her solitary Tea,
> Or o'er cold coffee trifle with the spoon,
> Count the slow clock, and dine exact at noon;
> Divert her eyes with pictures in the fire,
> Hum half a tune, tell stories to the squire;
> Up to her godly garret after sev'n,
> There stare and pray, for that's the way to heav'n.

Yet the town and the country were not stark opposites but, rather, complementary. Most towns – settlements like Hertford, Stratford-upon-Avon or Guildford, of one to two thousand souls – were markets, servicing rural hinterlands: centres for dealing in grain, livestock and provisions, for horse-trading, for making and mending tools, homes for such professional agents of gentlefolk as attorneys, surveyors and doctors. Towns offered diversions for countrymen, from taverns to theatres. Small-town manufactures relied upon the produce of the countryside: brewers, tanners, shoemakers, carpenters, masons and textile workers made up the backbone of their craftsmen. Moreover, in contrast to the French courtier's proverbial terror of catching rusticity, the English liked to think of themselves as wedding civic to country tastes. *Rus in urbe* and *urbs in rure* were cherished ideals. Edward Cave, the founder of the best-selling *Gentleman's Magazine*, astutely christened his persona 'Sylvanus Urban'. Townsmen enjoyed their gardens and kept pigs (brewers fattened hogs on their spent mash). There was less in England of the continental peasants' accusation that towns were bleeding the country white, or, among famished townsmen, that growers were holding them to ransom.

And if town and countryside were not at odds, it would be equally misleading to carve up the early-eighteenth-century economy rigidly into industrial and agricultural sectors. England's economy functioned well precisely because the two went so utterly hand-in-glove. Skilled workers and their families could achieve modest comfort through dual occupations, by combining a smallholding or kitchen garden with spinning, glove-making, straw-plaiting, lace-making, or framework-knitting. Cornish miners abandoned their picks in the autumn to go pilchard-fishing. By the integration of summer and winter, outdoor and indoor jobs, the chronic seasonal and climatic underemployment that hamstrings pre-industrial economies was overcome. By-employments and homegrown or home-collected food together enabled craftsmen to tide themselves over periodic price and demand fluctuations. For its part, large-scale agriculture was increasingly run on industrial lines, with sophisticated estate-management, division of labour and cost-paring.

Yet certain regional contrasts *were* profoundly important. One was the axial divide between the South-East and the North-West. South-east of a swathe running roughly from the Severn estuary to the Humber lay the best arable land and hence prosperous counties such as Middlesex, Surrey, Buckinghamshire, Hertfordshire, Bedfordshire, Northamptonshire and Oxfordshire. Counties in this band were also traditionally the most densely populated: in 1700 Northamptonshire, Bedfordshire, Wiltshire, Buckinghamshire and Suffolk were all more thickly peopled than Lancashire, Cheshire, Derbyshire, Leicestershire and Nottinghamshire, not to mention the Lake Counties and the Borders. Wages were higher in the South.

Around 1700 a labourer earning about £25 a year in London might have got about £15 10s. in the West Country for the same job, and in the North about £11 5s. Furthermore, the South-East housed most of the major settlements. London aside, towns such as Tiverton, Colchester, Ipswich, Bury St Edmunds and Cambridge were bigger in 1700 than Sheffield, Bradford, Preston, Wolverhampton or Derby, each of which was to out-strip them before the century was out.

All of this registers the fact that, around 1700, the triangle inscribed by Bristol, London and Norwich not only contained the prosperous corn-belt but was heavily industrialized as well. Iron-founding, boosted by military contracts, was still concen-trated on the woodlands of the Weald and the Forest of Dean; naval dockyards – the largest hives of workers in the realm – clustered around the Thames, Medway and Solent; the heartlands of cloth manufacture were Devon, Norfolk (chiefly around Norwich), the Essex–Suffolk border and the Cotswolds, though the West Riding was fast emerging. Luxury trades such as coach-building, watch-making, silk-weaving and couture were concentrated upon London. The dawning century was about to witness an unparalleled relocation of industry, towns, population and wealth.

A second basic division around 1700 lay between coastal and inland areas, or, more precisely, between places by navigable water and those not. Before canals or railways, and while roads remained disgraceful, coastal shipping and river navigation – much improved in Stuart times – remained far the cheapest, safest and often the speediest means of conveying freight. Hence ports were vital, not just as nodes of long-haul trade (for the colonies, Ireland and Europe) and nurseries of the navy, fisheries and the whaling fleets, but as the points where internal traffic criss-crossed. All the front-rank towns in the kingdom (including London) were either seaports or had easy river access to the sea. It was to this that Bristol, Exeter, Lowestoft, Great Yarmouth, Boston, King's Lynn, Newcastle and Whitby all owed their eminence. At first it was still North Sea ports that predominated: they were convenient for Europe, they straddled the grain trade passing up and down the Trent, the Fenland rivers and the Thames, and they were vital for the coastal traffic in Newcastle sea-coal, carried by water into the heart of the South and East.

Areas with poor water communications, such as the West Midlands around Birmingham, were hampered until the canal age.

A third contrast is between 'lowland' and 'upland', marking the distinction between open and wooded country, between arable and pastoral, between nucleated villages and scattered settlements, between densely and thinly populated parts. English prosperity had traditionally been lowland, the great settlements being crossings in broad-bottomed river valleys. The grain-belt lay on the low-lying vales of the Midlands and central southern England. Celia Fiennes, Daniel Defoe and other travellers around 1700 still saw highlands as wastelands and found them disagreeable. 'Forest' regions were bywords for lawlessness. 'The vicinity is filled with poachers, deer-stealers, thieves, and pilferers of every kind,' commented Arthur Young on the inhabitants of Wychwood Forest in Oxfordshire, 'offences of almost every description abound so much that the offenders are a terror to all quiet and well-disposed persons.'

All this was, however, in flux. As wood for building and firing grew scarcer, timbered areas rose in economic attractiveness. With the expansion of worsted, calicoes and cottons, the fast-flowing streams of the West Riding Pennine slopes proved important assets. Defoe glowed about the textile manufacturing settlements around Halifax:

wherever we pass'd any house we found a little rill or gutter of running water, if the house was above the road, it came from it, and cross'd the way to run to another; if the house was below it, it cross'd us from some other distant house above it and at every considerable house a manufactory or work-house, and as they could not do their business without water, the little streams were so parted and guided by gutters or pipes, and by turning and dividing the streams, that none of those houses were without a river, if I may call it so, running into and through their work-houses.

The foothills of the Pennines and the Peak, and the scrubby undulating grasslands of Staffordshire and Shropshire, were developing a versatile mixed economy. Grazing and herding left labour time free for domestic industry. Underemployed families holding settlements on heath and moorlands adapted themselves to new economic openings as smiths, wheelwrights, nailers,

cloggers or weavers. As the century progressed, upland areas
proved the nodal points of growth in manufacturing and extractive industries.

Lastly, how far was there a segregative geography of rank?
Obviously, metropolitans tended to be 'posh' by contrast to
provincials, and townspeople more fashionable than country
'bumpkins'. The barrel-scraping playwright could always jux-
tapose urbanity and rusticity (though cits were targets as well as
hicks). But the distinctions can be overplayed. An Englishman's
castle was his home. Unlike his French counterpart, *milord anglais*
revelled on his estate, building, landscaping and creating in the
heart of the country a sanctum of civilization. Yet the rural great
felt ambivalent about being too conspicuous in the countryside,
and many embarked upon a disappearing act, secluding themselves from the neighbouring commonality. Mansions were increasingly built back off the road, miles away from the gaze of
the vulgar (a few lords moved whole villages to ensure privacy).
Plantations, walls and gates raised a *cordon sanitaire*, as in their
own ways did travelling in coaches (rather than on horseback)
and in sedan chairs (rather than walking). In the same spirit,
from 1712 onwards the Lord Mayor of London rode in a coach
instead of on horseback for his installation parade.

Early in the century provincial towns were still too small to
support spacial elaboration. Most people lived where they
worked. Domestic servants, apprentices and journeymen lived-in
with their employers, often under the eaves (though living-in
was discouraged from mid-century). Class-segregated suburbs
had not yet developed (Edgbaston, Birmingham's 'aristocratic'
suburb, was beginning to be built by the Calthorpe family at the
end of the century). London was the sole exception, because of
its sheer size. And it just kept on growing. In the 1720s Defoe
was impressed to find 'Great Russell Street is a fair way to shake
hands' with Tottenham Court – what would he have felt sixty
years later when Horace Walpole reckoned 'there will soon be
one street from London to Brentford'?

The Thames was London's great artery, pulsating with shipping, wharves lining its banks. The contrast between north and
south banks was total. Around 1700, there was only stinking
industry – distilleries, rope-works, tanneries, shambles and ship-

yards – south of the Thames, punctuated with bear-baiting and bawdy-houses, hogs and fogs. Fashionable gardens, such as Vauxhall, and up-market suburbs, such as Camberwell or Streatham, where Henry Thrale the brewer was to live, came later. The West End/East End divide was just as striking. On the Thamesside, and stretching to the east of the business headquarters of the City of London, there were sooty shanties, shipping, crime and hordes of common people, adjacent to City counting-houses. West of the City, elegance was spreading its golden grids. Bloomsbury Square was built in 1680. It was followed by Grosvenor Street (1695), Red Lion Square (1698), Golden Square (1699), Queen Square (1704), Hanover Square (1713), Cavendish Square (1717), Portman Square (1764), Bedford Square (1769), Portland Place (1778) and Russell Square (1805) – all developed not by the Crown or government, but by titled investors and speculative builders. This development of an elegant, leisured, purely residential quarter proceeded steadily, culminating during the Regency in John Nash's stuccoed swathe which snaked from Piccadilly, via Regent Street, to Marylebone and Regent's Park. And yet the dregs still festered too near the dukes for comfort. Piccadilly was just a stone's throw from the thieves' kitchen of Seven Dials. Bloomsbury bigwigs battled to boot Welsh cattle drovers, Smithfield-bound, off their elegant, wide leafy thoroughfares. In London the contrasts were stark. 'The East end,' noted the Prussian, von Archenholz, in 1780,

especially along the shores of the Thames, consists of old houses, the streets there are narrow, dark and ill-paved, inhabited by sailors and other workmen who are employed in the construction of ships and by a great part of the Jews. The contrast between this and the West End is astonishing; the houses here are mostly new and elegant; the squares are superb, the streets straight and open – If all London were as well built, there would be nothing in the world to compare with it.

(There would also, the Prussian might have reflected, have been no tradesmen to feed it, no urchins to sweep mud off the crossings.) Furthermore, London's fashionable contrasts were not just between residential and manufacturing quarters, for the City itself was undergoing segregation and secession. Tycoons were moving domicile from their City premises to turn themselves into a pseudo-landowning pseudo-gentry, building airy villas in the new commuterlands of Twickenham, Richmond, Kensington and Primrose Hill. Within the City, divisions between workshops and offices, between finance and crafts, were widening all the time.

At the dawn of the eighteenth century, English society was highly differentiated. In matters such as religion, occupation, gender role and legal status, contrasts were strong, variations legion, and inequalities vast. Yet even the discontented and oppressed often felt passionate loyalty to their place in the order of things. Despite a degree of geographical and social mobility, inheritance of stations in life reinforced jealously guarded territoriality. The social fabric was intricate, its complexity mirrored by a deep-rooted economic division of labour and by the moral inertia of custom and precedent. Diversity and localism, entrenched rights and customs, were to stymie attempts by England's rulers to streamline and steamroller their rule, just as they also forestalled the formation of nationally effective resistance among the ruled. And, however complex and interdependent the society, one thing was clear: the gulfs between ruler and ruled, rich and poor, propertied and unpropertied, dominated life.

2. The Social Order

An eighteenth-century Englishman acquired his sense of public identity in relation to his birth, his property, his occupation and his social rank. Most women were defined by the honour of their presiding male. The power conferred by wealth, rank, office and status created tensions with people's basic equality under common law and within the family of man.

English society was a pyramid, with few at the top and many at the bottom. Towards the end of the seventeenth century, Gregory King estimated that the nation was divided up as follows (the percentages include families and dependants):

1.2% – landowners
24.3% – farmers and freeholders
3.4% – professionals, including clergy
3.7% – merchants and shopkeepers
4.4% – artisans and handicraftsmen
26.8% – labouring people and out-servants
29.4% – cottagers and paupers
6.8% – the armed forces

These figures are clearly defective: there were far more merchants, shopkeepers, artisans and craftsmen than King noted, and domestic servants – such a large section of the population – do not appear as a separate category. Nevertheless the general profile is suggestive.

Distinctions in wealth between top and bottom were vast. Poorer labourers were receiving about £10 a year; a great peer would be getting over £10,000. Even a prosperous knight, on around £800, could spend in a year what his threshers or mowers earned in a lifetime. Extreme distinctions in wealth were sometimes sealed by attitudes which almost denied that rich and poor came from the same species. Thus the Duchess of Buckingham loathed Methodists because 'it is monstrous to be told that you have a heart as sinful as the common wretches that crawl on the earth. This is highly offensive and insulting and at variance with high rank and good breeding.' Yet the gaps between adjacent links on the chain of income and status were microscopic, and this gave the order as a whole great strength. Examining the gradient of English society early in the nineteenth century, David Robinson found cause for eulogy:

In most other societies, society presents hardly anything but a void between an ignorant labouring population and a needy and profligate nobility . . . But with us the space between the ploughman and the peer is crammed with circle after circle, fitted in the most admirable manner for sitting upon each other, for connecting the former with the latter, and for rendering the whole perfect in cohesion, strength and beauty.

The English social ladder was indeed precisely graded. The distinctions between being a servant in or out of livery, a kitchen maid or a lady's maid, below or above the salt, lower deck or quarterdeck in the navy, between being called Mrs or Madam, were delicate, but they mattered at their own levels in creating status differentiation no less than the pecking-order between baronets and earls, marquises and dukes, as the Leveson-Gowers doubtless carefully noticed as they clawed their way up from the baronage (1730) to being earls (1746), and finally ending up as dukes (1833).

Likewise in the professions. Physicians looked down on surgeons, but surgeons were a cut above apothecaries (who in turn were snooty about druggists). All these nice distinctions, and the supercharged snobberies surrounding them, shaped a social order whose gross inequalities were landscaped in gentle gradients rather than in giant steps.

Unlike in certain parts of Europe, no iron curtain of law or blood permanently divided bondman and freeman, trade and land, commoner and noble. Mobility was considerable, eroding traditional ideas of deference. 'Subordination is sadly broken down in this age,' bemoaned Dr Johnson, 'there are many causes, the chief of which is the great increase of money . . . The shoeblack at the entry of my court does not depend on me.' What it took to be reckoned a gentleman was not legally fixed but flexible, a matter for negotiation, for by long tradition English gentility was but ancient riches. When Defoe jingled,

Wealth however got in England makes
Lords of mechanics, gentlemen of rakes

he broadly described what happened. People made bold to style
themselves 'gentlemen merchants', 'gentlemen clothiers', 'gentlemen of the road' – and of course there was 'Gentleman' John
Jackson, prize-fighter *extraordinaire*. 'An English tradesman is a
new species of gentleman,' opined Dr Johnson. Wealth that
dressed itself up in liberal behaviour and gave itself airs
commonly passed muster for gentility, Guy Miège thinking 'the
title of gentleman is commonly given in England to all that
distinguish themselves from the common sort of people by a
good garb, genteel air or good education, wealth or learning.'

England was a society in which the fences dividing social ranks
were, in theory and in practice, jumpable. Scope for upward
personal mobility prevented ossification and obviated the structural tensions dangerous in too rigid a society. Unlike, say,
Spain, England did not seem to comprise a number of mutually
exclusive estates. The English clergy, for example, were not an
estate apart in ways comparable to their celibate continental
Catholic counterparts (Dissenting clergy often doubled up occupations). Similarly, no English Sieyès could plausibly identify the
Commons as a third estate, rendered a 'nothing' by their exclusion, yet capable of becoming 'everything'.

Even so, it would be equally wrong to suggest that the
Establishment welcomed intrepid social climbers with open arms.
Recent research has shown how hard it was to break into landed
society at the highest level. And for the people at large, Dr
Johnson's words rang true: 'Slow rises worth by poverty deprest.'
It was easy to rise *towards* the portal of the next status group.
Crossing the threshold was more difficult, and required special
visas. Tradesman, however rich, were debarred from becoming
magistrates unless they first bought estates. Similarly, a common
sailor could rise to become lieutenant, but hardly ever to command (James Cook, son of a day labourer, who entered the navy
as an able seaman, was a superb exception). Perhaps ninety-nine
negroes in a hundred never escaped being slaves, servants or
seamen (though the exceptional English black became a prize-
fighter, like Tom Molineux or Bill Richmond, or a gigolo, like
Soubise).

Yet common coals occasionally burst into glorious fire. 'Men are every day starting up from obscurity to wealth,' wrote Defoe. A few rocketed to riches, such as prize-winners in the national lottery, or the crews of warships which captured Spanish argosies (prize money was shared out disproportionately, but even an able seaman might get a couple of hundred pounds). Others made good. Ralph Thrale, who became a great London brewer, was a farm worker's son; John Baskerville, the printer, started life as a footman, as did Robert Dodsley, the publisher. William Wordsworth was the son of a yeoman; one of his two brothers became Master of Trinity College, Cambridge, the other a sea captain. Archbishop Potter's father was a draper, Bishop Thomas's a drayman. Charles Hutton, the mathematician, had a coal-miner for a father. Lancelot ('Capability') Brown, the sublime landscape gardener, was the son of a small tradesman. By the age of twenty-four he had risen to become head-gardener at Stowe; his son in turn became an admiral. Englishmen dreamed of destiny. 'In my mind's eye,' wrote Nelson, 'I ever saw a radiant orb suspended which beckoned me onwards to renown' – and Nelson's mistress, Lady Hamilton, had herself been born a Cheshire nobody, starting her career as an artist's model and good-time girl in London.

But such rags-to-riches stories were highly exceptional, often involving a stroke of fate as well as great talent. Thrale had a rich, childless uncle who set him up, Cook the good fortune to be apprenticed to a Whitby coaster-owner. Spectacular ascent often required the magic wand of patronage, a fortunate marriage or a chance inheritance. Stephen Duck, the Wiltshire thresher poet, was discovered by gentlefolks and patronized right up to Court (where he was made a yeoman of the guard, before drowning himself in a trout stream). Many people made money; but it was hard to buy your way into high society. It was easier to marry a peer than acquire a peerage. The ascent towards the Lords was slow, arduous and costly, though for a few lawyers, such as Macclesfield, Hardwicke, Camden, Thurlow and Eldon, there was a fast route through the Lord Chancellorship. National heroes such as Clive got their coronet reward. But *nouveaux riches*, however *riches*, did not easily become ennobled. They could not buy a peerage – peerages were just about the one thing not for sale in Georgian England. Nor could moneybags themselves count on marrying peers' daughters,★ though in the next generation they might net a younger son of a needy peer as a match for their daughter, if she had a bulging dowry. It was the alliance of a gentleman's son with a merchant's daughter, the landed embracing the loaded, that was *mariage à la mode*. Peerage-ogling plutocrats had to play a waiting game. First they had to buy rolling acres – and ready-made, consolidated, prestige estates were hardly two-a-penny – establish a county family and political pull, and finally assiduously cultivate friends in high places. Even then, obstacles persisted. The fabulously rich Jewish financier and government contractor Sampson Gideon converted to Anglicanism, but it was his son who became a baronet.

What's more, the channels of social fluidity were in some ways silting up. True, as many foreigners noted, England was exceptional in that peers' younger sons entered trade (with primogeniture, only the eldest son inherited title and usually land); caste was not thereby lost. Lord Townshend's younger brother Horatio was a City merchant: the Earl of Oxford's brother was an agent in Aleppo. Yet only certain forms of money-making were honourable, principally large-scale overseas trade or finance (domestic wholesale or retail business was *infra dig.*). In any case, the tradition of Septimus or Decimus serving at the counting-house was in decline, as political patronage hoisted more younger sons of peers safely up into the army, Church or diplomatic service. It got harder for *parvenus* to break into front-bench politics, high office and high society.

People accepted the social ladder and tried to climb it. They studied and aped the manners of their superiors ('plain' Quakers were among the few who resisted). Ralph Thrale, the self-made brewer, sent his son Henry to Eton and Oxford – which proved predictably catastrophic for the future management of the brewery. The same happened when his rival, Samuel Whitbread, sent his own son to Eton and Cambridge, and on the Grand Tour. The son became a politician, near-bankrupt and eventual suicide. But if all knew the steps leading up and down, and experienced daily social frictions, there was little agreement as to

★ De Quincey wrote that John Palmer had 'accomplished two things very hard to do in our little planet. He had invented mail-coaches, and he had married the daughter of a duke.'

how precisely to picture the social structure as an entirety. Daniel Defoe suggested a sevenfold division, based on wealth and consumption:

1. The great, who live profusely
2. The rich, who live plentifully
3. The middle sort, who live well
4. The working trades, who labour hard, but feel no want
5. The country people, farmers etc. who fare indifferently
6. The poor, who fare hard
7. The miserable, that really pinch and suffer want

Hoping to probe more deeply, historians have debated whether Georgian England was a 'class' society (however snobbish, it certainly was not a 'caste' society – one which rivets people in place by blood, pedigree and birth). Contemporaries of course thought of the 'upper orders', the 'middling ranks' and 'labouring men'. Yet – as Defoe's scheme suggests – they did not think of their society in a way anticipating Marx as turning upon *struggle* between *three* distinct classes, defined essentially in relation to ownership and deployment of capital: landowners, bourgeoisie and proletariat. Analysts tended to lump and split groups more in terms of clutches of interests – wealth, occupation, region, religion, family, political loyalty and connection.

And in practice, when social conflict and political disturbances flared, lines were drawn between different faiths, between Government and particular socio-economic interests (such as the cider-makers), or between rival trades themselves, at least as often as between capital and labour. Interest groups – say, 'ins' and 'outs' – confronted each other more than 'class' against 'class'. The Marxist schema could hardly apply, in any case, to a nation in which smallholders, yeomen, self-employing tradesmen and craftsmen still comprised much of the workforce. Early in the century, apprentices could expect to rise to become small masters in their turn. Social position hinged upon a person's stage in the life-cycle. Much work was still family-based (what *is* the class position of women?), or sub-contracted out to teams of independent workers. A society with such characteristics does not readily fit into a three-class model. The mesh of terms such as 'nobility', 'bourgeoisie' and 'proletariat', or upper, middle and lower class, lets too many fish through, and over-concentration on them always risks obscuring the vast differences in wealth and status which individual health, luck (especially that of being first-born), effort or success could make, even within one family. Among the Hales family, for instance, one brother became a baronet, another, Stephen, entered the Church and remained curate of Teddington all his life, though becoming a distinguished scientist, but the third died in Newgate, a convicted forger. Richard Gough's survey in 1700 of all the inhabitants of the Shropshire parish of Myddle shows a remarkably fluid community, with rapidly fluctuating prosperity and impoverishment depending on application, astuteness and the luck of marriages and health. Every Quality family was forever keeping poor relations at bay.

Identification by social class was not the prime means of social self-description. Not least, people saw their standing in the world in concrete terms, in respect of local loyalty, occupation or family. 'I welcomed a friend with a shake of the hand,' reminisced the bookseller James Lackington, about his early business days,

but a year later I beckoned across the way for a pot of good porter. A few years after that I invited my friends to dinner, and provided them with a roasted fillet of veal, in a progressive course, the ham was introduced and a pudding made the next addition to the feast. For some time a glass of brandy and water was a luxury; raisin wine succeeded, and as soon as two thirds of my profits allowed me to afford good red port, it appeared on my table, nor was sherry long behind.

England's elite was a tight, privileged ring of landowners. Of course, European societies from feudal times down to the First World War were headed by such nobilities, but the titled proprietors of Georgian England were rather exceptional. In part this was because the absolute ascendancy of the landed nobility was something newly re-established. Dukes and earls had been axed by Henry VII's and Henry VIII's drive to secure the Tudor dynasty. New Tudor creations had not kept pace with natural wastage, though the early Stuarts diluted the Lords by elevating favourites, many of whom were needy Irish and Scots adventurers, lacking local power-bases. For many, the bills of luxuriant living outstripped incomes, resulting in what Stone has called the 'crisis of the aristocracy', in which the peerage was ground, politically and economically, between the upper and nether millstones of the Crown and a confident gentry.

As an order magnates did not perhaps fare much better in the post-Restoration political cockpit; rather a succession of individual careerist peers, such as Clarendon and Danby, Sunderland and Oxford, climbed the greasy pole to greatness. The empire of even the towering politicians at the turn of the century – Somers, Godolphin, Wharton, Montagu – was essentially personal. Nevertheless, the solidarity of propertied interests in rejecting James II heralded greater cohesion to come, and the pursuit of capitalist High Farming and High Finance was beginning to pay dividends for great landowners. Firmer control over elections and new game laws were already signalling oligarchic tendencies in politics. Thus, by early in the eighteenth century, the tide was turning in favour of the magnates. They were to become, for the next two centuries, the most confident, powerful and resilient aristocracy in Europe.

The English aristocracy had the great advantage of being small and stable in numbers. By European standards the English second estate was minuscule, largely because – unlike elsewhere – only eldest sons inherited titles. In 1688 there were just 160 lords temporal and twenty-six lords spiritual (elsewhere they ran into tens of thousands, some half a million claiming nobility in Spain). There were perhaps a further eighty to a hundred non-noble families of great leverage, owning 10,000 acres or more – men such as the agricultural improver, Thomas Coke of Holkham in Norfolk (who eventually consented to become Earl of Leicester). The size of the Lords remained remarkably steady until the 1780s, when Pitt became more open-handed with ermine. There was however no rash of Lilliput titles, or ennobling of small fry. Unlike the French, or even the Scottish, the English peerage carried few passengers; rather it possessed impressive corporate unity.

English grandees had no need to be preoccupied by legalistic jealousies over rivals' privileges – the divisive squabbles of old, indigenous titles against new royal creations, 'sword' against 'robe', landlords against administrators, courtiers against provincials, or moneybags against the impoverished, which sapped the strength of the French nobility, found little echo in England. Almost no English peers were down at heel. The grandees' world was a charmed family circle radiating out from great houses such as Stowe, Bowood and Chatsworth. Everyone knew everyone else, and the warp and woof of marriage-ties were closely interwoven. In five successive generations of the Guilford family, the eldest son married an heiress; Lord North's father, in fact, married three: Lucy, the daughter of Lord Halifax, Elizabeth, widow of Viscount Lewisham, and Catherine, widow of the Earl of Rockingham. From the late seventeenth century, four of five successors of the Grafton estates married heiresses. The Earl of Nottingham married six out of his seven daughters to peers. In such ways were prestigious estates, fabulous riches, and political connections strung together like ropes of pearls. Yet the occasional alliance to a millionaire commoner's daughter could be equally advantageous. The Bedford fortunes were cemented by the marriage arranged in 1695 between the young Marquis of Tavistock and Elizabeth Howland, a London merchant's daughter. The second Viscount Palmerston married a wealthy City merchant's daughter. Peers, by contrast, certainly did not want to marry their *daughters* into trade, lest estates fell into mucky hands.

Family continuity was the keynote of magnate success; the individual title-holder was the baton-carrier in the relay race of family destiny. Inheritance was paramount in a legal system in which male primogeniture ensured that estates were not broken up. Eldest sons came into lands *en bloc*. By contrast, younger sons got a relatively meagre consolation prize of money and a leg-up into a profession. Thus the Duke of Devonshire gave his two younger sons £1,000 each to dabble in politics, and Ralph Sneyd, a substantial Staffordshire gentleman, gave his six younger sons £1,000 each: two went into the Church, two into the army, one into the navy, and the last into the East India Company.

Grandees drew their vigour not primarily from pedigree but from being, in Perkin's characterization, 'an open aristocracy based on property and patronage'. 'What distinguishes it from all others is the ease with which it has opened its ranks,' noted Tocqueville, looking back with hindsight from the vantage of post-revolutionary France. Yet to stress such openness risks being misleading, for, as Lawrence and Jeanne Stone have recently emphasized, it took vast wealth and adroit manoeuvring for new families to implant themselves within the ranks of landed grandees. Indeed, the towering strength of the proprietorial order lay in their comprising a tight, self-reproducing oligarchy of the extraordinarily wealthy and influential, a club exceedingly difficult to join. As Speck observes, 'If anything, the English aristocracy was more of a closed circle in the eighteenth century than at any other time in history.'

They lorded it over every corner of life. Economic trends smiled upon them. Landownership and agriculture were admittedly not money-spinners through the entirety of the century, but land values and rents were buoyant at the beginning and rose markedly from the 1760s, as did profits from the produce and materials they marketed. Overall, between 1690 and 1790, in what was increasingly a sellers' market, land values about doubled. Most important, the economies of agrarian management encouraged great landowners to consolidate their estates geographically and cut labour costs on their home farms. The age of low grain prices between about 1710 and 1750 hit them less severely than small owners, who lacked capital to fund cost-cutting improvement or to see hard times through, and whose restricted estates impeded diversification of techniques and crops. Better prices after about 1760 prompted a surge of magnate-led enclosure and cemented the partnership between great landowner and the go-ahead farmer to whom he rented out his lands, an alliance which promoted extensive innovation in estate management, stock-breeding, and crop rotations. Between 1776 and 1816 Thomas Coke of Holkham doubled his estate's rental.

The profits of landowning were not the only area in which the aristocracy prospered (no peer had all his eggs in one basket). Many grandee families were 'amphibious', having for generations also owned urban estates, especially in and about London. In the Georgian building booms, land values and rentals soared as peers laid out fashionable metropolitan sites. The Bedfords for example developed their Bloomsbury lands, collecting £2,000 from their London properties in 1700, £3,700 in 1732, and £8,000 in 1771. The Grosvenors' London properties yielded £2,000 in 1772, £7,000 by 1779, and £12,000 by 1802.

Magnates also became what Cobbett termed 'fundlords', investing enthusiastically in Government stock, the Bank of England, and the great trading companies. The Earl of Sunderland, for example, had £75,000 in stocks and shares in 1722. And not least they gained hand-over-fist from industrialization. The greatest landowners were predictably sitting on the richest mines, including the Dukes of Argyll, Hamilton and Devonshire, Earls Gower and Fitzwilliam, Lords Middleton, Mostyn, Egerton, Dalaval and Lowther, and the Bishop of Durham. Lord Foley had mines worth £7,000 a year on top of an estate worth £21,000 and £500,000 in the funds. Great estates yielded building-stone, slates, sand, brick-clay and timber. Peers developed ports and promoted transport improvements such as turnpike trusts. It was the Duke of Bridgewater's itch to sell more of his Worsley coal in Manchester which launched the canal age. And some peers involved themselves directly in industrial ventures. James Brydges, Duke of Chandos, undertook mining projects, huge building enterprises in Bath, pearl-fishing off Anglesey and mineral-prospecting in New York (most of these failed); he took shares in the Covent Garden playhouse, was a leading figure in the York Building Company and equipped his own personal laboratory. The English peerage made money enthusiastically and without shame (in many continental nations, for nobles to engage in trade jeopardized legal caste and honour).

Crucially to their success, grandees had their jaws locked upon the profits and perquisites of the state. Peers monopolized cabinets from Walpole onwards, appropriating office, patronage and revenues. By 1720 one quarter of the peerage held Government or Court office. Positions at Court (such as being a 'gentleman of the bedchamber'), pensions and sinecures were valued prizes for titled families. Horace Walpole, the Prime Minister's son, was granted a Tellership of the Exchequer, alone worth £1,200 a year, and two other sinecures besides, the Clerkship of the Escheats and the Comptrollership of the Pipe. Under Pitt the Younger, George Rose had sinecures which brought him £11,602 a year. The soldier Lord Irwin was made Governor of Barbados while being allowed to keep his regiment, which, his wife candidly wrote, 'will be a great advantage to him in paying off his debts'. In mid-century a Secretaryship of State yielded about £6,000–£9,000 a year in clear profit. Many offices further allowed the incumbent to take commission from contractors, to accept *douceurs* and to handle astronomical sums of public money, with which they would play the Exchange privately for the duration. The humdrum work they entailed was farmed out to poorly paid deputies.

The post of Paymaster General made the fortunes of Marlborough, Cadogan, Amherst, Sir Robert Walpole, Bubb Dodington, Henry Fox, James Brydges and others. Brydges cleared £600,000 from his tenure of that office between 1705 and 1713. Top men sometimes crudely put their hand in the till. Lord Chancellor Macclesfield was unfortunate enough to be caught, and was impeached for mishandling £100,000. He was fined £30,000, which he paid off within six weeks. Not all such rake-offs, however, were narrowly personal; family, friends and neighbours benefited, and plagues of strangers clamoured for crumbs. Prime Minister Lord North showered his stripling half-brother, Brownlow North, with ecclesiastical offices, explaining that if Brownlow had to wait till he was older he might no longer have a Prime Minister for his brother. Brownlow became Dean of Canterbury at twenty-nine, Bishop of Lichfield at thirty, Bishop of Worcester at thirty-three and Bishop of Winchester at forty. Taught by experience that charity began at home, this precocious bishop in turn made his own elder son Master of St Cross Hospital, his younger son Prebendary of Winchester, and a grandson Registrar of Winchester diocese (at the age of seven), and spent £6,000 on his own residence.

In short, many factors combined to ensure the prodigious wealth of the peerage. Around 1700 their wealth may have averaged some £5,000 to £8,000 a year. Some were soon to enjoy annual incomes topping £20,000. In 1715 the Duke of Newcastle, whose lands straddled thirteen counties, grossed £32,000.

This tide of wealth, however, flowed out almost as fast. Newcastle dissipated his fortune on Whig politics. Sir Robert Walpole's private expenditure between 1714 and 1718 totalled £90,000. Walpole and his guests at Houghton Hall in Norfolk downed about £1,500 a year in wine, itself the income of a flush gentleman. Just lighting his house cost Walpole £15 a night in candles. In 1771 Bedford House had forty-two servants who cost £859 a year. Political and electoral expenses ran into thousands, and tens of thousands changed hands in gambling. Marriage settlements – dowries, portions, jointures – became heavier drains on fortunes. And vast capital fortunes were sunk in building.

Holkham Hall cost the Earl of Leicester £90,000 to put up; improving Audley End cost the Nevilles £100,000. Woburn was rebuilt between 1747 and 1763 for £84,000. The Marquis of Rockingham spent £83,000 on Wentworth Woodhouse (upkeep cost him another £5,000 a year). The Duke of Buccleuch kept two London houses for when he wearied of his eight country residences. The Duke of Devonshire owned Hardwick Hall, Chatsworth, Bolton Abbey, Lismore Castle and Compton Place, and, in London, Burlington and Devonshire Houses. Prodigal peers and their heirs ran up astronomical debts – and mortgaging and other legal devices allowed them to do this without imperilling their estates.

Their lifestyle glittered with eye-catching grandeur. Magnates ransacked Europe – the globe itself – for paintings, sculpture, furniture, jewellery. They patronized artists and poets, and collected antiques, scientific instruments and books by the roomful. The second Viscount Palmerston snapped up 300 old masters for a bargain £8,000. Aided by landscapers such as William Kent, 'Capability' Brown and Humphry Repton, they redesigned Nature, on occasion flattening entire settlements which spoilt the view. In landscaping Castle Howard, Vanbrugh drowned the village of Hilderskelfe. That champion of political liberty, Viscount Cobham, razed the village of Stowe, shunting its denizens off to Dadford. Thomas Coke re-sited the hamlet of Holkham – though perhaps later regretting his decision: 'It is a melancholy thing to stand alone in one's own country,' he commented. 'I look around, not a house to be seen but for my own. I am Giant, of Giant's Castle, and have ate up all my neighbours.'

The Duke of Chandos kept ninety-three household servants at Canons and his own private twenty-seven-piece orchestra under *Kapellmeister* Pepusch. Peers introduced tropical plants, bred livestock and bloodstock. Many invested in kennels of pedigree hounds to woo connections down for hunting parties. They were dictators of fashion and taste (explaining Henry Fielding's sardonic definition of 'Nobody' as 'All the people in Great Britain except about 1,200'). This veritable orgy of conspicuous consumption was partly for personal pleasure, partly with an eye to publicity (extravagant levées would be the subject of society gossip), but, perhaps above all, to consolidate personal stature within the world of politics.

For great landlords maintained their pre-eminence by means of an unshakeable grip upon political power: 'dominion follows property', as Mandeville wrote. Because none could rival their acres, the magnate class basked in a long hot summer of unthreatened political superiority, seemingly treating the state as a kind of trust devised on their behalf. On the one hand, the soaring price of politics in an age dominated by management, patronage and the spoils system, raised the price of high office beyond the clutches of mere squires (and, in any case, the first two Georges were ultra-dependent upon the cooperation of the Whig 'Venetian' oligarchy). On the other, the bark of radical and popular politics proved worse than its bite. No one realistically challenged the magnates' grip upon power.

In the driving seat, peers doled out offices of state to reward the loyalty of friends, family and clients, and to buy off the disaffected. Eligible posts at Court, and in the Church, bureaucracy, consular service, administration and, more obliquely, the armed forces, became marked in the patronage lists of such party managers as the Duke of Newcastle. In 1762 John Boscawen Savage was made an ensign in the 91st Foot Regiment at the age of two. 'Patronage was a social nexus,' writes Perkin, 'less formal and inescapable than feudal homage, more personal and comprehensive than the contractual relationships of capitalist cash-payment.' The state at their disposal, grandees pioneered the art of political asset-stripping.

The Church of England's plums in particular were once more gobbled up by peers and their minions. In Stuart times it had not been honourable for men of noble family to take the cloth. This changed. 'Our *Grandees* have at last found their way back into the Church,' observed William Warburton in 1752. 'I only wonder they have been so long about it . . . The Church has been of old the cradle and the throne of the younger nobility.' Under the early Stuarts, up to 25 per cent of bishops had been plebeian in origin; by George III's reign, this had dropped to some 4 per cent. The change came about partly because competition intensified for choice openings in other liberal walks of life, the Church being a safe stronghold for the staider sort (Lord Chesterfield thought it ideal for a 'good, dull and decent' young man). But the return to the Church was speeded partly because the emoluments and tithes for the higher clergy were becoming more attractive. The Archbishop of Canterbury could reckon on £7,000 a year, the Bishop of Durham £6,000, the Bishop of Winchester £5,000. A cathedral stallholder would receive a comfortable £350; and 'the life of a prebendary,' as Edmund Pyle reflected from personal experience, 'is a pretty easy way of dawdling away one's time: praying, walking, visiting – and as little study as your heart would wish.' Many well-born clergy took a second – or third – helping by pluralism. Bishop Richard Watson's bag of some £2,200 a year was made up from tithes of two churches in Shropshire, two in Leicestershire, two in Llandaff, three in Huntingdonshire, five other impropriations to the Bishopric of Llandaff, and two to the Archdeacon of Ely. Above all, clerical advancement to sees was designed to provide dependable pro-ministerial voting fodder in the House of Lords. Certain prelates, such as Benjamin Hoadly, were rewarded for being indefatigable government pamphleteers; others rose by connection, family and sheer importunacy.

The state underwrote magnate parasitism in another crucial way: through the law. By contrast to continental regimes, legal privileges *per se* for English lords (such as the right to trial by one's peers) were paltry; nor were English peers exempt from taxation. But the law and its devices were tireless allies in maintaining grandees' estates, in sanctioning primogeniture, and also in generating, after the Restoration, the invaluable instruments of mortgage, strict settlement and entail. Mortgaging estates enabled landowners to raise capital to make improvements, settle offspring or pay off debts, without having to shed acres. Entail blocked occupants of estates from selling them; the inheritor became in effect a life tenant on behalf of his family line. Recent research suggests that these devices probably did not result – as was once thought – in vast further agglomerations of estates: the biological and psychological fortunes of families were too up-and-down for that. Too many grandees died without male heirs, too many sons died prematurely, too many wayward sons were disinherited; counter-claimants always had to be satisfied – in short, the centrifugal forces were clamorous and ceaseless. Yet these legal arrangements certainly stabilized estates, a vital service at a time of rising claims upon property, such as jointures (an annual income provided for a wife), portions (a lump sum paid to a daughter) and cash settlements to younger sons – all drastic drains on an estate's annual yield. The net result was that Georgian landlords were making more, spending more and piling up vaster debts, yet few estates had to be liquidated and dispersed.

The law also privileged the great landowner in other ways. The game laws provide the classic instance. Under an Act of 1671 the right to take game, even on one's own land, was restricted to proprietors of estates worth more than £100 a year: thus even substantial farmer-tenants and freeholders were disqualified. The game laws were remarkable in privileging grandees even against other members of the landed orders.

But this is not surprising. For magnates were laws unto themselves in their own shires. One of the most profound consequences of the Civil War (1642–6), the Restoration (1660) and the Glorious Revolution (1688) was the consolidation of magnates almost as satraps of local communities, hardly impeded by Crown, Church or any equivalent to the French *intendants*. Magnates monopolized high local office, active and honorific, from the Lords Lieutenancies to the Chancellorships of the universities – and all of them carried authority and patronage. They pulled the strings at the hustings and carved up electoral contests through influence, interest, the creation of votes and other chicanery, and, where need be, bully-boys. They headed charities, and acted as trustees for canal projects. Their home-base power as consumers, employers and fountains of favour – though bitterly resented – almost defied challenge, except by rival peers. 'The idea I gave Lord Rockingham of this county,' wrote a Nottinghamshire correspondent in 1769, 'was four Dukes, two Lords, and three rabbit warrens, which I believe, in fact, takes in half the county in point of space.' (Not all counties, however, were like this: Kent had few peers.) The lion's share of parliamentary legislation comprised magnate-sponsored local private bills – for enclosure, canals, imparking, regulating trade. Indeed, Parliament itself, thought Trevelyan, was a kind of Grand National Consolidated Quarter Sessions. The Great House was the powerhouse, avatar of dominion.

The aristocracy's prepossessing role as rural patriarchs rang true because they revelled in country life on their property. 'Banishment alone will force the French to execute what the English do for pleasure,' remarked Arthur Young, '– reside upon and adorn their estates.' 'The multitude of gentlemen's houses, scattered over the country, is a feature quite peculiar to English landscape,' observed Louis Simond, '– the thing is unknown in France.' Magnates threw themselves into blood sports – 'they are all quite mad about them,' wrote La Rochefoucauld: 'A-hunting we will go!' They patronized agricultural improvement and cultivated their tenantry. While travelling deep in the French countryside, Arthur Young pointed a contrast:

At an English nobleman's there would have been three or four farmers asked to meet me, who would have dined with the family amongst the ladies of the first rank. I do not exaggerate when I say that I have had this at least a hundred times in the first houses of our islands. It is however a thing that in the present manners in France would never be met with from Calais to Bayonne.

Young was right about England. Lord Hervey recorded that Walpole invited friends down to Houghton in Norfolk 'to hunt, be noisy, jolly, drunk, comical, and pure merry during the recess', detailing a typical Walpolean dinner:

We used to sit down to dinner a little snug party of about thirty odd, up to the chin in beef, venison, geese, turkeys, etc.; and generally over the chin in claret, strong beer, and punch. We have Lords Spiritual and Temporal, besides commoners, parsons, and freeholders innumerable.

Lower down, the Duke of Norfolk gave a supper to 350 of his labourers in 1764. It was with fraternizings such as these in mind that Trevelyan remarked that 'if the French noblesse had been capable of playing cricket with their peasants their chateaux would never have been burnt'.

But how real was 'paternalism'? Complacent magnates doubtless liked to regard themselves as – in Burke's words – the 'great oaks that shade a country', but the veneer of patriarchalism was often stained by the brutality with which great landowners emparked, enclosed, exploited the game laws and rode roughshod over customary tenant and villager rights. Contemporaries were not fooled. Rural violence, the crescendo of poaching, and the snarl of anonymous threatening letters all testify to the defensive bush-war which communities sporadically had to wage against rapacious landlords. 'If every man who wears a lace coat was extirpated,' questioned no less an idolator of rank than Dr Johnson, 'who would miss them?'

Magnates were on the horns of a self-created dilemma. Acquisitiveness urged them to maximize agrarian profit, pride to bask in undisturbed private grandeur – yet both would undermine their hegemony over the community. The richer they got, the more they cultivated tastes – Palladianism, French fashions, Italian music and artistic connoisseurship – which risked distancing them from their natural right-hand men, homespun squires and freeholders. Patricians grew more snooty about the vulgar world, many itching to suppress popular festivities, wakes, church-ales and fairs as being silly and troublesome nuisances. And yet popularity was the kiss of life. Lacking private armies, in the end they had to court popularity and rule by bluster and swank. Authority could be upheld only by consent, through a tricky reciprocity of will and interests, give and take. As political bosses and parliamentary candidates, grandees wooed ratepayers and cajoled tenants for their votes before they bullied them, for, as Josiah Tucker commented, 'without the assistance or approbation of the people, they cannot be considerable either in the Senate or out of it'. The fraternizing game, however nauseating, however phoney, had to be played. At election time, acording to the Earl of Cork,

our doors are open to every dirty fellow in the county that is worth forty shillings a year; all my best floors are spoiled by the hobnails of farmers stamping about them; every room is a pig-stye, and the Chinese paper in the drawing room stinks so abominably of punch and tobacco that it would strike you down to come into it.

Horace Walpole was thus amused by the palaver of standing as a parliamentary candidate at King's Lynn in 1761:

Think of me, the subject of a mob, who was scarce ever before in a mob! addressing them in the town-hall, riding at the head of two thousand people through such a town as Lynn, dining with above two hundred of them, amid bumpers, huzzas, songs, and tobacco, and finishing with country dancing at a ball and sixpenny whist! I have borne it all cheerfully; nay, have sat hours in *conversation*, the thing upon earth that I hate, have been to hear misses play on the harpsichord, and to see an alderman's copies of Rubens.

Even safe in his own sanctum, no less, the lord knew at bottom he needed to buy the goodwill of wheedling tradesmen (after all, he lived on credit) and of his own domestic servants ('the greatest plagues on earth'), ever troublesome behind the mask of deference. The façade of elegance was never very secure. ' 'Tis not my dairy maid that is with child,' spat Elizabeth Purefoy in 1738, 'but my cookmaid, and it is reported that our parson's maid is also with child by the same person who has gone off and showed them a clean pair of heels for it. If you could help me to a cookmaid as I may be delivered from this, it will much oblige.'

Grandees were faced with a polarizing tendency in rural society that was of their own creation. To cope, many stage-managed a studied theatre of power: conspicuous menace (and mercy) from the Judge's Bench; exemplary punishment tempered with silver linings of philanthropy, largesse and selective patron-age; a grudging and calculating display of *noblesse oblige*: 'This is the day of our fair,' sulked Sir Joseph Banks in 1753, 'when ac-cording to immemorial custom I am to feed and make drunk every-one who chooses to come, which will cost me in beef and ale near £20.'

Therein lay the sly magic of authority. But behind the show, the underlying power was real. By 1800 the notables were absolutely and relatively wealthier and more united than their grandfathers. In 1700 peers had owned about 15–20 per cent of England's landed wealth; by 1800 the figure was probably be-tween 20 and 25 per cent, and a score of peers owned over 100,000 acres each. From mid-century rent-rolls were rising, in many cases doubling between 1790 and 1815, and peers were sitting beneficiaries of industrialization. And the French revolu-tionary wars conveniently underscored their virility as the war-rior champions of Church, State and Britannia. It was indeed a good time to be a lord. The success story of the grandees explains the phenomenal tenacity of the English social hierarchy.

Beneath the magnates stretched down some 15,000 further landed families. These 'gentry' (proprietors who did not per-sonally have to till the soil) were lordlings, combining local clout and office with – for some at least – national stature as the backbone of the backbenchers. They ranged from baronets, who in 1700 might have over £1,500 a year (by 1800 perhaps £4,000), down to the squire feeling the pinch on as little as £300. In England, however, there was no class of endemically threadbare gentry, like the Spanish *hidalgo* who 'ate black bread under the genealogical tree'.

These were, however, times when the economics of consolidated, capitalized agriculture and the nip of the land tax helped big gentlemen to get fatter while speeding smaller ones, and spendthrifts, towards bankruptcy and even the debtors' gaol. By 1800, £300 would no longer support a squire. On the other hand, especially when they cultivated commercial interests alongside agriculture, gentlemen could live snug. Early in the century the Archers of Warwickshire, topping up their landed income with the profits of forestry and iron forges, were netting close on £3,000 a year. The Whitbreads began the century as small Bedfordshire squires; by the end, they had £8,000 a year from their London brewery as well as £22,000 from land. The coal trade was the road to gentrification for northern families such as the Cooksons, the Liddells and the Curwens. By contrast, other gentry lines – such as Sir Watkin Williams Wynn's in Denbighshire – were ruined by the rocketing bills of politics; the Verneys of Buckinghamshire met disaster by their unsuccessful bid to wrest the county's political primacy from the aristocratic Grenvilles. To Gibbon's intense annoyance, gracious living on Hampshire estates burned a hole in his father's pocket. And many a small Tory squire – especially crypto-Jacobites – skulked biliously or went broke under the early Georges, having been ejected from local office and favour.

Squires did not come in one standard type. Booted, bloated, and bigoted Squire Westerns were real enough. Horace Walpole called their Norfolk counterparts 'mountains of roast beef'; 'their mornings are spent among the hounds,' wrote Lady Mary Wortley Montagu, 'and their nights with as beastly companions – with what liquor they can get.' Hannah More confirmed this image of the squire:

> He dreaded nought like alteration
> Improvement still was innovation.

Yet such purblind traditionalists were easily counterbalanced by astute businesslike figures such as Colonel Walpole, JP and MP in North Norfolk, father of Sir Robert. As J. H. Plumb has observed:

The two Walpoles, father and son, illustrate some of the more interesting aspects of English social and political life from 1660–1760; the prudent, intelligent, but essentially homespun father, with his ambition adjusted to those ends that were well within his reach – an increased estate and the leadership of his county – was so typical of all that was best in the gentry of his day: whereas the brilliant son, greedy for power, greedy for riches, yet creative in all that he did, was limitless in his ambition; in the brilliance of his taste and the grandeur of his opulence, he outshone the aristocratic world in which his ambitions lay.

The squire's spiritual half-brother was the parson (the proverbially lean-shanked curates are another matter): men such as James Woodforde, who, being a bachelor, was comfortable on £400 per annum. Most rectors, farming the glebe and harvesting tithes, lived well. Anglican clergy politicked, tally-ho'ed, farmed, and dined with the squires. The two were often barely distinguishable. 'His size, and figure, and countenance and manner,' wrote Boswell of the Revd Dr Taylor, 'were that of a hearty English Squire, with the parson super-induced.' Some such 'squarsons' were probably no more sober than mere squires. Yet there were learned and scholarly clerics, too, and antiquarians and naturalists such as the Rev. Gilbert White of Selborne, and hosts of other sober, decent men. As the century wore on, incumbents were increasingly in demand as Justices of the Peace, being thought to discharge their duties with greater punctilio than their lay counterparts.

Below the gentry, English landed society forked: there was a line of owner-occupiers reaching down through yeomen freeholders to copyholding smallholders; and a breed of tenant-farmers also came into prominence. In 1688, Gregory King thought freeholders, numbering some 100,000 and making £50–£100 per annum, were better off than farmers; just over a century later, Patrick Colquhoun thought the opposite. Farmers probably did indeed overtake freeholders in fortune during the century – though many individual yeomen rose into the gentry. As a breed, common freeholders lacked investable funds to compete with capital-intensive progressive agriculture. The modest owner-occupier did not, of course, disappear. Indeed in some areas, such as the Lake District, sturdy yeomen remained the dominant group, and, contrary to an older historical view, smallholders normally had their rights confirmed in enclosure awards. But, except in unusual boom conditions (for instance,

during the shortages of the French revolutionary wars), the lives
of petty owner-occupying families got tougher. 'I regard these
small occupiers as a set of very miserable men,' wrote Arthur
Young. 'They fare extremely hard, work without intermission
like a horse . . . and practise every lesson of diligence and frugality without being able to soften their present lot.' Tenants of
tiny farms did little better. 'The small farmer is forced to be laborious to an extreme degree,' remarked the Rev. John Howlett:

he works harder and fares harder than the common labourer; and yet
with all his labour and with all his fatiguing incessant exertions, seldom
can he at all improve his condition or even with any degree of
regularity pay his rent and preserve his present situation. He is confined
to perpetual drudgery, which is the source of profound ignorance, the
parent of obstinacy and blind perseverance in old modes and old
practices, however absurd and pernicious.

By contrast, substantial tenant-farmers had the opportunity to
prosper. For instance George Culley, a Northumberland stock-
breeder who had learnt his trade with Robert Bakewell, had an
income of £4,000 a year by 1801, and bought up Fowberry
Tower. 'Whenever I am at Fowberry,' he mused shortly afterwards, 'I am struck with astonishment when I reflect on our
beginning in Northumberland forty-three years ago. To think of
my son, now inhabiting a *palace*! although his father in less than
fifty years since worked harder than any servant we now have
and even drove a coal cart.' Tenant-farmers succeeded partly
because prudent landowners valued businesslike tenants, and
were prepared to rent them attractively large holdings (up to
five or six hundred acres), grant long leases and underwrite capital
improvements. Farmers slip-streamed magnates along the turnpike road of improvement.

By 1790 about three quarters of England's soil was cultivated
by tenants. The tenant-farmer – a species rare elsewhere in
Europe – was, for many commentators, the pride of English
agriculture. Farmers did well, their rising wealth and importance
being reflected in the barrage of moralizing resentment they
drew as they 'gentrified' themselves, rebuilding farmsteads and
investing in fine china and furniture, silver plate, sprung carriages
and vintage cellars. 'Sometimes I see a piano forte in a farmer's parlour, which I always wish was burnt,' exploded Arthur Young:

a livery servant is sometimes found, and a post chaise to carry their daughters to assemblies; these ladies are sometimes educated at expensive boarding-schools, and the sons often at the University, to be made parsons. But all these things imply a departure from that line which separates these different orders of being [gentlemen and farmers]. Let these things, and all the folly, foppery, expense, and anxiety, that belong to them, remain among gentlemen: a wise farmer will not envy them.

A pair of rhymes satirized the social pretensions of the farmers:

1722	*1822*
Man to the plough;	Man tally-ho;
Wife to the cow;	Miss piano;
Girl to the sow;	Wife silk and satin;
Boy to the mow;	Boy Greek and Latin;
And your rents will be netted.	And you'll all be gazetted.*

Cobbett warned of the wider effects: 'When farmers become *gentlemen* their labourers become *slaves*.' The reality, however, was that tenant-farmers were one of the success stories of Georgian England, and they marked their good fortune by claiming their share of the good things in life.

Down a peg from the landowning Quality, England could boast more prosperous folk than perhaps any nation other than the Dutch Republic: self-employed masters, owning businesses, savings and movable property, men of money. Sandwiched between the 'rise of the bourgeoisie', which Marxist historians traditionally locate in Tudor and Stuart times, and the steam-powered advance of manufacturing wealth in the age of the Great Exhibition, these middling men of Georgian England have remained in historical limbo – oddly, since it was an age of rapid urban growth and prosperity in trade and manufactures. One difficulty is that we don't accurately know what portion of the community the moneyed and making classes made up. Around 1700, Gregory King thought that their numbers and yearly family incomes were as follows:

1,500 persons in liberal arts and sciences	£60
5,000 shopkeepers	£45

* Gazetted = bankrupted

5,000 big office-holders	£240
5,000 lesser office-holders	£120
2,000 big merchants	£400
8,000 lesser traders	£198
10,000 men in law	£154
2,000 higher clergy	£72
8,000 lower clergy	£50

But these figures – both aggregate numbers and incomes – seem to be underestimates, spectacularly so in some cases (excise records tell us, for instance, that by the mid eighteenth century there were some 150,000 retail outlets in the country, so King's 5,000 shopkeepers looks very peculiar). Of course, few men of liquid wealth could match landowners in assets; nevertheless, recent research has shown that, around 1700, 22 per cent of London freemen had estates of between £1,000 and £5,000, and 5 per cent had estates valued at £5,000.

Before the days of the great entrepreneurs, when Manchester became Cottonopolis, middling folk made their money in the shadows and kept a relatively low political profile (unlike in France, there was no 'Jacobin' revolution). Certain historians, notably E. P. Thompson, have discussed Georgian society mainly in terms of struggles between 'patricians' and 'plebeians'; and within a polarizing scenario of this kind, middle-men are largely pictured as operating behind the scenes, running a client economy servicing the Great.

Of course, this is just what very many did. Thousands of master-craftsmen and small manufacturers made their living primarily out of the Quality market: jewellers, tailors, decorators, carriage-builders, peruke-makers, dress-makers, milliners and providers of culture, from the blind musicians who fiddled at aristocratic orgies up to top portrait painters such as Joshua Reynolds. Landed estates yielded bumper crops of litigation for lawyers, and physicians cashed in on gouty peers, especially in spa towns such as Bath. Every gentleman needed his penumbra of bailiffs, attorneys, clergy, surveyors, stewards, mortgage-brokers and horticulturalists. Directly and indirectly, the livelihoods of journalists, artists, poets, architects, designers and tutors all lay in the palms of the Great.

Middling men loathed being thus reduced to superior flunkeys in a client relationship which required cringeing sycophancy.

Economic dependency was humiliating and nerve-racking, especially because the nobs expected boundless and endless credit from their suppliers (who revenged themselves by charging through the nose). Even if all bills were finally honoured, the system meant that tradesmen were in effect being forced to invest in their betters, like a personal version of the National Debt. Those who could, cut the strings of clientship. 'A patron is a man who looks on with unconcern at a man struggling for life in the water, and when he reaches the bank, encumbers him with help': Dr Johnson's blunt verdict upon Lord Chesterfield's uselessness as the patron of his *Dictionary* expressed the silent rage of many. Johnson was one of the fortunate few who managed to swim for himself.

Throughout the century, however, many tradesmen and artists were condemned to fawning. Yet imitation was also the sincerest form of flattery. To what else did the emulative bourgeois aspire than to be welcomed into genteel society? As Cannadine has written, 'The ultimate proof of success in business was the ability to leave it.' When Adam Smith observed, 'Merchants are commonly ambitious of becoming country gentlemen', he was mouthing a platitude.

In moneyed men's attempts to become gentlefolks, a good marriage could often do the trick. Sir James Bateman, governor of the Bank of England and director of the East India Company, saw his son wed the daughter of the Earl of Sunderland and become Viscount Bateman. Acquiring land could achieve the same. City plutocrats had traditionally bought up acres in the Home Counties (Defoe's fictional Robinson Crusoe finally settled in Bedfordshire) – though a token estate, such as a gardened villa at Chiswick, would increasingly do. In Leeds – where merchants tended to be Tory and Anglican, aligning not *down* with textile manufacturers but *up* with the country gentry – merchant princes, such as the Gotts, Milneses and Denisons, realized their dreams by purchasing estates and having their portraits painted by artists such as Benjamin Wilson and Romney. But the upstart entrepreneurs of the Industrial Revolution aspired to gentility no less. Apart from anything else, it made good business sense. Jedediah Strutt the hosier informed his son about the pounds, shillings and pence of ingratiation:

You are not to be a nobleman or prime minister but you may possibly be a tradesman of some eminence and as such you will necessarily have connections with mankind and the world; and that will make it absolutely necessary to know them both: you may be armed if you add to the little learning and improvement you have hitherto had, the manners, the air, the genteel address and polite behaviour of a gentleman, you will absolutely find your act in it every transaction of your future life – when you come to do business in the world.

But it was also a matter of vanity and emulation. Manufacturers rushed pell-mell into land: Strutt himself, Marshall of Leeds, Arkwright, Horrocks and Peel all bought estates, and thereby status. Land was at least a secure investment, though yielding meagre profit – but it wasn't bought for profit. And with the estate went its accoutrements: 'The merchant,' wrote Soame Jenyns, 'vies all the while with the first of our nobility in his houses, table, furniture, and equipage.' Gentility of bearing was important too. Strutt sent his son Billy a copy of Lord Chesterfield's *Letters to His Son*, advising, 'It is almost as necessary to learn a genteel behaviour and polite manners as it is to learn to speak or read or write.' Was Strutt aware that Dr Johnson thought the *Letters* taught 'the morals of a whore and the manners of a dancing master'?

In all ways 'the middle class of people in this country', as Chesterfield himself put it, were 'straining to imitate their betters'; to turn, if not into landed gentlemen, at least into a paragentry who could put 'Esq.' after their names without a blush. When Josiah Wedgwood started to design fashionable pottery, he looked first to conquer the Quality market, coining brand names like 'Queensware', partly with the aim of later appealing to the much larger market of the middle-class snobs.

Moneyed society wanted to cover its tracks; to show it was no vulgar 'shopocracy' but a rightful guest at the Quality ball. One sign of this outlook is that it did not unite to form its own exclusive political ideology, party or machine. The multifarious interests of the mercantile community never saw eye-to-eye on matters such as war and foreign policy. Explicitly middle-class political activism came in sudden thunderstorms (their grandsons, by contrast, could boast of being the bedrock of political wisdom by Victorian times). But it was not absent: City radicals were giving tradesmen and shopkeepers their political education in self-awareness, as when William Beckford, the London alderman, explained in 1761, 'When I talk of the sense of the people, I mean the middling people of England ... the manufacturer, the yeoman, the merchant, the country gentleman, they who bear the heat of the day' (though Beckford's yoking together of rather disparate groups is itself highly revealing).

Various political causes rallied tradesmen and masters against ministries. Though frequent and boisterous, such attacks were usually triggered by highly specific grievances, especially trade downswings; now they were pro-war, now anti-war, though they were constantly anti-Spanish, anti-Court and anti-excise. Tradesmen's consciousness fed on a sense of Them and Us, Ins and Outs. Their resentments and anxieties about arbitrary power and privilege found voice early in popular Toryism and then in the pro-Wilkes agitation, in London and the provinces, in the 1760s. But the adventures of this gadfly in the Establishment ointment proved but a *détour de force*: Wilkism did not give rise to a sustained widespread campaign for the empowering of the middle class. Radical movements such as the Society for Constitutional Information, snapping at the heels of a corrupt legislature, won urban support; yet their leaders were aristocratic, and their demands remained couched in the traditional constitutional rhetoric of cleansing the ancient Constitution. Business leaders in the mushrooming industrial communities of the Midlands and North gave no lead on parliamentary reform. They resented their own lack of direct political clout, yet they held no brief for a 'democracy' which would encourage the mob's para-political disturbances and debauched aristocratic carpet-baggers alike. Bourgeois political radicalism was sporadic and partial. For every Friend of the People, there were a dozen friends of property, and a score more who were interested in politics only as it affected trade. Middling men were not born little Whigs – or Tories for that matter (though most Dissenters were Whiggish). Classic liberal-bourgeois nostrums, such as the career open to talent, or 'utility', were for the future.

In politics, the mercantile classes chose to operate a system which, though not theirs, could provide them with leverage at strategic moments. In Parliament, neither nabobs and businessmen, such as Henry Thrale the Southwark brewer, nor MPs for mercantile constituencies such as Bristol sought to de-

velop middle-class alliances. Instead they promoted the interests
of particular trades, either through pledging their services with
ministries as place-men or contractors, or, via back-bench lobby-
ing, currying ministerial favour. Even when they set up the
(soon abortive) General Chamber of Manufacturers in 1785,
master manufacturers such as Samuel Garbett, Josiah Wedgwood
and Matthew Boulton argued for their preferred commercial
policies in the snuff-filled ante-rooms of Westminster, not on the
streets or at the hustings.

To eyes familiar with the massed ranks of the Victorian bourgeoisie, the middling folk of Georgian England thus appear
rather protean. This applies equally to their vocational aspirations,
which defy modern stereotypes. Professional pride of the kind
later prominent in the Victorian civil service code of 'duty'
meant little. In liberal callings such as medicine and the law,
there was no great parade of idealistic *esprit de corps*, concerned
to uphold 'public service' standards of training, probity and
responsibility. Chartered professional corporations such as the
College of Physicians or the Inns of Court operated as closed,
oligarchic monopolies, jealously guarding their privileges. There
were only forty-five Fellows of the College of Physicians in
1745, and fewer than 400 practising barristers. Entry into the
higher echelons was not by proven merit but by rites of passage:
one qualified for the Bar by eating dinners at the Inns of Court.
Though the professions were monopolistic – all barristers had to
be called to the Bar – most workaday practitioners of medicine
and law were excluded from their governing bodies and privileges. Thus by statute, only doctors licensed by the Royal
College of Physicians could legally practise 'physick' in the
metropolis. Surgeons were licensed only to operate (and only
surgeons could operate). An Oxford, Cambridge or Dublin
degree was the entrance requirement for admission to the fellowship of the Royal College of Physicians (although the top
medical schools were Leiden in Holland, Edinburgh and Glasgow). Apothecaries, of vast and increasing importance as general
practitioners, and attorneys (solicitors) were trained on the job
by apprenticeship, like craftsmen. Though many attorneys were
the younger sons of gentlemen, the occupation had little éclat.
Dr Johnson once remarked that 'he did not care to speak ill of
any man behind his back, but he believed the gentleman was an

attorney'. Yet attorneys, their fingers in every pie, fixing mortgages and acting as bankers and political agents as well as handling
litigation, oiled the wheels of business. Outside the courts, they
were much in demand as informal arbitrators, conciliators and
honest brokers. Their numbers swelled and many got rich. By
1800, Bristol and Liverpool both had over seventy attorneys.
The Sheffield attorney Joseph Banks, who acted as a money-
lender, put £40,000 into land between 1705 and 1727. A successful provincial doctor such as Erasmus Darwin at Derby could net
over £1,000 a year in fees.

Most middle-class occupations were pursued in an *ad hoc* way,
unregulated by professional bodies. Valuers, architects, land-
agents, auctioneers, dentists, engineers, schoolteachers and civil
servants – all groups which became haunted in the nineteenth
century by the quest for professional security and status –
remained unincorporated: without academic training, exams and
paper qualifications, without codified professional ethics, without
a closed shop. Their status was often low. No surgeon was
knighted until 1778; no engineer until 1841. But the financial
rewards climbed. Outside holy orders, and the medical and legal
top brass, middle-class occupations remained fluid and personal.
Admission was by apprenticeship, not college and exams. Much
'white-collar' administration was done by unpaid amateurs or
part-timers: MPs, JPs, overseers of the poor, and philanthropists.
By later standards, the tally of Whitehall civil servants scratching
their quills in fusty offices was tiny (as distinct from the hated
revenue officers, who had shot up to about 20,000 by the end of
the century). In 1743 the Treasury staff was twenty-three; eight
clerks manned the Admiralty. (France by contrast had tens of
thousands of hereditary bureaucrats whose families had invested
in office.) Entry was essentially personal through recommenda-
tion, patronage or nepotism. Yet recent work by John Brewer has
shown that – despite the Benthamite stereotypes – parts at least of
Georgian Whitehall were in reality rather efficient, adapting
themselves well to the needs of an administration handling vastly
increased sums of money and running a global empire.

Many 'service' employments also remained low in status. It
was a vicious circle. Nurses in the London hospitals were low-
paid and untrained, and were regularly dismissed for tipsiness;
schoolmasters were often young unbeneficed clergy, kicking

their heels. Both lived down to expectations. Walter Gale, failed fabric-designer, sign-painter and hop-farmer, was taken on at £12 a year by Mayfield parish in Sussex to run the village school. Tom Paine, stay-maker by training (and later revolutionary), had spells as schoolmaster and excise-man. Next to nothing was done for threadbare curates on £10 or £15 a year. (Queen Anne's Bounty helped a little.) No one thought a job such as prison warder could be a social-service vocation; a blind eye was turned if holders treated such jobs as licences to milk inmates of fees.

Thus white-collar occupations did not breed the corporate professionalism ubiquitous today; but why should they? Their practitioners were content to be men of business, guineas jingling in their purses. Upward mobility was individual rather than collective. It was no-holds-barred in the clamour for advancement. Competition was fierce among doctors for patients and for fees (medical ethics remained ill-formulated), but the rewards were great (the leading surgeon, William Hunter, spoke of the 'happiness of riches'). A successful London physician, such as the Quaker John Lettsom, could pocket up to £12,000 a year in fees. Lord Kenyon, who began his career as an attorney, took £80,000 in twelve years as Master of the Rolls. Lord Chancellor Eldon's fees in 1810 amounted to £22,730 (he died worth £700,000, with land on top).

If professionals had an ambiguous identity, businessmen and tradesmen (as Peter Earle has shown) presented a much more solid front. Abroad, most bourgeois comprised bureaucrats, from mandarin crown servants down to clergy and schoolmasters. England by contrast had a swelling and confident middle rank dedicated to making money: manufacturers of all shapes and sizes, from the ubiquitous workshop master to the emergent factory owner; wholesale and retail tradesmen, speculators, investors and scriveners – to say nothing of butchers, bakers and candlestick-makers. Many had but a patchy academic education and none paper qualifications, but all knew how to seal a deal. Though lacking national political power, they had a nose for business, and making money needed little excuse: 'I soon came to a resolution of making this launch into the wide world, repairing to *London*, in order to SEEK MY FORTUNE,' declared John Cleland's fictional heroine, Fanny Hill. Except in the highest circles, trade was respectable. 'Our tradesmen are not as in other countries,' explained Defoe, 'the meanest of our people. Some of the greatest and best and most flourishing families, among not the gentry only but even the nobility, have been raised from trade.' Defoe's claim was widely seconded, by fastidious scholars such as Gibbon ('Our most respectable families have not disdained the counting house or even the shop') and by businessmen themselves, such as that Birmingham jack-of-all-trades, the Dissenter William Hutton ('the man of business is the man of liberal sentiment; a barbarous and commercial people is a contradiction').

Middle-class wealth stretched from the high plateaux of the money mountain down to the base of the foothills. In 1750 one was said to need a capital of £20,000 to set up as a banker, £2,000–£10,000 to be a brewer and £1,000–£5,000 to be a woollen draper; but a mere £10–£100 would start you off as a butcher. At the top, the pick of the plutocrats lived in London, many of them Huguenots or Sephardic Jews – Janssens, Lamberts, Da Costas, Medinas, Salvadors, Pereiras. Sampson Gideon subscribed £300,000 to the Government loan of 1744, bequeathing a fortune of over £500,000. Lord Mayor of London in 1724, Sir Peter Delmé held £122,000 in South Sea stock and £118,000 in Bank stock. Insurers, brokers, discounters, jobbers, contractors – men whose wealth multiplied in their sleep – crowded into Wren's City. Over 90 per cent of those holding more than £5,000 Bank of England stock at the beginning of the century lived in London and the Home Counties. Aside from the boom world of the money market, fortunes rocketed most easily in overseas trade. John Pinney, born into a family of West India merchants, started with £70,000 and turned it into £340,000. 'Some merchants,' wrote César de Saussure in 1727, 'are certainly far wealthier than many sovereign princes of Germany or Italy.'

But merchant princes – 'the life, spring and motion of the trading world', according to Addison – also flourished outside the metropolis. Indian nabobs turned themselves into country gentry, buying parliamentary seats to forestall investigations of their business skulduggery. Bristol had tobacco barons and slave-traders such as the Colstons, Yateses and Youngs; Liverpool had its Rathbones and Gladstones. The Liddells, Blacketts and Ridleys were the kings of the coal vent in Newcastle. King's Lynn trade was controlled by the Turner family, relatives of the Walpoles.

These cohorts of the upper-middle class – there were perhaps 2,000 in 1700, rising to 3,500 in 1800 - intermarried, pooled capital as partners and bequeathed their businesses, especially when religious scruples, as with the Quakers, foreclosed a stampede into land. Debarred from the fashionable roads to ruin, thrifty Friends such as the Lloyds, the Gurneys and the Darbys lasted for generations, accumulating all the time. And everywhere flourished fast-increasing numbers of men and women of some capital – many of them retired – who lived off annuities and investments.

Beneath people who dealt in money were countless petty traders, horse-dealers, builders, inn-keepers and manufacturers who excelled in turning a penny for themselves: men prepared to graft, adapt to the ups and down of the market, put their irons in many fires and drive hard bargains. As one of the kings of the cutthroat Newcastle coal trade put it, it was 'every man for himself and God for us all'. In Newcastle competition often erupted into gang violence among the hired thugs of the top merchants.

Prospects were particularly good for wholesalers as markets widened, fairs declined as potential sites of competition, and haulage improved. Good pickings were in the offing in transport itself. William Chaplin's coaching service in Regency London employed 2,000 men and used 1,800 horses. Pickford's ran ten canal boats and fifty waggons in the 1790s. Opportunities were there for those who could take them. 'Each man has his fortune in his own hands,' intoned the Birmingham businessman William Hutton, quoting Francis Bacon. He knew from experience. Born in 1723, son of a Dissenting wool-comber, and apprenticed at seven (his tales of child labour make chilling reading), Hutton came to Birmingham in 1741 seeking work as a stockinger. Whereas the father 'had no ideas of business or economy', the son was ambitious. He set up a small bookshop and circulating library; on the profits he tried bookbinding, paper-making and then land-dealing. By 1768 he was worth £2,000; he had property worth over £8,000 destroyed in the Birmingham Riots of 1791. The career of Francis Place, son of a dissolute but energetic baker, is comparable. Place began work as a breeches-maker. Through thrift, self-control and entrepreneurial talent he rose to be one of the top manufacturing tailors in London, earning

£3,000 a year. Parallel success stories are legion. William Strahan, apprenticed to an Edinburgh printer, came to London in 1738 to try his fortune. He made friends with the literati, published Hume, Johnson, Gibbon and Adam Smith, became the king's printer, and died worth £95,000. Another who learned the lessons of the industrious apprentice was the Newcastle merchant William Cotesworth. Starting out as a mere tallow-chandler's apprentice, at his height he traded 'for upwards of £30,000 a year in anything he could gain by'.

Others did well at more modest levels, Abraham Dent of Kirkby Stephen in Westmorland was primarily a grocer and had a turnover of £1,000 a year from his shop. But – a pluralist like so many others – he also made money as a brewer, bill-broker, small landowner and wholesale hosier, supplying locally woven stockings to Government contractors in London (slipping in Westmorland hams as juicy *douceurs*).

In other words, quite independently of the much-trumpeted rise of the factory-masters, small businessmen who could blaze a trail found rich rewards in the ebullient commercial climate. In 1774 James Lackington, self-educated ex-cobbler and Methodist, set up in business at Finsbury Circus as a second-hand bookseller, aided by a loan of £5 from his co-religionists. He modernized the book trade by standardizing prices, issuing catalogues and pioneering cut-price remainder-selling. Unusually for a trades-man, he gave no credit. By 1791 he was selling 100,000 volumes a year, and with slim margins, giant turnover and the philosophy of 'Small profits, bound by industry, and clasped by economy', was making an annual profit of about £5,000 through being 'the cheapest bookseller in the world'. No wonder he could compla-cently boast: 'Small profits do great things.'

England thus teemed with practical men of enterprise, weather-eye open, from tycoons to humble master-craftsmen. Richard Savage, wrote Dr Johnson in sardonic vein, 'having no profession became by necessity an author'. In the 1740s the impoverished curate at Broughton in Yorkshire kept a pub. Some, especially Dissenters, were dour and penny-pinching, pursuing the moral rules for business spelt out by Hogarth's prints ('The Industrious Apprentice') and by Defoe's and Frank-lin's writings ('Early to bed, early to rise . . .'). But many breezed along in a more free-and-easy way, living convivially from day to day – Defoe fretted about shopkeepers' 'ostentation of plate'. As Giuseppe Baretti noted, 'The English do their utmost to make money: but once they have made it, they spend it freely.' Few saw business as a science (in his pursuit of strict accountancy, Josiah Wedgwood was probably the exception rather than the rule), and with labyrinthine credit networks, speculative investments, coin shortages, irregular cash-flow and large outgoings on property and family, traders commonly had little control over the wheel of fortune. Taking profits and losses as they came, great businessmen such as Henry Thrale often had to go round cap-in-hand to their friends. And bank crashes and credit collapses meant that even sound businessmen were always at risk of finding themselves bankrupt or whisked off to the debtors' gaol.

What fired the trading classes was the itch to make money, and thereby a name. 'Oh, what pleasure is business,' exclaimed Thomas Turner, a Sussex shopkeeper. 'Here lies Jedediah Strutt' – the industrialist ordered to be chiselled on his gravestone – 'who without Fortune, Family or friends raised himself to a fortune, family and name in the world.' As he himself acknowledged, money was the motor. 'I was this day through Cheapside, the Change, etc.,' he wrote in 1767, spontaneously reflecting that

the sole cause of that vast concourse of people, of the hurry and bustle they were in, and the eagerness that appeared in their countenances, was the getting of Money, and whatever some divines would teach to the contrary, this is true that it is the main business of the life of man.

They put their trust in industry. 'The orders I have made,' insisted the iron-founder Ambrose Crowley, 'are built upon such a rock that while I have my understanding it shall be out of the power of Satan and all his disciples to destroy them.' And beneath the big fish such as Strutt and Crowley were shoals of small businessmen and master-craftsmen who played a vital role in the economy.

Not least in importance were shopkeepers. Long before Napoleon, Adam Smith had called England 'a nation of shopkeepers' – by late in the century they totalled upwards of 170,000. Shops and small businesses were everywhere. Petworth was a Sussex town of about 1,000 inhabitants, serving the local farming community and provisioning the house and estate of the Earls of Egremont. About 5 per cent of its population consisted of professionals – clergy, doctors, lawyers. A further 20 per cent were of the commercial middle class – merchants, shopkeepers, inn-keepers, retailers, millers, maltsters, peruke-makers, vintners, tanners, butchers, surgeons, barbers, schoolteachers. The inventories of such tradesmen show about 30 per cent left goods and property worth between £100 and £500. Birmingham directories list the following tradesmen in the 1770s:

248 Innkeepers	46 Brassfounders
129 Buttonmakers	39 Shopkeepers
99 Shoemakers	39 Bucklemasters
77 Merchants	36 Gunmakers
74 Tailors	35 Jewellers
64 Bakers	26 Maltsters
56 Toymakers	24 Drapers
52 Platers	23 Gardeners
49 Butchers	21 Plumbers/Glaziers
48 Carpenters	21 Ironmongers
46 Barbers	

It was these swarms of the petty bourgeoisie who helped make the English economy special. For, antedating and quite independently of the Industrial Revolution, England had a bustling economy built upon the commercial enterprise of hundreds of thousands of craftsmen, masters and dealers, while home consumption among those self-same middling families proved a bellows for what Maxine Berg has termed the 'age of manufactures'. 'It is not . . . an excess of property to the few,' Patrick Colquhoun concluded,

but the extension of it among the mass of the community, which appears most likely to prove beneficial with respect to national wealth and national happiness. Perhaps no other country in the world possesses greater advantages in this respect than Great Britain, and hence that spirit of enterprise and that profitable employment of diffused capitals which has created so many resources for productive labour beyond any other country in Europe.

As the century wore on, new occupations found niches for themselves between the plutocrat and the humble shopkeeper. Whereas Gregory King clearly had not thought it necessary to list 'manufacturers' as a separate occupational group, later social statisticians such as Joseph Massie and Patrick Colquhoun registered their growing numbers: Colquhoun estimated there were

25,000. Geoffrey Holmes has written of the emergence of journalists. The male obstetrician was a new specialist. The term 'manufacturer' itself began to shed its traditional generalized meaning of 'craftsman', becoming narrowed to apply to large-scale owners of plant and employers of labour.

More people also carved out careers as technical specialists. Agricultural experts such as Arthur Young, guidebook writers and handbook compilers earned livings by the pen. Surveyors, technicians, civil engineers, instrument-makers, cartographers, mill-wrights, turnpike-builders (such as Thomas Telford, the 'Colossus of Roads') swelled in number as the economy demanded greater technological expertise. Samuel Bentham, brother of the Utilitarian Jeremy, set the manufacture of ships' biscuits for the navy on a production-line basis. Whereas technologists on the Continent generally formed a state salariat or held military rank, in England most were self-employed entrepreneurs of expertise. For instance William Smith, England's pioneer geologist, was a self-educated land surveyor, canal engineer and mines prospector. And fresh openings were continually appearing for writers, commercial artists, industrial designers and impresarios of the arts. Thomas Bewick, the Newcastle engraver, bird painter and writer, was an astute commercial artist, cashing in upon local demand for trade cards, etc.

Finally, towards the end of the century, and building upon the foundations of Grub Street, something like a self-conscious Enlightenment intelligentsia was coming into being: writers such as Joseph Priestley, Richard Price, James Burgh, William Godwin, Thomas Holcroft, Mary Wollstonecraft, William Hazlitt and Arthur Aikin, making livings by teaching, journalism, lecturing, editing, publishing, reviewing, and translating; mostly young, astringent in tone, temperament and belief, many of them connected with religious Dissent. Clustering round radical publishers such as Joseph Johnson and the North East London Dissenting academies, they were associated with budding Romanticism, heterodox religion and philosophical radicalism. This avant-garde (and similar coteries elsewhere, such as the Dissenting communities in Warrington and Manchester) was a political force only obliquely: they were concerned more with ideals, and exposing privilege and corruption rather than with wresting power. Yet they formed the nerve centre of a new cadre of professional thinkers and communicators (Coleridge's 'clerisy'), experimenting in alternative lifestyles – on the whole, earnest rather than Bohemian – from vegetarianism to Coleridge's own arcadian dream of establishing a pantisocratic utopia on the banks of the Susquehanna.

In the nation as a whole, the sway enjoyed by moneyed men was economic rather than political, though many commanded great local influence within corporations and vestries. Gathering together in clubs, masonic lodges and tavern 'free-and-easys', they celebrated the values vital to commercial success: confidence, conviviality, credit, connection and consumption. Through their clubs, constitutional societies and debating societies, where they howled against interference and taxation, and their experience of service on vestries and parishes, they achieved the self-respect (respectability came later) typified by the tradesmen who swaggered down Hogarth's Beer Street. Many would have replied 'hear, hear' to Joseph Priestley's sunny view that 'there appears to be much more happiness in the middle classes of life who are above the fear of want, and yet have a sufficient motive for a constant exertion of their faculties'.

Beneath moneyed men came craftsmen and artisans, labourers and the poor. There was nothing homogeneous about the lower orders, who ranged from weavers to watermen, from ostlers to shepherds, from ploughmen to piemen, from crossing-sweepers to coal-miners. Women traditionally did similar jobs to men; they also washed clothes, sold milk and greens, stitched gowns and were wet-nurses and prostitutes. Above all, women span, kept house and raised children. Working families very commonly eked out a living by piecing together a variety of seasonal, part-time and casual employments, combining the land and the loom, hop-picking, spinning, fishing, barking timber, weeding, etc. And below them came vagrants, paupers, the old, the sick, the unemployed and society's flotsam and jetsam – and their multitudinous young. Labouring people's strength was sapped for little reward and no thanks. In most other countries the bulk of them were serfs or peasants: in England they were largely wage-labourers (though still called 'servants' by their masters). Although droves of self-employed workers remained – thatchers, woodcutters, tinkers and knife-grinders, to name just a few – by mid-century between 40 and 50 per cent of all English families were wage-earning. Those who did not control their own labour but worked for others included farmhands, a growing body; journeymen in manufactures and building; and spinners, carders, rovers, weavers and stocking-knitters in large-scale putting-out industries run by capitalist clothiers, subsequently in factories. Such workers included most women and children (who worked in subtle or direct dependency upon husbands, fathers and masters), servants in husbandry, and domestic servants – predominantly young and unmarried and easily the largest single occupational group, numbering between 600,000 and 700,000. England was traditionally 'the purgatory of servants', and the jurist Blackstone called master and servant – meaning employees in general – one of the three great relations of private life. Also included in this group were apprentices, living in, who received board but scant remuneration.

Within the traditional handicraft economy, the standing and earning-power of workers in many trades rose with age and experience. Teenagers were sent into service or apprenticed for seven years to a trade. In their twenties they would become journeymen and marry; some would in time become small masters. Yet, with growing capitalization, in many industries the gap between owners and labourers was widening and becoming unbridgeable. In mining for example, where shafts became deeper and more costly to sink, self-employing gangs of workers gave way to capitalist owners of winding and pumping gear, employing labourers. In the second half of the century, moreover, the rising population produced a pool of labour which tipped the economic power balance in favour of employers. Guild restrictions on entry into trades were smashed, the supply of day labourers swelled, and a greater proportion of working people spent their whole working lives as mere hands, becoming something akin to a modern proletariat.

Such polarization caused anxiety. Working men's 'motives to industry, frugality and sobriety are all subverted by this one consideration,' wrote Dean Tucker, discussing the highly capitalized Gloucestershire cloth trade, 'that they shall always be chained to the same oar, and never be but journeymen.' Apprentices likewise were often little better off than galley-slaves. Maltreatment of child apprentices was not infrequent; especially vulnerable were the London waifs and orphans farmed out to contractors and manufacturers. In 1764 a farmer from near Malmesbury was indicted for maiming and castrating two apprentices. It was alleged that, having received the premium for them, he tried to kill the boys by giving them smallpox.

Duty hours were gruellingly long, especially for servants-of-all-work. Dawn to dusk was a common span, though in certain trades journeymen's combinations had secured a ten-hour day. Household servants were hardly allowed lives of their own. Working conditions were often hellish – the flames and sulphurous fumes of vats and furnaces, the lethal damps and gases of the coal-face, the perils of the sea, made worse still by undermanned, waterlogged, but well-insured, vessels. Workmen in physical trades such as sawing became prematurely wizened, succumbing to ghastly industrial diseases; fumes and dust brought on lung and bronchial conditions, lead-miners contracted plumbism, and no new legislation protecting against occupational diseases and hazards was introduced. Around ports, common seamen were never safe from the shanghai'ing press-gangs.

Earnings were poor, and women received only about two thirds men's wages for the same work. There was no compensation against slumps, seasonal underemployment or lay-offs, when snow, floods or drought halted trade (he was a fortunate working man who was in employment twelve months in the year). Men were subjected to brutality from their masters (soldiers and sailors were flogged as matters of routine), women, especially servants, were prey to sexual exploitation. Further hardships were piled on, for instance payment by 'truck' not coin, or long in arrears (though this did enforce a form of savings). Even Dean Tucker, a friend of capitalism, admitted that in some industries the relationship between master and worker 'approached much nearer to that of a planter and slaves in our American colonies than might be expected of such a country as England'.

The well-to-do feared the labouring poor, yet many also acknowledged their steadfast skills and counted themselves fortunate that England was not beggar- and bandit-infested like other places. The American traveller Louis Simond offered a crumb of comfort: 'the poor do not look so poor here as in other countries,' yet humanitarians could see that many of the labouring classes could hardly subsist. 'I found some in their cells, others in their garrets,' wrote the scandalized John Wesley in 1753, 'half starved with cold and hunger, added to weakness and pain. But I found not one of them unemployed who was able to crawl about the room. So wickedly, so devilishly false, is that common objection, "They are poor because they are idle." '

The working masses bore the luxury of the well-to-do on their shoulders. 'I never see lace and embroidery upon the back of a beau,' wrote a correspondent to the *Northampton Mercury* in 1739, 'but my thoughts descend to the poor fingers that have wrought it ... What would avail our large estates and great tracts of land without their labours?' Or, in the disarming phrase of that high priest of capitalism, Adam Smith, 'In a civilized society the poor provide both for themselves and for the enormous luxury of their superiors.' Under these circumstances, although the polite reviled the insolence of what Horace Walpole dubbed 'our supreme governors, the mob', the wonder was they were so tractable. 'The sufferings of the poor are indeed less observed than their misdeeds,' wrote Henry Fielding. 'They starve and freeze and rot among themselves, but they beg and steal and rob among their betters.' Probe deeper, he suggested, and it would be clear how the labourers' lives were sacrificed on the treadmill of toil. Many hardly lived outside work (miners often slept down the pit). As a haberdasher's assistant, Robert Owen often worked till two in the morning. Abigails and apprentices were expected to be chaste; their private lives were under surveillance. Servants might even lose their own names, being dubbed (like pets) 'Betty' or 'John Thomas'. Most of their remuneration came indirectly, not in money wages, but in bed and board, cast-offs, shelter, perks and tips. A maid-of-all-work might be paid a princely £3 a year.

The workplace was exhausting: there was no incentive to develop labour-saving machinery because labour itself was abundant and cheap. Yet it could also have its compensations – often more so than home life. In those long-established urban trades such as tanning or tailoring which were covered by the Elizabethan Statute of Artificers, guilds and companies were still strong. Their rules and traditions restricted entry and upheld apprenticeship (enforcing the seven-year term and limiting the number of apprentices per master), and by-laws empowered magistrates to enforce established rates of pay and terms of work. Indentured apprenticeship requirements gave qualified journeymen in effect a closed shop, a property in their skill. Regulatory statutes gave muscle to collective bargaining: workers were demanding only their legal due. Thus freemen of London companies often appealed to the Lord Mayor's court – a kind of industrial tribunal – for relief against masters who introduced blacklegs.

In such protected trades, teams of skilled journeymen enjoyed their own time-hallowed rituals of collective strength and con-viviality, with their ribald work-songs and traditional horse-play. Trades had their own coats of arms, regalia, slang, annual parades and licensed fooleries; they ran sports competitions and set up benefit and friendly societies in taverns. In town, events such as executions or mayors' parades were cues for time-off, dressing-up and revels. In many trades ancient usage protected the rate for the job and fringe benefits, and journeymen dug in their heels against encroachments – often with success. Strikes, though localized, were part of the fabric of industrial relations and could be backed up by intimidation – anonymous threatening letters, effigy-burning or machine-smashing. John Kay's home was attacked in 1753 by workers protesting against his 'flying shuttle'. A few years later Blackburn spinners destroyed Hargreaves's spinning jennies. Nottinghamshire hosiers smashed hundreds of Arkwright's stocking frames in 1779 after failing to secure a minimum wage (significantly the workers won their point, and there were no successful prosecutions against the wreckers). As the century wore on, combinations (trade unions), mostly clan-destine and masked by 'box-clubs', increased. Journeymen tailors and stay-makers ran the most powerful London combinations, but they were also strong among carpenters, joiners, bricklayers, masons, shipwrights, lightermen and wool-combers, and in other trades besides.

Protection of labour within a 'moral economy' worked well enough for craftsmen in the first half of the century when labour was in relatively short supply. Later, things got more difficult. With inflation climbing from the 1760s, workers increasingly needed to press to raise wages. Thus, in 1775, Islington hay-makers, customarily on 1s. 4d. a day, struck for 1s. 6d.: they got it. But the flooding of the labour market as population rose, and technological innovations requiring less skilled operatives, put craftsmen's backs against the wall. For example, late in the century in the Cotswold cloth industry, capitalists were introducing mechanical gig mills to replace properly apprenticed skilled labour. The workers resisted fiercely but lost. Strikes against new machinery and the undermining of apprenticeship regulations grew more frequent. Government responded by repealing legislation protecting apprenticeship and work conditions (statutory apprenticeship was abolished in 1814). In any case, the Elizabethan protective legislation had never applied to 'new' trades, such as cotton-spinning and calico-printing. Under the 1799 and 1800 (anti-)Combination Acts, workers forming illegal combinations could be summarily gaoled for three months, after appearing before only one magistrate.

Working people won some control over their lives – and some relief – in two ways. First, many of them took advantage of the fringe benefits of working under the noses of their betters, domestic servants above all. Appreciating what Gibbon called 'the indispensable comfort of a servant', no gentleman wanted to be waited upon by lousy, stinking ragamuffins. It was in masters' interests to supply wigs and bodices, medical treatment, and even some education, for those who served and waited. While deploring their impertinence, many wished to use such 'gentlemen's gentlemen' and lady's maids as confidantes, accomplices, go-betweens, and even companions. William Hogarth painted his. A few eccentric families, notably the Yorkes at Erddig in North Wales, took loving care of their staff, writing verses about them, keeping their portraits, and generally treating them as part of the family (though they still paid them badly). Upper servants such as John MacDonald might be choosy about their employers – he got through twenty-seven masters. For the likes of MacDonald, service was a priceless opportunity for foreign travel and raffish sexual adventure – and it finally left him savings enough to establish a hotel. Ex-butlers often set up inns. Charles Fortnum, once a footman of George III, founded the provisions emporium. Nor were servants slow to exploit their immense blackmailing potential. What the butler saw frequently came out in testimony against their masters in court, especially in adultery cases, and sometimes their silence had to be bought. They quizzed low life above stairs, and mimicked high life below.

In any case, custom gave servants many perks. Cooks were allowed to sell off dripping and cinders, and they expected commission from shopkeepers; maids inherited clothes when mistresses died. Live-in servants ate well (some pilfered adroitly too). So thumping were the tips (called 'vails') which servants expected from house-guests (some would take only silver) that a campaign to abolish 'taking the vail' went as far as the Commons – provoking servants' riots in 1764. In the intricate hierarchy of servants' hall, upper servants assumed airs, wielding their own authority. Not least, the exceptional maid might – like Pamela in Richardson's novel – marry her master. Boswell knew an attorney who wed his cookmaid 'because she dressed a lovely bit of collop'.

Servants' lives had their degrading side; they were always on call, their personal life was stifled, and jeopardizing their good character could spell ruin. Yet masters' complaints about pert servants (where could trusty ones be found?), and servants' own high job mobility, prove they had real bargaining power. Many undoubtedly used service as an entry into a superior world.

Thus certain jobs provided a degree of freedom. But in general the lower classes relished freedom from work. They knew labour did not ennoble *them*. Few possessed the so-called 'bourgeois' spirit of thrifty accumulation (not too many of the bourgeoisie did, either). This was quite rational: with wages low and labour long, increasing earnings significantly would have been a pipedream for most. People commonly preferred leisure to working harder and saving, and they spent what they had (again rational: those with savings disqualified themselves from poor relief). Because out-work paid by the piece, artisans could generally work their own hours. They commonly took Monday off (St Monday – the devout honoured St Tuesday too), and then they worked like maniacs through to Saturday, when payday brought a binge. Also – as Benjamin Franklin bemoaned – Englishmen downed tankards while they worked.

Because of their irregular work habits, labouring men were always being cursed as feckless. 'When wages are good,' prated Defoe, 'they won't work any more than from hand to mouth; or if they do work they spend it in riot or luxury.' In short, he concluded, 'we are the most lazy-diligent nation in the world.' His views found echo fifty years later. 'If a person can get sufficient in four days, to support himself for seven days, he will keep holiday the other three, that is he will live in riot and debauchery.' Labourers fretted the employing classes, because they kicked against their allotted life of drudgery, preferring ale and letting off steam. Workmen, complained Dr George Fordyce, are 'always idle when they have any money left, so that their life is spent between labour ... and perfect idleness and drunkenness.'

But, as with the pauper problem, punitive solutions only bred fresh problems. Whereas the far-sighted Adam Smith advocated a high-wage economy, to give labourers inducements to work and save, the cautious believed Dr Johnson's retort: 'Raising the wages of day labourers is wrong for it does not make them live better, but only makes them idler.' Yet reducing wages sapped incentives, hit consumption and threw more upon the parish.

Anxiety over the lower orders' improvidence was greatest in respect of those least dependent upon regular pay packets: seasonal and casual workers, self-employed pedlars, and all those wild-fowlers, mole-catchers, charcoal-burners, and hurdle-makers who constituted the secret people, living on the waste or in coppice-clearings, getting a living out of the commons in a 'scratch-as-scratch-can' way. A hundred thousand cottagers' families subsisted chiefly in scrubby woodland areas and were widely believed to top up their income with petty crime – sheep-stealing, poaching, receiving, coining. Dwelling outside villages, they more than most escaped the disciplinary eye of magistrates, neighbours and the Church (not that Anglicanism or Old Dissent had much sway over the lives of many of the lower orders). Colliers formed a substantial group who, huddled around isolated pits, were reckoned unusually wild and lawless. In some of these communities – for instance among the tinners of Cornwall and the colliers of Kingswood Forest near Bristol, thought 'an un-governable people' – popular Methodism began to exercise a sobering influence later in the century.

Collectively at the workplace, labouring men could give a show of independence. Males in particular could spend their wages in the dram-shop buying oblivion. Spirits were always cheap. Early in the nineteenth century Francis Place recalled, 'Until lately, all the amusements of the working people of the metropolis were immediately concerned with drinking – choir-clubs, chanting clubs, lottery clubs, and every variety of club, intended for amusement, were always held at public houses.' By contrast, plebeian home life must generally have been pinched. As the century wore on, the professional and landed orders cultivated a new domesticity and invested in home comforts, but the lower orders' harassed domestic economy left little room for the graces. In fact, home life for many grew even starker. As more country workers lost common rights and became proletarianized, fewer had wood for firing, a cow for milk or hens for eggs. Fewer brewed and baked for themselves: even country folk were eating shop-bought bread. Checking the diets and living standards of the poor became an improving pastime for their voyeuristic betters (as did collecting their ballads and folklore). Without exception, such philanthropic snoopers found country workers – especially in the great arable belt of central southern England – reduced to a cheerless breadline: bread, cheese, cold fare; Lent all the year round. Better off than many – note the princely outlay on tea and sugar – was an Oxfordshire rural labourer, near the end of the century, who laid out each year for himself and three children:

4½ peck loaves a week at 1s. 2d. each	£13 13s.
Tea and sugar	£2 10s.
Butter and lard	£1 10s.
Beer and milk	£1
Bacon and other meat	£1 10s.
Soap, candles, etc.	about 15s.
House rent	£3
Coats	£2 10s.
Shoes and shirts	£3
Other clothes	£2
Total expenses	£31 8s.

As a carter and digger he earned a beggarly 8s. or 9s. a week. His expenses thus exceeded his income by over £5 a year. The parish partly made this up; but he was £5 in debt.

How much did the lot of the labouring poor change? The horrors of a peasantry multiplying while food production and job openings remained static were gripping much of rural Europe in the late eighteenth century, leading to serf revolts, mass vagrancy, beggary and the flooding of the starving into towns such as Naples. England avoided the worst of this. The expansion of manufactures and marketing opened new employment. Many more families found full-time or part-time work spinning, weaving and stocking-knitting, dotted throughout the countryside or concentrated in sprawling industrial villages. A loom of one's own promised independence and self-respect. In the Black Country and South Yorkshire the metal trades forged ahead. Where relatively unskilled work (for example, weaving) was plentiful, couples tended to marry earlier, producing more children. In such areas the steep population rise of the last third of the century was a response to the tonic of job openings.

Elsewhere, in less prosperous areas, unemployment and parochial dependence were probably the precipitants of earlier marriage and larger families. There was a steady, creeping migration from rural hinterlands towards the manufacturing districts. The move to the towns was not, however, a direct consequence of husbandmen being turfed off the land by enclosure. In fact, enclosure for pasturage, so common in the Midlands from the 1750s to about 1780, created both short-term and long-term employment. Industrial areas, rather, were magnets offering better employment prospects, and the demand for labour in manufactures forced up wage-rates in the Midlands and the North. These gains were wiped out, however, by inflation and taxation in the 1790s, when wartime disruption of export trades also created crippling unemployment. Women and children were in great demand for factory work, and wage-levels were attractive (though, of course, entrepreneurs picked female and child labour because it was cheaper than male). Technologically sophisticated textile factories in turn created demands for ancillary labour. Spinning factories thus multiplied the need for home-loom weavers, whose wages were reaching short-lived halcyon levels (sometimes over £3 a week at the end of the century).

Were industrial working conditions deteriorating? The new factories were steamy, full of unguarded machinery and disciplined by martinets and the ceaseless throb of the engine. Yet factories accounted for a tiny fraction of the labour force. Labour at home or in the workshop was itself often performed in cramped, dusty, dingy conditions, under a tyrant master or husband. Industrialization doubtless multiplied crippling occupational diseases, and deeper mine shafts spelt more colliers' widows. Yet new villages such as Cromford and Styal planted by textile magnates in the rural valleys of Derbyshire, Cheshire and Lanca-shire were garden-town models of enlightened planning, with stone houses, shops and allotments. However we assess urban conditions in industrializing areas, the flow of labour was all in their direction.

It was workers on the land whose prospects were unambigu-ously eroded as the century progressed. In the seventeenth, and through much of the eighteenth, century, farm labour was chiefly performed by 'servants in husbandry', young, unmarried workers who lived-in with farmers, usually on an annual con-tract. In time, however, farmers reduced this practice, not want-ing their 'improved' farmsteads polluted by labourers, and finding it cheaper to hire labour only when occasion arose, at harvest for instance, by the day or task. The decline of living-in made farm labourers more dependent on money wages, while also leaving many without employment for much of the year. Such pressures were exacerbated where enclosure further reduced inde-pendence by depriving labourers of customary access to common land, which had helped them eke out a living from firing, grazing, nuts and berries, and the odd rabbit. The Revd Richard Warner, touring the southern counties, mused, 'Time was when these commons enabled the poor man to support his family, and bring up his children. Here he could turn out his cow and pony, feed his flock of geese, and keep his pig. But the enclosures have de-prived him of these advantages.' Furthermore, in the rural south-ern counties, only the more poorly paid forms of by-employment (such as sock-knitting in Hampshire) tended to be available, and the lack of large industrial towns nearby made it more difficult for families to migrate in search of work (surrounding parishes would boot them back to their place of settlement, fearing a charge on the rates). The underemployed thus became more dependent upon outdoor relief. Numbers swelled (by 1800, 28 per cent of the population was in receipt of poor relief), and costs soared (but it was still cheaper for farmers than paying wages all the year round). £532,000 had been paid out per year in 1680; by 1780 the figure was almost £2 million, and rising fast. As Cobbett vividly described, the southern rural proletariat was becoming demoralized. Not only were they afflicted in the midst of plenty, but even when they were in employment they could not command a living wage. The Revd David Davies

wrote in 1795, 'In visiting the labouring families of my parish
... I could not but observe with concern their mean and
distressed condition ... Yet I could not impute the wretchedness
I saw either to sloth or wastefulness.' Arthur Young, long the
most enthusiastic supporter of enclosure, by 1801 characterized
the fatalism of the rural displaced:

Go to an ale-house of an old enclosed country, and there you will see
the origin of poverty and poor-rates. For whom are they to be sober?
For whom are they to save? (Such are their questions.) For the parish? If
I am diligent, shall I have leave to build a cottage? If I am sober, shall I
have land for a cow? If I am frugal, shall I have half an acre for
potatoes? You offer no motives: you have nothing but a parish officer
and a work-house! – Bring me another pot!

The most intractable labour problem of the next century was
staring people in the face: rural pauperism.

Finally, Georgian England had its underground people, its
concealed world of beggars, small-time thieves, gipsies, dossers
and vagrants, sharpers and cheats, who got by on practically
nothing. Long before Mayhew, the German traveller Lichtenberg
described such destitute, dangerous shanty-town people:

... persons born in the fields, generally near the brick-kilns round
London ... They grow up without learning to read or write, and never
hear the words 'Religion' or 'Belief', and not even the word 'God',
excepting in the phrase 'God damn it'. They gain their livelihood by all
kinds of work in the brick-kilns, helping the drivers of hackney coaches,
and so forth, until the old Adam in them is aroused: then they take to
stealing and are generally hanged between the ages of 18 and 26. A short
life and merry one is their motto, which they do not hesitate to
proclaim in court.

Outside London, however, professional criminals were few.
Many of the men who took to petty theft (fewer women did)
were labourers who stole to get over hard times.

But, alongside, a permanent body of proletarianized paupers
was gathering: proletarians in that they possessed no source of
income save their labour, no customary rights over the land, no
roots; paupers in that they had no work (often through old age,
illness, disease or infirmity) or only casual work, or – very often
– because wages would not support a household. Particularly in

the last years of the century, price inflation was outstripping wages. Wheat had cost 34s. a quarter in 1780; it was up to 58s. in 1790 and 128s. by 1800. Although Adam Smith and his acolytes sanguinely prophesied that the march of capitalism would eradicate poverty, the reverse was happening. To the trapped poor, Burke offered cheerless, though realistic, belt-tightening advice: 'Patience, labour, sobriety, frugality, and religion, should be recommended to them: all the rest is down-right fraud.'

Did it suit the propertied to be surrounded by the lumpenproletariat? In some ways, not at all: they proved a bottomless pit into which poor rates were poured; they harboured disease, crime and disorder; they did not pull their weight as consumers; they were the tinder of disaffection awaiting a spark. That is why Malthus advised the poor to breed less. Marx argued that expansive, profit-hungry, free-market capitalism needed such people as a plentiful reserve army of labour, to plug gaps in the workforce and depress wage-levels in general. In a sense the proletarianized poor did constitute such a reserve army: industrial capitalism was not asphyxiated at birth by labour shortage. Yet what use were the urban riff-raff and country yokels to employers? Outside the workforce they were not serviceable; they were merely a residue, the left-overs of such economic change as enclosure, the cast-offs of a cutthroat society in which atomized and myopic administration adopted callous policies and no one shouldered ultimate responsibility. As Frederick Eden observed, 'It is one of the natural consequences of freedom that those who are left to shift for themselves must sometimes be reduced to want.'

The Georgian age did not witness any dramatic transformation of the social structure, rather a gradual change. Several groups swelled in importance – especially the capital-deploying trading classes and the proletarianized poor – but the league table of wealth and status, headed by great landowners, was much the same in 1800 as a century earlier. The complex fabric, in which social power was compounded of many factors, including family, clientage, privilege, inheritance, status, occupation, and regional, political and religious connections, had by no means boiled down by 1800 into a society where clear-cut class armies glowered at each other across industrial battlefields. So long as landowning remained profitable as well as prestigious, there was no prospect of upset at the top; below, so long as mass concentrations of workers remained highly exceptional and the Poor Law regulated rural society, there was no imminent threat to stability. Limited access to upward mobility and the rise in tandem of aggregate wealth and social pretensions ensured that the social order neither collapsed nor was overthrown.

3. *Power, Politics and the Law*

Georgian England has often been pictured as an Eden of ease, elegance and equipoise; George Saintsbury coined the phrase 'the peace of the Augustans' to evoke its supposed majestic, imperial calm ('*Quieta non movere*' was after all the key to Robert Walpole's statecraft). Such pastoral interpretations would have us see England as a happy hierarchical hunting ground of Toby-jug squires and their dogs, paternalist grandees flanked by deferential retainers, the great aristocratic oaks sheltering the bumpkin multitude. It was – one historian tells us – 'an age when the less fortunate classes still meekly accepted their lot in life'. 'The early part of the eighteenth century has something of the glamour of Arcadia,' wrote Dorothy George. 'We think of it as the last age of old England, of solid, stable, rural England.' In particular, Sir Lewis Namier and his followers have portrayed mid-Georgian politics as the apogee of oligarchy, when public affairs were handled as the family business of a closed clique of clans. There was a solid maturity about high politics, the argument runs, because bigwigs dropped all the rant and cant about principles and programmes, and made no bones about concentrating instead upon the nitty-gritty of power, intrigue and management.

More recent historians, however, have discarded any such idyllic views. Struggle, tension and conflict have been restored stage centre by political historians of all stripes, both those who stress popular protest and those who underline the perduring allure of 'divine right' Toryism and Jacobitism. And the same goes for social and cultural historians, who have stripped off the civilized veneer of the 'age of reason', revealing that beneath the perfectly powdered wig, emotional and psychological disorder seethed. This was after all the century in which the deeply misanthropic Dean Swift has his hero, Lemuel Gulliver, see men as monkeys and decide to go and live with his horses. In one of his despairing, drunken fits, James Boswell hurled a lighted candelabra at his beloved wife. Clive of India, an opium addict, was one of many who despaired and took his own life (England became notorious as the world suicide capital). Dr Johnson went in fear of losing his wits, and the poet William Cowper analysed his own psychological shipwreck:

> No voice divine the storm allay'd
> No light propitious shone,
> When, snatch'd from all effectual aid
> We perish'd, each alone;
> But I beneath a rougher sea
> And 'whelm'd in deeper gulfs than he.

Out of doors, crime was rife and often bloody: smugglers had little compunction about slaying excise officers. And, from the rough-house of the crowd to the dragoons' musket volley, violence ran through public and political life, as English as plum pudding. Force was used as a matter of routine to achieve social and political goals, smudging hard-and-fast distinctions between the worlds of criminality and politics. Indeed bigwig politicians were often represented as petty bruisers and bullies writ large. The gang-leader Jonathan Wild thus achieved sardonic glory as the minnow who got caught, while the pestiferous sharks of high society, such as Prime Minister Walpole, were let off the hook: the theme of *The Beggar's Opera* and countless satires. An 'Advertisement Extraordinary' in the Wilkite *Middlesex Journal* for 1769 harped on the same theme:

Whereas a gang of notorious robbers have for some years past infested the neighbourhood of St James and the Treasury, and have in a daring manner, and in open defiance of the laws of the land, plundered the public of several millions sterling, to the great loss of his majesty's liege subjects; and have lately absconded loaded with their plunder. These are therefore to require all good and well disposed people, born on this side of the Tweed, to apprehend such traitors and robbers, and bring them to justice, and in so doing, shall on conviction and execution, receive the reward due to the distinguished Patriots of Old England and be recorded in history for future generations.

Highwaymen were sometimes romanticized – not without irony – as 'gentlemen of the road', smugglers fêted because excise-men were hated (why should imports be taxed? – especially when the establishment itself, from Walpole to Parson Woodforde, bought up contraband, Walpole using an Admiralty barge to run his smuggled wine up the Thames?).

Upright citizens – not just blackguards and bravoes but the village Hampden too – did not shrink from force to get their due. There was a cacophony of verbal violence: newspapers, cartoons and street ballads blasted their targets with scabrous insults and Billingsgate scurrility; political sermons thundered from pulpits. And frequently just the whiff of rough stuff was sufficient. Casanova was astonished when Drury Lane patrons, finding a different play performed from the one billed, threatened to wreck the theatre unless the manager, David Garrick, abjectly apologized: 'On your knees,' they yelled; Garrick knelt. Even so, Drury Lane was wrecked by riots in 1743, 1750, 1755, 1763, 1770 and 1776. To celebrate popular causes such as the Wilkite triumphs, London mobs would order householders to light up their windows under threat of pulling down the frontage. And crowds often took the law into their own hands. Brothels were rifled by disgruntled punters, homosexuals stoned to death in the pillory. Corpses were sometimes hacked down from the gibbet and snatched away by friends and family in hope of revival and to prevent anatomical dissection by surgeons (itself another form of violence, which formed one of Hogarth's 'Four Stages of Cruelty'). Crowds, often led by women, would use force to stop dealers selling corn above fixed prices or contrary to market regulations, or would attack mills and granaries, sometimes brandishing firearms, to prevent grain being bulk-shipped elsewhere in times of shortage. Bread and food riots were common, not least because they were successful. In 1740 disturbances paralysed Norwich for five days over the price of mackerel. Bloody food riots in Somerset and Wiltshire in 1766–7 involved attacks on stores and looting: 3,000 troops were sent in. Turnpike gates, hated as a new concealed tax, were uprooted. Severe turnpike riots occurred in Gloucestershire, Yorkshire and Nottinghamshire (in one at Beeston ten people were killed by the military). In 1749, reported the *Gentleman's Magazine*,

about 400 Somersetshire people cut down a third time the turnpike gates on the Ashton Road ... then afterwards destroyed the Dundry Turnpike, and thence went to Bedminster headed by two chiefs on horseback ... the rest were on foot, armed with rusty swords, pitch-forks, axes, pistols, clubs.

Strikes for higher wages, and machine-breaking to halt the installation of new technology, were commonplace. The entre-preneur Matthew Boulton was set upon by Cornish tin-miners in 1787, having to buy them off with 20 guineas for drink. Over 400 labour disputes have been documented during the century.

The lava flow of violence ran through the political landscape, sometimes underground, sometimes on the surface. Unpopular politicians were often ragged, peers' carriages pelted and rocked, and their windows smashed, as they left Westminster – whereas heroes such as Henry Sacheverell or Charles James Fox were cheered and chaired. Minorities were tempting targets. Meth-odists were treated as cockshies (John Wesley saw it as a mark of Divine favour that no brick hit him personally), as were homo-sexuals, witches, bawds and Frenchmen. The Act of 1753 legal-izing the naturalization of Jews brought baying anti-Semitic mobs on to the streets: it was immediately repealed. Irish-baiting and Scots-baiting were national sports. Fear of popery sparked the Gordon Riots in London in 1780, though targets broadened to include the rich, Lord Mansfield, breweries and Newgate gaol. The City lay paralysed at the mercy of 'King Mob' for a week; £100,000 of damage was done to property (ten times as much as in Paris throughout the French Revolution) before troops restored order at the cost of 290 citizens' lives: twenty-five looters were later executed. Prejudices against Dissenters, especi-ally Unitarians, led to insults against them and attacks on their property, particularly in the 1790s, when Tom Paine was also often burnt in effigy by loyalist crowds, egged on by constables. When John Wilkes presented himself in the 1760s as St George rescuing fair English liberties from the dragons of general war-rants, Lord Bute, George III and Parliament, crowds flocked onto the streets, marched, cheered, badgered the support of bystanders – for instance, forcing publicans to stand toasts – and intimidated opponents. During the explosive 1790s, ministers quaked, terrified that violence might erupt just about anywhere.

Alarm was well founded, partly because the machinery of law enforcement was patchy. Most parishes boasted only an amateur constable or two: aided by community vigilance, these could cope with petty crime but not with disturbances. Faced with disaffection, mayors and JPs sometimes trembled to act: their own sympathies sometimes lay with anti-government or anti-middlemen rioters. They themselves risked prosecution if they overstepped the letter of the law. In any case they lacked disciplined, readily mobilized forces, for there was no national police to summon. In the event of riots, magistrates were unwilling to call upon the Home Secretary to send in troops: it was an admission of defeat, invited centralism, and in any case they quickly learnt that a platoon of soldiers billeted on their borough created more disruption than it quelled. Bristol Corporation sought troops from the Secretary of State to deal with labour disputes in 1791. When similar troubles broke out in 1794, it decided it could deal better with rioters itself.

Disturbances were alarming because they were so often sudden and swift. Black-faced nocturnal bands ripping up fences or burning ricks were hard to catch or convict. What further perturbed the authorities was that rioters were not typically hardened criminals, agitprop demonstrators or the scum of society – all of whom might have been easily identified and punished without compunction. For even rock-solid citizens resorted at times to militancy and law-breaking as a means of collective bargaining by direct action: artisans, master-craftsmen, yeomen, stevedores, smallholders, ex-soldiers or sedan chairmen, often led by someone of higher standing, a publican or a maverick gentleman for instance. Thus, it was the English at large who were an ungovernable people. Nor were riots just spasms, brought on by extreme hunger. Demotic disturbances were often political acts, howling down injustices and the abuse of power and championing traditional values: No General Warrants! Wilkes and Liberty! 1688! No Scots! Old Prices! The blasphemous anonymous letters pinned upon the doors of bailiffs, millers and magistrates threatened blood, but threatened it in the name of Freedom, the British Constitution or Christian Justice – witness this instance from Rossendale in 1762, addressed to James Bailey, a JP:

This his to asquaint you that We poor of Rosendale Rochdale Oldham Saddleworth Ashton have all mutaly and firmly agreed by Word and Covinent and Oath to Fight and Stand by Each Other as long as Life doth last for We may as well be all hanged as starved to Death and to see ower Children weep for Bread and none to give Them nor no liklyness of ever mending wile You all take Part with Brommal and Markits drops at all the principle Markits elceware but take This for a shure Maxon, That if You dont put those good Laws in Execution against all Those Canables or Men Slayers That have the Curse of God and all honest Men both by Gods Laws and Mens Laws so take Notice Bradshaw Bailey and Lloyd the biggest Rogue of all Three I know You all have Power to stop such vilonas Proceedings if You please and if You dont amaidatley put a Stopp and let hus feel it the next Saturday We will murder You all that We have down in Ower List and Wee will all bring a Faggot and burn down Your Houses and Wait Houses and make Your Wifes Widdows and Your Children Fatherless for the Blood of Shul de hill lyes cloose at Ower Harts and Blood for Blood We Require.

Take Care. Middleton.

Rioters thus saw themselves as avenging angels, Robin Hoods of redress. Their political savvy was high and often couched in Biblical cadences. Theirs was an allegiance to an Old England of popular rights, customary law, neighbourliness and roast beef. The *vox populi* uttered its demands through the sympathetic magic of slogans, riddles, graffiti, effigies, songs and caricature. Excluded from Westminster, the lifeblood of popular politics coursed through the propaganda media of newspapers, handbills, ballads, posters and cartoons, through tavern and coffee-house debate, and spilt onto the streets.

Disorder pockmarked Georgian England – foreigners were astonished at the licence permitted to the people. They found the English extraordinarily politically well-informed and assertive, from peers down to shoe-blacks and the millions in between, crowding around the outworks of the official political nation. 'There is scarce any man in England,' observed Joseph Addison early in the century, 'of what Denomination soever, that is not a free-thinker in politics, and hath not some particular notions of his own . . . Our nation, which was formerly called a nation of saints, may now be called a nation of statesmen.' Continentals found the people's participation in political street life unparalleled at home. 'When one sees how the lowliest carter shows an interest in public affairs,' commented the Prussian, Moritz, in the 1780s:

how the smallest children enter into the spirit of the nation; how
everyone feels himself to be a man and an Englishman . . . as good as his
kind and his king's minister . . . it brings to the mind thoughts very
different from those we know when we watch the soldiers drilling in
Berlin.

Yet this political fabric – endlessly abused, spat upon, pulled,
torn, tattered and patched – was never ripped to pieces. If the
socio-political nation really had been weak, fragile and verging
on dissolution, surely the Jacobite rebellions of 1715 and 1745, or
the Gordon Riots, or the radicalism of the 1790s, would have
precipitated that final conflagration. But crypto-Jacobite sympathies – though widespread – did not lead to a rush to arms in
England; the Gordon Riots did not spread beyond London; and
key radical bodies of the 1790s such as the Friends of the People
(1791) and the London Corresponding Society (1792) expected
to carry the day through Reason – by education, pamphlets and
petitioning. Piecemeal violence never erupted into general insurrection.

Why? One reason lies in the mentality of the riot. Protesters'
aims were usually concrete, defensive and limited: they wanted
bread at old prices, the restoration of long-standing wage-rates,
the clearing of rights of way. Their appeal was to a traditional
order, to be restored by society's traditional leaders. The crowd
did not want to direct the grain market itself, still less abolish
private property in grain; it wanted magistrates to enforce the
regulatory statutes. In place of Lord Bute, Wilkite crowds did
not demand a National Convention, still less a Committee of
Public Safety, but English liberties. And once a mob had aired its
grievances – uprooted a toll gate, destroyed a recruiting office –
it dispersed. Crowds had no programme of revolutionary socialism, or even democracy, no manifesto for modernity. Riots
were dramatic, and, like theatre, similarly cathartic and finite.
They were demonstrative enactments, symbolically lancing the
festering body politic, exposing corruption, venality, toadyism
and tyranny. The crowd created icons of iniquity and images of
justice: the cuckold's horns, a loaf of bread wrapped in mourning
crêpe, the Liberty Cap, the scales of Justice. John, Earl of Bute,
was demonized into a Jack Boot. Disturbances expressive but
circumscribed in nature made sense in a society where protesters

experienced grievances closest to the bone in local contexts, where – alongside a spatter of violence – the surest hope for redress lay in appeal to law, customs and magistrates.

The ruling order sometimes took disturbances on the chin, generally responded with a kid-glove approach, and emerged essentially unscathed. It survived so well partly because of its own resilient union of social, economic and political strength, and partly because political leaders, ever mindful of the lessons of 1642, did not again commit suicide by warring against each other.

The solid alliance of monarchy and magnates which successfully governed the ungovernable people was in many respects nothing strange, finding parallels throughout *ancien régime* Europe. The Tudor era had seen the Crown elevate itself against rival princelings, and the Reformation made the monarch Supreme Head of the Church. Contemporary socio-economic trends had also helped consolidate an effective landed class. The early disappearance of serfdom encouraged an agrarian capitalism in which proprietorship, profit and power interwove; and then the political broils of the Stuarts, culminating in 1688, checked the dangers that divine-right monarchy might have posed to the autonomy of the county community, and left property absolutely secure.

Yet the Hanoverian state boasted two special strengths. First, the partnership between Crown and grandees proved unusually harmonious. Second, between them these ruling elements commandeered an expanding state apparatus, which paid big dividends to its beneficiaries, while securing property and political stability.

The marriage between crown and magnates was partly one of necessity. By the seventeenth century, the nobility no longer possessed assured private *military* strength – armies, retainers, the skills of command. The king, served by the flower of the nobility, had lost the Civil War on the battlefield; in no other state had rebels been so successful in arms. Yet, as counterbalances to military decline, the leading proprietors in mid-Stuart times had not yet evolved new instruments of political control. Squabbles with the Crown (for instance with Charles II in the Exclusion Crisis) had split the magnates, leaving them *as a body* without automatic access to Court. Especially over religion, deep rifts had opened between the Court, great nobles and the solid gentry.

Magnates needed the protective armour of state power. Yet even under William and Mary, and then Anne, the struggle for mastery in high politics produced turbulence, sectarian conflict and factionalization. The generation straddling the new century was strife-torn. Both William III and Anne had regal wills of their own. The prospect of a disputed succession after Anne loomed as a Doomsday threat, polarizing and paralysing the nation. Would Anne ever produce an heir who outlived her? If not, would the Hanoverian succession succeed? Or would they be toppled? And if so, would the Stuarts return? In religion, how exclusive, privileged and autonomous was the Anglican Church to be? How much toleration would be granted to Dissenters and Catholics? All such profound issues splintered the loyalties of the ruling order at the turn of the new century, creating rabid infighting and schism. Gambling on the political future was make-or-break for career politicians such as St John, Harley, Stanhope and Walpole. Whig and Tory, Low and High Church, landed and moneyed property, pro- and anti-war, pro- and anti-Hanoverian factions tore at each other's throats like fighting cocks. Factions factionalized, and polarized all arenas of life. In London, even the coffee houses and theatres became sucked into party whirlpools. Tory theatre-goers patronized Drury Lane, Whigs the Haymarket; Tories went to the Cocoa-Tree coffee house, Whigs joined the Kit-Kat Club. The commission of the peace was dramatically purged for political reasons in 1696, 1700 and 1710. Political dissension *within* the ruling order – 'the rage of party' – had not been so cutthroat since the Civil War. Moreover elections held every couple of years (an unprecedented ten elections were called between 1695 and 1715), vitriolic propaganda and street mobs meant that the fight within the ruling order for power and its spoils spread to embroil – and divide – the localities and the masses. This was especially because the electorate had expanded to some 300,000 voters (maybe one in six adult males), and a large portion of constituencies were being contested: twenty-six counties went to the polls in 1705, twenty-three in 1710.

When the new century dawned, the pattern of future politics in England – above all, the relation between the Crown and the political nation – was profoundly unresolved. Stuarts and

Hanoverians were both waiting in the wings, and many hedged their bets. Whoever became king, he would not be very English, in birth, religion or outlook. And the very personality of the monarch could still make all the difference. After all, William of Orange had distrusted English politicians, followed a continental strategy, Dutch rather than English in orientation, and had far outstripped the success of any Stuart in developing the Crown as an effective instrument of government. Relations between state and society hung in the balance. Another century of prolonged Stuart constitutional conflicts might have polarized and impoverished English landed society or castrated the Crown, turning England into a France, a Spain or a Poland.

And yet it was a time when control of power offered sunnier prospects than ever, for the spoils were greater. Above all, government revenue was soaring, partly through the rise of customs receipts thanks to commercial expansion, and increasingly through the facilitation of borrowing. The Charter of the newly founded Bank of England (1694) authorized the Bank to advance £1.2 million to the Government, a sum increased in 1709 by a further £2.9 million. Between 1690 and 1700 total Government borrowing amounted to £11.7 million. Exchequer income also rose through the soaring taxes – direct and indirect – levied to finance continental war. In the 1690s alone, some £45 million were collected. Much of this revenue found its way, through various channels, to ministers and their henchmen and supporters.

Indeed, the Government establishment itself was snowballing. Warfare required more army and navy commissions, more contracts and concessions. Growth, as Brewer has stressed, meant new openings in the colonies and the excise, the expansion of Treasury clerkships, cashierships and controllerships, and the setting-up of the Board of Trade – all carrying with them jobs in the Government's pocket: by 1718 there were 561 full-time and another 1,000 part-time customs officers in the Port of London alone. The official salaries of every post could be doubled by fees and perks; and most office-holders had their deputies. Not least, the enlargement of sophisticated credit finance associated with the National Debt gave the backroom boys of the Government, those fingering the bills and calculating percentages – men such as John Aislabie and James Craggs – plenty of scope, above and below board, for manipulation and pickings.

In short, the plums of office – the opportunities for personal enrichment and for rewarding supporters – were becoming ever choicer. Yet so were the costs of winning and holding them. Fierce competition, frequent elections, the need to win voters over – all gobbled up money. And party vendettas showed no signs of cooling. In 1710, the Whig Government put the High Churchman Henry Sacheverell on trial. Succeeding Tory Governments met spite with spite by curbing the civil liberties of Dissenters with the Occasional Conformity (1710) and Schism Acts (1714). Political costs and struggles for power were threatening to get out of hand: the Sacheverell crisis alone produced over 1,000 controversial salvoes.

Yet, in the event, the early years of the century proved to be the *molto agitato* overture to several generations of growing political stability. For events fell out in such a way as to permit the executive to tighten its python grip on the political nation. Above all, the once populist Whigs, having come to power with the Hanoverian succession, began to transform certain oligarchical tendencies into a full-blown system of government. The Tory Stamp Act of 1712 had already dampened publications; the Whig Riot Act of 1715 was meant to clamp down on street politics. Power became concentrated in varied ways. Legislation of 1710 imposed a land qualification of £600 for county MPs and £300 for borough MPs. Soaring electoral costs began to restrict politics to the wealthy. In 1689 Pepys had spent £8 5s. 6d. on an election at Harwich, but by 1727 Viscount Percival needed £900 for the same constituency: electioneering was becoming a rich man's sport, and many independent gentry families of long political standing got squeezed out by the cost. Sir William Fostwick, MP for Bedfordshire from 1698 to 1713, ran up £26,000 in political debts: he had to sell up and leave the country.

Furthermore, as the costs of politics rose, there was a greater premium upon not wasting money, but shepherding political investments better. The Septennial Act (1716) gave MPs seven years' tenure on a seat, not three as before, and with elections only every seven years, the heat was taken off somewhat. But less frequent polls in turn had the effect of putting up the price of a seat still further (at the Oxfordshire election of 1754 the Tories spent no less than £40,000 to unseat the Whigs – and failed).

And with electoral costs threatening to go sky-high, it made sense to avoid a contest wherever possible, especially in the counties, where electorates were large and freeholder voters often truculent. So advance deals were increasingly struck to secure candidates' election unopposed; two-member constituencies were often carved up by agreement between Whig and Tory. At the same time borough-mongers tightened their grip on small constituencies. Political management grew in sophistication. With costs and rewards so high, the arts of fixing seats, bribing voters, placing supporters, cultivating influential interests, and not least resorting to gerrymandering, graft and legal chicanery became a major part of the Hanoverian statesman's manual. All such developments – the emergence of efficient political management techniques – partly explain why, by contrast to the preceding century, the age of the Georges turned out to be one in which the ruling order was never unsaddled, or even seriously threatened. At times, oligarchic control was so successful that electoral politics were very quiet indeed. In 1761 only eighteen out of 201 borough constituencies with fewer than 500 voters actually went to the polls. Between 1754 and 1790 twelve counties never polled at all.

Oligarchic tendencies had been in the air ever since the Restoration, with grandees cultivating their electoral interests in boroughs and corporations. But the arts of management were first comprehensively and successfully exercised by Walpole, who steered the political nation out of the South Sea Bubble crisis. Walpole and the Duke of Newcastle together built a system of control on the assumption that local grandees – not all but enough – needed access to political power and favours, hence craved inclusion, and so had their price. Establishing precisely which individuals were to be those favoured insiders was an accident of the manner of the Hanoverian succession. Once the Tories dithered over giving the Hanoverians firm support, the Whigs – at that time a vociferous, ambitious minority, bent upon political survival – grabbed the Crown and exploited the Jacobite rising of 1715 to launch a witch-hunt against the Tories. Under the first two Georges, Tory diehards came to be permanently proscribed from office, central and local – Tory squires, for example, were purged from the Commission of the Peace, and officers from the army. Tories continued to command deep grassroots support, yet the costs of permanent exclusion from office were so damaging that, from the late 1720s, a trickle of Tories cut their losses and came in from the cold, deserting to the Whig and Court party. The outcome was the consolidation of a broad-bottom coalition of pro-government politicians, proprietors, and their clients (nominally Whigs), united above all by their desire to be where the power and rewards were, so as to advance both personal and local interests.

Walpole's overbearing ministries, muzzling critics and deploying spies, informers and propagandists, financed by secret service funds, were reviled by backwoods squires and vocal opinion at large – by those who believed that 1688 had been the revolution to purge centralism and corruption, not to reinforce it. All century long, bitter populist hatred of ministries and monarchs continued, readily appropriated by opportunist demagogues such as Wilkes. Yet low food prices and good employment opportunities helped to head off any coalescence of plebeian and gentry disaffection. As perhaps with the stock exchange nowadays, the political nation was far more eager to play the political system – survival depended upon success – than to seek to change it. In the end, oligarchic one-party government was not just possible but ultimately – though great tact and acrobatics were required – plain-sailing. 'The rage of party gave way to the pursuit of place,' as Plumb put it: 'Place was power; patronage was power,' and patronage 'scarcely bothered to wear a fig leaf'.

Georgian ministerial politics concentrated on managing the influential and milking society at large. This was achieved partly through control of elections. In some boroughs (for instance naval dockyards such as Chatham) the Court itself could pressurize electors, since voters were government employees and voting took place in public. In others, candidates (and, behind them, their borough-monger patrons) cajoled voters by bribes and threats, or bought up properties carrying the franchise. In 1768 Marlborough obtained a seat at Oxford after helping to pay off the corporation debt of £5,676. The Last Determinations Acts (1696, 1729) aided corporations and borough-mongers, who aimed to limit the size of electorates, by deeming that, in cases of dispute, the most recent electoral roll should stand (notwithstanding contentions that it was customarily broader).

Management and manipulation brought a political cynicism

into the open, which defused tensions amongst the elite by concentrating attention on the division of spoils. Many candidates were opportunist carpet-baggers. Bubb Dodington thus recorded in his diary his contest of the Bridgwater election in April 1754:

> April 11. Dr Sharpe and I set out from Eastbury, at four o'clock in the morning, for Bridgewater, where, as I expected, I found things very disagreeably framed.
>
> 12. Lord Egmont came, with trumpets, noise, etc.
>
> 13. He and we walked the town; we found nothing unexpected, as far as we went.
>
> 14., 15., 16. Spent in the infamous and disreputable compliance with the low habits of venal wretches.
>
> 17. Came on the election, which I lost by the injustice of the Returning Officer. The numbers were for Lord Egmont 119, for Mr Balch 114, for me 105. Of my good votes 15 were rejected: 8 bad votes for Lord Egmont were received.
>
> 18. Left Bridgewater – for ever.

Especially in boroughs, the typical franchise holder, exercising his dwindling opportunities to vote, could be relied on to plump for Mr Most. The Duke of Richmond thus called the constituency of New Shoreham a 'new whore that is anybody's for their money'. Not all seats could be controlled, however – some boroughs such as Westminster, and many counties, had electorates of several thousands. Bath had just thirty-two voters – the corporation – yet they were notoriously obstreperous. But most boroughs with electorates of a few hundred or less were safely in the pockets of patrons. In mid-century about 255 out of 405 borough seats were under oligarchic control. The Walpoles had Castle Rising in Norfolk as their pocket borough, and substantial interests in King's Lynn and Yarmouth; the Lowthers controlled some seven seats in Cumbria; the Duke of Newcastle disposed of up to twelve. Electoral management was child's play in Scotland, where electorates were tiny. In 1788 Scottish counties had a combined electorate of just 2,662 voters. But management was usually successful, pre-empting any real choice and power among voters. Shropshire had no contest between 1722 and 1831, Wiltshire only one poll between 1713 and 1818. In 1780 only two English county seats actually polled. In short, Georgian governments became exceptionally secure against the electorate. A diminishing number of seats actually came up for contest, and of those that did, a majority of boroughs could be fixed in advance.

The other arm of management lay within Parliament itself. There, judicious dispensing of Court patronage and pensions, and the cultivation of clients' interests and family alliances, were skilfully used to build up safe ministerial majorities. Sinecure-holders might not have much official business to do, but they were expected to be loyal and politically active to earn their keep. In 1742 the Commons contained 139 placemen; by 1780 the number was up to 180. For their part, top politicians clustered into family cabals, in 1761 the Commons boasting five Townshends, five Mannerses, four Cavendishes and four Yorkes. Behind such big guns the Whit ministries of Walpole and the Pelhams marshalled great landlords, with their immense local influence, but also contractors, civil servants, City financiers, Low Churchmen and Dissenters.

Even though the Whig 'Old Corps' was derailed early in George III's reign, nothing disturbed the continuity of magnate government. The soft furnishings of the house of oligarchy were shifted around, but the foundations hardly trembled. Though an interregnum of ministerial reshuffles perplexed the 1760s, the regimes of North, Pitt the Younger and Liverpool piloted what was effectively a one-party state safely into the 1820s. Of course, ministries and oppositions, 'ins' and 'outs', roused themselves to oratorial paroxysms about despotism, demagogy, nepotism, anarchy or the Church being in danger. But it was all ultimately shadow-boxing, because no inside political connection poised on the threshold of power wanted to kill the goose that laid the golden eggs, and political agitation 'outdoors' remained ineffectual.

Prudent ministries patched up family alliances and applied balm which healed rifts and mollified malcontents: a sinecure here, a pension or a promise there. John Gay the writer became Commissioner of the State Lottery; Edward Gibbon was made a Lord of Trade on £800 a year, and, though never making a speech, voted obediently for Lord North's ministry ever after. Though there was never enough to go round, men great and small begged for tempting scraps of offices and perks. In such circumstances, to be a Trimmer, a vicar of Bray, a political yes-man, was no disgrace; such conduct was not merely worldly wise, but perhaps even family duty.* Politics were mercenary, and though moralists on the sidelines huffed and puffed about 'corruption', few refused to feather their own nests. For the state was their lifeline, providing those who clung on with security and prospects in the forms of favour and pensions (defined by Dr Johnson – soon to accept one himself – as 'pay given to a state hireling for treason to his country'). Office was especially welcome to younger sons, who, because of primogeniture, had to wave goodbye to the family estates. Furthermore, the very ties of importunity and gratitude, of begging and granting, the queue which political patronage created all the way down the scale, satisfied honour and civilized hungry ambition. 'I think it my duty,' wheedled Thomas Newton to the Duke of Newcastle, 'to acquaint your grace that the Archbishop of York lies a-dying and, as all here think, cannot possibly live beyond tomorrow morning if so long; upon the occasion of two vacancies, I beg, I hope, I trust your Grace's kindness and goodness will be shown to one who has long solicited your favour.' There was of course endless disappointment, but that remained personal, and it neither killed hope nor dashed the system.

Despite endless territorial bickering over jurisdictions and spoils, the different limbs of the political nation worked harmoniously together. Limited, constitutional monarchy was an important unifying force, powerful enough to calm great proprietors' fears of any resurgence of Cromwellian republicanism, but not so strong as to threaten magnate property or independence itself. True, the Hanoverian kings hardly warmed the nation's heart. George I and II were graceless domestic tyrants, addicted more to Hanover than to England (people thought it fitting when George II died in the privy). George III, who at least was English, gained some sympathy after he went mad, and some popularity as Farmer George. Their courts were mean, their taste was drab, their family feuds vindictive. Yet they were active and determined rulers, anxious to keep the Court the centre of politics, and – their trump card – they were indelibly Protestant.

Maintaining the Protestant succession was one of two tenets all

---

* The epitaph of Mrs Bates stated that 'by means of her alliance with the illustrious family of Stanhope, she had the merit to obtain for her husband and children twelve several appointments in church and state'.

Englishmen could support in politics (the other was, in the last resort, to trust kings rather than politicians). The Crown, as head of the executive, still appointed the leading ministers and courtiers, and had a direct hand in policy, especially in foreign and religious affairs. George II personally led his troops into battle, if only once. The king's extended family held key appointments, particularly in the armed forces. The monarch disposed of a privy purse and immense powers of patronage at Court and through the civil list (there were over 1,000 appointees connected with the royal household). Only diehards prepared to risk being permanent castaways (Jacobitical squires in the 1720s and a sprinkling of reforming Whigs in the 1790s) dared forsake currying royal favour. With the possible exception of the inexperienced George III in the 1760s, the Georges did not make the Stuart mistake of neglecting politicians' goodwill; their aim was not to construct a Versailles or rule through mere creatures. The first two Georges accepted Whig domination: George III clung to Bute, North and Pitt the Younger. The Crown was not dramatically weaker in 1800 than in 1700, nor had its scope for political manoeuvre been eroded.

During the century, the grandees tightened their hold on the headquarters of state. By 1800, 11 per cent of navy officers came from titled families and a further 27 per cent from landed families; the army recruited its officers from the sons and friends of the ruling elite to an even greater degree. Above all the Church of England was increasingly annexed to the state, its prize livings occupied by numinous families. Clerics were advanced to prelacies because they would loyally go through the government lobbies in the Lords. 'No man,' lamented Dr Johnson, 'can now be made a bishop for his learning and piety; his own chance of promotion is his being connected with someone who has parliamentary interest.' Under Queen Anne it had fleetingly seemed possible that clerical high-flyers would resist the absorption of the Church within the state. The Whigs, however, by proroguing Convocation and advancing their minions, nipped Church–state friction and ecclesiastical independence in the bud until the Oxford Movement.

The blueprint for this snug fit between the proprietorial classes and their protective, insulating shell of state (symbolized by the Crown) was the Constitution. The governing classes were proud

of the British Constitution (which supposedly had existed 'time
out of mind') as 'the most beautiful combination ever framed'
(the phrase is George III's), glorying in the time-hallowed jur-
isdictional distinctions between Crown, Lords and Commons,
between executive, legislature and judiciary, between Church and
state: 'Herein consists the excellence of the English government,'
asserted Blackstone in 1765, 'that all parts of it form a mutual
check upon each other.' Not least, they portrayed MPs as
independent representatives, not delegates.

All of these constitutional finesses – or fictions – they vaunted
as free-born Englishmen's guarantees against despotism. The
conservative revolution of 1688 had rescued liberty from danger:
in turn the 1688 settlement must itself be preserved. Even anomalies – rotten boroughs such as Old Sarum and Gatton, bereft
of voters – were properties making for healthy diversity, and
could not be invaded without risking wholesale erosion of ancient
rights. Traditional liberties – politicians argued – were best
protected by traditional grandees, who, by virtue of their ownership of freehold estates, were not creatures of the Court. 'I
cannot help feeling,' argued that stalwart friend of the people,
Charles James Fox, 'that in this country at least, an aristocratic
party is absolutely necessary to the preservation of liberty.'

Of course, this sedative rhetoric of constitutional liberty (with
its polite fictions such as 'virtual representation', devised to prove
that the disqualified were just as properly represented as the
enfranchised) rationalized the hegemony of the great proprietors.
Within this mythology, it was their guardianship of property
rights that was in turn every Englishman's security against despotism and demagogy alike:

> The nations, not so blest as thee,
> Must, in their turns, to tyrants fall,

chorused magnates who gloried in being the sultans of their own
shires. Or, in Arthur Young's formulation, 'The principle of our
constitution is the representation of property, imperfectly in
theory, but efficiently in practice . . . the great mass of property
both landed and moneyed and commercial finds itself represented.' In other words the landed classes did not just com-
mandeer political *power*. Rather the constitution glossed their
own essence (that is, property) as *rights*. Realist as ever, however,

Adam Smith would have none of this humbug: 'Civil government . . . so far as it is instituted for the security of property, is in reality instituted for <u>the defence of the rich against the poor.</u>' Of course, despite the vaunted checks and balances and separations of power which allegedly forestalled tyranny, all branches of effective power sprang from one single trunk. Crown, ministries and Commons were in league, intermingled, and it was the executive that pulled the legislature's strings. The king's choice as first minister could expect to piece together a parliamentary majority. Management in the shires and boroughs meant that no ministry lost a general election for over a century after 1714, and the Commons was kept obedient partly by subaltern ministerial placemen, and partly from the Lords via the plethora of sons and relatives of peers sitting in the Lower House.

Georgian society was thus controlled by an extraordinarily united and stable ruling order monopolizing political authority. What impact, then, did the organs of state have on society at large? To twentieth-century eyes the things the state didn't do are highly conspicuous. Kings and their ministers did not set out to implement progressive programmes of social justice or reform. They didn't pursue comprehensive and long-term industrial and agrarian policies or promote programmes of education and welfare. 'Providence has so organized the world,' explained Lord Shelburne, 'that very little government is necessary.' But the actions of the state did underwrite social trends independently at work, not least by redistributing income. Stuart government had been very cheap. It had to be, because the Commons had fought tooth and nail even the shoestring taxes the Stuarts had demanded. Eighteenth-century rule, by contrast, became immensely costly. In 1700 the Government had raised £4.3 million in revenue; by 1800 it levied £31.6 million. Put another way, central government spending was about 7 per cent of the Gross National Product in 1715, about 16 per cent in 1783, and as high as 27 per cent in 1801. But Parliament came to vote taxes more readily. This was partly because the political nation now controlled spending and was the major beneficiary from taxation. Taxes financed profitable wars, officers, sinecures and pensions, and above all underwrote government credit, guaranteeing the National Debt, stabilizing the currency and keeping the growing army of rentiers content. With sound borrowing facilities, ministries could embark on imperial conquest and borrow almost limitless sums (Britannia's wars were won on credit). Between 1688 and 1697 governments had raised £16 million by loans; between 1793 and 1815, £440 million. Taxes were increasingly earmarked for servicing the National Debt, which stood at £14.2 million in 1700, had reached £130 million in 1763 and rocketed to £456 million in 1800. By 1784 the cost of debt-servicing alone was £9 million a year, by 1801, £20 million (Charles II's entire Restoration state had had to run on just over £1 million a year). Parliament thus now had a cardinal stake in maintaining public credit, for finance had become the soul of England's enterprise, and no government could survive without the City's support. 'The stability of the Bank of England,' explained Adam Smith, 'is equal to that of the British government ... It acts not only as an ordinary bank, but as a great engine of state.'

Proprietors could thus contemplate higher taxation with some equanimity, partly because their own contributions came back to them in the form of office and interest, but also because their own share of the tax load was diminishing. In 1700 the chief direct tax was the land tax, generally levied at 20 per cent. Because assessed valuations were not indexed to actual values, the land tax actually bit less hard as time went on, except against freeholders and minor gentry without alternative sources of revenue.

Per capita taxation more than doubled between 1715 and 1803. Yet liquid capital as such escaped, and investment incomes of financiers and industrialists got off scot-free. Income taxes had long been deemed inquisitorial (though finally raised by Pitt the Younger in 1797 in wartime emergency). Hence most new levies were indirect taxes upon consumption. Thus in the late seventeenth century 35 per cent of taxation had been direct: by 1790 that had dropped to 18 per cent. Indirect taxes fell on luxuries such as carriages but they also hit the people. Heavier excises were laid even on certain basic commodities. In 1769 a foreigner remarked that

the English are taxed in the morning for the soap that washes their hands; at 9 for the coffee, the tea and the sugar they use at breakfast; at noon for the starch that powders their hair; at dinner for the salt that savours their meat; in the evening for the porter that cheers their spirits; all day long for the light that enters their windows, and at night for the candles that light them to bed.

He unaccountably omitted bricks, coal, leather and glass. William Blake was enraged: 'Lawful Bread, Bought with Lawful Money, & a Lawful Heaven, seen thro' a Lawful Telescope, by means of Lawful Window Light! The Holy Ghost, & whatever cannot be Taxed, is Unlawful & Witchcraft.' Contrary to the patriotic stereotype, the common people of free, parliamentary England were surrendering more in taxes than their French *ancien régime* counterparts.

Taxation policy indicates how the state functioned blatantly as the patrimony of grandees and their clients, both protecting their interests and serving as a carcase ripe for parasites to gorge off. Fiscal opportunism was everywhere. A new Knight of the Garter had to pay £400 1s. 7d. in fees. Even George I discovered he had to slip 5 guineas to the man who fished his carp out of St James's pond. This translation of politics into jobbery, though not universal, was ingrained and unashamed. 'If I were asked, at this moment, for a summary opinion of what I have seen in England,' wrote Louis Simond at the turn of the nineteenth century,

I might probably say that its political institutions present a detail of corrupt practice – of profusion – and of personal ambition under the mask of public spirit, very carelessly put on, more disgusting than I should have imagined.

Exposure of 'corruption' was, of course, often oratorical rant, yet it highlights the fact that the system was oiled by venality and benefited those at the top and on the inside, and all their hangers-on. For example, when a nobleman wished to enclose a common, divert a watercourse, develop a harbour, or – more difficult – divorce his wife, a private Act of Parliament legitimized what might otherwise be seen as an act of robbery or injustice. Parliament operated largely to do private and sectional business – 'a mere quarter session', declared Horace Walpole, 'where nothing is transacted but turnpikes and poor rates.' It protected established rights and defended the shores, but beyond that, to twentieth-century eyes, its responsibilities to its citizens were few, practically all matters of social policy devolving upon local government. Indeed, with the rise of a *laissez-faire* lobby, Westminster abandoned its longstanding mercantilist paternalism, one by one repealing laws regulating wage-rates, employment conditions and markets, which impeded the free play of capital. Some thought it fortunate that the Government was so lackadaisical, for, in Arthur Young's words, 'everything is well done in England, except what is done with public money' (much of which ended up in private pockets).

The Georgian state was thus personal, venal and often nepotistic; yet this was in many ways appropriate to a relatively face-to-face society, marked by immense local diversity, where familiarity and 'pull' really did count for more than abstract expertise. In any case, we should not take the root-and-branch denunciations of 'corruption' by back-bench politicians and Utilitarians at face value; they were in their own ways self-serving (the Utilitarians, for instance, wanted to substitute a corps of professional bureaucrats, i.e. themselves). The penalty of venality, however, was that abuses remained deep-rooted. There was concerted resistance to reform, orchestrated by landed proprietors themselves, and to any encroachments by centralized government upon time-honoured jurisdictions or vested interests. Thus standing armies were despised because they involved mercenaries and barracks, and, despite rising fear of crime and disorder, the idea of professional police and salaried magistrates met immense opposition, for those stank of jobbery and tyranny. Even in the wake of the Gordon Riots, a Government proposal in 1785 to set up a London police of 225 men was defeated. In 1753 Thomas Thornton, MP, helped to defeat the Bill to conduct a national census, declaring, 'I hold the prospect to be totally subversive of the last remains of English liberty.' Responsibilities remained individual, local, private. It was for colonels to dredge up soldiers for their own regiments. They employed recruiting officers, themselves small businessmen, who often pocketed £5 for every soldier who took the king's shilling. Colonels clothed and fed their own regiments, profiteering on the side. Naval commanders were laws unto themselves on board their own men-of-war (crews, not the state, took captured prize money). Parish officers got 5s. for every vagrant arrested. Paying rewards to individuals who brought criminal prosecutions commended itself as the cheapest and least tyrannical way of catching law-breakers (it was also, perhaps, quite efficient). Criminal informers got a 'Tyburn ticket' which excused them from the burdens of civil office – these tickets themselves becoming transferable pieces of property with a market price. In the clampdown against 'Jacobin' radicalism in the 1790s, a motley crew of dregs and zealots received under-the-counter funds to serve as spies, informers and *agents provocateurs.*

The agencies of state were patchy and often bungling, partly because – despite vast expansion in highly efficient departments such as the Revenue – key areas, like the embryonic Home Office, remained skeleton-staffed. In 1792 the Home and Foreign Offices each had staffs of nineteen. Incompetence was sometimes exposed to devastating effect, as in the War of American Independence, yet reformist demands to separate career bureaucrats from party influence (for instance by excluding civil servants from the Commons) made scant headway before the 1780s. Bentham's Utilitarian aim of reforming administration on rational, centralized lines was thought to smack of continental absolutism. Admittedly, overbearing oligarchy and the tyrannies of tax collectors and press-gangs were hated by the people at large. The 'despotism' of Walpole and Bute, and the maladroit handling of the American crisis in the 1770s, drew furious protest. But parliamentary reform movements received only fitful and opportunist backing from within Parliament itself, and pressure out of doors was neither sufficiently organized, continuous, nor influential to succeed. Wilkes's whirlwind movement sought to reinstate certain fundamental freedoms (such as his own right to his parliamentary seat), but to do so *within* the existing scheme of government. In his motion Dunning noted – rightly – that 'the influence of the Crown has increased and is increasing', arguing it ought to be diminished, and the Yorkshire Association hoped to achieve this end through some redistribution of parliamentary seats, mainly to raise the leverage of county gentry. But no excluded rival bloc, no 'alternative government' – as manufacturers were eventually to fancy they were – was as yet breathing down the necks of the political nation. In any case, no true challenge came to the real powerhouse, the House of Lords, lair of the dynasts. Moreover, the last thing many reformers wanted was to make government stronger, more centralized or bureaucratic. Radicals such as William

Godwin in the 1790s thought there was a surfeit of government already, and aimed to pare it down to a minimum.

Nevertheless, reform was in the air by the 1780s, in part because the old generation of politicians – Newcastle, Chatham, North – had finally been replaced by juniors such as Charles James Fox and the younger Pitt. Some token reforms were brought in. Burke's Act abolished 134 offices, Shelburne's Act 144. In 1789 Pitt abolished 765 jobs. Revenue officers were disfranchised and royal household expenditure brought under control. In 1780 the Commissioners for Examining the Public Accounts were set up. But though some sinecures went, there was no electoral reform, no shift of power. The machinery of placemen and patronage, factions and juntos at Westminster, and borough-mongering in the localities, steamrollered on into the nineteenth century with what Plumb has called 'adamantine strength and profound inertia'. And all the while Parliament was becoming even more unrepresentative: by 1801, four out of the seven largest towns in England had no MP. The apparatus of state reinforced and exacerbated the social division of power. Why was it not challenged more effectively?

In part, it was because the state was ramshackle enough not to be consistently oppressive. Power checked power, the most articulate interests could find a protector. So long as England was for many a land of economic opportunity, in which the state did not thwart enterprise and prosperity, pressures for reform from moneyed men were piecemeal and intermittent. Not least, the long arm of patronage offered loaves and fishes to enough people right down the social scale, and crumbs of comfort kept others' hopes alive. Benefiting in this way, the poet Edward Young sycophantically salaamed before Walpole:

> My breast, O Walpole, glows with grateful fire.
> The streams of royal bounty, turn'd by thee,
> Refresh the dry domains of poesy.

The very pervasiveness of patronage and dependence set up expectations that gave the system its strength and durability.

Unlike France or Prussia, eighteenth-century England was a polity in which grandee power flowed from the shires up to the capital. The Revolutionary Settlement had guaranteed landed proprietors a lot of rope for running local affairs, and lesser people probably preferred it that way as well. Smallholders, traders and cottagers might have little love for the carriage folk, but automatically closed ranks with them against such central interference as the imposition of a new cider tax, higher militia levies or threats to tamper with the corn bounty. They knew which side their bread was buttered.

Atomistic decentralization and rabid regional chauvinism were recipes for administrative pluralism. Local government units formed a jungle whose only rationale lay in history. Beccles in Suffolk for instance was governed by the owners of its fen; Haverfordwest in Pembrokeshire enjoyed the same privileges as the City of London, with its own Lord Lieutenant and Keeper of the Rolls. In the Palatine County of Durham, the Bishop had powers resembling those of a German ecclesiastical prince. Moreover, as population expanded and migrated, the skin of legal authority was being stretched out of shape and split by community growth. Mushroom towns were still being run by manorial courts which had once served feudal manors. By 1750 Halifax parish had 50,000 inhabitants yet still no acting JP. In Manchester administration was still by court leet bearing the vestiges of baronial jurisdiction. Here and there, in the interstices of higher jurisdictions, private manorial and hundred courts survived, dealing with infractions of by-laws, nuisances, and tenure disputes.

Furthermore, reforms – to improve street lighting or policing, or to clamp down on scavenging – themselves sprang from local initiatives, piloted by private self-help rather than by central direction. This was both a boon and a bane. Local legislation was generally sensitive to local needs, but it could not cope with problems that were fundamentally regional or national. The upshot was a crazy patchwork of new administration stitched piecemeal over the threadbare fabric of the old. There was no national rhyme or reason in the siting of new turnpike roads or poor law unions: such things were never decided nationally (except for roads of military importance: the London to Holyhead road was improved, for it was the troop route to and from Ireland).

Great landowners, and merchant oligarchs in towns, exerted vast fields of force because of their pull as employers, consumers, and dispensers of favour and patronage. Those who were also politically strong-armed, such as peers, MPs and their henchmen, exercised further authority, acting as ears and mouthpieces between the local community and Westminster, as protectors, supplicants and negotiators. But above all it was the local offices, hogged by the regional elite and backed by law, which dictated the destinies of communities.

The top tier of county office was the Lord Lieutenancy. The post was largely honorific, with few day-to-day chores, yet the Lord Lieutenant recommended JPs for appointment and commanded the militia (sometimes called out to enforce civil order). Carrying great prestige, the Lord Lieutenant had powers of patronage, appointing to such offices as the Clerkship of the Peace (especially prized as it was tenured for life). Ministerial and Court directives filtered down through him into his shire. The lieutenancy was an office vital for party management, increasingly coveted by national political bosses. For instance, the Duke of Bolton was Lord Lieutenant for Hampshire, Dorset and Carmarthen, the Duke of Newcastle for Sussex, Nottingham and Middlesex. Beneath him, the sheriff, and their respective deputies, carried out similar functions on a lower level. Sheriffs had real political sway, being responsible for the protocol of electoral polls, their siting, timing, conduct and supervision (all carrying vast scope for abuse).

The workhorse of everyday magistrate power was the Justice of the Peace, who combined his own clout as a landed gentleman (from 1732 JPs had to have an estate of £100 a year) with extraordinarily wide and unsupervised judicial and administrative powers. Acting summarily on their own, JPs issued warrants for arrest and punished offenders for scores of misdemeanours such as drunkenness, vagrancy or profanity.

Magistrates had petty offenders such as poachers publicly whipped, fined or put in a house of correction; for more serious crimes – such as simple larceny and assault – they committed miscreants for trial at quarter sessions. Typical of their business were two cases handled by Wiltshire quarter sessions at Devizes in 1746:

Hannah Carrington of Corsham, spinster, for stealing one shift value 5s., the goods of John Peace – pleads not guilty, jury guilty, whipt and imprisoned for 3 months. Benjamin Winter of Devizes, weaver, stealing 2 hens and a cock value 2s. 6 of the goods of James Buckley – pleads not guilty, jury guilty, whipt and 3 months imprisonment.

A JP also had the power to commit suspects for trial by judge and jury at the county assize courts, which circuited the country twice a year and which had the power of life and death in criminal cases. A brace of justices could exercise summary jurisdiction over alehouses, bastardy suits and runaway servants and apprentices. In addition to their role in bringing offenders to justice, JPs also fixed wages and prices, regulated apprenticeships, swore in constables, ordered highway maintenance, suppressed nuisances, oversaw markets, assessed county rates, and licensed – or banned – fairs and amusements. In executing the poor law, JPs made settlements, heard depositions, conducted examinations, ordered removals and assessed ratings.

JPs were unpaid, and their duties were onerous and sisyphean, though some were more zealous than others. Henry Purefoy, a Buckinghamshire JP, found all his time disappeared attending to the nerve-fraying housewifery of his community: disputed wills, settlements, appointments to vestry offices, obstructions to highways, the destruction of woods, runaway servants, etc. Yet many relished their role as village Solomons. After all, they were backing their own interests with legal sanctions: a justice might well be punishing poachers of his own game. Hardly supervised from above, their discretionary powers were enormous. 'They played ducks and drakes with the law when it suited them,' Plumb has noted, 'breaking with impunity what they were supposed to maintain' – though suits could always be taken out against them by a plaintiff at the King's Bench.

In the countryside, the JP and an oligarchical parish vestry of property-owners; in the borough, the corporation. Most great towns of early Georgian England – places such as York, Exeter and Coventry – were incorporated (though many unincorporated townships raced past them in size during the century, Birmingham being a prime example). Corporations exercised wide regulatory powers over residents, owning property, levying rates and rents, managing town lands, licensing trades and administering charities. As magistrates they passed by-laws. They also manipulated borough politics and patronage (frequently the aldermanic bench held all the parliamentary franchises). By the eighteenth century most corporations were co-opting, self-perpetuating and intent on taking advantage of their good fortune. Yet in certain places, elections to local offices, such as the mayoralty, were open and split the community right down the middle on party-political and religious grounds.

The prince of corporations was of course the City of London. Government of the City was shared between an upper court of twenty-six aldermen (elected for life) and a lower (the Court of Common Council) made up of 234 freemen elected annually from the various ancient livery companies. Against central government the City corporation jealously guarded its own jurisdictions and privileges, including those of electing its own sheriffs and commanding its own private militia, and championed the causes of commerce and finance. No ministry dared alienate the City. Yet disputes between the two chambers were endemic, partly because freeman radicalism was on the boil. Up to 12,000 Londoners voted in elections for their aldermen and councillors.

The bedrock unit of local administration was the parish (or, in the North of England, the township), of which there were about 10,000. It was at parish level that community feeling had to be harmonized with directives from above. Parishes were run by officers appointed annually by JPs or elected by ratepayers: churchwardens, constables, the surveyor of the highways, and overseers of the poor (and humbler figures too, such as the pinder, who kept the cattle pound). Being unpaid and often unwilling, some officers recouped their lost time in junketings and in making huge 'expenses' claims. The overseers of the poor at St Martin-in-the-Fields once laid out £49 13s. 9d. on a dinner for themselves ('Every parish officer,' complained Francis Grose, 'thinks he has a right to make a round bill on the Parish during his year of power').

Most parish business was indeed parochial, part of the perennial negotiation of domestic interests, settling of grudges and restoring of neighbourliness, which were the everyday stories of countryfolk (and townsfolk too). In addition to apprehending offenders, constables had to ensure their parish's militia quotas were met (ballots were held, and those chosen might serve in person or find substitutes). Surveyors of the highway had a right to claim six days' unpaid labour from parishioners for road-mending.

Divergent trends in local government were operating in counterpoint. Established institutions were growing more exclusive, oligarchic and unrepresentative. Certain vestries ceased to be open and became 'select' (or co-opting) – for example in 'select' parts of London such as the West End. Closed institutions were not necessarily corrupt: the select vestry of St George's, Hanover Square, was energetic and public-spirited, whereas the open vestry at Bethnal Green, with 2,000 voters, was a veritable Tammany Hall. More corporations became self-perpetuating, with aldermen nominating their successors. To restrict entry, levies for becoming a freeman were raised. Within corporations the fiercest personal and factional rivalries flared over office and reward, but, legally secured from challenge from without, torpid corporations often became oblivious to public duty, basking in their privileges, fingering fees, eating dinners and exploiting the economic windfalls offered by their rights to build, regulate markets, administer land and property and admit freemen. Thus when public-spirited citizens of Leicester set about founding a hospital, the corporation merely looked on. Yet some corporations showed commendable activity in developing public utilities: sensing its own commercial interests, Liverpool Corporation built fine docks.

There was no popular agitation for a clean-sweep central reform of corporations or of JPs' powers. Suggestions for the appointment of stipendiary magistrates (a few already existed in London) were denounced as arrant jobbery. Overall, Roach has dubbed it an age of 'collective inertia' in local administration. Yet the needs of localities were becoming ever more complex and pressing. As population and industrial plant grew, providing new public utilities became priorities. Outlying fields circling towns had to be enclosed to allow expansion for new housing (where this was not done – as at Nottingham – appalling warrens of slums resulted). Towns had to be cleansed and drained, markets expanded, roads widened and crumbling city walls removed. Human excreta and industrial waste and effluent became festering nuisances and health-hazards. Parish constables could no longer cope with law-breaking where communities grew larger and anonymous, criminals more mobile, and 'capitalist crime' – property theft – increased. Six days' shirking labour on the highways could not keep the commercial arteries of the nation in trim.

Yet many vestries and corporations just bumbled on, and

Parliament did not force them to mend their ways. The result was that, in many towns, interested parties took the initiative in setting up private utilities in the interstices of existing authorities, coexisting with them rather than replacing or reforming them. Private Acts for particular towns were piloted through Parliament, sanctioning the setting-up of panels of commissioners or trustees, empowered to raise a rate to finance services such as sewerage and water. Between 1761 and 1765 the City of Westminster secured private Acts for paving and lighting. In 1769 an Act licensed the Birmingham Street Commissioners, a board of fifty – the property qualification for trustees was £1,000 – with power to levy a rate of up to 8d. in the pound, charged to regulate building. Here, as elsewhere, commissioners expanded the scope of their activities as time went on. Manchester obtained a Cleaning and Lighting Act in 1765, an Improvement Act in 1776 and a Police Act in 1792. Between 1785 and 1800, 211 such private Acts were passed. Private initiative also founded dispensaries, hospitals and other charities. In commercial centres such as Birmingham, small-debt and conciliation courts were set up to give summary, cheap and quick justice in trade disputes.

The migraine of local government were the poor. On the one hand England possessed a *national* statutory poor law (unlike most Catholic nations, where relief was left to alms-distribution by the Church: Ireland also had no poor law; in Eastern Europe relief of poverty was generally left to the extended family). On the other hand, as the Law of Settlement and Removal of 1662 confirmed, responsibility for relieving poverty was given to the smallest unit of *local* administration, the parish. The 1662 Poor Law, conceived with surveillance uppermost in mind, defined responsibilities with regard to each pauper. Every native was deemed to possess a 'settlement' in one parish, and in one parish only. Such a settlement – a typical English property right – could be established most commonly by (a) birth in a parish if a bastard, (b) having a father settled there, (c) marrying a husband there, (d) being hired as a covenant servant for a year there, (e) being apprenticed there, or (f) renting a house there. A person destitute on account of unemployment, sickness, incapacity to work, etc., had the right to relief in that parish and no other.

This policy had the merit of providing relief and identifying responsibility for it. It also had the aim of immobilizing the poor and forestalling droves of vagrant beggars, by encouraging residence in or about their parish settlement. In law a person needed a certificate before leaving his parish of settlement to seek work, though in buoyant times this was often waived, especially for healthy males, who were least liable to become a charge. Paupers in receipt of relief were to wear a 'P' badge on their clothes. But the right to a settlement was also an entitlement to remove. Officers had power to drive back to their native parish vagabonds and all those without a settlement liable to become a burden on the rates.

Entitling each person to a right in a stipulated parish (frequently, of course, the place of residence) had its virtues. Personal acquaintance could excite compassion for the unfortunate. Overseers were often sympathetic towards familiar faces, for whom dribbling payments of a shilling or two were made for house repairs, funerals, clothes, tools or medicines, or for tiding them over hard times. In 1788 the Oswestry overseers paid Mary, widow of Richard Francis, three years' rent and allowed her 3s. a week. She was also granted 1s. to have her garden hedged, 3s. to buy seed potatoes for the garden, and £1 for straw to thatch her cottage. Her family needing clothes, widow Francis received doles for shoes and stockings for her children, as well as for shoe repairs, and so forth. At Leytonstone in 1740 an understanding overseer gave Beck Mitton money 'to fetch her stays out of pawn'. In a multitude of small ways, the Poor Law served as a thorough-going system of support for – and control over – parishioners, complementing the family as the regulator of life. In the first half of the century in particular, overseers of the poor seem to have been paternalistically generous in their supplements to domestic income. As long as labour remained in relatively short supply, it made good sense to conserve the local workforce.

But there was a black side, too. Parishes would accept no responsibility for people without a settlement, and never hesitated to pass the buck. The poor, old and sick were ruthlessly driven on (or sometimes even bribed to leave). Unmarried pregnant women were treated barbarously: no parish wished to have a bastard 'dropped' on its doorstep, since thereby the baby gained a settlement. Women big with child were sometimes bullied into shot-gun weddings with bridegrooms from other parishes, for the baby would take its settlement from its father's parish. Performing such ceremonies distressed Parson Woodforde: 'It is a cruel thing that any person should be compelled by law to marry.' Yet he complied. Other women were hounded out of the parish even when in labour, in order to 'pass the baby'. Parish accounts record appalling brutalities:

1722 To a big bellyd woman several days and nights at Nursing at Robinson, & conveying her to Chigwell after she had gathered strength to prevent her lying in here, she fell to pieces in two or three days there 17/7d.

The terror of incurring liabilities produced bundles of costly litigation and even black comedy on occasion. East Hoathley in Sussex spent no less than £80 in settling one Thomas Daw in another parish – 'Yet I believe,' wrote the pennywise ratepayer Thomas Turner, 'it is a very prudent step,' for Daw was one-legged and had a blind wife. Overseers perfected petty bullying and developed ruses for profiteering and evading responsibility. One common device was to farm out pauper infants to minders or masters for a small premium. If the children then died, no one asked questions.

Enormous energies were expended in grappling with the problem of the poor, against the pressure of soaring rates. In 1700 the cost was between £600,000 and £700,000, and was even then thought to be a disgrace. By 1776 it had shot up to £1.5 million, and then it went through the roof: £2 million in 1786, £4.2 million in 1803. Part of this went on relieving the sick, the enfeebled, the unemployed; but more and more went on 'topping-up' the income of workers who couldn't support their families on skinflint wages, or who could find only seasonal employment. Following the Speenhamland ruling (1795), 'topping-up' was index-linked to keep pace with inflation. Scandalized magistrates groped for answers.

Every fresh 'solution' got tied in knots because attitudes towards the poor were so contradictory. The masses – ratepayers believed – were feckless; naturally idle, they would work no more than they must. The moment they had spare cash they would squander it, turning to drink, debauchery and crime. 'The miseries of the labouring poor arise,' pontificated the

philanthropist Frederick Morton Eden 'less from the scantiness
of their income (however much the philanthropist might wish it
to be increased) than from their own improvidence and un-
thriftiness.' Thus the authorities were exasperated by their own
impotence. Neither sticks nor carrots seemed effective. 'When
wages are good,' Defoe complained:

they won't work any more than from hand to mouth; or if they do
work they spend it in riot or luxury, so that it turns to no account to
them. Again as soon as trade receives a check, what follows? Why then
they grow clamorous and noisy, mutinous and saucy another way, and
in the meantime they disperse, run away, and leave their families upon
the parishes, and wander about in beggary and distress.

In the light of these considerations, magistrates believed that
wages should be pared down to keep labourers at work longest
(this suited employers). 'The only way to make the poor industrious,' judged William Temple, 'is to lay them under the necessity
of labouring all the time they can spare from rest and sleep, in
order to procure the common necessities of life.' 'Everyone but
an idiot,' echoed Arthur Young, 'knows that the lower class
must be kept poor or they will never be industrious' (though he
recognized that the poor also needed incentives to be industrious,
for: 'The great engine wherewith the poor may be governed and
provided for the most easily and the most cheaply is property').
But the problem with all such 'low-wage' solutions was that
they kept labourers only a farthing away from destitution's door:
the slightest accident, illness or trade downswing would instantly
turn a sturdy family into beggars, chargeable to the parish.
Furthermore, if the wages of the employed were at starvation
level, why work, rather than be maintained as a parish pauper?
Observers noted that institutionalized paupers often got better
food than independent labourers' families.

These problems were intractable, but sanguine schemers always
thought they had the solution. One much-canvassed, though
long-term, answer was to recondition minds: 'to train up the lower
classes in habits of industry and piety,' as Hannah More phrased it;
to break them in to habits of work, and make them thrifty and
frugal. Charity schools, sermons, titbit rewards for labourers who
served the same master for forty or fifty years – all would teach
that labour was a blessing, it was hoped. But this would take time.

One instant and radical way to keep people off poor relief entirely was to abolish it. This modest proposal, popularized by Joseph Townsend, Frederick Morton Eden and, to some degree, by Thomas Malthus, argued that relief, far from relieving, stoked poverty, because it robbed recipients of motives for self-respect, responsibility and providence. Remove the safety net and people *would* provide for themselves (some charity might be needed as a long-stop in cases of real misfortune, though there should be no doles as of right). 'Hunger will tame the fiercest animals,' argued the realist, Townsend, 'it will teach decency and civility, obedience and subjection to the most perverse . . . In general, it is only hunger which can spur and goad the poor on to labour; yet our laws have said they shall never hunger.' This audacious stroke, however, was never tried. Georgian statesmen, flattering themselves on their humanity and paternalism, shrank from it. Anyway, the measured dispensing of relief was a useful technique of control. The hand that fed would not be bitten, and the Poor Law served the important functions of regulating where labourers lived and immobilizing a workforce which was little charge to employers when there was no call to hire labour.

A favourite nostrum was the idea that hand-outs should have strings attached; notably, that to accept relief should mean loss of liberty. The *deus ex machina* was to be the workhouse – called by Jeremy Bentham 'a mill to grind rogues honest, and idle men industrious'. There the poor would earn their keep (thus sparing the ratepayers), and be taught skills, discipline and piety. All birds would be killed with one stone. A seventeenth-century development, large-scale workhouses were first tried in Bristol from 1697, and a couple of hundred other places subsequently, endorsed by the Knatchbull Act (1723), which gave discretion to curb the right to outdoor relief of anyone who refused to enter a house of industry. Workhouse management was often farmed out to contractors primarily interested in profit, for example Matthew Marryott, who was running thirty houses of maintenance in Buckinghamshire in the 1730s. The philanthropist Jonas Hanway took a black view of the practice of farming the poor: 'Parish officers never intend that parish infants should live.' He believed that an infant of one to three years might on average survive a month in a London workhouse. The death-rate in the workhouse of St George's, Middlesex, was 100 per cent. Out of

2,339 children received into London workhouses in the five years after 1750, only 168 were alive in 1755.

> Is it a holy thing to see
> In a rich and fruitful land
> Babes reduc'd to misery
> Fed with a cold and usurous hand?

No one answered Blake's accusation of the slaughter of the innocents.

As cheap and productive cures for poverty, workhouses proved duds. One problem was that the inmates were – by definition – the nation's most unpromising work-force: a rubbish tip including the very young and the aged, the chronic sick and infirm, rogues, vagrants and village simpletons. Many were unemployed because of trade slumps: it was moonshine to suppose that self-financing workhouses could somehow buck the economic trend. In any case, workhouses readily became nests of jobbery, run by contractors who pocketed allowances and provisioned them in their private capacity as tradesmen. Many blamed the failure of workhouses on the fact that the individual parish was too tiny a unit; so parishes banded together, particularly in East Anglia, to set up poor law unions, with joint houses of industry, a movement encouraged by the Gilbert Act (1782). But bigger workhouses just ran at bigger losses. Only a few hundred were founded. Their main 'success' was custodial – they shunted paupers out of sight. Parson Woodforde visited a Norfolk workhouse in 1781:

We dined at 3 o'clock and after we had smoked a Pipe etc., we took a ride to the House of Industry about 2 miles West of Dereham, and a very large building at present tho' there wants another Wing. About 380 Poor in it now, but they don't look either healthy or cheerful, a great Number die there, 27 have died since Christmas last.

Parishes floundered from expedient to expedient. Supplementary relief would be tried, and then abandoned in favour of a house of correction or an experimental workhouse, followed by contracting out to entrepreneurs, and then back to botched-up outdoor relief.

All these responses to poverty – both off-the-cuff and programmatic – fell short because they were treating superficial symptoms, not root causes. What is more, they were handling symptoms locally, when the problems were national. The economy itself, with its exploitative system whereby those who worked hardest got least rewards, was producing a pauper residuum; and this was a process economists thought vital for the nation's well-being: 'Poverty,' argued Patrick Colquhoun, 'is . . . a most necessary and indispensable ingredient in society, without which nations and communities could not exist in a state of civilization.' At the same time, through the spread of *laissez-faire* ideology, with its great god of competitive individualism, the political nation was washing its hands of responsibility for poverty, or at best resorting to punitive, incarcerative expedients. At the end of the century Malthus told the indigent they had only themselves to blame: they bred too fast. Endemic pauperism was one of the nightmare monsters begat by the Georgian century.

Elsewhere there might be the sultan's caprice, the *lit de justice*, judicial torture, the slow-grinding mills of canon law bureaucracy, and the *auto-da-fé* of the Inquisition. In England, by contrast, king and magistrates were beneath the law, which was ever even-handed as the guardian of every Englishman's life, liberties and property. Blindfolded Justice weighed all equitably in her scales. The courts were open, and worked by known and due process. Eupeptic platitudes such as these on the unique blessings of being a free-born Englishman under a common law derived from the Anglo-Saxons were omnipresent. Anyone, from Lord Chancellors to rioters, could be heard uttering them (though for very different purposes).

Subjects at large, and vulnerable minorities in particular, looked to the law for protection against the mighty – as well of course as being anxious to have their own life, limbs and property secured against cutpurses, sharpers, debtors and footpads. As formulated on the statute book and established by judicial precedent and time-honoured custom, the legal process truly offered redress to many plaintiffs (married women and children came off worst). Even the poor initiated civil litigation (often the aim was not a court ruling but to encourage out-of-court settlement in a long-running dispute). Wilkite radicals dazzlingly exploited the courts on points of law to trip up the executive. Even magistrates who ordered troops to fire on rioters occasionally found themselves prosecuted. In 1765 a soldier sued his colonel at the Court of Common Pleas for reducing him from a sergeant to a private – and won £70 damages. Mercantilist legislation had long regulated wages and prices, terms of apprenticeship, and the like. Habeas corpus guaranteed protection to the person. Freedom of worship (albeit incomplete) was enshrined in the Toleration Act (1690).

By contrast to most of the Continent, ministries could not even count on judges to be time-serving reserve arms of executive power. Following publication of the supposedly libellous issue 45 of the *North Briton*, John Wilkes was arrested on a government general warrant. Chief Justice Pratt had him released on grounds of his privilege as an MP, and cast doubt upon the legality of such warrants. Thomas Hardy and other radicals, tried for sedition in the 1790s, were acquitted. Cases against many a thief and murderer had to be discharged through loopholes and procedural defects in the prosecution – such as the misspelling of names in indictments. In felony cases Englishmen had the reassurance of being arraigned by their countrymen. Almost all prosecutions were privately laid; in court a defendant's family and friends could vouch for his character, and it was his peers serving as jurymen who reached the verdict (going before a jury was called 'putting yourself on your country'). Magistrates themselves constantly played roles as arbitrators in trade disputes. In short, from the hue-and-cry to the macabre carnival of the public hanging, the law and its execution were not just Government fiats or ruling-class weapons but an intimate part of community life.

Nevertheless the law was at bottom framed and enforced by those with power to cajole and coerce the rest, as Goldsmith's laconic monosyllables state: 'Laws grind the poor, and rich men rule the law.' There was clearly one law for the rich, another for the poor. 'Tippling in an ale-house may be punished,' noted a 'gentleman' in 1753, 'but not drinking in a tavern; bawdy houses may be searched but not bagnios; and in every other instance the laws themselves vindicate our tyranny over the poor.' One way the law was increasingly nipping the common people was through the encroachment of statute upon areas hitherto regulated by custom alone. In many crafts, custom allowed workers to keep scrap or sell leftovers, such as wood chips, of materials supplied by their employers. At employers' instigation, new embezzlement and theft laws were passed, outlawing such hitherto winked-at fringe benefits. An act of 1740 made it criminal for a worker to purloin materials entrusted to him; by 1773 this offence carried three months' gaol. Rights to search workers' premises were granted, and theirs was the burden of proving innocent possession. Between 1726 and 1800 eleven new embezzlement statutes were passed in the woollen, fustian and worsted trades (though they proved almost impossible to enforce). Breach of contract was turned in some instances from a civil into a criminal offence. Similarly, many cottagers without legal title had customarily occupied common and waste land. In enclosure settlements, such squatters received no rights or compensation, and in issues of grazing, gleaning or rights of way, the complex bundle of users' rights (usufruct) tended to be boiled down into questions of absolute property right, to the benefit of the ultimate landowner. Customary tenures were also assailed. In such ways, the law was being brought increasingly into line with the needs of new forms of property and securities in a sophisticated capitalist economy. The law of false pretences was introduced in 1757. Much case law on credit, contracts, paper money debts, bills and other vital commercial issues dates from the judicial decisions of Lord Mansfield at King's Bench between 1760 and 1788. Fresh forgery and counterfeiting statutes were brought in to protect the currency and credit: thus in 1771 the misdemeanour of coining copper coin was elevated into a felony. Two thirds of those convicted of forgery were actually executed.

Two other developments gave further twists to the class bias of the law. First, legislation made the penal code more ferocious. There had been fifty capital offences in 1689; by 1800 there were four times that number. Many specified death for small-scale theft such as pickpocketing goods valued more than 1s., or shoplifting items worth more than 5s. New capital offences covered such heinous activities as being out at night with one's face blackened, breaking down fish-ponds, cutting hop-binds, destroying turnpikes, sending threatening letters and destroying silk on the loom. The Waltham Black Act (1724) created fifty new capital offences at a stroke. Successive tightenings of the game laws meant that by the early nineteenth century offenders caught poaching were frequently transported; the poacher who let off a gun at a keeper committed a capital offence.

Second, the protection of property loomed larger in legislators' minds. Property was of course central to eighteenth-century society, residing in anything from mere goods, to rights (a vote or an apprenticeship was a property), or even persons. Negro slaves were openly sold as chattels – witness the *London Advertiser* (1756):

To be sold, a Negro boy age about fourteen years old, warranted free from any distemper, and has had those fatal to that colour; has been used two years to all kinds of household work, and to wait at table; his price is £25, and would not be sold but the person he belongs to is leaving off business.

Trade thrived in ornamental collars and padlocks for slaves. But prestige military commissions were bought and sold as well. The *Morning Post* advertised:

An Ensigncy in an Old Regiment returned from Egypt and now at Malta to be sold, £60 under the regulated price. There are several vacancies in that regiment which make it an eligible purchase.

In mid-century an ensigncy cost about £400, a lieutenant-colonelcy about £3,500.

Locke had enunciated, 'The great and chief end, therefore, of men's uniting into commonwealth and putting themselves under government is the preservation of their property'; and the governing classes went about doing this with a will, for 'economic crime' was on the increase. By 1736 servants who pilfered from their masters were liable to hanging; in 1741 sheep-stealing was made a capital offence (this became a much-used statute). Homicides might often be given nominal sentences or be acquitted (the great actor Charles Macklin slew a colleague in a fit of temper and walked out of the Old Bailey free, convicted of manslaughter, 'to be branded on the hand and discharged'). But convicted thieves, found guilty of felony, were generally sentenced to hang. The great majority of men and women 'turned off' were hanged for theft. In London and Middlesex between 1749 and 1771 only seventy-two out of 678 people executed were murderers. Crimes especially damaging to capitalism were punished with exemplary severity. Coiners and forgers were shown no mercy, for they endangered the system of credit from top to toe. In 1789 a woman was burned at Tyburn for coining (yet such was the shortage of legal tender that coiners – especially minters of copper money – helped to make the economy go round).

The law was capital's bulldog in many ways. From the 1720s statutes were passed restricting trade unions. Combinations were outlawed among tailors in 1721 and 1767, in the woollen trade in 1726, among hatters in 1777, and in 1797 among paper-makers. By the time of the general (anti-)Combination Acts (1799 and 1800), over forty Acts were already on the statute book forbidding combinations to raise wages. Above all, the game laws were made ever more savage. From 1671 no one without an estate of £100 a year was allowed to kill game (not even on his own land); but it was from around 1750 that game preserves were set up in large numbers and the war against poachers began, possibly because they were starting to use guns.

Under an Act of 1770 nocturnal poachers were liable to six months' imprisonment. A further Act of 1803 prescribed death for poachers resisting arrest with arms, and an 1816 Act recommended transportation even for an unarmed man caught with a net. From mid-century gentlemen set up Game Associations, to expedite prosecutions. By 1827 poaching crimes were accounting for one seventh of all criminal convictions in England. Even the panegyrist Blackstone believed that the game laws showed the protection of property quite out of hand, for they were founded on 'the ... unreasonable notion of a permanent property in wild creatures ... productive of ... tyranny to the Commons ... The game laws have raised a little Nimrod in every manor'. Whether or not the propertied grew more heartless, the need to protect property was certainly felt more urgently, for with the multiplication of material possessions, employers and property holders became more vulnerable. In certain putting-out trades, up to a twelfth of employers' materials were disappearing into workers' pockets. As communities grew and, like London, became more mobile and anonymous, it was easier for thieves to melt into the crowd. (Yet counter-developments made criminals' lives harder. For example, listings of stolen property and highway robberies in newspapers facilitated detection.) All species of property found champions in the courts, from deer to votes, from army commissions to slaves. Despite the much trumpeted Somersett ruling of 1774, even the rights to own Negro slaves in England remained stubbornly secure throughout the century.

Yet, just as the Poor Law did not prevent poverty, there is little sign that the proliferating terrors of the criminal code were effective in deterring crime. Many felons could not afford to contemplate the scaffold or didn't give a damn. Few made crime their career: many took to theft only when bad times had shut off other ways of survival. Trade slumps made crime rocket: craftsmen in the metal trades took to coin-clipping, and demobilized soldiers, finding no work, slipped into lawlessness. Children were inducted into pocket-picking by their elders. Abandoned girls became street-walkers (prostitutes tended not to be full-time 'professionals', but women who went on the streets when times were hard). In 1741 a nineteen-year-old, Elizabeth Hardy, was sentenced to hang for theft of goods worth 13s. 6d. Forsaken by her husband, she was a stranger in London who had stolen out of desperation. She got a last-minute reprieve and was transported.

The penal system was known to be ineffectual. At the end of the century the London magistrate Patrick Colquhoun summarized what reformers thought was wrong:

1. The Imperfection of the Criminal Code.
2. The Want of a proper System of Police.
3. The Want of a Public Prosecutor for the Crown.
4. The Unnecessary Severity of Many Punishments.
5. The Abuses of the System of Granting Pardons.
6. The Entire System of Imprisonment in Hulks.
7. The Want of a Proper Penitentiary House for the Employment and Reformation of Criminals.

As legal reformers such as Colquhoun and Jeremy Bentham insisted, laws indiscriminately prescribing execution for murder *and* for lifting handkerchiefs were unlikely to hinder heinous crime. Some magistrates were corrupt. In the London area so-called 'trading justices', having bought their offices, milked them through fees and bribes: Horace Walpole was not the only one to believe 'the greatest criminals of this town are the officers of justice'. Punishments neither deterred nor reformed. The hangman's victim had his tipsy moment of celebrity. Instead of being pelted, those clapped in the pillory – Daniel Defoe was one of them – were often lionized by the crowd. And, before the 1780s, few seriously expected prisons to reform miscreants – 'prison,' mused a shrewd writer in 1726, 'is a place fitter to make a rogue than reform him.'

Prisons were laws unto themselves, run on private-enterprise sub-contracting systems through which the governor and his underlings hoped to make tidy profits, for instance by selling liquor to inmates or renting out superior accommodation to those who could pay. Lord Derby owned Macclesfield gaol and made £13 a year from it. Many gaols were small and ruinous – even ale-houses might be used as lock-ups – and there was only fitful inspection from sheriffs. Gaols aimed to do little more with their inmates than confine them, and internal discipline was often exercised by groups of prisoners themselves (the King's Bench gaol had its 'college', or ruling clique of inmates). Prisoners were a mishmash of humanity, most awaiting trial or transportation, with no segregation of the sexes. William Smith described some occupants of Middlesex prisons in 1776 as 'vagrants and disorderly women of the very lowest and most wretched class of human beings, almost naked, with only a few filthy rags almost alive with vermin, their bodies rotting with distemper, and covered with itch, scorbutic and venereal ulcers'. Extortion, prostitution, and drunkenness were routine. Many rotted and died in the feculent conditions – gaol fever took more victims than did Justice. Yet many prisoners brazened it out. Racketeers found the inside of a gaol fertile soil for their dealings. At Lancaster Castle prison, inmates could ply their trade, bring in their families, and even keep pets (though pigs were banned from Newgate after 1714).

In any case, the law and the courts worked in mysterious ways. Thousands of debtors were clapped without trial into King's Bench gaol by their creditors. In the 1770s almost half the entire prison population were debtors. But they were confined at the creditors' expense – and by gaoling debtors, creditors risked wrecking their chances of repayment. Many debtors hardly minded being gaoled, for they could carry on their trade from prison (they were allowed out of King's Bench during daylight hours). So long as they were confined, their property was legally safeguarded.

The law, moreover, remained ineffective because catching lawbreakers was a hit-and-miss affair. England's police were unpaid, part-time and parochial, perhaps effective at handling street crime but useless at detection work. Petty thefts committed by neighbours or servants in a hamlet were relatively easily sniffed out (amateur criminals were rarely good at covering their tracks). But wheezy watchmen had a harder time in London and other big cities. In the late eighteenth century, the metropolis, its population nearing one million, had no more than 1,000 officers and 2,000 watchmen. (Paris, by contrast, had 7,000 officers and 6,000 Swiss guards, under greater central control.) The authorities relied heavily on private initiative. Citizens were encouraged to set themselves up as vigilante 'thief-takers' by the offer of a £40 reward for every highwayman turned in. The respectable front of the gang-boss and fence Jonathan Wild was as a thief-taker and restorer of stolen property.

Exceptional London magistrates, such as Thomas de Veil, Henry Fielding and his blind half-brother John, took steps to establish a more effective police force, Henry Fielding setting up the Bow Street Runners in 1749 with secret-service funds. Runners were paid a guinea a week, plus a share of the parliamentary reward for each criminal successfully prosecuted. Patrick Colquhoun's Thames Police dated from 1798. But parliamentary funding was sporadic, because of disquiet lest a paid central police became an executive tool. Hence citizens formed vigilante groups to plug the gap. Many Societies for the Prosecution of Felons were formed in the second half of the century, particularly among urban employers. Similarly in 1792 the inhabitants of Hoxton, on the outskirts of the City of London, formed a 'military association for the protection of their persons and properties against the attacks of ruffians'. Desperate for remedy against body-snatchers, mourners set spring-guns around graves.

Finally, the law and the penal system worked inefficiently because of the hiatus between crime and punishment, what statutes prescribed and what courts did. Magistrates, judges and juries hesitated to enforce the full terror of the law, preferring to earmark atrocious penalties for vicious blackguards and in occasional exemplary circumstances. The bench winked at undervaluing stolen goods so as to slim down grand larceny – a hanging offence – into petty theft. Masters would often plead successfully in court for clemency towards servants or poor relations. Overkill would erode respect for the law. Theatrical use was made of mercy and pardons to set Justice in a better light. Hence the paradox that in Georgian England capital statutes certainly grew, and crime probably increased, but hangings steadily decreased from their Stuart peaks. In the late eighteenth century some twenty people were being hanged a year in London and Middlesex, compared with about 140 early in the seventeenth century. Though there were 200 capital statutes, no more than about 200 people a year were hanged in England and Wales. Similarly, many of the new statutes against labour were little used in the event: employers found it simpler to settle by negotiation. And reprieves were common: in late-eighteenth-century London, only about one in three people sentenced to death was actually hanged.

Agitation mounted about the supposed crescendo of crime, in particular the emergence (alongside shoals of small-fry swindlers, fences and con-men, and their trollops, molls and jades) of organized big time racketeering in London. Nevertheless, through most of the country professional crime remained rare, banditry was almost unknown, and premeditated assaults against the person uncommon. The moral watch exercised by communities made for a law-abiding attitude. And compared with the legalized violence, exploitation and extortion carried out by society itself (in the form of press-gangs, military discipline, taxation, enclosures, whippings at home, workhouses and workshops, and unchecked looting and rape in the expanding empire), criminal activities were a pinprick. As the rhyme asked,

> A sin it is in man or woman
> To steal goose from off the common
> But what, then, is his excuse
> Who steals the common from the goose?

Nevertheless, urban society became more anonymous, and the security of capital and goods more critical, fears of crime grew, and toleration of disorder – both criminal and plebeian – diminished. Towards the end of the century, reformers were coming up with blueprints of social machinery to police society, to clamp down on crime and to regenerate rogues. The accent moved from prosecution to prevention, from punishment towards reform, from instant physical pain to long-term institutional management. The age in which penitentiaries would be seen as the keys to social discipline was just around the corner.

*

To say English political and legal institutions favoured the propertied and privileged is truistic. More significantly, they formed a suit of legal armour protecting and empowering the already independently weighty body of the propertied, par-ticularly in the localities. Georgian England had no autonomous absolutist centralized 'state', staffed by a distinct *Stand* of bureau-crats, cutting across their interests – that was exactly what the landed orders had quashed in the previous century. Yet precisely because the 'state' as an independent being had been attenuated, it was possible for divers groups to use public institutions such as the law for various own ends, and also for new bodies (as in local government) to spring up between the cracks. In such circum-stances, social conflict remained piecemeal and dispersed, allegi-ances in flux. While parish control could be oppressive, the eighteenth-century central state was lax, a beanfeast to those in power, more than a tyrant lash upon the backs of the ruled. Its more grievous exaction was taxation, and since England's produc-tive classes were multiplying and wealth was increasing, this was a burden the grumbling hive could bear.

4. *Keeping Life Going*

Two mirages float up before unwary eyes attempting to picture everyday life in pre-industrial times. Both must be dispelled. One is the image of some wholesome 'community', where people were engaged in satisfying creative craft-work, and peasants lived snug within the bosom of the extended family. Recent researches, however, have destroyed the myth of the extended peasant family – and even of a peasantry itself – at least for Georgian England, and perhaps for the whole of English history. Certainly, the *family* was a key institution,* the elemental unit of living and dying, reproduction and socialization, education and business, love and hate. Gregory King significantly tabulated the English population not by individuals but by families. But the typical family was simple.

The basic and most common household arrangement among the working population was for the occupation of a house by just one married couple. Their young children would live with them, though sons and, slightly less so, daughters were likely to move out as soon as they were apprenticed to a trade or sent into service in their early teens. But a married couple did not normally have their parents living with them (if they were still alive – and very many would be dead – they would continue to live in their own dwelling), and it was exceptional for a married pair to be living under the roof of their parents. Courting couples did not generally marry until the man could support his wife and set up home. It was unusual for in-laws or members of the wider family to be living-in, except temporarily. By contrast it was normal for domestic servants, apprentices, unmarried farm servants and paying lodgers to live with the family. Even quite poor

---

* Though in England, as in much of north-western Europe, family loyalties were sharply circumscribed. Even brothers might feel little obligation to get each other out of a financial scrape. And not all families were happy families.

tradesmen and smallholders would employ young household servants, for they were plentiful and cheap, and working households ate up labour. For teenagers from poor families, going into service was a normal thing. In families, husbands ruled; contrary to the practice of some continental peasant societies, family decisions were not taken by the wider family acting in conference.

The second and contrasting mirage is that pre-industrial societies should be compared to a present-day, under-developed 'third world' country. It is sometimes assumed (among those who hold this gloomy view) that before heavy industrialization, the primitiveness of technology, hygiene and medicine, together with illiteracy, population pressure and sheer exploitation, meant lives verging on starvation and complete hopelessness for the masses. But this was not so in Georgian England. Life for the working population was certainly infinitely gruelling, pains far exceeded pleasures, and upwards of one family in five received poor relief. Yet there is plenty of evidence that even needy labourers had some disposable income, participated in the money economy and exercised some say in the patterning of their lives. They possessed a few heirlooms and went in for the odd luxury: tea-drinking was to spread well down the social scale. Labouring men possessed skills, initiative and their own 'appropriate technology', and – unlike serfs East of the Elbe – they enjoyed some mobility in employment and domicile. Theirs was not at all the expropriated, hopeless, begging-bowl destitution of parts of the present-day third world. The ordinary Georgian working family did not bask in a folksy golden age; neither, however, did it have one foot within the refugee-camp.

For working people, life within the household and the community followed tightly organized, highly regulated, businesslike rounds of routine drills, plotted from the cradle to the grave. Prudent performance of what was allotted and expected made all the difference between merely surviving and living better, between failing and thriving according to one's lights. Through moral precepts, authority figures, family demands and work-routines, communities effectively applied continual physical, moral and emotional pressure upon their members to conform to certain tried and tested ways of living. Everybody's life involved harmonizing regulations imposed from above (such as the requirements of the law or the commands of employers) with peer-group pressure and with personal hopes and ambitions. Sometimes achieving the adjustment was easy, sometimes agonizing. What youth would not leap at the chance of marrying his master's daughter or widow (as did Robert Owen's brother, William)? But how many daughters wanted to stay at home and nurse crotchety parents? The community's wishes were often accepted, internalized and put into practice, because they were the well-established and approved ways of getting on. Sons knew that, if they were dutiful, they would eventually inherit; runaway apprentices, by contrast, would lose their 'character'. Debating whether to marry against his father's wishes, and finally, prudently, deciding not to marry, Edward Gibbon experienced similar pressures: 'I sighed as a lover; I obeyed as a son.' Quakers who married out knew they would be expelled from the meeting; unneighbourly old women were branded as witches.

Creating community cohesion was vital where people had to operate in harmony. Husbandmen tilling open fields had to agree on crop rotations, or on when to allow post-harvest stubble-grazing. Ploughs and ox-teams were shared, as were wells and pumps. The rival claims of millers, farmers and bargees upon running water had to be reconciled. Many jobs involved cooperative physical labour, pulling in unison: sawyers, for example, worked in teams. Work songs such as shanties kept team efforts in time.

Codes of basic values captured in proverbs and wise sayings aimed to make people's vital interests converge. Families needed to win for themselves and their dependants a livelihood, struggling against nature and economic rivals. But they also needed ways of negotiating personal relations so that mutual rights and duties would be allocated and disputes settled (from tiffs right up to vendettas), and these made solemnly binding on future generations. The warp of self-preservation had to be interwoven with the weft of neighbourliness. Pressurized by want and need, villagers abided by the time-honoured proprieties, and heads often had to rule hearts. Thus working mothers swaddled their babies or farmed them out to wet-nurses; such practices were necessary because they couldn't afford their work to be interrupted by toddlers' demands. A certain cool-headedness was needed when it came to choosing company, a spouse, a trade.

Two activities regulated particularly tightly were work and sex. For production and reproduction had to be kept in fine balance. Too few able bodies, and the depleted workforce would not sustain well-being. Too many mouths, and pauperism would edge in. Below leisured society, everybody could expect to be put to work, and few retired until forced by incapacity. Infants might tread washing; from the age of four or five some would scare crows or keep cows from the corn, or would be doing domestic work in textiles. Defoe admired the economy of the West Riding of Yorkshire because he found 'hardly any thing above four years old, but its hands are sufficient to itself'. Once they reached their teens, boys were commonly apprenticed – to shopkeepers, craftsmen, or, even younger, to chimney-sweeps. Once in his twenties, a journeyman would begin serious courting with a view to setting up on his own, using his wife's labour and that of the anticipated children.

Within the working family, domestic arrangements had to be practical. Our glimpses of petty bourgeois and artisan domestic life reveal level-headed relationships, in which adults took priority over children and men over women in meeting the needs of production. William Hutton, who was to become a flinty Birmingham businessman, records that he was never hugged or kissed by his Nonconformist mother: this is probably not untypical. When his mother died, his nanny upbraided his tears: 'Don't cry, you will soon go yourself.' Hutton wrote, 'I was an economist from my cradle.' Sentiment was a luxury which many could not afford.

Few craftsmen or professional men were so impetuous as to marry until they had saved enough to set up home or had inherited their father's tools or holding (mere labourers, blessed only with their strength, had less reason to delay). Many men married women older than themselves, often widows. Widows were proven mothers and housewives, and were more likely to have a nest egg. To marry an older woman was also a hedge against having too many children. In this practical vein, Matthew Boulton advised, 'Don't marry for money, but marry where money is.' Above all, men needed wives to be (in Richard Gough's words) 'prudent, provident and discreet'; Defoe thought that in seeking a bride a man might well choose 'the homeliest and eldest' out of a bunch, for 'it was application and business they were to expect assistance in'. And, by today's standards, men themselves married quite late. Teenage marriages were uncommon. Early in the century, journeymen generally wed after apprenticeship in their mid or even late twenties; professional men often married in their thirties. Their brides were a little younger. This pattern of late marriage, special to northwestern Europe, meant that about half of all parents never lived to see their children grown up. Overall it was a society in which economic prudence strongly regulated family formation – and, early in the century in particular, many never married at all. Though contraceptive appliances were hardly used, family size was kept in check, partly by delayed marriage, sometimes by sexual restraint within marriage and other practices (delaying weaning a previous child was known to hinder fertility). A marriage bond, once formed, generally held together until the death of one of the partners. Thereafter, few widowers remained unattached for long: they needed a spouse to look after the home and children.

If among ordinary folk matrimony was postponed until starting a household and family became prudent, pre-marital sexual experience itself was very commonly forgone, particularly among women. Of course, many dashing young men sowed their wild oats, actors and soldiers being notorious for loving and leaving, and every village had its molls who were known to go with men. But most young maids probably went without. Considering that a decade or so commonly separated puberty and matrimony, there were few bastards (for most of the century they amounted to about 2 per cent of recorded births). Of course, recorded bastards are a far from perfect index of pre-nuptial sex. Many illegitimate births went unrecorded (stillbirths, early mortality and infanticide silenced plenty), and in any case, in an age when fertility was low, sex did not often result in conception. Bastardy, however, went up in the second half of the century. The prudence and prohibitions which in late Stuart times had powerfully dictated delayed marriage and curtailed pre-marital sexual activity, and had meant that many remained single, were all loosening. As a rising proportion of the population married, and married younger, so the disadvantages and stigmas of bearing bastards were also reduced. And a rising percentage of marriages themselves became contracted after pregnancy.

The rising bastardy rate may also indicate that fertility was improving, perhaps accompanying better health and nutrition, and hence that sex – outside marriage as well as within – was more often leading to pregnancy. It may often mark anticipated marriages falling through. Couples frequently began having sex once they were courting in earnest, with the assumption that a formal wedding would take place when circumstances were right:

> Bobby Shafto's gone to sea
> Silver buckles on his knee
> When he comes back he'll marry me.

But if an accident, such as a war or unemployment, put obstacles in the way of marriage, the woman might be left holding the baby. Bastards were thus frequently the wages not of promiscuity or casual sex, but of serious courtship which failed to result in marriage.

The rising bastardy figures are also possibly a consequence of the stricter definition of legitimacy following Hardwicke's Marriage Act (1753). Upon pregnancy, it had been customary in many communities to recognize established couples as *de facto* man and wife ('consensual marriage'); even many clergymen had looked upon the offspring of such unions as legitimate. The 1753 Act, however, made a regularly conducted church wedding the sole proof of marriage. Henceforth, parish clerks were much less likely to regard children of such 'consensual marriages' as legitimate.

All in all, the low bastardy rate and the desire of many cohabiting couples not legally married to have some public recognition of their union show that village and small-town communities were ones in which individual behaviour largely kept in step with community values. Except in big towns or right off the beaten track, people were continually in the public eye, and censure was shameful and disabling. The pressures to conform were great. Shorter is probably right to suggest that 'sexuality in traditional society may be thought of as a great iceberg, frozen by the command of custom, by the need of the surrounding community for stability at the cost of individuality, and by the dismal grind of daily life.'

People certainly trimmed their wills to their ways and means.

Trade downswings resulted in postponed marriages. By contrast, in the Midlands and the North, economic effervescence in the last third of the century encouraged faith in the future and thereby boosted population. In the framework-knitting centres of Leicestershire and Nottinghamshire, for example, couples began to marry earlier, confident that work would be available and anticipating that, with the growth of manufacturing, large families would be a boon rather than a bind. As Arthur Young expressed it, 'It is employment that creates population: marriages are early and numerous in proportion to the amount of employment.'

Parents, kin, masters, friends and communities all expected to have a certain say over the private lives of individuals. Many people never escaped direct dependency (marriage would bring a *man* full membership of society, but his *wife* only switched superiors). The private lives of domestic servants were highly supervised and often exploited. Servant girls who bore a bastard – often their master's – were liable to have their name besmirched and hopes of respectable marriage dashed, for once dismissed as an outcast, such a girl's life was easily reduced to a harlot's progress. Mothers and nurses, no less than fathers and masters, habitually inflicted physical punishment. Young Francis Place was frequently beaten by his father until the stick broke: 'a word and a blow, but the blow always came first'. John Wesley's mother, Susanna, positively boasted of her babies, 'when turned a year old (and sons before) they were taught to fear the rod, and to cry softly'. Autobiographies show that children from the lower orders in particular experienced parents as figures of direct power. In many families, youngsters were often still expected to stand silently in their parents' presence, and obedience was the child's golden rule. Many children had been constrained from birth by months of swaddling. 'I lay very quiet,' (thus, at the beginning of the century, Richard Steele imagined a newborn babe thinking), 'but the witch [i.e. the nurse] . . . takes me, and binds my head as hard as possibly she could; then ties up both my legs, and makes me swallow down an horrid mixture. I thought it an harsh entrance into life, to begin with taking physic; but I was forced to it.' John Locke, philosopher and tutor, was as concerned to drill children to go to stool as go to school, and alongside rigorous toilet-training, cold baths came into vogue to strengthen the fibres. Girls of genteel family were fastened into backboards, corsets and stays to improve posture. For being naughty, Fanny Kemble was imprisoned for a week in a toolshed, Charlotte Charke was tied to a table leg. Children were traditionally made to feel their place.

By virtue of their seniority parents compelled submission; but did age command respect, or even love? Gibbon frankly thought the young were relieved when their parents died. 'Few, perhaps, are the children who, after the expiration of some months or years, would sincerely rejoice in the resurrection of their parents,' he candidly commented, 'and it is a melancholy truth that my father's death . . . was the only event that could save me from an hopeless life of obscurity and indigence.' For, with long apprenticeship, professional training and late marriage, young men were financially insecure and could be kept under their elders' thumb for half their days. For many tedious years the future Lord Kenyon, training in the law, languished on £50 a year from his father. The old could be irksome because they didn't retire (most could not afford to, having no insurance for old age: Tom Paine was an early advocate of old-age pensions). Overall, it was not an era which revered grey hairs. Ageing Georgians tried to look young rather than to appear like long-bearded patriarchs: wigs and cosmetics, used even by men, were to keep an appearance of youth. The outlook of the Age of Reason led old Henry Fox to bring up his son, Charles James, to believe that 'the young are always right, the old are always wrong'.

Tensions between the generations were not surprising in a society where most people were young and clamouring to get on. Over 45 per cent of the population was under twenty: there were juveniles galore. Yet there was an extra-fast lane to power for the privileged young: Pitt the Younger could rise to be Prime Minister at twenty-four; Brownlow North was a bishop at thirty; Wolfe got his army commission at fourteen and was a major at twenty.

Ceremony and show were overt and powerful regulators of life: witness the complex degrees of formal mourning attire. Distinctions in dress offered cameos in code of status and occupation. Thus butchers wore distinctive aprons and physicians had different wigs from everybody else and carried gold-headed canes – while wearing swords to show that they were gentlemen.

But clothes also signalled much other private and public information, from the schoolmaster's gown of authority to the cap
donned by the ageing spinster to show she had withdrawn from
the marriage market. Charity school uniforms, provided free,
were badges of poverty. In days before savings banks, people
invested more of their wealth in fine and formal clothes. Even
wigs, accessories and stuccoed cosmetics, and nuances of dress
and undress, could reveal rank, age, and party politics (where
precisely ladies stuck their face patches was a clue to whether
they were Whig or Tory). The lace tongue of the fan could
scandal-monger, or it could seduce. Up to the 1770s it was
unfashionable for men not to wear a wig; then suddenly even a
tonish servant such as Fag in Sheridan's *Rivals* would not have
been seen dead wearing one. As a peer, Lord Ferrers, who had
murdered his steward, went to his execution in his wedding suit
embroidered with silver, begging to be hanged with a rope of
silk. Clothes had their own language.

Life was animated and punctuated by the festive calendar,
many days of the year having their own distinct rituals. Hair was
still cut at full moon, blood was let in the spring. Feeling
continued to run strong against marrying in Lent, traditionally
forbidden by the Church, and parishes seem to have had their
own preferred months for weddings and baptisms. Birthdays
were times of private jollification but also reminders about one's
body and getting old. Thus Thomas Turner, a schoolmaster,
recorded in his diary in 1755: 'This day being my birthday, I
treated my scholars with about five quarts of strong beer and had
an issue cut in my leg': beer and blood flowed together. Festivities
marked off the stages of the farming year – Plough Monday,
sheep-shearing, rush-bearing, harvest home. Trades had their
annual processions – weavers marched on St Blaise's Day, for
instance – giving licence for apprentices' high jinks. In boroughs,
mayoral processions, like mini-coronations, signalled a change of
authority. César de Saussure noted:

The Lord Mayor's day is a great holiday in the City. The populace
on that great day is particularly insolent and rowdy, turning into
lawless freedom the great liberty it enjoys. At these times it is almost
dangerous for an honest man, and particularly for a foreigner, if at all
well dressed, to walk in the streets, for he runs a great risk of being

insulted by the vulgar populace, which is the most cursed brood in existence.

Some holidays were holy days – although religious festivities such as Christmas, Twelfth Night and Shrove Tuesday were celebrated with pagan good cheer, eating, merriment and wassailing. On Shrove Tuesday men played football, youngsters shied at cocks. Whitsun overlapped with the summer wakes and was the season of well-dressing. 'On Good Friday,' wrote Samuel Bamford about his native late-eighteenth-century Lancashire, 'children took little baskets neatly trimmed with moss, and went "a pace-egging", and received at some places eggs, at some places spiced loaf, and at others half-pennies, which they carried home to their mothers.' Other rural festivals enacted pagan and magical lore, such as the Helston Furry (or Flora) Dances or the horn dance at Abbots Bromley in Staffordshire, palimpsests of Christianity and nature worship. A carnival puppet, Jack O'Lantern, was tossed around on Ash Wednesday, celebrating the death of Winter. Christening was a sacrament, but it was also believed to ward off sickness. Folk wisdom held that Christian confirmation was a specific against rheumatism (nothing doctors gave you did any good). Good Friday bread was preserved for months to be used as a remedy.

Customs, feasts and mummers' pageants kept traditional beliefs alive and kicking. People danced round maypoles, and morris men jangled their bells, rode hobby horses, hoisted corn dollies and sang refrains about 'the Green Man' and other fertility and virility symbols. 'Tom Poker', 'Old Shock', 'Will o' the Wisp' – such ancestral bogeys and ghosts thread in and out of popular stories, frightening children on dark nights. Games such as barley-break and the nine-men's morris were bedecked with legend. Rituals, such as those of St Valentine's Day and May Day, gave personal emotional release and perhaps helped tongue-tied young people to initiate courting. 'On the eve of the 14th of February, St Valentine's Day,' explained Henri Misson,

a time when all living nature inclines to couple, the young folks in England, and Scotland too, by a very ancient custom, celebrate a little festival that tends to the same end. An equal number of maids and bachelors get together; each writes his or her true or some feigned name upon separate billets, which they roll up and draw by way of lots, the maids taking the men's billets, and the men the maids'; so that each of the young men lights upon a girl that he calls his Valentine, and each of the girls upon a young man which she calls hers. By this means, each has two Valentines; but the man sticks faster to the Valentine that is fallen to him, than to the Valentine to whom he is fallen. Fortune having thus divided the company into so many couples, the Valentines give balls and treats to their fair mistresses, wear their billets several days upon their bosoms and sleeves, and this little sport often ends in love.

May Day gave a maid a chance to pay her addresses to a youth, but it was also when Shropshire colliers battled with farm labourers for possession of the summit of the Wrekin, and London chimney-sweeps swaggered around on parade. On other gala days, people danced round maypoles and girls were crowned Queen of the May. Most festivals allowed children to scrounge cakes and half-pennies, and let off steam for once in a while.

In Georgian England, the holiday calendar was heavily political and dynastic. There were fireworks for the king's birthday and bonfires for Guy Fawkes' Day (5 November was also providentially the anniversary of William of Orange's landing at Torbay); 23 April was St George's Day, 28 May marked the birth of George I (for Jacobites, 10 June was the birthday of the Old Pretender). These rituals, with their parades and bonfires, stoked up the fires of patriotism. Rites of inversion – such as pupils locking masters out of school – allowed authority to be mocked with impunity one day a year, though in the end they served to reinforce authority itself. MPs' footmen held their own mirror Parliament, prisoners staged their own mock assizes.

Carnival customs gave chances for release – for tipsiness, or paying off old scores – and ritual play put a smile on the back-breaking drudgery which was the curse of working life. Fasts were ended with feasts, solemnities with sport. 'Some two or three weeks before Christmas,' recalled Samuel Bamford about his late-eighteenth-century childhood,

it was the custom in families to apportion to each boy or girl weaver a certain quantity of work, which was to be done ere his or her holidays commenced. An extra quantity was generally undertaken to be performed, and the conditions of the performance were such indulgences and gratuities as were agreeable to the working parties. In most families a peck or a strike of malt would be brewed; spiced bread or potato custard would be made, and probably an extra piece of beef, and some good old cheese would be laid in store, not to be touched until the work was done. The work then went on merrily. Play hours were nearly given up, and whole nights would be spent at the loom, the weavers occasionally striking up a hymn or Christmas carol in chorus . . . Before Christmas we frequently sang to keep ourselves from sleep, and we chorused 'Christians, awake' when we ourselves were almost gone to sleep . . . Christmas holidays always commenced on the first Monday after New Year's Day. By that day every one was expected to have his work finished.

Sunday was a day apart. A vestige of the Puritan day of enforced godliness, it was still a time of enforced inactivity. Even before the Evangelical sabbatarian crusade late in the century, most trading, work and entertainment were banned. As Dr Johnson put it, Sunday 'should be different from another day. People may walk, but not throw stones at birds'. Yet he himself had suffered 'heavy' Sundays as a child, when his mother droned to him *The Whole Duty of Man*. 'Nothing is more wearisome, more silent, more gloomy than an English Sunday,' concluded the Swede, Erik Gustaf Geijer.

The formalities and transitions of life – the times for living, loving and dying – were ceremoniously acted out to emboss them upon the public memory. Rites of passage marked the openings and closures of chapters in individual lives – vital enactments in a society which set less store by calendar age than by stage of development. Boys, for example, would be publicly 'breeched'. When in Laurence Sterne's novel Tristram's father declared, 'We should begin to think, Mrs Shandy, of putting this boy into breeches,' he created a domestic furore, because the transition from wearing skirts to wearing breeches signalled the close of a mother's reign over her son. The induction of new apprentices would be marked with elaborate and often barbaric pranks. Weddings involved customs such as kissing the bride, bedding the couple, and a battle over the bride's garter. Many couples who did not want to go through a regular church marriage (perhaps because a partner, previously married, whose spouse had disappeared, feared bigamy) wanted community recognition to mark their union, and there was always a sympathetic – or unscrupulous – cleric to be found to give his blessing to popular moral feelings. How a man departed this life was a matter of public example. 'See in what peace a Christian can die,' boasted Joseph Addison to his stepson, while James Boswell haunted the death-bed of the sceptic David Hume hoping to find recantation or terror. Imposing death-bed scenes, last words, and stately and lavish funerals aimed to fix an indelible final image of the departed and to forestall the family rifts that the will might create: burials were far more formal than weddings.

Particularly in the countryside, where so many of the vital arrangements of life were not written down but guaranteed by long-standing memory, the solemn, conspicuous and symbolic reiteration of rights of way, boundaries, terms of work and mutual rights and responsibilities was paramount. For example, parishioners annually 'beat the bounds' around the perimeter of the village to assert their territory. When the rules of this 'moral economy' were broken, the community stepped in to restore propriety. 'Rough music' – raising a din and parading indecent effigies – was the neighbours' way of shaming shrewish wives or cuckold husbands into putting their houses in order. By contrast, at Great Dunmow a flitch of bacon was awarded yearly to the happiest married couple. Acts of communal defiance greeted tradesmen, bailiffs and gamekeepers who infringed traditional rights and customs: they might be tarred and feathered or receive threats in riddles; farmers might have their ricks burned and cattle maimed. And with its inventive mimic street theatre, the people's culture mercilessly deflated the *poseur* pomp of the mighty. For instance the mock election of the 'mayor' of Garrett in Surrey (where men qualified for the broad franchise if they had 'enjoyed a woman in the open air in the district') burlesqued the corrupt farce of parliamentary hustings and the bare-faced lies of politicians.

Overall, community wisdom felt the need for peace, neighbourliness and harmony deep in its bones (it had to, for communities were highly disputatious and even litigious). Ringing through popular feeling was the chorus of Hospitality. The flowing bowl, the pipe of tobacco, the songs of 'Begone dull care' and John Barleycorn, processions, oaths, healths, toasts, pledging – these were the ways people sought to patch quarrels and keep neighbours sweet, or hoped to sugar the bitter pills of life. 'The people of this neighbourhood are much attached to the celebration of wakes,' observed the Revd A. Macaulay about Claybrook, near the end of the century:

and on the annual returns of these festivals, the cousins assemble from all quarters, fill the church on Sunday, and celebrate Monday with feasting, with musick, and with dancing. The spirit of old English hospitality is conspicuous among the farmers on these occasions.

In the tone of extreme unctuousness, however, which paragons of respectability were beginning to assume, Macaulay wanted to suppress this communal release from care:

But with the lower sort of people, especially in the manufacturing villages, the return of the wake never fails to produce a week, at least, of idleness, intoxication and riot; these, and other abuses, by which these festivals are so grossly perverted from the original end of their institution, render it highly desirable to all the friends of order, of decency, and of religion, that they were totally suppressed.

English *bonhomie* gelled into the distinct form of the club. 'Man is a sociable animal,' wrote Joseph Addison, 'and we take all occasions and pretences of forming ourselves into those little nocturnal assemblies which are commonly known as *clubs*.' These ranged from august bodies such as the Whig Kit-Kat Club and Dr Johnson's Literary Club (Johnson deemed the mark of a gentleman lay in being 'clubbable'), down to the Ugly Clubs, the Tall Clubs, Farters' Clubs, Surly Clubs, burial societies and tippling clubs of ordinary men. Lancashire weavers won fame for their musical societies, and gardening clubs flourished.

Quintessentially English was the Sublime Society of Beefsteaks, a convivial club dedicated to the eating of beefsteaks, founded in 1735. Anticipating the Lunar Society of Birmingham, the farmers of Aveley in Essex set up a 'Lunatick Club' in 1763 to meet monthly at full moon (riding home merry was safer then). Some were orgiastic, from the Hell-Fire Club of the rakes down to a London club which the German Lichtenberg described in 1770:

it consisted of servants, journeymen, and apprentices. On these evenings every member laid down fourpence, for which he had music and a female gratis; anything else had to be paid for separately. Twenty of the girls were brought before Sir John Fielding; the beauty of some of them aroused general admiration [Sir John, alas, was blind].

The rise of private aristocratic clubs, like White's and Almack's, whose gaming tables were the sepulchres of fortunes, tolled the knell of coffee houses. Fashionable 'speculative' freemasonry also took root, combining the all-male cheer of the club, the fraternity of trade, and non-denominational lay piety (English lodges were not politically radical, as they were on the Continent). Secret signs and mumbo-jumbo bound masons together – chiefly men in trade, hoping to find a degree of commercial stability in unity. Other clubs, such as the Spitalfields Mathematical Club, were more intellectual and educational. Trade guilds provided conviviality in health and benefits in sickness. Their freemen were bonded together by their initiation rites and oaths of secrecy and by trade cant for materials, tools and processes (preventing outsiders from breaking in and industrial spies from understanding the 'mystery'). And friendly societies ('box clubs') mushroomed among the lower orders, offering mutuality and rudimentary social insurance, and serving as a front for trade-union activities. By 1800 friendly societies had well over 600,000 members.

Clubs created identity and partisanship. Political clubs (like the Calves' Head) cheered either the Whigs or Tories, Hanoverians or Jacobites, rowdies carrying these allegiances out on to the streets with their flags, cockades, sashes, colours and chants. More than most, minorities banded together to safeguard their identity. Expatriate Welshmen and Cornishmen in London, for instance, were already forming exiles' associations. Particularly in London, fringe religious communities gathered and dissolved like clouds – Sandemanians, Swedenborgians, Muggletonians, Moravians. The London Negro population (numbering up to 14,000; mostly slaves, personal servants and sailors) had its own musical bands, taverns and meeting places, and London's Germans had their own churches. Ghetto areas formed. Thus immigrant Huguenot silk-weavers cocooned themselves in Spitalfields.

All in all, the make-or-break of working people's lives lay in their success in adjusting to the day-to-day routines of earning a living, maintaining a family and coping with the occasional but critical watersheds of existence. Ordinary people were accustomed to tailoring their individual lives to community expectations (enforced in the end through the parish Poor Law). Many of the customs of everyday life were traditional; some (like friendly societies) were new and fulfilled new needs. In pacing their life and work rhythms, the lives of common people were not wholly dictated by squire and parson. The metabolism of communities was more self-regulating. Popular wisdom, a living manual for maintaining life's fabric and reproducing it for the generations to come, kept going strong.

✓ Possibly unlike today, most eighteenth-century learning went on outside officially designated systems of instruction. Education was neither organized by the state nor compulsory, and was not geared to precise age groups. For very few people did exams or paper qualifications count: finding a good patron and being able to pen begging letters were far more useful. Few jobs were won by open public competition. Most education was learning for living, in particular for earning a living. For the elite, Greek and Latin Classics inculcated politeness, style, the graces, and a habit of superiority. At humbler levels, nursery rhymes taught home truths to toddlers and helped the young to learn to count; decks of cards taught the ABC and numbers, and shop and tavern signs and church interiors familiarized people with words and their associations: scraps of history, morality, mythology and the Commandments. Mothers, aunts, nurses and friends taught brides about baby-care; masters imparted know-how to apprentices, elder children taught younger. Rhymes, lullabies, songs and riddles jingled all you needed to know about the weather, money, omens, charms, home cures, cooking and courting – endless sayings like

> If you marry in Lent
> You'll live to repent.

Crossing knives on the table, killing crickets or money spiders, chopping down holly trees, putting anything other than a prayer-book on top of a Bible, passing someone on the stairs – all these, this hand-me-down wisdom warned you, were unlucky. It was bad luck to say your prayers at the foot of the bed, but (who would have guessed it?) lucky to fall downstairs. Put milk on the fire and the cows will go dry. All such proverbial wisdom invested everything with significance, inevitable in a society in which accident and disaster struck often without warning or explanation.

Sewing samplers taught girls how to be good even as they meticulously stitched the letters:

> Patience is a virtue
> Virtue is a grace
> Both put together
> Make a very pretty face.

Elizabeth, daughter of the Kirkby Stephen shopkeeper Abraham Dent, copied into her handwriting book stern but improving sentiments such as 'Knowledge procures general esteem', 'Labour improves wealth', 'Misfortunes are a kind of discipline', 'Quarrelsome people are dangerous', and 'Youth is the best time for learning'. During the century more and more of this traditional lore was also being reproduced in cheap teach-yourself books, though, alongside these, the old favourites – chapbooks such as *Jack and the Beanstalk*, *Guy of Warwick* and *Tom Thumb* – remained well-thumbed.

Countless people – certainly not just the poor – picked up their book-learning not in school, but by finding out for themselves as children or adults, browsing through the family bookshelf, or being taught by kin and friends. There were proud autodidacts galore, such as the mathematician Charles Hutton and the novelist Thomas Holcroft. The pioneer canal engineer James Brindley was taught by his mother and worked out many of his designs in his head, while lying in bed. Lack of nice accomplishment did not necessarily hold men back. 'Give me leave my lord,' Admiral Pye begged Lord Sandwich,

to make one Observation more and I have done – that is When you peruse Admiral Pye's letter you would please not to scrutinize too close either to the speling or to the Grammatical Part as I allow my self to be no proficient in either. I had the Mortification to be neglected in my education, went to sea at 14 without any & a Man of War was my University.

In any case, formal schooling itself was no guarantee of an education. Many parents sent their children from pillar to post. Poet-laureate-to-be Robert Southey attended no fewer than six different schools. Other literati such as Coleridge delved into books to *escape* their schooling. After an unhappy home upbringing, where Molly, the family servant, 'hated me' and his brother Frank 'had a violent love of beating me', he was sent to the famous London charity school, Christ's Hospital, where 'the school boys drove me from play and were always tormenting me – and hence I took no pleasure in boyish sports but read incessantly'.

The trade in cheap improving works – teach-yourself books, pocket imprints of the classics, instruction manuals (*Reading Made Quite Easy* and the like), dictionaries, primers for handwriting, accounts and foreign languages – expanded beyond recognition. When young William Cobbett left home to tramp to London for work, he spent his last three pence on Swift's *A Tale of a Tub* and read it from cover to cover, entranced. Cobbett, eventually to become England's leading journalist, seems never to have gone to school. It was easier to be a successful autodidact than ever before. But people didn't need to be, for the century also saw a huge expansion in school places. This was no thanks to central or local government, which recognized little brief for teaching. Moreover, many old endowed academic institutions were in the course of atrophy. 'Whoever will examine the state of the grammar schools in different parts of the kingdom,' complained Lord Kenyon in 1795, 'will see to what a lamentable condition most of them are reduced. If all persons had equally done their duty, we should not find, as is now the case, empty walls without scholars, and everything neglected but the receipt of salaries and emoluments.'

Some of these grammar schools decayed because they were myopically bound by statute to a Classical curriculum for which the demand was waning, for parents in trade increasingly wanted an education including 'modern' and 'useful' studies, such as arithmetic, accounts, French, handwriting, navigation, shorthand, commercial methods, and maybe a spot of science. Other grammar schools, however, did move with the times, teaching more mathematics and practical subjects; still others moved up-market, taking fewer parish boys but converting themselves into fee-paying boarding schools for sons of the genteel and the aspirant. The public school super-league – Westminster, Eton, Harrow, Charterhouse, Rugby, Winchester – consolidated itself, enhancing its reputation partly by a self-perpetuating sleight-of-hand: classy people attended such schools because other classy people had – old school ties were already strong. Yet they truly offered the intimate liberal and Classical grounding patricians valued, their cadets being 'lashed into Latin by the tingling rod'. Life in the Georgian public school, as in its gaols, was regulated not just from above but also from within, by a senate of senior boys who tyrannized over the younger. Vicesimus Knox, headmaster at Sevenoaks, wrote that, while a pupil at Merchant Taylors', he had 'lived as a fag under a state of oppression from my school-fellows unknown to any slave in the plantations'. Beyond lessons and a rather brutal discipline, which included flogging, the masters did not interfere much in boarders' lives. (The idea that every second of schooldays should be timetabled with improving activities such as 'sporting' team games was the invention of the nineteenth century.) Public-school culture was an initiation into the life of a gentleman: boys drank, gambled, rode, fought, and gained precocious bisexual experience. Not infrequently they rebelled: the militia had to be called in on one occasion to storm Eton (all manner of battles were won and lost on its playing fields).

Public schools, thought Henry Fielding, were 'the nurseries of all vice and immorality'. Yet this kind of schooling was reckoned a good baptism in English freedom for the nation's junior rulers. 'I shall always be ready to joyn in the common opinion,' judged Gibbon, who had attended Westminster:

that our public schools, which have produced so many eminent charac-ters are the best adapted to the Genius and constitution of the English people. A boy of spirit may acquire a praevious and practical experience of the World, and his playfellows may be the future friends of his heart or his interest. In a free intercourse with his equals the habits of truth, fortitude and prudence will insensibly be matured: birth and riches are measured by the standard of personal merits; and the mimic scene of a rebellion has displayed in their true colours the ministers and patriots of the rising generation.

Like most grammar schools, the two English universities – still all-male, celibate and Anglican – had declining numbers of matricu-lants. Christ's College, Cambridge, had just three freshmen in 1733. By mid-century, Oxford's intake had fallen to fewer than 200 freshmen a year. Oxford and Cambridge came to be attended principally by sauntering young gentlemen filling in time with rather desultory studies (few troubled to graduate), and by penurious scholarship boys, many of them curates' sons, seeking ordination into the Church. It was grinding tutors and slumbrous pedants who made an academic career in the colleges. Most of the great scholars of Georgian England – the law reformer, Jeremy Bentham, historians such as Edward Gibbon, Archdeacon Coxe and Charles Burney, and scientists such as Joseph Priestley and Henry Cavendish – were not in academic life. Oxford dons, suggested Gibbon's malicious vignette, were steeped in port and privilege:

'decent easy men', who supinely enjoyed the gifts of the founder; their days were filled by a series of uniform employment; the chapel & the hall, the coffeehouse & the common room, till they retired weary and well-satisfied, to a long slumber. From the toil of reading, or thinking, or writing they had absolved their conscience. Their conversation stagnated in a round of college business, Tory politics, personal anecdotes & private scandal: their dull & deep potations excused the brisk intemperance of youth.

Oxford (for Horace Walpole, a 'nursery of nonsense and bigotry') and Cambridge (which Lord Chesterfield deemed 'an illiberal seminary') became more genteel, luxurious and expensive, and so deterred poorer students, except those who gained scholarships. Oxford's crypto-Jacobite politics repelled some, as also, however, did the ultra-modern curriculum based on geometry, mathematics and Newtonian science which Cambridge evolved. The torpid universities hardly transformed themselves, though Cambridge was introducing written exams at the end of the century, and no reform was imposed from outside. Ministries let sleeping dons lie.

Those who needed higher education for a profession such as medicine usually went elsewhere. Early on, medical students flocked to the Dutch universities; later Edinburgh University became extremely popular, being open to Dissenters and training surgeons as well as physicians. As centres of literary and intellectual ferment Oxford and Cambridge were eclipsed by the metropolis (significantly, Richard Porson, the great Cambridge professor of Greek, chose to live in London). The ancient English universities became rather pocketfuls of patronage and the starting line in the race for Church livings. Fellowships were prized as remunerative pieces of property, often entailing no teaching responsibilities, and, at the very least, handy to be going on with for a fledgling clergyman with his eye upon a choice parsonage – many of which were in the colleges' gift. Lively minds and ambitious fellows would move on. 'A fellowship is an excellent breakfast, an indifferent dinner, and a most miserable supper,' judged George Faber.

The skyline of learning was changing with the needs of the times. Many liberal families mistrusted the public school and the university, with its diet of birch, boorishness, buggery and the bottle, and put their trust instead in private tutors (aided by music teachers and and dancing masters), with a European Grand Tour thrown in as icing on the cake. Lady Leicester of Holkham obligingly bribed her great-nephew with £500 a year if he would take a Grand Tour rather than be ruined at one of 'those schools of vice', the universities. Grand Tours of France, Italy, Germany and Holland gobbled up money, costing up to £5,000 for three years.

Nonconformist boys from the trading classes, excluded by religious tests from Anglican grammar schools and universities, generally went to Dissenting Academies. Many of these, such as Kibworth, Taunton, Daventry, Kendal, Warrington and Mile End, presided over by such distinguished scholars as Philip Doddridge and Joseph Priestley, became justly famous: by their sheer quality they even attracted Anglican students. Mainstream Old Dissenters, and in particular Presbyterians, were not too 'precise' to appreciate polite learning (though many 'plain' Quakers were), and they set out to blend canonical Classical studies with 'useful' and 'modern' subjects such as geography, shorthand, arithmetic and science (bound by no charters, such foundations could be flexible). The long-term social importance of the Academies lay in the fact that, ironically, they became fifth columns, undermining orthodox Dissent. They were privately run by the schoolmasters themselves, without statutes or day-to-day supervision from Nonconformist church elders. These schoolmasters themselves often felt leanings towards a more heterodox theology, rejecting Calvinism, and they explored open and 'rational' teaching methods that encouraged doubt and question. The upshot was a revolt of Dissenting youth against orthodoxy. Hackney and Hoxton schools in particular became hotbeds of theological ferment; Calvinism was undermined, Socinianism taking its place. Thus, though initially brought up in strict Sandemanian learning, William Godwin was admitted to Hoxton Academy and proceeded to become a pantheist and anarchist. Burke dubbed

Hackney Academy 'the new arsenal in which subversive doctrines and arguments were forged'. Prestige academies such as Hackney, Warrington and Hoxton were forced to close when church elders could no longer stomach doctrinal anarchy. By the end of the century, Dissenting schoolmasters and their ex-pupils were floating away from orthodoxy, buoyed up by the hot air of free-thought.

'It is here not uncommon,' wrote Pastor Moritz, 'to see on doors in one continued succession "Children educated here", "Shoes mended here", "Foreign spiritous liquors sold here", "Funerals furnished here".' Moritz's acid *in memoriam* on the 'pupils' progress' spotlights the forest of private-enterprise commercial schools shooting up all over England. These catered to the same social ranks as Dissenting Academies – business-minded families – but lacked their religious commitment. Hundreds of younger sons, beneficeless clergy and penurious writers set up day schools and boarding schools, teaching anything from the alphabet, to Classics, gunnery and navigation, and laying heavy emphasis upon the drills of spelling, handwriting, mathematics and casting accounts. Their wives and sisters commonly acted as matrons. Such schools were frequently short-lived, and many mercifully so, yet they met a need in giving boys (and, though less so, girls) from craft and petty-bourgeois backgrounds the practical skills needed for earning a living or entering an apprenticeship: bookkeeping, a little law, commercial practice, writing business letters, arithmetic, technical drawing. Not least, such schools were cheap. A sound boarding education could be had in the North of England for as little as £10 a year. Boys from the middling orders were getting a more down-to-earth and applicable education than in any previous century. When they were a little older, it was just these people who formed the audiences for another major new venture in free-market instruction: popular lectures. For a few shillings, young men could enrol in the larger towns for evening courses – often delivered by itinerant lecturers – both in vocational subjects like navigation and in cultural pursuits such as natural history and antiquities. Sometimes women were admitted.

The number of schools for girls went up as well by leaps and bounds, though many, such as the one set up at Newington Green by Mary Wollstonecraft, taught little more than some reading, sewing and drawing, being glorified child-minding establishments. Jane Austen, for example, attended three boarding schools, starting at the unusually early age of seven, but picked up most of her education from her clergyman father. Polite society did not take girls' minds very seriously. 'I don't think so much larning becomes a young woman,' declared Sheridan's Mrs Malaprop; and she wasn't alone. The more refined girls' schools aimed to groom their pupils for their future compliant and decorative role in fashionable society, teaching manners, deportment, religion, French, arts, graces and even cards.

Lower down the social scale, parents were perhaps less eager to send their children to school: they could ill afford the fees, or to forego their labour. But more schools were being provided for them, free or at nominal cost, by philanthropists. Not that everybody agreed that the poor ought to receive schooling. Some feared they would get ideas above their station, become idle and be seduced into sedition. 'The more a shepherd, a ploughman . . . know of the World,' suggested Mandeville with his habitual cynical, paradoxical turn, 'the less fitted he'll be to go through the fatigue and hardship of it with cheerfulness and content.' Soame Jenyns judged ignorance 'the opiate of the poor, a cordial administered by the gracious hand of providence', or as Davies Giddy, a later president of the Royal Society, argued in 1807,

Giving education to the labouring classes or the poor would be prejudicial to their morals and happiness; it would teach them to despise their lot in life, instead of making them good servants in agriculture and other laborious employment. Instead of teaching them subordination, it would render them fractious and refractory.

But promoters of schooling for the masses reassuringly countered that the education offered would be cheap, wholesome and indoctrinating, and enumerated the expected benefits. Schooling the poor would teach godliness and subordination, drill them for work, impart craft skills, and ensure that the commonalty would not be a drain upon, or a threat to, society. 'It is through education,' assured John Evans, 'that the poor become acquainted with the duties they owe to society.'

One spur to setting up charitable schools for the poor came from religious bodies such as the Society for the Promotion of

Christian Knowledge (SPCK), founded in 1699. Such charity schools were generally financed by subscribers, mostly laymen, and run by shareholders on joint-stock principles. Some were inter-denominational within Protestantism. Other schools had sprung from bequests. Thus at Hallaton in Leicestershire early in the century there was a school for poor children, financed out of a bequest, where a master taught twenty children the catechism and led them to church on Sundays. The town also had a small Dissenting school. Later the scheme of holding school on Sunday won favour (in 1787 one estimate put the number of children attending Sunday school at 250,000). Sunday school did not interfere with the working week, and would keep children out of mischief on their free day.

Methodists also set up schools for labourers' children, principally giving religious instruction. 'Our method of educating our children is this,' explained Mary Fletcher, a Methodist schoolmistress, in 1764: 'As our design is to fit them for good servants, we endeavour as early as possible to inure them to labour, early rising, and cleanliness.' She let pupils have fifteen minutes a day recreation in the garden, but ensured 'they do so with a degree of seriousness and they know it is for their health'. No indulgences were allowed: 'We never use the term play, nor suffer any to give those toys or playthings, which children are usually brought up to spend half their time in.'

Charity schools for the lower orders formed part of a tissue of conspicuous philanthropy. Upwards of 1,700 were set up. Many clothed their pupils, free or cheaply, in a distinctive uniform, and annual church services were held to praise God and the subscribers (a mammoth congregation was held at St Paul's). Taking boys and girls together, they taught a straight and narrow curriculum, principally reading and Scripture. Catechizing was the staple fare. Some instructed in writing as well, though others forbade it as prejudicial. The emphasis was above all on discipline: pupils were made to chant rhymes like

> It is a sin
> To steal a pin.

Mechanical methods of instruction and repetitive drill were taken up, partly to simulate workshop discipline and partly for economy. In the last years of the century Andrew Bell's system of rote teaching using pupil monitors offered itself as 'the Steam Engine of the Moral World'.

What, then, was the impact of education? Neither the state nor the Church enforced a uniform system of indoctrination; educational licensing had effectively broken down. The result was a pot-pourri of distinct sorts of schoolings, ranging from dame schools to Eton, and not omitting fashionable Rousseauism, pioneered by Thomas Day and Richard Edgeworth. In this educational free market, the instruction children got, determined by parental choice and pocket, tended to *reinforce* existing social, cultural and gender distinctions rather than break them down and make new ones. This was not a century in which there were masses of eager but 'over-qualified' scholarship boys trying to storm the citadels of state, or heavy 'graduate unemployment'. Literacy rates were gently rising (though they slumped again among the masses in the years of rampant population increase and social disruption during the early industrial revolution). Almost all males from the middle class and above were literate, but little more than half the population of labouring men (women were proportionally less literate).

Literacy was, however, counting for more: with the emergence of newspapers and magazines there was more to read. The ploughboy could still rap on the farmhouse door asking for work, but skilled operatives would also scan the 'situations vacant' section of the newspaper. More widespread reading made the culture more metropolitan, more immediate, uniform and modern. Yet literacy was certainly not indispensable. Much was then committed to memory which we now commit to writing. 'Bridging' processes, such as reading out loud to others, brought the written word to the illiterate. It was a century in which rising demand for education, and, awareness of its manipulative uses, called new schools into being; but the schooled were far from the sum of the educated. The bedrock of literacy and learning came not from school but from self-help, the family or the community.

It is hard to judge the impact of the more blatantly manipulative charity schools. Their managers were themselves in a cleft stick: should they emphasize literacy, numeracy and Scripture? Or should they chiefly run schools of industry, where children would repay expenses by spinning, picking oakum, beating hemp, knitting or performing similar menial chores? Schools of industry in the event failed to pay for themselves. Furthermore, there was the dilemma of how schools could simultaneously teach subordination while whetting ambition. Did charity and Sunday schools successfully teach the poor respect and play a normalizing function? What seems beyond doubt is that charity schools did not succeed in winning the loyalties of the lower orders to Anglicanism. The danger of sowing dragons' teeth was ever present. It was far easier to teach people to read than subsequently to direct their reading.

Like the discipline of family and school, religion indoctrinated people for life. It gave divine reasons for social relations, spelling out mutual responsibilities, the bonds between the dead and the living, the duties of the present generation to the unborn. Divinity explained the riddles of existence and taught salvation through Christ crucified, but the Georgians knew piety was also social medicine – or at least a placebo. Marx's 'discovery' that worship was an opiate would have been greeted with barely stifled yawns. 'It is certain,' wrote Addison,

> the Country-people would soon degenerate into a land of Savages and Barbarians were there not such frequent returns of a stated time, in which the whole village meet together in Church with their best faces, and in their cleanest habits, to converse with one another upon indifferent subjects, hear their duties explained to them, and join together in Adoration of the Supreme Being.

Many Georgians rarely went through a church porch between their christening and burial. Yet practically everyone, in his own fashion, had faith. Much of it was a fig leaf of Christianity covering a body of inherited magic and superstition, little more than Nature worship (the polite, doctrinally correct form of this was known as 'natural religion'). But everyone had his own vision of a Creator, of a 'place' in Heaven, and convictions of Good and Evil, reward and punishment. Though many were careless about performing their devotions, Dr Johnson was right to say 'there are in reality very few infidels'. Deism – belief in a non-personal Deity, lacking Christianity's historical Incarnation – made headway among intellectuals early in the century, sickened by sectarian fanatics, Popery and clericalism. But once Christians allowed their sword of persecution to sleep in their hands, the particular attractiveness of Deism and free-thought waned. The most prickly intellectual challenges to the foundations of belief were to come not from atheists but from heretics on the inside. The most notorious Georgian materialist was not some flash *philosophe* but the Bible fundamentalist and millennialist Joseph Priestley. Debate *within* theology remained heated, Anglican theology oscillating between rationalism and obscurantism, Dissenters divided over free-grace and Calvinist predestination. The reason for this was that it was difficult to adjust literalist dogma to the new material prosperity, science and freedom of inquiry. Religious divides went deep – this is evident from the reams of sermons and theological polemics published and avidly read – and only bashing the old bogey of Romism ('No Popery!') could unite Protestants.

Contemporaries voiced fears that the age was mumbling Christianity's *nunc dimittis*: worship had diminished, but ought to be increasing. 'There is less appearance of religion in England,' bemoaned Joseph Addison at the dawn of the century, 'than in any neighbouring state.' Visiting England, Montesquieu glossed this view: religion in England 'excites nothing but laughter'. Devotions withered. 'I was at home all day,' Thomas Turner confessed to his diary one Sunday, 'but not at church. O fye! No just reason for not being there.' Whereas in 1714 seventy-two churches in the metropolis had offered daily services, in 1728 the number had dwindled to fifty-two, and by 1732 there were but forty-four. The liturgical temperature sank. Parson Woodforde almost never held services except on Sunday. The Revd William Holland in early-nineteenth-century Somerset fretted over his thin congregations. Among Anglicans, family prayers became uncommon. 'Oh! may religion once more rear up her head in this wicked and impious nation,' beseeched Thomas Turner, without seemingly doing much about it himself.

Yet beneath all the rationalism, worldliness and indifference, religious urges remained deep and strong. Samuel Johnson was terrified of damnation (by which he meant being 'sent to Hell, Sir, and punished everlastingly'). Searching for identity in his teens, Gibbon fleetingly became a Catholic convert, as did Boswell. Many instinctively believed in special providences and omens. When his razor snapped while shaving one Sunday,

Parson Woodforde confided to his diary, 'May it be a warning to me not to shave on the Lord's Day, or to do any other work to profane it, *pro futuro*.' Even people who had no dispositions towards Damascus experiences knew religion was a charm to ward off ills and a social glue, rather as Lord Chesterfield commended at least lip-service to his son:

Depend upon this truth, that every man is the worse looked upon & the less trusted, for being thought to have no religion, in spite of all the pompous & specious epithets he may assume, of esprit fort, free thinker or moral philosopher; a wise atheist (if such a thing there is) would, for his own interest, & character in the world, pretend to some religion.

Georgian faith was practical and moderate. No less than Anglicans, mainstream Dissenters thought godliness should complement worldly virtue and prudence, rather than demanding abandonment of this vale of tears. Less was heard of original sin or of saintliness. Piety (preachers urged) ought to be natural, commonsensical, easy, the workaday world in Sunday suits. Near the close of the seventeenth century, the influential Archbishop Tillotson set the tone for Georgian moderate Anglicanism by thus characterizing Christ: 'His Virtues were shining without Vanity, Heroical without anything of Transport, and very extraordinary without being in the least extravagant.' Spellbinders who preached demonic possession and ecstasy, devils and spirits, the new birth, grace abounding, or even the transforming power of the Cross, were now treated with great suspicion as 'fanatics' by new 'Latitudinarian' churchmen and laymen alike. 'Enthusiasm,' concluded Joseph Butler, Bishop of Durham, 'is a very horrid thing.'

Opinion-leaders complimented themselves on their religious moderation: there had been much, they believed, in religion in need of being moderated. Faith ought to be a force for restraint and civilization. Desperate for security after generations of blistering sectarian strife, Georgians saw meekness as the Gospel's first commandment. In a sermon delivered in 1715, the Bishop of Gloucester accused zealots of wreaking 'more cruelty, wars, massacres, burnings, more hatred, animosity, perverseness, and peevishness' than almost anyone else. Fanatic Puritans had fomented civil war a century earlier, making a mockery of Christ's ministry of peace. And Papist Jacobites were inveterate plotters, designing to topple the state. By contrast, 'His commandments are not grievous' and 'Be not righteous overmuch' became hallowed texts for the Latitudinarian 'Christianity without tears' sermons read from Anglican pulpits throughout the century, syncopated (so Hogarth depicted) to the snores of their slumbering congregations.

Georgians could urge that the spirit of religion was peace, not the crusading sword, partly because the epoch of persecution was indeed ceasing. Though animosities continued, the Act of Toleration (1690) had guaranteed religious freedom, with certain strings attached. The Anglican Church was, admittedly, established by law (bulging tithe barns were its witness). Anglicans were privileged: choice areas of the state, such as the universities and civil office, were out of bounds to those beyond the Anglican communion, and Catholic recusants still paid mulcts. In reality, however, Protestant Dissenters who could stomach the palaver of occasionally taking Anglican communion need not have their ambition thwarted. Nearly forty 'occasionally conforming' Dissenters became MPs during the century, many others becoming London aldermen; for a span of sixty years the mayors of Nottingham were Dissenters, and in London, a number of Jews even held local government office.

And if the front door of the state was still only just ajar to non-Anglicans, less stigma was now attached to those who sported their minority religion like gentlemen. Witness the Catholic Lord Petre, an aristocrat of easy spirituality, who, though of Jacobite descent, entertained George III at Thorndon in 1779, and confirmed his influence as a borough-monger. 'I have lived here above thirty years,' the Catholic Sir Henry Arundel pointed out to his friend Lord Hardwicke, 'and thanks to the lenity of ye government, without ever having had the least molestation given me.' Nonconformists and Anglicans cooperated on philanthropic and missionary endeavours. True, stiff-necked sectaries were liable to be vilified and – like Defoe – occasionally set in the pillory. But this amounts to little when it is remembered that the entire Protestant population was expelled from France in 1685, and heretics were still being burnt throughout the century in Catholic Europe, Pietists likewise in Calvinist Switzerland.

In England private faiths were tolerated: 'each man,' so Defoe put it, 'goes his own byway to heaven.' It was a land of a hundred sects (even if – as Voltaire's quip went – there was only one sauce). And since, as Voltaire also observed, a single religion in a country spelt tyranny, and two, civil war, but a plurality meant peace, England's was a highly enviable situation:

Enter the London stock exchange [wrote Voltaire], that place more respectable than many a court. You will see the deputies of all nations gathered there for the service of mankind. There a Jew, a Mohammedan, and the Christian deal with each other as if they were of the same religion, and give the name of infidel only to those who go bankrupt; here the Presbyterian trusts the Anabaptist, and the Anglican honours the Quaker promise. On leaving these free and peaceful assemblies, some go to the synagogue, others to drink; this one goes to have himself baptized in the name of the Father, the Son and the Holy Ghost; that one has his son's foreskin cut off and Hebrew words mumbled over the child which he does not understand; others go to church to await the inspiration of God, their hats on their heads; and all are content.

Toleration was not just good for religion: it was good for commerce as well.

The Anglican Church was the nation's largest and wealthiest institution, spearheaded by twenty-six bishops, each occupying a cathedral in which deans, canons and prebends officiated (the higher clergy numbered some 1,000 in all). Beneath these, there were some 10,000 parishes – the whole of England was emparished. The Church's local pull was, of course, enhanced by the fact that the ecclesiastical parish also doubled as the cell of local government (parsons were appointed as JPs in increasing numbers).* Rectors and vicars – now almost all graduates – were presented to livings by ecclesiastical and lay patrons (in mid-eighteenth-century Oxfordshire only 11 per cent of advowsons actually lay in the Church's gift), getting their income out of tithes and by farming the glebe. Many parsons were non-resident and pluralist, having installed cut-price curates to perform their ministry (these got 'leavings' not 'livings'). About a quarter of parishes did not have a resident minister, and this situation worsened. In Devon in the 1740s just over half the rectors were non-resident; by 1780 that had risen to nearly 70 per cent. The Church maintained its own system of spiritual courts, though

---

* It is revealing that when Richard Gough set out to survey all the inhabitants of Myddle, a Shropshire village, in 1700, he described the people pew by pew.

these were waning, and also a monopoly grip on English universities. Only subscribing Anglicans could graduate, and almost all dons were in holy orders, as were most grammar-school masters. Yet if the Church had a strong grip on society, government had a stronger grip upon the Church. From 1717 central Church government (Convocation) was prorogued by the Whigs, fearing the rabid Toryism of its lower house. Thereafter the Church had no independent, corporate spiritual leadership of its own, for prelates were generally thick as thieves with the politicians who were their nursing fathers.

As an institution, the Church kept its books in comfortable balance through the century. Input was adequate: there was no shortage of ordinands. Tithes grew in value. By mid-century a few episcopal incomes were topping £5,000 a year (Archbishop Hutton made a clear £50,000 out of twelve years' tenure at York). Output was also maintained. Few Anglican clergy failed to perform their undemanding duties. Parsons may have been, as Crabbe styled them, 'cassock'd huntsmen and fiddling priests' ('ropes of sand' in Wesley's words). But they intoned their weekly sermons with correct diction, married couples, baptized their children and buried the dead (occasionally even saying prayers on saints' days). This may have been all they did, but few parishioners expected them to be red-hot evangelists, or even very saintly shepherds of their flocks (though they had to be blameless and make up a rubber at whist with the squire). Georgian parsons were thought none the worse for not believing that faith was something you wrestled with. George Pryme recollected that, in his youth in the 1780s, 'if a rector performed the service on a sunday, and visited the sick *when sent for*, it was thought quite sufficient.' At Weston Longueville it was an innovation when, in 1777, Woodforde said prayers on Good Friday.

Most bishops were businesslike diocesan managers, efficient at conducting visitations and holding mass confirmations. Above all, the higher clergy served their political masters well. 'He resides as much as any bishop in his diocese,' Viscount Percival complimented Bishop Willcock of Gloucester in 1730,

at least four months in the year, and keeps a very generous and hospitable table, which makes amends for the learning he is deficient in.

Though no great scholar nor a deep man, he is a very frequent preacher and this with his zeal for the government, good humour and regular life, makes him very well liked by the government and all that know him.

If few parsons were saints, few were utterly scandalous – though a handful were highly eccentric, including Laurence Sterne, author of *Tristram Shandy*, and Martin Madan, passionate advocate of polygamy as the answer to society's ills. The fabric of churches was often allowed to fall into picturesque disrepair, but parsonages were improved. Gentlemen of the cloth kept their genteel patrons happy, comfortable in their private, curtained, upholstered box pews, heated if not with spirit at least with stoves. They preached obedient deference, and not just to God. Because preachers readily supposed that virtue, temporal success and heavenly prospects formed a harmonious Trinity – the politically or socially radical parson was a rare bird indeed – very few of the pedigree flock deserted the Anglican fold to browse in heterodox pastures.

Yet the Established Church did not have a very positive hold on the hearts and hopes of ordinary parishioners, many of whom were at best a surly captive congregation (under the squire's eye, in the lady's retinue), or were absentees – in some cases worshipping elsewhere. Masterless men – many of the urban tradesman class, for example – found Protestant Dissent sympathetic. The gentry fretted at the heathenism of the common people (and specifically at their non-Anglicanism). Even in the depths of the countryside, the bulk of the population (many of whom loathed parsons as gentrified tithe-gatherers) may not have been regular church-goers. Slapton in Devon had only thirty-two communicants out of 200 families; nearby Churchstow had forty-three families, just four of whom were communicants. In mid-century Oxfordshire, only about one person took communion for every three families. And things were getting worse. Thirty Oxford parishes which between them had 911 communicants in 1738 had just 685 in 1802. Only about one in ten English people took Easter Communion with the national church in 1801. But little was done to change things. Parishioners could no longer be prosecuted for not going to church, and curates, some paid less than £10 a year by absentee rectors, commonly could not afford

to reside in their parishes, riding over every so often to take a service.

The spectre of lower-class unbelief worsened with population
rise and redistribution. As Midland and Northern hamlets mushroomed into industrial centres and ribbon settlements spread up
valleys, the old jigsaw of parish boundaries bore ever less resembl-
ance to actual population. Industrializing Lancashire and Cheshire
had only 156 parishes; Essex, Suffolk and Norfolk had 1,634.
Concentrations of people were left with grotesquely inadeqate
church accommodation. Manchester, with some 20,000 people in
1750, had one parish church. In 1800 Marylebone had a population of 40,000 but one sole Anglican church, seating 200. By
1812 there were just 186 Anglican places of worship in London,
compared to 256 Dissenting. And within churches, space-eating
box pews, providing comfort to the rich, could not be replaced
by bench-pews, for they were sacred private property.

The Church of England thus made it easy for Dissenting
congregations to move in. Their form of church government
was devolved, voluntaristic and flexible, their ministers maintained by the worshippers, though they might have to top up
their income by schoolmastering. Red tape and property rights
made it so much more difficult for the Church of England to
adapt to a new society. Building new churches meant endowing
new parishes to support incumbents, thereby reducing others,
robbing St Peter's to pay St Paul's. Plans drawn up by reformers
such as Edmund Gibson, Bishop of London, for rationalization
of church income met successful resistance. The London Churches
Act of 1711 set money aside to erect churches, but only ten out
of a projected fifty were actually constructed, largely because the
trustees opted for a small number of architectural gems rather
than the full quota of functional ones. The year 1800 dawned
with the Anglican Church ill-equipped to serve the nation.

How much was it missed? Many Dissenting ministers spoke
direct to common people's hearts, and certain Anglicans had
long been alert to this need. Anglican voluntary societies (such as
the Society for the Propagation of the Gospel and the Society for
the Promotion of Christian Knowledge) sought the ears of
ordinary people, through charity schools, tracts and, later, Sunday
schools. Masses of cheap Anglican literature, from the *New
Whole Duty of Man* to Hannah More's uplifting tracts, peddled

religion to the poor. But was this fare palatable? Did the poor really take to heart prayers like this one from the *New Whole Duty of Man*?

Oh God, I believe that for just & wise reasons thou hast allotted to mankind very different states & circumstances of life, & that all the temporal evils which have at any time happened unto me, are designed by thee for my benefit: therefore, though thou hast thought fit to place me in a mean condition, to deprive me of many conveniences of life, & to exercise me in a state of poverty, yet thou hast hitherto preserved & supported me by thy good providence, & blessed me with advantages above many others . . .

One movement within Anglicanism undoubtedly had the common touch. That was Methodism. Wesley was far from the only evangelist in the eighteenth-century Church, the religion of the heart speaking in many different tongues. There was Wesley's silver-voiced co-worker George Whitefield (who thought Archbishop Tillotson had known no more about religion than Mahomet), and William Law in Oxford; there were field preachers such as Samuel Walker of Truro, John Berridge of Everton, the Yorkshireman William Damey, and in Wales Hywel Davies, Daniel Rowland and Howell Harris; and from the 1770s a powerful Evangelical revival got under way. But Wesley was unique as an Anglican evangelist in preaching to the savage 'pagans' of society ('poor almost to a man', as he described his congregations), while organizing his ministry as a national missionary movement. 'I love the poor. In many of them I find pure genuine grace, unmixed with paint, folly & affectation.' In the sentiments of his brother Charles's hymn,

> The rich and great in every age
> Conspire to persecute their God.
> Our Saviour by the rich unknown
> Is worshipped by the poor alone.

John Wesley was a true-blue Anglican. He was Arminian in his theology, believing in salvation for all; High Church and High Tory in his politics, a paladin of the Crown and the law; and loyal to the Church of England to his dying day (he detested Dissent and stood out against Methodists separating, wanting at most to institute a church within a church). But his religious practice was everything the Church's wasn't. An itinerant preacher who saw the whole world as his parish, Wesley put England's new turnpikes to the test, riding during his long career some 25,000 miles and preaching 40,000 sermons, many in the open air. A fanatic 'brand plucked from the burning', he was an arch-critic of Mammon's profligates. 'To speak the rough truth,' he wrote, 'I do not desire any discourse with any person of quality in England.' His 'vital religion', flaming out in mesmerizing sermons and passionate hymns, melted the hearts of scoffers and the indifferent. Hardbitten mining communities and fishing villages immune to charity schools, tracts and other forms of soup-kitchen religion from above embraced Wesley's heart-cleansing salvationism.

Of course, Wesley taught resignation, obedience and subordination. 'He who plays when he is a child, will play when he is a man,' he pronounced; 'avoid all lightness as you would avoid hell-fire.' His way with children was short: 'Break his will now, and his soul shall live, and he will probably bless you to all eternity.' Disorder haunted him: 'Mend your clothes, or I shall never expect you to mend your lives.' Yet he was also self-critical, seeing how easily, how inevitably, Methodist spirituality might fossilize into numb, worldly respectability. 'In every place,' he noted with concern,

the Methodists . . . grew diligent and frugal; consequently they increase in goods. Hence, they proportionally increase in pride, in anger, in the desire of the flesh, the desire of the eyes, and the pride of life. So, although the form of religion remains, the spirit is swiftly vanishing away.

Methodism's importance must not be pre-dated. There were only 24,000 Methodists in 1767 and 77,000 by 1796. Hence it is only through an optical illusion that certain historians see Methodism as having 'saved' England from a 'French Revolution' – or indeed as having almost caused one. Nor did it remain unified. By the end of the century, Wesleyanism was recruiting in more presentable quarters, thereby speeding its own fissure into authoritarian and populist elements ('Primitive Methodists'). Yet Methodism became the century's most fertile new national organization, sustained from the grassroots if inspired, commanded and dogmatized over from the centre, for each congregation had its own governing cell sending delegates to an annual conference, at which Wesley passed down the tablets of the law. It challenged the Establishment more than any contemporary political movement, because it had the power to generate enduring self-respect and self-government among its converts, and because Methodist ministers escaped the obloquy of being parasitic tithe-gatherers. The Wesleyan connection proved fertile in many directions, leading to the political radicalism of many Primitive Methodists and the sturdy self-help culture of the artisan lay preacher.

Those who attacked Wesley – many with stones – were correct to see his 'inner light' teachings, his hysteria-raising sermonizing, his lay preachers, his passionate eucharistic love feasts (practices, judged Dr Johnson, 'utterly incompatible with social or civil society'), as time-bombs planted under complacent Latitudinarianism. Augustus Toplady (Evangelical author of the hymn 'Rock of Ages') condemned Wesley's views as 'an equal portion of gross heathenism, Pelagianism, Mahometanism, popery, Manichaeism, ranterism, and antinomianism'. Squires and parsons incited mobs to pelt 'Pope John' – Wesley noted how the gentry often 'headed the mob in person'. Ladies such as Elizabeth Prowse dismissed servants who attended meetings.

Methodism, of course, suffered inner contradictions: a populist movement led from above by an egoistical and authoritarian prophet; a spiritual and transcendental faith which insisted on worldly discipline and industry. Yet the ostrich-like scions of the Church believed they did not even need to grapple with these paradoxes, thinking they could just anathematize Wesleyanism and ignore what it galvanized. Wesley challenged the bishops to come to terms with independent religious witness at the grassroots. Their response was to drive it out of the Church. Thereafter the national church largely parted with popular faith.

Many denominations carved out niches for themselves in Georgian England. Because religion was as concerned with orderly conduct as with faith or theology, confessional allegiances typically reinforced, rather than cut across, social boundaries. Thus, for example, in addition to its old recusant communities, English Catholicism was increasingly identified with immigrant Irish labourers. The number of Catholic gentry fell, as many made the pilgrimage to Canterbury. For it was a strain to be a gentleman without being an Anglican. Once-Catholic lords such as Sefton, Molyneux, Gascoyne and Montague, unwilling to remain on the social margins, converted, and with them went their flocks. The 115,000 Catholics of 1720 had shrunk to a mere 69,000 by 1780. Even gentry who remained Catholic reintegrated themselves into the community; fewer sent their daughters abroad for a nunnery education. Nicholas Blundell, impenitent head of a prominent family of Lancashire Catholics, served on the Anglican vestry.

Similarly, the old Puritan gentry trickled over into Anglicanism. Dissenters being second-class citizens, the cream of them were under pressure to convert: as the cynic put it, 'The Dissenter's second horse carried him to Church.' Wealth and status seduced even some of the normally stiff Quakers. The Gurney family, for instance, gave up being 'plain' and became 'gay' (worldly), and successful Quaker businessmen such as Ambrose Crowley and the Barclays went over to Anglicanism. Dissenters faced the dilemma of being neither persecuted nor privileged. The letter of the Corporation and Test Acts disqualified them from the trophies of office; yet, in the absence of persecution, Old Dissent lost its spur to zeal and minded its own business, and the grandchildren of revolutionary Puritans became quietist, inward-looking and even lukewarm, as worldly in their own prim way as Anglicans. Early in the century there were about 179,000 Presbyterians, 59,000 Independents (or Congregationalists), 58,000 Baptists and 38,000 Quakers. Many sidled over to conformity or just became indifferent. The tally of Dissenters may have fallen by up to 40 per cent between 1700 and 1740.

Dissenters tended to be a good deal more strait-laced in lifestyle than their Anglican brethren, but their worship – especially Presbyterians' – became equally moderate, anti-enthusiastic and morality-minded. Their church government, with its prominent place for lay 'elders', was hierarchical. As with Anglicans, wealthy Dissenters owned their own pews or raised seats (servants sat at the back) and exercised patronage. Many meetings required a guinea a year subscription to qualify for a say. Since elders and their friends were paying for their ministers, they called the tune even more directly than rich Anglican parishioners usually could. Old Dissent was essentially bourgeois. 'The main body of Dissenters are mostly found in cities & great towns among the trading part of the people,' reflected John White in 1746,

& their ministers are chiefly of the middle rank of men, having neither poverty nor riches . . . If I had a son brought up in any trade & had no consideration either for him or myself in another world, I should be ready to say to him at setting up, – *my son, get Money & in order to do that, be a Dissenter.*

In 1730 the Dissenting leader, Philip Doddridge, candidly admitted in tell-tale terms that Nonconformity was not catering for 'the plain people of low education and vulgar taste'. His own very correct meeting-house expelled members for 'failing in the world', through bad debts or extravagance.

Bourgeois Nonconformity contributed something unique to English culture: scruple. Theirs was an earnest, conscientious desire to exercise control – over self and others alike – for righteousness's sake. To a liberal conscience they added a demure seriousness that could teeter towards self-righteousness and casuistry. They were the great discoverers of 'deserving causes'. The prominent Dissenting writer Mrs Barbauld was one of many who gave up sugar in protest against slavery. They stood out as reformers, doctors and educators of youth, dissenting practitioners being conspicuous in towns such as Liverpool, Manchester and Chester in campaigning for better public health, hospitals and the moralization of the poor. Quakers in particular mobilized opinion against the slave trade, before its abolition was piloted through Parliament by Wilberforce, the Anglican Evangelical leader.

Most Protestant Dissenters, from skilled artisans up to the most opulent merchants, professional men and manufacturers, were townsfolk. Nearly a third of the populations of Bristol and Norwich were Nonconformist. Country areas noted for weaving, especially in the West Country, also had high Nonconformist concentrations. In certain parliamentary constituencies, for instance Tiverton, Dissent formed an electoral lobby with real leverage. In politics, Dissent, with its own pressure group, the Dissenting Deputies, was prepared to trail the coats of Whiggery even though Walpole had failed to repeal the Test and Corporation Acts (Tories were implacably hostile to Dissent). Walpole placated Dissenters with money out of the privy purse for ministers' widows. Dissenters wanted civil equality and redress, but their zeal for socio-political reform should not be exagger-

ated. The prominent Nonconformist, John Aikin, characteristically dismissed Tom Paine: 'he is not like a gentleman'. Not
till the 1780s, and then only among a hothead minority, did
Nonconformity show a potential for political radicalism.

Escape from the harassment suffered under the later Stuarts took
the millennialist strain out of other Dissenting groups such as the
Baptists and Congregationalists (though they remained believers
in a Calvinist elect), and overall numbers of all Dissenting sects
dropped. Rural districts were worst hit. Hampshire, which had
forty Presbyterian chapels in 1729, was down to two in 1812.
Unlike Anglicanism, however, Dissent was always in ferment. Its
fabric was open-textured. Dissent had early spawned a plethora of
sects and schisms, and (though each group had its own 'tests') there
was no single test of orthodoxy, unlike the Thirty-nine Articles
within the Anglican Communion. Dissenting conventicles were at
bottom self-governing. Hence Nonconformist fission constantly
produced its own dissidents, a very diverse brood. At one extreme
there sprang up Antinomians and Millennialists, Moravians and
Sandemanians, and other tiny, exclusive pentecostal cells, empha-
sizing scriptural literalism, personal conversion and emotional,
participatory worship. At the other end of the spectrum, some
became more rational and liberal, gravitating towards Arianism,
Socinianism and Unitarianism – all more or less repudiating the
divinity of Christ, the Trinity and the miracles and mysteries of
Christianity. Joseph Johnson, the radical Unitarian publisher, had
been brought up as a Particular Baptist; Joseph Priestley, the
leading Unitarian, was of a Calvinist Independent background.
William Godwin, son of a Dissenting minister, moved via Sande-
manianism to pantheism. (Though most Unitarians had journeyed
through Dissent, some had started off Anglicans, such as Theophilus Lindsey and Gilbert Wakefield.) By the close of the century
Unitarians were an articulate minority seeking to purify and
rescue religion by purging it of all but liberal politics and middle-
class morality. Whether seen as Protestant radicalism (fidelity to
one's intellect and scruples) or as what Erasmus Darwin called a
'feather bed to catch a falling Christian', Unitarianism, which
early in the eighteenth century had been a clerical fringe, drew a
growing lay following, especially among such expanding professional groups as scientists, publishers, writers, reformers, campaigners and educators – the grandfathers of Victorian honest doubters.

Because Dissent had not sunk into a morass of livings, rights to present, tithes and patronage squabbles, it was flexible, with scope to adapt and expand. In the last third of the century, a 'New Dissent' gained ground, recruiting down the social order, wooing and winning artisans in fast-growing industrial areas. The 15,000 Congregationalists of 1750 had swollen to 35,000 by 1800; the Particular (that is, Calvinist) Baptists went up from 10,000 to 24,000. The race for the souls of the emergent labour aristocracy finished in a dead-heat between Dissent and Methodism. Evangelical missions of New Dissent had success in the countryside too. 'Almost the whole country is open for village preaching,' proclaimed the Baptist John Rippon in 1798.

In Georgian much more than Stuart times, religious communion generally cemented pre-existing social bonds. Anglicanism was polite society, or the squire-dominated village, at prayer; Old Dissent was the meeting of craftsmen and solid provincial traders in their Sunday best; Methodism became the faith of isolated workforces such as colliers. Rarely did religious affiliation *create* independent social adhesion where none had existed before. Fringe sects, however, promised just this. Cellular congregations of the 'perfect', led by born-again prophets, attracted urban lost souls. New Worlders of the 1790s such as the disciples of Joanna Southcott (who claimed she was to give birth to Shiloh, to 'rule all nations with a rod of iron') and Richard Brothers (self-styled nephew to the Almighty), remind us that many Georgians, castaway upon the anonymous, lonely seas of megalopolis, found hope in rebirth and religious utopias. Drawing upon a common disgust with the Babylonical times, their leaders took such sentiments to lengths of logic and literalness that few would follow. Sectaries saw visions of a New Jerusalem, even a green and pleasant Albion. Lord George Gordon, one-time fanatic anti-papist, became a long-bearded convert to Judaism. James Graham, former pedlar of health through sex-therapy and mudbaths, later founded the 'New and True Christian Church', practised Adamic nakedness, and died insane. Prophetic anger flamed into art in the pen and brush of William Blake, baptized in the streams of mystical underground religion. The most stable group whose religious protocols created a tight community set apart were the Quakers. Rather like the Jews (of whom there were about 10,000), Friends segregated themselves by their distinctive, aggressively humble manners, antiquated sombre dress and plain speech ('theeing'), and above all by the requirement of marrying in. Those who married out were thrown out, as were culpable bankrupts. Quakers were not proselytizers; they became closed and quietist and declined in numbers from about 38,000 in 1700 to about 20,000 in 1800. But this evaporation left them socially more select: the proportion of merchants and professional men rose, while that of artisans declined.

Friends were in a quandary. Their origins lay in persecution and in George Fox's noble egalitarianism; they rejected war and despised the insolence of rank and the idiocies of Vanity Fair. There were no Friends in high places. Yet in the workaday world many were bankers, corn-dealers, brewers and arms-manufacturing iron-masters, with money coming out of their ears: the Peases, Barclays, Frys, Reynoldses, Perkinses. They contained these contradictions by scrupulous plain dealing (Quakers pioneered fixed-price retailing), industriousness, loyal support of other Friends, family solidarity, philanthropy and blamelessness. Firms such as the Quaker London Lead Company championed industrial welfare for their employees. Quaker meeting-houses were 'schools for the inculcation of business and clubs for encouraging the practice of them'. The long-lasting family firms of the Gurneys, Lloyds, Wilkinsons, Darbys, Backhouses and others form a muster of undissipated industrial talent unmatched elsewhere in the eighteenth-century world.

Religion in Georgian England rubber-stamped social, power and property relations, generally ingrained already. Denominational boundaries sanctified social divides more than they cut across them. Stuart religious fervour had sowed dragons' teeth, producing sectarian strife, civil war and visionaries awaiting the Second Coming. Georgian piety by contrast ambled along with society. Yet this detracts neither from religion's sincerity nor its importance. Religion was still the language people spoke in earnest, on oath. For all the self-congratulatory rationalism of the Enlightenment, it was Christian zealots who were the selfless reformers of abuses: John Howard – the Captain Cook of the prisons – Thomas Clarkson and Granville Sharp, campaigners against the slave trade. What first galvanized large sections of the workforce into self-help and self-respect were not polite letters,

Enlightenment rationalism or Deism, but Methodism and New Dissent. And when polite society itself felt the earthquake tremors of revolution at the close of the century, it was to religious scourging and revival – to God – that it turned. Religion was still the idiom of the people, though its accents and dialects were many. By 1800 English piety was decisively shaped by social rank. Denomination itself had become a litmus of social position.

5. *Getting and Spending*

Every country and every age has dominant terms, which seem to obsess men's thoughts. Those of eighteenth century England were property contract, trade and profits. [Sir Lewis Namier]

Long before the eighteenth century the English economy had ceased to supply mere subsistence. Their ability to harness the surplus wealth-creating labour of wage-earners had long consolidated propertied ruling elites dominating production. The business of family formation, and of instilling values through education and religion, the interlocking of family, ownership and labour, production with reproduction, individual with community – all these ensured regular inheritance of capital goods, skills, drills and know-how from generation to generation. These self-adjusting mechanisms provided against catastrophe.

But on top of all this, there was a busy buzz of activity in Georgian England. The market economy went forth and multiplied, especially from mid-century, generating an effervescent atmosphere which encouraged individuals to try their fortune and prosper. There were fresh openings for men (and it was chiefly *males*) who were competitive, mobile, ambitious, resourceful or simply lucky enough to possess some capital or skills in demand. Economic expansion of course brought tensions and hardships. Economic individualism had centrifugal effects which threatened those least able to fend for themselves. The enrichment of farmers and manufacturers often involved the impoverishment and displacement of the labouring poor. But those who took the panoramic view saw prosperity smiling over the fast-changing landscape. 'You would not know your country again,' Horace Walpole told his friend Horace Mann, late in the century. 'You left it as a private island living upon its means. You would find it the capital of the world.' Especially after manufacturing industry got up steam from the 1780s, the wealth of England admitted no doubters. As the republican French traveller Meister wrote, with very mixed feelings, at the close of the century:

Why is the soil of England so well cultivated? It is because England is rich. Why is England the seat of liberty? It is because England is rich. Why does England at present pay so little regard to the attainments of art and literature? It is because England is too rich . . . Why is England not more peaceable and happy? It is because England is too rich. Gold is the sun of the nation.

But long before, it had become a platitude that England was an unusually prosperous island, her trade robust, bustling and success-ful. 'The great British Empire, the most flourishing and opulent country in the world,' trumpeted Defoe: 'no clothes can be made to fit a growing child.' Two foreigners he met at Bushey Heath confided to him, 'England was not like the other countries, but it was all a planted garden.' In the 1760s Smollett could purr, 'I see the country of England smiling with cultivation: the grounds exhibiting all the perfection of agriculture, parcelled out into beautiful enclosures, corn fields, hay pasture, woodland and commons.' Henry Homer agreed: 'Everything wears the face of dispatch; every article of our produce becomes more valuable.' In the business community, confidence mounted.

The English supplanted the Dutch as the commercial top-dogs who scurried around buying, selling and money-making. 'There was never from the earliest ages,' thought Dr Johnson, 'a time in which trade so much engaged the attention of mankind, or commercial gain was sought with such general emulation.' The new discipline of political economy blessed the pursuit of profit, above all in Adam Smith's *Wealth of Nations* (1776), which advocated a high-production, high-consumption, high-wage eco-nomy. Anything that would turn a penny was tried. In London you could hire spy-glasses for $\frac{1}{2}$d. to view the Jacobite heads spiked on Temple Bar, and souvenir Tyburn rope fetched 6d. an inch. Getting and spending was everyone's business – at least everyone who could afford it. 'So great is the hurry in the spirit of the world,' lamented the Quaker John Woolman – though Quakers were certainly no exceptions – 'that in aiming to do business quickly and to gain wealth the Creation at this day doth groan.'

More than potential rivals such as Holland, England had the

right catalysts for sustained economic improvements. Vital raw materials were to hand, most on England's own doorstep, some from the colonies. Extractive industries flourished, coal (for heating, power and smelting in the non-ferrous metal trades) being especially plentiful, and in some places it was readily dug open-cast. In 1700 London used 800,000 tons of coal, in 1750, 1,500,000 tons, and by 1790, 2,500,000 tons, mainly for domestic and industrial heating.

Furthermore, England's political and legal infrastructure was favourable. With the fleeting exceptions of the '15 and the '45, English soil was not a battleground. There were no swingeing internal customs duties, like those that hamstrung traffic between German states and within France (though of course turnpikes and later canals took their toll). Great Britain was Europe's biggest common market. Adam Smith further highlighted the absolute protection that English law gave to private property:

That security which the laws in Great Britain give to every man that he shall enjoy the fruits of his own labour, is alone sufficient to make any country flourish ... In Great Britain industry is perfectly secure, and though it is far from being free, it is as free or freer than in any other part of Europe.

Thus commentators believed the state wasn't a clog to trade, as elsewhere – though commercial lobbies were perennially grumbling. There was no profits tax, no capital gains tax, no 'value added tax' on most manufactures. The policies of successive ministries switched tariffs to protect home manufactures and cheapen exports. So in 1700 import of silks and printed calicoes was banned, and Combination Acts forbade skilled craftsmen from emigrating. Most wars were waged in pursuit of trade. A smaller proportion of national wealth was being squandered on a dropsical bureaucracy, a giant permanent standing army or a pyrotechnical court than in most states. In 1783 Berlin housed 57,000 officials and soldiers among a total population of 141,000: its commercial and industrial bourgeoisie was insignificant. By contrast, in the boom towns of England, few people were not directly involved in the cash economy.

The economic infrastructure also met the needs of business well. This was, above all, the age of *commercial* capitalism. The techniques of exchange grew faster, cheaper, more reliable. The potential had long been present; for centuries nowhere had been very far from a market, a fair, even a crossroads. Thus Northampton had long been a thriving market for horses (as was Barnet fair), Uttoxeter for cheese, and Guildford for the bark used in tanning. But the Georgian century saw exchange quicken. 'An estate is but a pond,' wrote Defoe, 'but trade is a spring.' Quietly and piecemeal a comprehensive and flexible credit network took shape. The stability of the Bank of England — *parliamentary* not *Crown* credit — gave confidence to the fast-growing fraction of the public investing in the Funds or the chartered companies. Authorized to receive deposits and lend them out at interest, especially to the government, the Bank became so secure that it was able to draw large funds from abroad, particularly Holland. City banks — there were about twenty early in the century — accepted deposits, issued notes ('promises to pay') and discounted bills. They specialized in dealings with the aristocracy, particularly in raising mortgages and handling government securities. The paper-money economy grew. Bills of exchange passed into circulation from clients to shopkeepers, from retailers to wholesalers, from manufacturers to their raw-material suppliers. All forms of credit-worthy paper — even lottery tickets — tended to become negotiable and pass into circulation. In the provinces, merchants, goldsmiths and attorneys became bill-brokers and discounters (they often grumbled, yet such transactions proved profitable).

Credit transactions were vital, not least because England was endemically short of circulating coin (entrepreneurs resorted to issuing trade tokens which passed as money: the iron-master John Wilkinson's tokens were so valuable that they attracted forgers). Credit enabled business to expand by trading upon expectations, even if collapses often landed unfortunate parties in the Clink. Interest rates, moreover, remained low — fluctuating just above 3 per cent — because capital was plentiful. Whatever the project — land improvement, turnpikes, canals, building or colonial trade — cheap money appeared to finance it. Most businesses were stoked with privately raised family capital; manufacturers tapped hoarded wealth by begging their relations, entering into partnerships, or making judicious marriages. Thus Josiah Wedgwood got his initial capital through marriage to his cousin Sarah, daughter of a Cheshire cheese-dealer. Mortgaging enabled landowners to raise capital for building, enclosures, drainage, to underwrite jointures – or to pay off gambling debts! Turnpike trusts and canals got most of their capital from local shareholders, from grandees down to the £50 shares bought by scores of inn-keepers and widows. Modestly affluent people now found it more trouble-free to put their nest-eggs in secure capital invest-ments than in bits and pieces of land with all the attendant problems of management. Local attorneys, brewers, and merch-ants commonly acted as catalysts in raising and releasing capital. Such men had long provided informal banking facilities, but in the second half of the century country banks proper emerged, issuing their own notes. Coutts' bank was founded by an Edinburgh corn-dealer, Gurney's by a Norwich worsted-manufacturer. In 1750 there were just twelve country banks, by 1797, 290 (though they were not as secure as City banks, and many crashed). The development of insurance further safeguarded prop-erty. The Phoenix (1680) and the Sun Fire (1708) pioneered fire insurance in London; the Royal Exchange Assurance and Lloyds looked after marine insurance. Helped by actuarial science, life assurance was beginning to make headway.

England's successful trafficking economy was energized by highly favourable overseas trade, especially with the fast-growing empire. The merchant marine almost trebled from about 3,300 vessels (260,000 tons) in 1702 to about 9,400 ships (695,000 tons) in 1776. As Atlantic ports expanded, London's share declined from over 40 per cent to just under 30 per cent. England's grip on major primary producers – such as the Caribbean, Canada and India – tightened, and the Navigation Acts enforced a monopoly of carrying and entrepôt trade with the colonies. At the beginning of the century England was legally importing about £6,000,000 worth of goods each year and exporting about £6,470,000. By 1770 imports had doubled to about £12,200,000 and exports increased to £14,300,000. (The clandestine ledger of contraband would dramatically swell these figures.) Surviving records of shopkeepers, such as Abraham Dent of Kirkby Stephen, show that even in the depth of the countryside customers were daily being served with produce from the corners of the globe: ginger, molasses, cinnamon, quinine. Dent sold forty different types of cloth. In turn, English goods went to distant parts: Cheshire cheese was shipped to the Falkland Islands, Burton ales to the Baltic.

A thousand other developments expedited trade. For instance, foreigners complimented the English on their retailing. 'The magnificence of the shops,' wrote Von Archenholz, 'is the most striking thing in London.' Defoe underlined the key distributive role of shops (bright, glass-fronted and bow-windowed) in serving householders with goods from the length and breadth of the country – hangings from Kidderminster, a looking-glass from London, blankets from Witney, rugs from Westmorland. He rhapsodized over their sheer number: 'I have endeavoured to make some calculation of the number of shop-keepers in this kingdom, but I find it is not to be done – we may as well count the stars' (yet the old Puritan in him begrudged the outlay lavished on their tinsel display). Advertising swelled enormously, especially in newspapers. Between 1747 and 1750 Bottely's *Bath Journal* carried 2,740 advertisements, between 1780 and 1783, well over twice as many. Provincial newspapers especially alerted readers to metropolitan tastes. Thus a North Walsham staymaker told lady readers of the *Norwich Mercury* in 1788 'that he is just returned from Town with the newest Fashions of French and Italian Stays, Corsetts and Riding Stays . . . their Orders will be executed in an Height of Taste not inferior to the first shops in London' (who could resist?). A Newcastle-on-Tyne lady was demanding a Wedgwood dinner service with an 'Arabesque Border' before her local shopkeeper had even heard of it; she insisted on that precise pattern, having discovered it was 'much used in London at present', and refused to be fobbed off with substitutes. In 1777 Abigail Gawthern noted in her diary that she 'used a parasol for the first time . . . the first in Nottingham'. Advertising's role in puffing demand was clear to all. 'Promise, large promise, is the soul of advertisement,' wrote Dr Johnson, who believed 'the trade of advertising is now so near perfection that it is not easy to propose any improvement'. Advertising's allure whipped up demand for knick-knacks, curios, and all manner of disposable items, bought upon whim, and increased turnover in fashion. Handkerchiefs were hawked with Marlborough's five great victories painted on them; other designs celebrated Dr Sacheverell or the Peace of Utrecht. The radical John Wilkes's squinting face was plastered over mugs, jugs, teapots, plaques and plates.

England teemed with middlemen. The Tudor statutes governing marketing regulations for grain had almost denied the need for middlemen (traditionally branded as parasites), producers being required to sell in small quantities directly to the consumer at market. By the eighteenth century this system was increasingly obsolescent. More merchandise was being bought and sold in bulk, through advance contract, by wholesale capitalist butchers, drovers, grain-dealers, millers, brewers, maltsters and, not least, mere speculators. Though consumers, looking to the traditional 'moral economy' of the face-to-face regulated market, with its just price, decried such dealers as profiteers, in fact they were the inevitable off-shoots of concentrated production and the remorseless geographical broadening of the market. Only substantial middlemen could satisfy bulk demand from buyers such as government contractors (who required stockings for soldiers in lots of ten thousand) or the great brewers (who demanded thousands of bushels of barley of constant tip-top quality).

Last, communications improvements – even before the canal age – made exchange easier, widening markets and mobilizing effective demand. Engineering works extended navigable rivers from about 960 miles in 1700 to about 1,110 in 1726. The Aire and Calder navigation was improved to aid the Yorkshire woollen industry, the Weaver deepened to get Cheshire salt down to the Mersey. By 1750, the Don was made navigable up to Sheffield. But above all, the movement to turnpike roads gathered momentum. England's old roads were atrocious, largely because the bulk goods hauled in huge waggons rutted them, and livestock droves turned them into ribbon dungheaps. Foul roads long kept England a land of pedlars and packhorses.

Turnpike-building, by local private enterprise, started around London in Stuart times. Further afield it was patchier. As late as 1740, there was no turnpike on the London-to-Edinburgh road north of Grantham, and the journey could still take over a fortnight (it was quicker by sea). By 1750, however, the trunk roads connecting London to such major cities as Manchester, Bristol, Birmingham, York and Dover had all been turnpiked.

These Georgian 'motorways' produced their own booming sub-economy of inns, ostlers, coachmen and coaching services, highwaymen and illicit game-dealers. Foreigners complimented the English on their hostelries (though some remained insufferable: 'God sends meat,' spat John Byng, dining at one, 'but the

Devil sends cooks'). Turnpiking also spurred horse-breeding – the eighteenth century has rightly been called the 'age of the horse'. Cleveland bays were the favoured coach horses, though Suffolk Punches and Clydesdales were preferred as shire beasts. Better roads made haulage quicker, safer and more efficient. Henry Homer estimated in 1767 that 'the carriage of grain, coal, merchandise, etc., is in general conducted with little more than half the number of horses' formerly used. Regular passenger stage-coach services were established. Another spin-off was the setting-up of a reliable and swift (but not cheap) mail delivery.

'Good roads, canals and navigable rivers are the greatest of all improvements,' judged Adam Smith. Visitors certainly admired English highways. 'These roads are magnificent,' wrote César de Saussure in the 1720s, 'being wide, smooth and well kept.' Not all were, of course – some left the agricultural writer Arthur Young apoplectic: 'The country from Tetbury to Oxford is extremely disagreeable, barren, wild, and almost uninhabited. The road is called, by a vile prostitution of language, a turnpike, but christened, I apprehend by people who knew not what a road is.' There were 109 Turnpike Acts between 1720 and 1750, 389 from 1751 to 1772. In 1750, 143 turnpike trusts covered 3,400 miles, by 1770, 500 trusts administered in 5,000 miles of roads.

Turnpikes were new, and supposedly better maintained, but not until late in the century did engineers like Blind John Metcalfe, Thomas Telford, and John MacAdam substantially improve surface quality, reduce gradients, and replace fords and ferries with bridges. And turnpikes certainly didn't make bulk freight or travelling cheap (canals did): coaches charged 2d. or 3d. a mile; in 1774 it cost Parson Woodforde a stiff £4 8s. to cover the 100 miles from Oxford down to Castle Cary in Somerset by post-chaise. Yet road improvement assuredly axed travelling times, as the following list of times (in hours) taken to get to London shows:

	1700	*1750*	*1800*
Norwich	50	40	19
Bath	50	40	16
Edinburgh	256	150	60
Manchester	90	65	33

Road improvements encouraged more traffic, producing a socio-economic multiplier effect. Thus, though an important market town, up to mid-century Leicester possessed almost no scheduled links with other cities. Public passenger traffic began in 1753, when a chaise was sent up to London (as the owner put it) 'on Monday, Tuesday, Wednesday or Thursday'. In 1759, a thrice-weekly coach service from London to Leicester, Nottingham and Derby was added. From 1765 a 'flying machine' was doing the journey between Leicester and London all in one day, at 25s. for an inside passenger, 12s. 6d. for an outside; this soon became a daily service. By the end of the century Leicester's communications network with other provincial towns had been etched in. A Manchester coach was set up in 1776, one to Birmingham in 1781 (it took thirteen hours), followed by others to Sheffield and Carlisle. Similarly in 1740 there had been only one stage-coach a day from Birmingham to London; by 1763 there were thirty. All in all, improvements in roads sped turnover and the pace of life, and sucked the dark corners of the land into the hectic economy of exchange and consumption. 'I wish with all my heart,' fumed the crusty conservative John Byng, 'that half the turnpike roads of the kingdom were ploughed up, which have imported London manners and depopulated the country.' Arthur Young, however, saw the other side, celebrating:

The general impetus given to circulation; new people – new ideas – new exertions – fresh activity to every branch of industry; people residing among good roads, who were never seen with bad ones, and all the animation . . . and industry, which flow with a full tide . . . between the capital and the provinces.

Until late in the century, output operated almost exclusively through small-scale crafts, cottage and workshop industry. Expansion did not hinge on revolutionary innovations in technology, but on the steady sucking of accumulated wealth into circulation, better use of labour reserves, and new techniques facilitating exchange of goods and services. The heroes of this steady, inexorable march of commercial capitalism are largely anonymous: rank-and-file distributors, hauliers, shippers, transporters, and thousands of humble waggoners, packmen, tinkers, carters and hucksters. Up to 1760, no decisive breakthroughs had occurred in mechanization, in work organization, in the scale of the workplace, in sources of industrial power. The agricultural sector remained paramount, the fluctuating price of corn still largely dictating the tempo of commercial and industrial activity. Thus when agricultural profits were low in the 1730s, turnpiking tailed off. In mid-century, two thirds of British iron was still being used for agricultural purposes.

Even profit-conscious expanding trades continued to organize their labour force in traditional ways, often within guild or company rules. Such regulation after all ensured stability and rarely proved a brake upon expansion. Manufacturing typically remained in workshops, based on the work-unit of the household. Putting-out was perfect for expansion in textiles. Master-clothiers supplied workers – carders, rovers, spinners, weavers – with materials, usually a week's supply, which they worked up on their own premises, using their own or rented wheels and looms. This system was a cost-effective use of capital. The capitalist needed to freeze little fixed capital in plant, and had flexibility in hiring and firing labour. Sub-contracting remained ubiquitous as a mode of employment and industrial organization, for instance in the 'butty' system used in shallow Midlands coal-mining. It shared investment risks, profits and the problems of managing the workforce. (Publishing books by subscription could be seen as a parallel case, obviating the need for the author and printer to lock up too much capital in the project.) Where metal extraction was regulated by ancient court jurisdictions, as in Cornish tin-mining and Peak District lead-mining, each sinking was undertaken by a gang supplying its own capital and equipment, and getting its return, not in wages, but in shares of ore sales. In all such trades, 'middle management' had hardly emerged as a regular profession. Most intermediaries in businesses were not salaried foremen or 'executives' but were part of the family, bosses in their own right. Employment was direct, responsibility personal, rewards proportionate to success.

Industry remained largely labour-intensive and skill-intensive. Weaving, smithying, hat-making, the furniture and cutlery trades, metal-working and thousands more besides expanded by recruiting more hands. When demand was high it was easy to take up the slack (and especially from mid-century, population pressure made the labour market a buyers' market). Women and children in particular could easily be drafted into the labour force.

There were, of course, a handful of mammoth factories in the first half of the century. Thomas Lombe's silk-throwing mill in Derby employed 500, his twenty-three-foot water-wheel driving 26,000 spindles. But this was highly exceptional – and not very successful (nor indeed original: Lombe merely copied Italian factories). There were also a few colossal entrepreneurs. Around 1700, Ambrose Crowley, the iron-master who got rich on navy contracts, commanded a workforce of nearly 1,000 and pioneered the techniques of shop-floor organization, discipline and welfare taken up in later generations by industrialists such as Josiah Wedgwood (Crowley had no alternative: he directed his Tyneside works by letter from London). In his 'Law Book of the Crowley Ironworks', all instructions begin 'I DO ORDER'. Crowley knew it paid to take pains over workers. He housed his employees on company property – but enforced a 9 p.m. curfew – and provided a doctor and poor relief, but the recipients had to wear a badge inscribed 'Crowley's Poor'. Yet such a man was utterly exceptional – a 'giant in an age of pygmies' as his biographer has called him. Only a vast purchaser such as the wartime navy could create such concentrated demand: civilian consumer requirements did not support titan captains of industry so early. Even with later industrialization, the expansion of great iron firms such as the Carron Works, Walkers, and Wilkinsons depended largely on military contracts. Indeed, only naval dockyards themselves had a comparable scale and division of functions. 'The building-yards, docks, timber-yard, deal-yard, mast-yard, gun-yard, rope-walks; and all the other yards and places, set apart for the works belonging to the navy, are like a well-ordered city,' was Defoe's comment on Chatham in the 1720s, 'and tho' you see the whole place as it were in the utmost hurry, yet you see no confusion, every man knows his own business.'

Furthermore, in the first two thirds of the century, it was highly exceptional for technological innovations to revolutionize a trade. The development of the coke-smelting of iron by the Darbys of Coalbrookdale was, of course, to prove vital in facilitating mass iron-casting. But, despite rising charcoal prices, this innovation made slow headway (the Darbys kept it secret). New textile machinery such as Kay's flying shuttle also came in slowly. Newcomen's steam engine was used almost solely for pumping mines, and industrial power still came from animals, hands and feet, wind and water. Improvement occurred through the piecemeal modification of existing technologies within traditional employment structures. England consolidated her skills-base. By mid-century she led the world in timepieces and scientific instruments; eventually she dominated in piano manufacture.

Typical of the piecemeal expansion of traditional industry was the extraction of mineral riches. English non-ferrous metal-mining reached its zenith, Cornish tin and copper in particular prospering. Over 5,000 tons of Cornish copper and 3,400 tons of tin were being mined a year by the end of the century. Pennine lead-mining expanded, from Allendale south to the Peak. Aided by Newcomen's steam pump, coal shafts around Newcastle reached depths of over 100 fathoms. Coal-mining, sometimes under the sea, brought new wealth to Cumberland. Yet on most fields pits remained shallow – in the West Midlands, frequently less than 100 feet deep – and were worked in time-honoured ways by a gang of men, a few auxiliary women and children, and a horse. But more hewers spelt higher output. In 1660 2¼ million tons of coal were mined, 4.3 million in 1750, 6.4 million in 1770, and almost 14 million by 1800. The South Lancashire coalfield's output leapt from 78,000 tons in 1740 to 680,000 in 1800, yet all on traditional methods. 'What signify all your Balls, Ridottos, etc,' demanded Sir Henry Liddell, 'unless navigation and the coal trade flourish?'

In some sectors, growth took place by streamlining, reducing waste. Many parts of rural England saw more effective integration of agricultural and industrial labour, families pursuing multiple trades when just one wouldn't win a decent living or couldn't be followed all the year round. Buckinghamshire attained prosperity through its mix of lace-making, felt-making and straw-plaiting with cattle-droving and dairying. Bedfordshire families combined husbandry with lace-making, osier basket-weaving and brick-firing. Suffolk and Norfolk villagers made sailcloth; paper was milled in the Mendips and in Kent.

Rising profits could be won by steady expansion and cost-efficiency within existing industrial techniques, know-how and organization. Brewing was a growth industry, not through sudden technological transformation, but because heavier capitalization facilitated economies of scale. This was partly because porter became a popular drink, for, being more stable than ale, it could be stored longer, transported further, and hence bulk-brewed. Thereby limits upon market-size were overcome. Such developments favoured big producers. In 1700 there were 174 London brewers; by 1799 only 127. Already by 1760 Ben Truman's plant was valued at £30,000, and he had a floating capital of over £100,000.

The success of the Black Country affords a signal example of regional piecemeal growth. West Midland towns – from leaders such as Birmingham down to pint-sized Wednesbury, Darleston and Bilston – were dominated by small masters in the hardware trades, working their own forges and smithies, making nails, buckles, locks, hinges, pots, buttons, tools, guns and a thousand and one other articles. Supplies of coal and iron-ore were to hand. Because there were no guilds and corporations, it was easy for masters to adjust to market openings. Growing division of labour made for efficiency, as was known long before Adam Smith. In 1758, Dan Tucker admired the efficiency of production techniques:

In many provinces of the Kingdom, particularly *Staffordshire, Lancashire,* and certain districts of *Yorkshire*, with the Towns of *Manchester, Norwich,* and some others, the labour ... is very properly proportioned ... so that no Time shall be wasted in passing the goods to be manufactured from Hand to Hand, and that no unnecessary Strength should be employed. For an instance of both Kinds, take one among a Thousand at *Birmingham*, viz. When a Man stamps on a metal Button by means of an Engine, a Child stands by him to place the Button in readiness to receive the Stamp, and to remove it when received, and then to place another. By these Means the Operator can stamp at least double the Number, which he could otherwise have done, had he been obliged to have stopped each Time to have shifted the Buttons: And as his Gettings may be from 14d. to 18d. and the Child's from a Penny to 2d. *per* day for doing the same Quantity of Work, which must have required double the Sum, had the Man alone been employed; this single Circumstance saved alone 80 or even 100 *per cent* at the same Time that it trains up Children to an Habit of Industry, almost as soon as they can speak.

Such developments enabled a few Midland manufacturers to become very big fish. Matthew Boulton – Boswell christened him 'the iron chieftain' – was employing 500 at his metal-works by the 1770s. Yet, right through the century, the workshop, owned by a master, with a fistful of journeymen and apprentices, remained the norm in the metal-trades. Middling prosperity depended less on new machines than upon energetic, resourceful and ambitious men, with a nose for gain, trying their luck in a buoyant sector of the economy. Arriving in Birmingham in 1741 looking for work, William Hutton was impressed by its hum of activity:

I was surprised at the place but more so at the people: They were a species I had never seen: They possessed a vivacity I have never beheld: I had been among dreamers, but now I saw men awake: their very step along the street shewed alacrity. Every man seemed to know & prosecute his own affairs.

Such a man was Peter Stubs. Born in 1756, Stubs was a Warrington file-maker who attained prosperity, though not because of any revolution in file-making. He benefited from a lively market: in an age before standardization, all machine parts had to be filed to size by highly skilled 'fitters': almost all trades needed files. He profited from favourable credit arrangements: he could obtain his Sheffield steel on long-term credit, and his customers bought from him on tick. He took advantage of the excellent communications network which had just emerged, winning orders from London and overseas as well as from local customers. He expanded business by taking on more skilled workers, most of whom he employed by putting-out. Though steady workers were hard to find, their debts and his tough bargains made them, once found, tractable: Stubs could bind them with contract indentures. Furthermore, like so many bouncy minor industrialists, Stubs had many irons in the fire. He dabbled in property, kept an inn, and was a successful brewer.

The brisk competitiveness of the market, and especially the growing surplus of labour from mid-century, gradually eroded economic regulation. Furthermore, new trades were not covered by the restrictions (for example, on apprenticeship) in the Elizabethan Statute of Artificers. In these circumstances, previously backward but unrestricted regions could thrive at the expense of traditional ones, for it was a contemporary commonplace that guilds or corporations held back enterprise: 'A town without a charter is a town without a shackle.' Thus in guild-free towns such as Manchester, opined Lord Kinnoul in 1767, 'genius had free scope, and industry is exerted to the utmost without control, check or interruption'. The absence of guild protection did not hit workers badly in the developing North and Midlands, because employment prospects were good and wages competitive.

Every region grew in its own way, but the trend was expansive. Before 1700, the far North-West of England, the Lake counties, formed a self-contained, poor region of husbandmen, which had actually suffered mortal famines in Stuart times. During the Georgian period the great natural wealth of the Cumberland coalfield was tapped by the Lowther, Senhouse, Christian and Curwen families. The harbour of Whitehaven was built by the Lowthers, to become for a time one of the half-dozen biggest ports in the country, largely through the coal trade, but also because of its tobacco imports and its convenience for traffic to the Isle of Man and Ireland. Walter Lutwidge, its greatest tobacco merchant, a Whig and Dissenter, rather unsubtly called one of his vessels the *Walpole*. Along the same coast, Workington and Maryport were developed respectively by the Curwens and the Senhouses. Inland, agriculture was meshed into the wider national market, with cattle-rearing thriving. The population of Kendal, a modest 2,000 in 1700, had leapt to 8,000 by 1800, as a result of the prosperity of quite traditional industries such as stocking-weaving, tanning, glove-making and gunpowder manufacture. By 1784 Kendal had at least twenty shops. It was run by an oligarchy of Dissenting merchants (many of them Quakers) who dominated local government and gave the town an air of culture by supporting an illustrious Dissenting Academy (headed by Caleb Rotheram), a newspaper, a book club, a subscription library and a theatre.

In some cases, it was geography that had the last word in thriving or failing. Salt helped Cheshire to prosper. Brewing clustered where water was sweet, as on the Trent. Smuggling gave moonlighting employment along the coastal strip and in distribution networks inland. Naval expansion was the making of Chatham, Portsmouth and Plymouth. Early in the century the most spectacular growth points were west-coast ports such as Liverpool and Bristol (though not until the eighteenth century did Bristol break out of its medieval boundaries and town-plan). Both combined the advantage of being well placed for Ireland and the colonies (both were slave-trade centres) with command of an industrial hinterland. Bristol was the mart for Somerset and

Kingswood coal, Mendip lead and the South Wales copper-smelting trade. It controlled the Severn and Avon, and supported important potteries, glass-blowing, bottle-making, soap-boiling, zinc and distilling industries. This business centre was, for Horace Walpole, 'the dirtiest great shop I ever saw' – a town where 'the very clergy talk of nothing but trade and how to turn a penny and are in a hurry, running up and down with cloudy looks and busy faces, loading, carrying and unlading goods and merchandizes of all sorts from place to place.'

But Bristol was in turn overtaken by Liverpool. As industry nosed up the Severn valley to the Midlands, Bristol's industrial pre-eminence was captured by Worcestershire, Shropshire and the Black Country. Abraham Darby, the leading iron-smelter, moved his works from Bristol to Coalbrookdale in Shropshire. Later in the century, the pattern of canals tended to make the natural outlet for the West Midland industries the Mersey and Liverpool rather than the Severn and Bristol. Bristol delayed building docks; Liverpool seized the moment.

Though it had a population of under 10,000 in 1700, Liverpool had become by 1800 the second largest town in England. It thrived on overseas merchant investment, specializing in tobacco and slaves ('Methinks, I everywhere smell the blood of slaves,' commented the painter Fuseli), but then its wholesale merchants cornered the market of Lancashire cottons. Its corporation energetically improved harbour facilities, building the first wet-dock as early as 1715 (London's main docks were not built until the close of the century). Liverpool's corporation acted like a private company. The Rathbones and other merchant oligarchs prudently funnelled some of their wealth into civil utilities such as dispensaries, theatres, pleasure gardens, libraries, alms-houses and charity schools.

Industries were migrating all the time. High labour costs and guild restrictions pressed London manufacturers to look elsewhere: shoe-making moved out to Northamptonshire, stocking-knitting to Nottinghamshire, silk-throwing to Derbyshire (in some cases the high-quality finishing part of the trade remained in London). In 1700 the major textile centres had still been the towns of southern England – Exeter, Tiverton, Frome, Taunton, Colchester, Norwich – and villages such as Woodchester and Nailsworth nuzzling in steep Cotswold valleys. In these places, manufacturing was still tightly regulated by apprenticeship rules and workplace customs, and labour organization was robust. They made high-quality products but were resistant to change. During the century rivalry increased, above all from the West Riding, where wage rates started lower and capitalists faced fewer restrictive practices when trying to modify and cheapen products to suit the customer. Many markets long supplied by the South-East, such as Spain and the Mediterranean, stagnated, whereas West Riding mercantile enterprise seized the vastly expanding trade with the colonies and later the United States. The consequence was the downfall of textiles in Devon and Essex. The bottom fell out of the weaving trade in Colchester, Braintree and Bocking, and many once-prosperous Essex weaving areas remained ghost towns throughout the nineteenth century. (Norfolk fared better, though Arthur Young in 1771 found trade in Norwich 'neither brisk nor very dull'.) Yet so buoyant was the economy that some towns could bounce back despite the decay of their prime industry, often by becoming service centres for gentry consumption – housing bankers, estate agents, tailors, attorneys, and gunsmiths, and sprouting assembly rooms and theatres – or by developing processing industries, such as brewing, leatherwork and milling. Already in the 1720s Defoe noted such economic gentrification in Bury St Edmunds in Suffolk:

Here is no manufacturing in this town, or but very little except spinning; the chief trade of the place depending upon the gentry who live there, or near it, and who cannot fail to cause trade enough by the expense of their families and equipages among the people of a country town.

The economic infrastructure and tonic atmosphere of eighteenth-century England put prosperity within the reach of many. Obviously, growth was neither universal, uniform, nor linear. Trade moved in cycles. Capital investment, building, etc., fluctuated from boom to gloom and back again. Ebullience depended largely upon uncertain factors such as harvests and warfare, which affected prices, interest rates and the pulse of markets. Perhaps at some point during the century, the trade cycle supplanted the harvest as the heartbeat of the economy.

In an economy as regionally diverse, great dangers lurk in proposing general, national trends: one risks masking more than is revealed. One place's meat was another's poison. Chester's decay as a port – the Dee silted up – was given the *coup de grâce* by the growth of Liverpool. The Worcestershire town of Bewdley stagnated after its merchants missed the boat of canal development. Nearby Stourport became a canal junction and outstripped it. In any case, it is folly to be categorical about economic movements: our statistics will not bear it.

Nevertheless, certain patterns of long-term development are discernible. The century dawned on an expansive note. Population, which had fallen between 1650 and 1680 and remained stagnant until the end of the seventeenth century, was beginning to climb once more. A population of only slightly over 5 million in 1700 had become 5.2 million by 1710. Commodity imports and exports were rising. The War of the Spanish Succession meant fat government contracts on items such as weapons, ships, uniforms and boots. Furthermore, imperial and commercial expansion was multiplying overseas trade outlets. From 1707, the Act of Union opened free trade with Scotland, providing ready markets for England's manufactures. Not least, the early century was a time of hectic activity in the City. Because the Bank of England seemed to have made credit secure by linking investment with government, speculation in shares, and, above all, investment in government securities soared to new peaks. More companies were floated. The rich were gambling with surplus wealth rather than leaving it idle. The brisk business in patents indicates great expectations.

In the late 1710s and 1720s, however, this movement evaporated. Not all sectors were affected. Thus exports continued to move ahead. Worth £6.4 million in 1711, they went up to £7.5 million in 1721, £8.4 million in 1731, and £9.1 million in 1741, the increases being due mainly to a steady rise in manufactures. Over 100 ships were leaving Bristol a year on the slave trade, with capacity for about 30,000 slaves. Between 1714 and 1760, imports rose 40 per cent and re-exports 50 per cent.

Yet in the 1720s the population rise ceased, in part because of waves of lethal epidemics ravaging the country. Typhus, typhoid and other fevers struck repeatedly, 1718–19, 1727–31 and 1740–42 being particularly severe spells. In a single year an epidemic could wipe out in a locality the population gains of a decade. Dr Hillary at Ripon reported the poor dying like flies in 1727: 'Nor did any other method which art could afford relieve them; insomuch that many of the little country towns and villages were almost stripped of their poor people.' Largely because of such epidemics, there were about 100,000 fewer people in England in 1730 than in 1720. Falling population checked consumer demand. Shortage of labourers and consequent high wage-rates meant sunny times for artisans, but did not encourage capital holders to embark upon expansion. Furthermore, from 1713 the coming of peace had eased back demand for military and naval supplies. The financial boom broke. Company flotations had never been very stable: ninety-three joint-stock companies existed in 1695, but by 1712 only twenty-one were left. But it was the bursting of the South Sea Bubble in 1720 which killed off investment mania. Subsequent laws restricting company formation (a royal charter was required) nipped in the bud any possible stock-market for industrial projects. Eighteenth-century industrial investments remained private, not corporate or speculative.

But arguably the greatest dampener in the 1720s and 1730s was low agricultural profitability (after all, so much of the national product and surplus capital came from the land). Improvements in agricultural techniques and management, and a run of exceptionally good harvests meant that grain production was outstripping operative home demand. Corn output went up from 13.1 million to 14.7 million quarters between 1700 and 1760. Much was exported – in 1750, a million quarters: as late as 1766 a Frenchman could still call England 'the granary of Europe'. More and more was distilled into spirits, especially gin (by 1743 spirits output was six times that of 1700). Overproduction drove grain prices down. For consumers, this was a godsend. Cereals became cheap – prices were about 30 per cent lower than in 1660, making the cost of living through much of the 1730s and 1740s over 10 per cent less than in 1700. People were better nourished, though since much surplus grain was consumed as 'Mother Gin', plenty actually spelt alcoholism and death for some. But cheap food and high wage-rates depressed profits, and bumper yields meant a sticky wicket for farmers. Minor gentry and freeholders unable to diversify felt the pinch most. Many farmers went out of business, others got into debt, the lucky being hauled through bad times by far-sighted landlords. Rents fell into arrears, or had to be lowered, some farms became tenantless, and incomes in the landed sector stagnated or dropped. Yet necessity is the mother of invention. Tight profit margins squeezed the go-ahead landlord or farmer into greater cost-efficiency and productivity, at a time when yields per acre were actually falling in parts of Europe, such as Brittany and Lorraine. Penny-pinching, not expectations of large profits, spurred agricultural innovation in the first half of the century.

Of course, improvement in husbandry had been going on at least since Tudor times, and was to continue throughout the Georgian period. There were many incentives (including simply the lure of novelty and experiment). But its main dimensions are clear. Of key importance was the aim of reducing labour costs. Where possible, farmers eroded the traditional annual contract for the labourer, hiring rather by the day or week. There was also the drive to maximize land use. Fens and waterlogged lands were being drained, wastes (which Gregory King thought covered a quarter of the country) were being brought under the plough. Fertilizers such as marl, seaweed and lime were being tested. The century's showcase estate for land reclamation was to be Thomas Coke's at Holkham, Norfolk. Over a lifetime (1752–1842) he transformed this region with the aid of his tenants and imitators, and – more importantly – gave rural improvement shining publicity. When he began farming in 1778 he found the country barren. By marling the sandy topsoil, he converted it within fifteen years into rich cornlands, raising the value of the estate from £5,000 to £20,000 a year. Yet Coke was by no means the earliest Norfolk improver. Families such as the Townshends and Walpoles had long been improving rotations, experimenting with marling and sowing wheat and barley.

Stock-breeding became more systematic. Robert Bakewell of Dishley in Leicestershire, the century's most prestigious breeder, viewed a sheep as 'a machine for turning grass into mutton'. Many of the great English breeds, such as Hereford and Shorthorn cattle, or Southdown sheep, date from this period. More attention was paid to diversifying crops to meet soil and climatic needs. Above all, crops such as legumes, sainfoin and clover, and roots such as turnips, swedes and mangelwurzels, came into use on light sandy soils, to improve the tilth and provide fodder crops for overwintering cattle. Livestock were energetically folded for their dung, regenerating the soil. In some areas water meadows were flooded in the spring to provide an earlier, lusher bite. And there was a long-term switch in the geography of production. The traditional corn-belt of the Midland clays steadily switched to livestock pasturage, partly because of the rising demand for meat. By 1790 William Marshall could describe Leicestershire as 'a continuous sheet of greensward'. By contrast, former sheep-grazing areas such as Oxfordshire, the Wiltshire downs, the Chilterns, Norfolk, and the North and South Downs, aided by convertible husbandry, were being put to the plough, especially late in the century. According to Arthur Young, 'half the county of Norfolk within the memory of man yielded nothing but sheep feed', but by the end of the century it was covered with fine barley, rye and wheat. In 1803 Thomas Rudge reported similarly on the Gloucestershire upland economy:

Within these last hundred years a total change has taken place on these hills. Furze and some dry and scanty blades of grass were all their produce, but now with few exceptions the downs are converted into arable enclosed fields.

Begun long before, flexible agricultural improvement of this kind, sensitive to soil and market demand alike, and aimed at cost-effectiveness, continued during the difficult years between the 1720s and 1750s. The innovators – the great landlords, in league with big tenant farmers to whom they granted long leases – had the required capital to press ahead. Such investment was a gamble to make farming pay.

In the short term, however, surplus production and low profits dictated a generation of circumspection from the 1720s among the economy's big spenders. Few major new fields of industrial investment were opened. The number of new industrial patents tailed off. Canal-building did not get under way until the end of the 1750s. The economy was not so much suffering a slump as continuing on a plateau.

From the mid-1740s, however, demographic and economic growth began an upswing which, with only the occasional hiccup, carried through into the Industrial Revolution. The reasons for recovery at this time are disputed. The first forty years of the century saw a run of low food and commodity prices – the cost of living was regularly less than in the late seventeenth century – yet rising incomes. It is likely that many had surplus disposable income; as this translated into higher consumer demand, growth in manufactures was stimulated. Relatively abundant food, helped by measures taken in 1751 to cut gin consumption, may eventually have produced a more robust and fertile population, more resistant to epidemic disease (though decreasing mortality was probably minor as a factor in demographic growth).

For whatever reasons, population began to creep up again from the 1730s. The total population of 5.3 million in 1731 was about the same as in 1650. But by 1741 it had risen to 5.6 million, by 1751 to 5.82 million. The wars of the 1740s gave an artificially induced, state-centred cash injection, and the Seven Years War (1756-63) secured new colonies (Canada, India, and islands in the Caribbean) which boosted trade.

From the 1750s there was no looking back (with the exception of a spell around 1780 when British losses in the War of American Independence seriously disrupted trade, panicked the money market and led to bank crashes, eroding confidence). Even before changes specific to industrialism, England was overcoming the age-old blocks to sustained population rise and economic growth. How?

Improvement may have been somewhat fortuitous. Mortality from epidemic diseases declined, not peaking again until appalling slum conditions in London and the new industrial towns early in the next century provided perfect breeding grounds for fevers and sustained the coming of cholera. This was perhaps a biological windfall, but better nutrition and environmental conditions – such as draining stagnant waters, paving towns, enclosing sewers, and the spread of piped water – probably helped. The enormously successful adoption of smallpox inoculation (whole villages were often inoculated at a time) and, later, vaccination saved many lives directly and may conceivably have resulted in a more fertile population (smallpox sometimes lowers fertility among survivors).

From the 1740s, population rise boosted home economic activity, increasing demand and cheapening labour. Rising demand required more hands, in turn encouraging further population expansion, for, as Arthur Young put it, 'the increase of employment will be found to raise men like mushrooms'. The 5.7 million English people of 1751 became 6.1 million in 1761, 6.4

million in 1771, 7.0 million in 1781, 7.7 million in 1791, and 8.7 million in 1801. A pool of cheap labour sprang up to serve industrial expansion. Such growth could continue unchecked, because abundant capital was available for investment; the century saw it put to fresh and more productive uses.

One channel of investment of profound impact was canals. In 1759 James Brindley completed for the twenty-three-year-old Duke of Bridgewater the first canal of industrial significance, carrying coal from his Worsley pits to sell in Manchester. From then on canal construction pressed ahead – both short-haul ones for single purposes (usually linking collieries to towns) and longer trunk canals linking navigable waters, such as the ninety-three-mile Grand Trunk, which connected the Mersey to the Trent and served the Potteries. Ninety out of 165 Canal Acts passed by 1803 were designed to serve collieries: 'A navigation,' said Bridgewater, 'should have coals at the heel of it.' The profits from Bridgewater's own mines shot up from £406 in 1760 to £48,000 in 1803, thanks to the fact that the canal halved the price of coal in Manchester.

Canals were sanctioned by Acts of Parliament, and financed by incorporated companies issuing shares, chiefly bought not by a general rentier public (as later with railway shares), but by interested local parties (shares often cost £200 each). The Duke of Bridgewater estimated that a canal cost up to 10,000 guineas a mile. The Grand Trunk Canal cost £200,000 in all. The Pennine Link was estimated at £320,000 but ate up much more. By 1795, £8 million had been invested in canals; by 1815, £20 million. Construction was undertaken by sub-contracting separate stretches – viaducts, locks, bridges, junctions – to particular builders, thus sharing the risks and avoiding the headache of centralized supervision.

Canals linked the Severn and Mersey by 1772; the Trent and Mersey by 1777; the Severn and Thames in 1789; and the Mersey, Trent and Thames in 1790. By 1790 (the start of a decade of 'canal mania'), Liverpool, Hull, Birmingham, Bristol and London were all linked up. Direct routes across the Pennines, however, linking industrial Lancashire and Yorkshire, were delayed. Canal-building created employment, directly for technicians and navvies, indirectly for supply industries. Above all it made inland transport cheaper and easier, especially for the bulk freight of industrial raw materials, such as coal, metals, stone, fire-clays, bricks and grain. Whereas a 6-ton waggon needed eight horses, one beast pulling a long barge could haul 25 tons. Canal freight was hence up to four times cheaper than road. Canals also made carriage of breakable goods such as ceramics safer, and so encouraged national markets in such wares. A town such as Reading, traditionally cut off by waterlogged roads from even the nearby Midlands, suddenly had ready access by canal. Canals provided an enormous boost to enterprise. Sometimes profitable to shareholders, occasionally not, canal construction was one of the key means whereby private initiative established the infrastructure of utilities upon which industrialization was based.

In two other areas basic capital investment gave the economy new momentum. The Georgian period saw unparalleled urban reconstruction. This made fat profits for property speculators and provided work for builders, surveyors, designers, decorators, joiners, cabinet-makers, painters and scores of other craftsmen, as well as timber suppliers and builders' merchants. Urban renewal meant more inns and shops, coaching-houses, theatres, assembly rooms and concert halls, which in turn created service employment, and provided venues where money was spent and business transacted, all releasing fresh capital into circulation. Dock construction got under way. Bridges, jetties and lighthouses were erected, and many ports developed warehouse and harbour facilities.

By channelling resources into productive use, enclosure was likewise a shot in the arm for the economy (though a kick in the teeth for many rural workers). Enclosure required costly surveys and parliamentary approval (involving fat lawyers' fees), and then new roads, fencing, walls, hawthorn hedges, farmhouses, barns, cottages and perhaps drainage systems. Enclosed land not only yielded fatter stock and heavier crops, but other fringe benefits as well. For instance, grazing animals haphazardly on vast open fields probably spread livestock diseases (contemporaries frequently associated open fields with sickly stock). Isolating infected stock was much easier on enclosed lands. Since certain animal diseases are transferable to humans – for example, tuberculosis via infected milk – enclosure may even have benefited health. Open fields dragged everyone down to the level of the least efficient.

Enclosure had been going on in the countryside for centuries: about half the cultivable land had been enclosed by 1700. The great area of fields remaining open early in the eighteenth century was the swathe running from the southern counties up through the Central and East Midlands to Lincolnshire and the East Riding of Yorkshire, including Dorset, Wiltshire, Oxfordshire, Berkshire, Buckinghamshire, Northamptonshire, Huntingdonshire, Cambridgeshire, Leicestershire and Nottinghamshire. Much of this was enclosed during the course of the century, as the following figures of the number of Enclosure Acts passed in each decade suggest:

1740–49	64	*1780–89*	150
1750–59	87	*1790–99*	390
1760–69	304	*1800–09*	574
1770–79	472	*1810–19*	422

Georgian enclosure was two-phased. First, the open-field clays of the Midland counties were enclosed, chiefly for pasturage, between about 1745 and 1780. Then, from the late 1780s, the open fields, wastes and commons of the South and the East were enclosed for cereals, as population increase pushed grain prices to record levels, boosting profit margins. Between 1760 and 1799 enclosures brought between two and three million acres of waste into cultivation.

Enclosure could properly be carried out either privately by 'agreement', at the prompting of big landowners and yeomen (in Adam Smith's words) 'sensibly dividing the country among opulent men', or by Act of Parliament (usual where much common land was at stake.). In fact, enclosure was sometimes bulldozed by a naked act of aggrandizement. In 1716 John Warren, Lord of the Manor in Stockport, on his own initiative simply started selling common land for building and industrial purposes. The one patch of land left as common he set aside as the site for a gaol, and some of the profits of enclosure were earmarked to build a workhouse for 170 people. Perhaps he had a clear-sighted vision of the plight of the people under enclosure.

Enclosing initiatives usually came from large landowners, since they stood to gain most (and not only in husbandry: in many parts, enclosing fields was an effective way of seizing absolute control of mineral rights, quarries or valuable building land on town perimeters). Much ink and passion have been spilt by historians debating the injustice and social consequences of enclosure, but the main lines of development seem clear. Open-field farming was not necessarily primitive or hidebound. Nevertheless, cultivating enclosed fields was generally more productive. Holdings were consolidated. Less land was wasted on baulks and headlands, and it lay fallow for less time. Stock was healthier, for even stinted commons were frequently overgrazed. Under enclosure it was easier for the individual agriculturalist to innovate or be flexible. The muck-spreading journalist Arthur Young was right to say that farmers on enclosed land were more go-ahead ('Enclosing has changed the man as much as it has improved the country').

Not just great landowners and enterprising tenant farmers but many freeholders secure in their possession of deeds to a sizeable holding were keen to enclose. Much enclosure was by agreement (though 'enclosure by agreement' might be a euphemism for 'enclosure by pressure'), and enclosure commissioners generally acted with equity to husbandmen who could demonstrate good title. Hence, as well as setting up handsome, consolidated farms (the broad-acred tenant farms which came to typify English agriculture, though almost unknown elsewhere), enclosure also planted thousands of compact holdings of perhaps 30–100 acres. Enclosure did not make the smallholder an endangered species, for their holdings were amply viable in the boom-years towards the end of the century and through the Napoleonic Wars. Many went bust, however, in the depression after 1815, but not until the 1870s did the smallholder really go to the wall.

Three groups suffered desperately from enclosure. First, those independent cultivators whose strips on the open fields were so minute as to make access to commons and waste (for geese, for grazing a cow or a pig, for wild food, twigs and bracken for firing) a vital supplement. On a diminutive enclosed holding, without further outlet to the soil, their livelihood became attenuated and precarious. Overheads – and often debts – were alarmingly increased by the need to fence and drain, and build a new barn, without compensating savings from economy of scale. Enclosure can rarely have benefited this class of smallholder. They were the first to be forced to sell up at the slightest misfortune or economic downswing.

The second group to suffer were the many cottagers who performed wage-labour on farms for part of the year while also following trades such as nail-making or hurdle-making. They had little or no holdings in the common fields, but by ancient custom kept a pig or a few hens on the common. By enclosure they lost an important economic safety net, as well as their sense of having a stake in the land. 'The poor man was rooted out,' Thomas Bewick observed *à propos* of enclosure, 'and the various mechanics of the villages deprived of all benefit of it.' In the judgement of the Revd David Davies, rector of Cookham in Berkshire, for a dubious economic benefit 'an amazing number of people have been reduced from a comfortable state of partial independence to the precarious condition of mere hirelings, who when out of work immediately come on the parish.'

But most calamitously hit were those who had hitherto been at best tolerated squatters occupying shacks on the common or waste. Without a share in the open fields, they scratched a living by seasonal agricultural wage-labour and by trapping rabbits, collecting wood or burning charcoal, and topping it up perhaps by petty theft, above all poaching. Without a 'right' to use the common (such a 'right' required forty years' occupancy), such families were simply ejected (ratepayers were often delighted to see them off the parish). Victims of what Arthur Young called the 'open war against cottagers', they became a landless (and often homeless) rural lumpenproletariat. Enclosure created temporary job openings for such people (there was a flurry of hedge-planting, fencing, road-construction and barn-building). But, turfed off the land and with no secure employment, many such families sank into pauperdom, drip-fed by parish doles under the eye of the constable and the overseer of the poor. In Arthur Young's words, 'By nineteen out of twenty Enclosure Bills the poor are injured and most grossly . . . The poor in these parishes may say with truth, "Parliament may be tender of property; all I know is, I had a cow, and an Act of Parliament has taken it from me."'

What did enclosure achieve? First, it fundamentally altered the landscape. The familiar chequer-board pattern of fields with ruler-edges, hedgerows, and wide, straight roads dates from enclosure. Second, it gave proprietors further encouragement to treat agriculture as a business. It turned the land into absolute private property and abolished usufruct, customary usages and commoners' and occupants' rights; it consolidated the great landowners – that is why the Hon. John Byng could describe enclosures as 'the greedy tyrannies of the wealthy few to oppress the indigent many'. It made capitalist wage-labour paid by the day or task the norm on the land, as factories were later to do in towns.

Third, enclosure boosted rural output and profits. Despite Malthusian fears, England remained astonishingly able to support its soaring population. The land was feeding half as many people again in 1800 as in 1750, and corn yields increased by about 43 per cent during the century. Perhaps three fifths of this increased production was due to higher efficiency, the rest to higher acreage (much poached off the commons). Fourth, enclosure dealt a fatal blow to a long-established lower-class domestic economy, in which access to fields and commons had given families a small stake in the land and enabled the resourceful poor to piece together a living. A striking but typical instance of rural collapse following enclosure is offered by the village of Wigston Magna in Leicestershire, enclosed in 1765. Long before enclosure, the inhabitants were already highly unequal in wealth; only three tenths of the villagers owned land, and, of those, five owned more than 200 acres each, while two thirds had less than 50 acres. Yet within sixty or seventy years of enclosure practically all the small owner-occupiers had disappeared. The lower orders had lost all ownership of the means of rural production and had been reduced to rural labourers or framework-knitters. In Wigston, pauperism became a grave problem for the first time. In 1754 just £95 had been spent on the poor rate. By 1802 the charge was £1,776.

Most observers believed that those rural poor who continued to enjoy a stake in the land were better off. Arthur Young wrote revealingly of the inhabitants of the unenclosed Isle of Axholme in Lincolnshire: 'Though I have said they are very happy, yet I should note that it was remarked to me, that the proprietors work like negroes and do not live so well as the inhabitants of the poor house: but all is made amends for by possessing land.'

Enclosure cast long shadows. The profile of the dispossessed rural proletariat, especially in central southern England, at the turn of the nineteenth century is of a group not merely impoverished but sinking – a charge on ratepayers and moving towards that desperate guerrilla war against the propertied which culminated in poaching, rick-burning, riot, incendiarism and rebellion. Dispossessed cottagers from Dorset, Cambridgeshire and Lincolnshire were not driven into northern factories. Indeed their tragedy was compounded by the fact that they stayed put, immobilized partly by the Poor Law and partly by hopelessness. The nineteenth-century poor, however, were haunted with a vision of repossessing the land.

During the first forty years of the eighteenth century, society and economy remained in equilibrium, and there were no great destabilizing pressures. Employment opportunities were restricted, marriage was late, reproduction was regulated. The rise of population was slow, and occasional severe epidemics reversed the process. From about the 1740s, however, the economy started to grow, and this growth accelerated, fuelled by population pressure. Economic expansion increased the national product, and the 'haves' – farmers, property-owners, rentiers and capitalists, from small masters right up to plutocrats – could all count on benefiting from rising prosperity. This was particularly so as consumer prices had been low since the beginning of the century, and price inflation did not begin to pinch till the last decades.

The accelerating pace of economic change, however, proved a mixed blessing for the 'have-nots', the mass of the working people. Population rise destabilized the terms of labour. Growing competition for jobs began to slice wage-rates, particularly on the land, and undermined customary work organization and restrictive practices. The old working life pattern in which the apprentice could hope to become a master was increasingly challenged by the rise of huge wedges of less skilled, less organized labour. A proletariat, and a lumpenproletariat, were forming. Yet, where manufactures were advancing, there was a brisk demand for labour, and wages had to be competitive. Without economic growth, England could not have supported her newly booming population, though it was a population in which a growing percentage were condemned to lives of toil and poverty as wage-labourers.

6. Having and Enjoying

The last chapter argued that the economy of eighteenth-century England was an abrasive one, scouring the face of the country, bringing some parts up bright:

Great towns decay, and small towns rise [wrote Defoe]; new towns, new palaces, new seats are built every day; great rivers and good harbours dry up, and grow useless; again, new ports are open'd, brooks are made rivers, small rivers navigable ports, and harbours are made where none were before.

But how, and how far, did economic change and rising national wealth affect the ways people lived, their material belongings and surroundings, their lifestyles? Four main currents of development stand out. First, there was a growth of well-being which filtered down, however unequally, to improve the standards and quality of living of much of the population (though often heightening contrasts between the 'haves' and the 'have-nots'). Second, much of this new wealth was being translated into personal goods, raising many households from subsistence levels to some comfort and style. Third, spare cash was widely laid out on entertainment and enjoyment. Easy-come, easy-go attitudes were widespread: people liked to take their pleasures noisily, effusively and in public (snooty critics were later to deem this the characteristic of 'plebeian' culture). Last, entertainment, art, letters and culture were becoming increasingly organized on a commercial basis, in response to the broadening of demand. All such developments opened up new vistas of material enjoyment, while introducing profound tensions into the relations between traditional and elite culture.

Not everything changed, not everybody benefited. Prosperity for some meant impoverishment for others. Yet, for many, economic buoyancy meant there were more sovereigns, or shillings, to be spent. Of course, this did not instantly revolutionize the quality of life. Surplus income generally went on more of the same old things: a new bonnet, another foaming quart of ale, half-a-dozen oysters (then a cheap snack, rather like crisps today). Much about material life changed very slowly indeed. In 1800, as in 1700 – or 700! – the fastest mode of locomotion was still the horse (except, perhaps, for daring balloonists). In 1800 affluent houses were still lit by candles, and hovels by rushlight and starlight. In these, as in other basic matters, revolutionary change was just around the corner. Gas lighting, the steam printing press, and then railway engines, horse-trams and the electric telegraph made the first half of the nineteenth century times of bold change in everyday living and perception.

In fundamental matters, the lifestyles of the 'haves' and 'have-nots' were very distinct; those distinctions were not eroded. Take housing. A shockingly large mass of the urban poor were still occupying lean-tos and cellars, with the rural poor inhabiting shacks made of wattle, turf and road-scrapings (to discourage poor-law settlements, many parishes demolished cottages and refused permission to build new ones). 'Mud without and wretchedness within,' was the Hon. John Byng's verdict on the way the poor lived in Warminster. At Bridgnorth things were worse, for they led troglodite existences in homes gouged out of the cliff face. With timber shortage and enclosure, many could not even afford a fire. 'Humanity shudders,' observed Thomas Davis, steward to the Marquis of Bath,

at the idea of the industrious labourer, with a wife and five or six children, being obliged to live or rather to exist, in a wretched, damp, gloomy room, of 10 or 12 ft square, and that room without a floor; but common decency must revolt at considering, that over this wretched apartment, there is only *one* chamber, to hold all the miserable beds of the miserable family.

Styles of town and country housing for the higher orders were not transformed out of all recognition during the century. Flat-fronted, brick-terraced town houses with vertical lines, handsome doors, sash windows and classical mouldings and fittings held sway. In other necessities, such as diet, the distinctions stayed much as before. Food ate up the bulk of the poor's budget. About two thirds of a working family's income would go on food and drink, the rest covering rent, fuel, clothes and boots.

Labourers' diets were at least as meagre and monotonous in 1800 as in 1700, bread and cheese predominating. The common people could afford little meat – and that mainly fat bacon. Adulterated tea, used over and again, tended to replace milk and beer (home brewing got more difficult, and fewer cottagers could keep cows). The spread of potatoes, however, improved nutrition, and even the poor had their aspirations to a better – or more fashionable – diet, such as a preference for white over brown bread, particularly in the South ('rye and barley bread are looked on with horror even by poor cottagers,' commented Arthur Young in 1767). The higher in the social scale, the larger the amount of meat eaten, especially the patriotic roast beef, carnivores lording it over granivores. As with architecture, eating habits among the affluent diversified somewhat. Prejudices against fruit and vegetables relaxed: pulses and greens were more widely served, and strains of fruit improved. Imported provisions such as coffee, tea and sugar ceased to be seen as luxuries, and suppliers' lists show handsome ranges of spices, exotic fruits and fish.

But the boards of the rich remained mountainous and unsubtle. French cooks were rare and often despised. Gastronomic patriotism meant loading your belly. 'The art of cooking as practised by most Englishmen,' judged the Swedish visitor Pehr Kalm in 1748, 'does not extend much beyond roast beef and plum pudding.' 'BLESSED BE HE THAT INVENTED PUDDING,' bantered the Frenchman Henri Misson, 'a propos of English goût, 'for it is a Manna that hits the Palates of all Sorts of People: a Manna better than that of the Wilderness, because the People are never weary of it. Ah, what an excellent Thing is an *English Pudding! To Come in Pudding Time*, is as much as to say, to come in the most lucky moment in the world.'

Satisfying hearty appetites was the soul of hospitality. Parson Woodforde recorded his annual tithe dinner in 1783:

I gave them for Dinner a Leg of Mutton boiled, and Capers, some salt Fish, plenty of plumb Puddings and a Couple of boiled Rabbitts, with a fine large Surloin of Beef rosted. Plenty of Wine, Punch and strong Beer after Dinner till 10 o'clock. We had this Year a very agreeable meeting here, and were very agreeable – no grumbling whatever. Total recd. this Day for Tithe 286. 15. 0.

Alcohol consumption remained high among all ranks. Liquor (even brandy, when smuggled) was cheap, sealed bosom companions and spelt out cheer and health. The tombstone of Rebecca Freeland (d. 1741) read:

> She drank good ale, good punch, and wine
> And lived to the age of ninety nine.

Early in the century, 11.2 million gallons of spirits were being drunk in London a year (about seven gallons per adult), sold from some 207 inns, 447 taverns, 5,875 ale-houses, and 8,659 brandy shops. Northampton, with a mid-century population of 5,000, had sixty inns and 100 ale-houses, and there were about 50,000 inns and taverns throughout the country. Though the Gin Craze eviscerated mainly the dregs of society, the rich liked their glass too. In 1774 the Lord Mayor's dinner at the Mansion House polished off 626 dozen bottles of wine. In 1733 Robert Walpole's household consumed over 1,000 bottles of White Lisbon wine alone: perhaps its thirst had been raised by the 1,200 lb. of chocolate he ordered a year.

Nevertheless, patterns of consumption were changing, most notably among people faring well, from craftsmen up to professionals and farmers. As studies of their inventories reveal, growing purchasing power was being laid out on greater ranges of goods, beyond mere necessities, which could be afforded partly because they were becoming cheaper. Prices at large dropped by some 10-15 per cent between 1700 and 1750. Sugar got cheaper: 200,000 lb. were consumed in 1690, 5,000,000 lb. in 1760. Tea halved in price over the same period. Moreover, real incomes were going up early in the century because demographic stagnation afforded skilled labour a strong bargaining position. A family could survive on 10s. a week, but such craftsmen as printers or Spitalfields silk-weavers were earning £2–£3 a week (and their family income would be topped up by the wages of their wife and children). At mid-century, Soame Jenyns reflected on the growing enjoyment of rising material comforts: 'The consumption of everything is also amazingly increased from the increase in wealth in our metropolis, and indeed in every corner of this Kingdom, and the manner of living, throughout all ranks and conditions of men, is no less amazingly altered.' Opportunities for spending increased, and social attitudes encouraged it. Easy credit, low interest rates, and lack of legal security for bank and friendly-society savings made spending more appealing than saving. In any case, the urge to emulation and ostentation was strong. 'Every man now,' wrote Defoe,

be his fortune what it will, is to be doing something at his place, as the fashionable phrase is, and you hardly meet with anybody who, after the first compliments, does not inform you that he is in mortar and heaving of earth, the modest terms for building and gardening. One large room, a serpentine river, and a wood are become the absolute necessities of life, without which a gentleman of the smallest fortune thinks he makes no figure in his country.

Commentators – some enthusiastic, others reproachful – remarked how feverishly rising standards and expectations were chasing each other's tails. 'Their tables are served as well as rich merchants were a hundred years ago', it was remarked in the 1770s of provincial shopkeepers, 'their houses good and ornamented. What formerly was a downfall gable end, covered with thatch, is now brick and tile.' In similar vein a commentator from mid-century Nottingham noted of the refinement of habits right down the social scale:

People here are not without their Tea, Coffee and Chocolate, especially the first, the use of which is spread to that Degree, that not only Gentry and Wealthy Travellers drink it constantly, but almost every Seamer, Sizer and Winder will have her Tea in a morning ... and even a common Washer woman thinks she has not had a proper Breakfast without Tea and hot buttered White Bread!

Of course there was nothing new in moralists berating lower-class luxury – though the object of attack switched from beer to tea-drinking. That true 'friend of the people', Richard Price, bewailed in 1773, 'The lower ranks of the people are altered in every respect for the worse, while tea, wheaten bread and other delicacies are necessaries which were formerly unknown to them.'*

Others, however, appreciated the economic, and even socio-moral, benefits of keeping up with the Joneses. Asking rhetorically, 'Is not the creation of wants the likeliest way to produce industry in a people?', Bishop Berkeley approved of the fact that householders were lately purchasing items previously only within reach of their betters: ceramic tableware (perhaps Spode or

* Ironically, wheaten bread might have been healthier than rye, because less subject to ergotism.

Royal Derby) to replace pewter mugs and platters; metal knives and forks supplanting wooden implements; iron hobs and grates, cushioned chairs, Axminster and Wilton carpets, kitchen ranges, wallpaper, framed prints for their walls, the latest delicate Sheraton furniture (no one wanted antiques) and brass ornaments. Veritable argosies of fabrics enticed housewives into the shops. In 1774 one draper had for sale:

Dutch ratteens, duffles, frizes, beaver coatings, kerseymeres, forrest cloths, German serges, Wilton stuffs, sagathies, nankeens, Silisia Cambricks, Manchester velvets, silks, grograms, double allapeens, silk camblets, barragons, Brussels camblets, princes stuffs, worsted damasks, silk knitpieces, corded silks and gattias, shagg velvets, serge desoys, shalloons and allapeens.

Even artisans' houses became better appointed. The inventory of a Colchester weaver in 1744 recorded her possessions as:

Two Bedsteads 2 Beds 1 pair of Curtains 7 Sheets 3 Blanketts 2 Coverlids 4 pillows 4 pair of Cases 2 Bolsters 2 Pair of Drawers 3 Tables 1 Copper Saucepan and Cover 1 small Boyler 1 Iron pot 1 Iron Kettle 2 Box Irons and heaters 2 Iron Candlesticks 1 Looking Glass 2 Jugs 1 pair Bellows 12 pictures 3 glass Ditto 1 pair Tongs Sifter poker and Fender 1 Frying pan 2 Chamber pots 1 Iron Tramell 3 Basketts 2 Earthern pots 1 Wash tub 1 pail 2 Bowl dishes 9 Glass Bottles 3 Dishes 16 plates 9 Basons 4 Tea pots 16 Cups and Saucers 2 Silver Spoons 3 Quart pots 1 Trunk 1 Sweeping Brush 3 pewter Measures half pint Quart Do and $\frac{1}{2}$ quart Ditto 1 Bird Cage 14 Gallon Cask 1 Bay [etc.].

People did not merely acquire more household goods. Fashions changed, and they invested in furnishings and ornaments which were lighter, more comfortable, more elegant or just simply newer. The architect John Wood noted this spring-clean. The traditional interiors – stately, sombre, built to last and marked by a patina of age – were being scrapped. Now

The floors were laid with finest clean deals, or Dutch oak boards; the rooms were all winscotted and painted in a costly and handsome manner; marble slabs, and even chimney pieces, became common; the doors in general were not only made thick and substantial, but they had the best sort of brass lock put on them; walnut tree chairs, some with leather, and some with damask or worked bottoms supplied the place of such as were seated with cane or rushes; the oak tables and chests of drawers were exchanged, the former for such as were made of mahogany, the latter for such as were made either with the same wood, or with walnut tree; handsome glasses were added to the dressing tables, nor did the proper chimneys of any of the rooms long remain without framed mirrors of no inconsiderable size; and the furniture of every chimney was composed of a brass fender, with tongs, poker and shovel agreeable to it.

Noting similar changes, the designer Robert Adam drew attention in 1773 to

a remarkable improvement in the form, convenience, and relief of apartments ... The massive entablature, like the ponderous compartment ceiling, like the tabernacle frame, almost the only forms of ornament formerly known in this country, are now universally exploded, and in their place we have adopted a beautiful variety of designs, gracefully formed, delicately enriched and arranged with propriety and skill. We have introduced a great diversity of ceilings, friezes, and decorated pilasters, and have added grace and beauty to the whole by a mixture of grotesque stucco and painted ornaments, together with the painted rainceau with its fanciful figures.

One aspect which barely developed, however, was sanitation. Plumbing changed little; except for aristocratic mansions, few houses had baths installed, and the massed ranks of urban back-to-backs had to share external pumps and privies.

For artisans, stone or brick houses increasingly replaced cob, lathe and plaster dwellings (very heaven for vermin). In the 1780s Gilbert White noted that all the villagers in Selborne now had brick and stone cottages. Georgian terraces have lasted well, whereas little built previously in vernacular materials has survived. Tens of thousands of standardized, two-up, two-down, sash-windowed houses were erected, costing from as little as £150, and building societies were floated to help small men to build and buy. Expectations about acceptable standards of comfort, cleanliness and decency were rising in all classes. Dr Johnson – himself, notoriously 'no lover of clean linen' –

could remember when people in England changed a shirt only once a week. Formerly, good tradesmen had no fire but in the kitchen; never in the parlour, except on Sunday. My father, who was a magistrate of Lichfield, lived thus. They never began to have a fire in the parlour, but on leaving off business or some great revolution of their life.

Growing pride in better material conditions was thus mirrored in domestic spruceness. Foreigners thought English houses the cleanest in Europe – except those in Holland. 'The amount of water English people employ is inconceivable, especially for the cleansing of their houses,' thought César de Saussure in the 1720s:

Though they are not slaves to cleanliness, like the Dutch, still they are remarkable for this virtue. Not a week passes by but well-kept houses are washed twice in seven days, and that from top to bottom; and even every morning most kitchens, staircase, and entrance are scrubbed. All furniture, and especially all kitchen utensils, are kept with the greatest cleanliness. Even the large hammers and the locks on the door are rubbed and shine brightly. English women and men are very clean; not a day passes by without their washing their hands, arms, faces, necks and throats in cold water, and that in winter as well as in summer.

The Duc de La Rochefoucauld, touring England in the 1780s, agreed: 'People take the greatest possible pains to maintain the standard of cleanliness.'

The impression that ordinary people could afford not just necessities but 'decencies' and novelties also impressed continental visitors, unused to this among their native peasantry. De Saussure, for example, was amazed that artisans – even, he believed, shoeblacks – lounged about browsing the papers in London coffee houses. Pastor Moritz found his London landlady read Milton and other literary classics: 'The English national authors are in all hands, and read by all people, of which the innumerable editions they have gone through are a sufficient proof.' Once a year this cultured widow treated herself to a visit to Ranelagh in Chelsea to stroll round the gardens and rub shoulders with the nobs. Out in rural Oxfordshire Moritz was equally impressed by the living standards of countrymen dressed 'not as ours [that is, the Germans] are in coarse frocks, but with some taste, in fine good cloth; and were to be distinguished from people of the town not so much by their dress as by the greater simplicity and modesty of their behaviour'. Madame du Bocage thought the same about English husbandmen: 'they have their houses well furnished, are well-dressed and eat well; the poorest country girls drink tea, have bodices of chintz, straw hats on their heads and scarlet cloaks upon their shoulders.'

Pulpits might thunder, but the flood of pinchbeck consumer

goods, and the surplus to buy them, were clearly reaching down the social scale. 'The labourer and mechanic will ape the lord,' complained Jonas Hanway in 1752, and John Trusler in 1796 bemoaned in a similar sourpuss manner, 'the great degree of luxury to which this country has arrived within a few years ... [is] not only astonishing, but almost dreadful to think of. Time was, when those articles of indulgence, which now every mechanic aims at possession of, were enjoyed only by the Baron or Lord of a district.'

If the lower orders were expressing similar desires to their betters, this was not least because advertising and salesmanship shamelessly exploited envy. Josiah Wedgwood opened London and Bath showrooms for his tableware, laying out tempting dinner sets, ready to eat off. Wedgwood and other manipulators of fashion prided themselves on their grasp of consumer psychology. '*Fashion*' is infinitely superior to *merit*,' thought Wedgwood, for promoting sales; 'and it is plain from a thousand instances that if you have a favourite child you wish the public to fondle and take notice of, you have only to make choice of the proper sponsors.' Wedgwood played on cultural aspirations – one might say snobbery – by promoting his Etruscan ware, based on neo-Classical designs, modelled on finds from newly discovered Herculanaeum.

The world of goods was endlessly publicized, and with it the delights of ownership. Newspapers, magazines and tea-table conversation dwelt on the latest fashions. Fops mannequinned fashionable outfits and accessories in public (it was still a peacock society). Fashion-conscious travellers scoured stately homes, anxious to discover the latest motifs in cabinets, fabrics and wallpaper (of which 197,000 yards were sold in 1713, 2,100,000 yards in 1785).

In this highly image-conscious and opinion-conscious society, could anyone afford not to 'improve' and 'arrive'? There were great pressures upon people to mimic their betters. 'I remember in Bedfordshire an old tenant of my brother's,' reminisced the Hon. John Byng in 1795:

who wore the same coloured coarse cloth all the year round, and tied his shoes with thongs; his son in succession, when I called upon him, in a morning about nine years ago, ordered the maid servant to bring a bottle of wine 'with black seal', and, pouring out a glass, said, 'There, colonel, perhaps there's as good a glass of claret as you ever drunk at St James's.'

Though moralists deplored how the 'effeminate' urge for comforts was sapping the nation's fibre, for business it was a matter of animating the wheel of trade by stimulating wider markets. In such processes, the well-off colluded. Gentlemen and ladies wanted their servants fashionably dressed, and servants expected cast-offs. Dean Tucker wrote, with some exaggeration:

Females of all Ages and Conditions hardly use any Woollens at present, except those of the finest Texture, and made of the finest Wools, Silks, Cottons, and Linens, combined in a thousand forms . . . are now almost the universal wear, from her Grace in the drawing-room down to the lowest Scullion in the Kitchen.

Moreover, metropolitan fashions were sucked down into the provinces. Many country areas had traditionally been isolated backwaters, out of the mainstream of the mode. Cobbett thus described the Surrey of his infancy in the 1760s:

As to politics, we were like the rest of the country people in England; that is to say we neither knew nor thought anything about the matter. The shouts of victory, and the murmur of defeat would now and then break in upon our Tranquility for a moment, but I do not remember ever having seen a newspaper in the house, and most certainly that privation . . . did not render us less free, happy or industrious.

But provincials, spurred by newspapers and turnpikes, and above all by the urge to shed their 'rustic' image, wanted to change all this.

Provincial towns put on London airs. Better communications sped London fashions into the regions, with results the smart found risible. 'Where the newest fashions are brought down weekly by the stagecoach,' chuckled the *Connoisseur* magazine in 1756, making fun of the provinces,

all the wives and daughters of the most topping tradesmen vie with each other every Sunday in the elegance of their apparel. The same genteel ceremonies all practised there as at the most fashionable churches in town. The ladies immediately on their entrance, breathe a pious ejaculation through their fansticks and the beaux very gravely address themselves to the Haberdashers bills glued upon the linings of their hats.

Provincial towns christened their pleasure-gardens Ranelagh and Vauxhall, their theatres Drury Lane. John Wood the Elder laid out grounds in Bath overtly 'in imitation of the Ring, in Hyde Park, near London'. Burghers made Handel the staple of regional musical life after his oratorio triumphs in London and Dublin. Edinburgh, Bath, Cheltenham and Bristol all built show--case new towns, abandoning regional styles and vernacular materials, and promoting international Classicism. From early in the century reading societies and gentlemen's clubs were set up in market towns such as Peterborough and Boston to imbibe the *Spectator*. Genteel provincials suppressed their dialects and affected London catch-phrases, cant and conversation. Always the eye was on the capital. 'The theatrical performances here,' announced the *Bristol Guide* of 1801, 'are little (if any) inferior to those in London,' and even the Bath Penitentiary for Reformed Prostitutes was the proud protégé of the London prototype.

Sophisticated shops sprang up – seedsmen, gunsmiths, high-class booksellers. 'I should not have expected,' exclaimed the startled Thomas Twining, visiting the West Riding in 1781, 'to meet with a bookseller (Mr Edwards) in Halifax who is one of the best and most elegant binders in England, and has a valuable collection of books and prints.' Eyeing London, provincials set up circulating libraries, theatres, concert-seasons, subscription balls, coffee-houses, musical societies, assembly rooms and freemasons' lodges, and the elite put on a philanthropic face, managing charities, infirmaries and dispensaries. Not least, masking slums and sewage stench, townscapes were improved with new utilities and amenities: squares and walks, bridges, paved and lighted roads, piped water, pleasure-gardens and new street-plans, not to mention grids of elegant town houses.

Plenty and panache of this kind gave a new zing to the provinces. In 1761 even the demanding Horace Walpole was impressed with what he saw of the denizens of King's Lynn: 'their language is very polished since I lived among them [1741]. I attribute this to their more frequent intercourse with the world and the capital, by the help of good roads and post-chaises, which, if they have abridged the King's dominion, have at least tamed his subjects.' John Byng, by contrast, told a tale of innocence corrupted: 'the country is only improved in vice and insolence by the establishment of turnpikes,' he thundered, 'I meet milkmaids on the road with the dress and looks of Strand misses.'

Georgian society took pride in the increasing range of material objects which were now falling within the pockets of a wider cross-section of society. Inventories even of ordinary people's belongings reveal hosts of items: tongs, bellows, prints, trunks, clocks, fenders, pans, copper kettles, saddlery, firescreens, trinkets, toys, mirrors. Many such belongings went beyond the basic necessities – stools and cooking pots and basins – that had made up the furnishings of so many Stuart cottages. Now people had far greater access to articles of fashion and amusement, from family games to magazines. In the 1750s Thomas Turner, the Sussex grocer, was bringing home scientific toys: 'I entertained my sister Sally, and my brother's wife, with the sight of the Modern Microcosm, which I think is a very pretty curious sight, for we see the whole solar system move by clockwork, in the same manner as they do in the heavens.' The stout heirloom Bible now had to share its shelf with tatty novels, newspapers and fashion pattern books. There was more impulse buying: there were more ephemera to buy.

Few manufactured goods were standardized and mass produced, as they became under the Victorians. Individual craftsmanship prevailed. Nor was there the dwarfing of people by possessions which set in with that clutter of furniture and domestic bric-à-brac ushered in by Victorian mass production and sentimentality about home. Georgian taste still favoured clean lines, simplicity, sparseness. Objects certainly fascinated the Georgians: they loved touring stately homes and factories, inspecting machinery, peering down microscopes, going to museums and galleries, travelling, collecting curios. Yet they were also mobile, valuing the freedom money gave for activity, and enjoying being out of doors and on the move. 'Home sweet home' is basically a nineteenth-century sentiment.

Georgian social life gravitated out of doors. Trades were carried on in yards, open-fronted workshops and booths looking out on to the world. People did their business, discussed their politics, and took their pleasures in the open air, in public spaces, to a much greater degree than in Britain today. Their letters and diaries record them constantly milling around in streets that bustled with flower-girls, pie-men, milkmaids (selling adulterated milk), patterers and ballad-mongers, street vendors, street-walkers, street-criers, street-urchins. Home had fewer attractions. Blessed were the convivial. Solitary people were pitied and diagnosed as morose, melancholic, boorish: sociability integrated people, invigorated the faculties, and knocked off rough edges. The Dr Johnson who thought Charing Cross offered the full tide of human life had no doubts: 'The true felicity of human life is a tavern.'

This public domain was growing increasingly secular. The Church's once overwhelming place in communal life was being eroded. In previous centuries church had been the only place in many settlements where there were paintings, books and learning; it had been the chief forum for news, discussion and community action (weapons were stored there). Vicars had dispensed herbal remedies and taught the ABC, and schoolmasters were generally clergymen.

In the eighteenth century, churches continued to fulfil these broad roles, especially perhaps for relatively closed Dissenting and Catholic congregations. The English continued to enjoy a good sermon. But churches were encountering alternatives and competition. Religious pluralism and toleration meant that no single place of worship could bring whole communities together. With growing religious indifference, people looked elsewhere. Privately owned, non-denominational schools sprang up, run by laymen. Hundreds of communities, even in small villages, set up their own secular book clubs, which for a guinea or two a year gave subscribers access to scores of volumes. Proprietary libraries were founded in Liverpool in 1768, Sheffield in 1771, Hull in 1775 and Birmingham in 1779. The English were still religious in their culture: witness the popularity of sacred music. Yet this was being divorced from worship. Handel's biblical oratorios were often performed not in church but at a concert and without liturgical function. The *Messiah* was sung at fund-raisers at the Foundling Hospital in London.

As an assembly place the church faced rival venues. With magistrates frowning on church ales, the church lost its centrality as a place of merriment. Coffee-houses blossomed, over 2,000 having been set up in London by 1700. With a wry sense of the turnabout, Goldsmith depicted clergymen snug in coffee-house nooks, penning their sermons; doctors used them for consultations; Addison wrote *Spectator* papers from Button's Coffee House. Some even had educational aspirations – William Hogarth's father set up such an establishment where Latin was to be spoken: *non floruit*. If the Puritan chapel had been the citadel of seventeenth-century freedoms, by the eighteenth the coffeehouse had become – in Prévost's words – the 'seat of English liberty' – because of the open political discussion held there. Unlike churches, they were open to all denominations (though few admitted women).

Pursuit of pleasure became more respectable. Calvinist taboos against indulgence were sloughed (Cromwellian Puritans became the killjoy stormtroopers of caricature). Not many seventeenth-century fathers would have advised a son, as Lord Chesterfield did, 'Pleasure is now, and ought to be, your business.' Travelling, when not for business, had once been holy, as religious pilgrimage, or therapeutic, for exercise to recover broken health. Now people were increasingly going on jaunts in their own right, partly because better roads, inns and coaches made it more pleasurable. Bath – labelled by Defoe 'the resort of the sound rather than the sick' – became the cynosure of elegance and one of Britain's top ten towns, its population of 2,000 in 1700 shooting up to 34,000 by 1800. 'Taking the waters' for medicinal reasons was the excuse, but in reality it was a holiday haven. Visitors flocked in to idle away time, ogle the exquisite, haggle matches for their daughters, and, above all, gamble. Unlike Restoration Tunbridge Wells, Bath was not a hotbed of sexual debauchery, possibly because Beau Nash, the *arbiter elegantiarum*, was heedful to preserve Bath's reputation – and took a rake-off from the gambling. Indeed, Bath was so properly organized as to be thought dull. 'The only thing one can do one day one did not do the day before,' confessed Elizabeth Montagu, 'is to die' – though for his part the Methodist Charles Wesley denounced the city as 'the headquarters of Satan'. Bath was in turn imitated all over the country: Malvern Wells, Cheltenham, Buxton, Harrogate, Scarborough, all offered glimpses of glamour for the more homespun. 'Here was the same specimen of company as usual,' complained the ever bilious John Byng about Cheltenham, 'widows wanting husbands, old men wanting health, and misses wanting partners.'

Coach tours also came into vogue as a secularized pilgrimage (the walking holiday was the discovery of the Romantic age). Abroad, grand tourists flocked to France and Italy, those magnificent museums of history, culture and civility. At home, the Peak fed the new love of natural sublimity, until it was rivalled by the Lake District and the Welsh Mountains. Like other Georgian delights, travelling was becoming the joy of a broader cross-section. 'Life has not many things better than this,' Boswell was informed by Dr Johnson as they bowled along the Stratford road. He hankered after spending his life, the doctor confided, 'driving briskly in a post-chaise with a pretty woman'.

Travelling became more agreeable partly because coaches improved in comfort, being sprung and upholstered. Chaises could be hired, but the Englishman's dream was to own his own (Regency bucks popularized the phaeton, the sports car of the horse age). 'In everything that concerns the stables', commented Arthur Young,

the English far exceed the French; horses, grooms, harness, and change of equipage; in the [French] provinces you see cabriolets undoubtedly of the last century; an Englishman, however small his fortune may be, will not be seen in a carriage of the fashion of forty years past; if he cannot have another, he will walk on foot. It is not true that there are no complete equipages at Paris, I have seen many; the carriage, horses, harness, and attendance without fault or blemish; but the number is certainly very much inferior to what are seen at London. English horses, grooms, and carriages have been of late years largely imported [into France].

The sea-side holiday was invented. Sea water was first prescribed for its therapeutic properties by Dr Russell of Brighton, who instructed that it should be *drunk* for health. Then *bathing* in the briny was urged as a cure, but soon it became accepted as a pleasure in its own right. George III patronized Weymouth, where he loved taking the salute. John Byng, by contrast, detested its affected vulgarity:

a sandy shore, being excellent for bathing, has first induced the neighbours to come; and since, by fashion, and by the Duke of Gloucester's having built a house, is become the resort of the giddy and the gay: where the Irish beau, the gouty peer, and the genteel shopkeeper blend in folly and fine breeding.

The Prince Regent popularized Brighton, where he built the pavilion and raced chariots with his friends along the strand. Londoners flocked to Margate, northerners to Scarborough. 'One would think that the English were ducks,' remarked Horace Walpole, 'they are for ever waddling to the waters.' At resorts opportunities for commercial expansion were seized, from hotels (though most people hired lodgings) and coaching services down to souvenir shops, bathing machines, and their attendant 'dippers'. Beneath the gentry, most who could afford holidays at all stayed with friends and relations. Londoners of slender means strolled out on Sunday picnics to Bagnigge Wells, Sadlers Wells or Hockley-in-the-Hole, where there were ornamental gardens, ponds, fishing, cream teas, glasses of purgative waters, and sometimes sport such as bear-baiting. The urban poor got away by going harvesting and hop-picking.

Holidays were thus finally ceasing to be 'holy days'. Less time out of work was being spent in religious activities, more on mere leisure. The other great transformation experienced in the Georgian age was that many forms of enjoyment which had previously been private, exclusive and monopolized by the very rich were becoming open and available to the paying public at large. 'It is evident,' observed Madame Roland, 'that any man, whatever he may be, is here reckoned something, and that a handful of rich does not constitute the nation.'

For much of the Tudor and Stuart centuries, the centres of gravity for poetry, music and theatre were the Court and certain aristocratic patrons. Noblemen would support a consort of viols or a company of players, or even keep their own jesters. Restoration courtiers had written and performed their own plays. Artists and performers, thinkers and poets, necessarily had an eye to patrons' hospitality — who else would support them? Great philosophers such as Hobbes and Locke did time as domestic savants, tutors to gentlefolks' children; Dryden received crown pensions of £200 a year as Poet Laureate and Historiographer Royal.

But this changed. Market forces — affluence, leisure, the fast-developing book trade — led to high culture becoming available, if not to the masses, at least to the many. One no longer needed to be a gentleman proprietor to saunter round ornamental gardens, because Vauxhall, immediately south of the river at

Westminster, and Ranelagh at Chelsea, made pleasure-grounds available to Londoners at a small charge. Now you did not have to own paintings to appreciate them, because public art exhibitions were held – at the Foundling Hospital, where Hogarth exhibited, and, from 1768, by the Royal Academy. Commercial galleries were common in London by the second half of the century (though the state was hardly involved: the National Gallery dates from the nineteenth century). Cheap engravings of Old Masters sold briskly in the print shops which were springing up everywhere.

There were many stages and dimensions to the popularization of what had once been reserved for the cognoscenti. For instance, in the seventeenth century, collections of antiquities and natural history typically had been privately owned, but their owners had displayed them to select visitors brandishing letters of introduction. By 1759 the British Museum had been opened, at the bequest of Sir Hans Sloane, as the first publicly owned, free-entrance museum in Europe. The second half of the century saw privately run museums opening their doors as commercial ventures in London and the provinces. Sir Ashton Lever's in Leicester Square took £13,000 at the door between 1775 and 1784. Similarly, all England's stately homes were, of course, private domiciles, yet proud proprietors threw them and their grounds open to visitors, strangers included. Some even sold teas, prints, guidebooks and souvenirs to visitors. At Wentworth, Arthur Young found Lady Strafford so obliging as to retire from a room so he could view it.

The exclusive cultivation of poetry, music and drama of course continued: the Duke of Richmond was famous for his private theatricals, and many polite families – Jane Austen's for instance – staged plays: play texts were bestsellers. Yet the performing arts developed well-established public arenas – a shift speeded by the Court's decline as a show-case and a forcing-house of the arts. Charles II had been a friend of the arts, and many Restoration wits – Wycherley, Sedley, Etherege, Rochester, Vanbrugh – were gentlemen at Court. Restoration Court culture had been intimate, innovative, *risqué*. Court art was lively art. But among the early Hanoverians, Court taste was more staid. The Georges loved gardens and built up high quality picture collections, but they were no patrons of literature. The first two Georges were known as Dunce the First and Dunce the Second. George III's literary taste was dull too. He disliked Shakespeare (though reading *King Lear* when mad), but he paid Benjamin West a handsome £34,000 for sixty-four paintings. Hanoverian Court dress lagged behind fashion. The leading-edge of artistic innovation and *avant garde* taste hence swung away from the Court and towards the public: significantly, popular styles were named not after monarchs but after craftsmen and designers – Sheraton, Hepplewhite, Chippendale, Adam. In any case, the English crown never had dictated to the arts and intellectual life in the manner of the Bourbon monarchs from Versailles, via institutions such as the Académie Française.

What were the implications of culture becoming more secular, and focused less upon the Court and more upon the public? In some ways, it signalled a change in taste and style. The Restoration theatre of bold wit, intimate allusion and in-jokes was inappropriate to eighteenth-century commercial theatre. The playhouses of Georgian London were huge: in 1794 Drury Lane held 3,611 people, and even Norwich's theatre seated more than a thousand. Popular playwrights – Cibber, Goldsmith, Colman, Lillo – had to write for middle-brows and mixed audiences, their hits being simple, moral and sentimental, with elements of pantomime, farce and music-hall. The new audience, paying the piper and calling the tune, was broadly middle class and middle-brow. To please them, drama shed the Frenchified gentlemanly-rakish taste of the Restoration, with its sly sexual innuendo, blasphemies and cynicism (Addison deplored 'the lewdness of the theatre'). Satire gave way to gentle and humorous comedy, sentiment replaced cynicism; morals and happy endings were wanted. A very English mongrel breed of musical comedy was born in plays such as George Colman's *Man and Wife*, *Man of Business*, and *Miss in her Teens* – light, domestic and going with a swing. And kitchen-sink melodramas of bourgeois life, such as George Lillo's Hogarthian moral tragedy *George Barnwell*, about an apprentice lured into murder by a drab, were staged. As Lady Mary Wortley Montagu complained, 'The heroes and heroines of the age are cobblers and kitchen wenches.' The emergent novel, with its psychological realism, its morality and its sentiment, touched middle-class hearts.

Those who provided art and pleasures became aware that they

had to appeal to enlarged audiences. Some viewed this vulgariza-
tion with disdain. 'The pleasures of a town life,' commented
Gibbon upon mid-century London, 'the daily round from the
tavern to the play, from the play to the coffee-house, from the
coffee-house to the —— are within the reach of every man, who is
regardless of his health, his money, and his company.' Others
were more enthusiastic about what they saw as the open participatory culture of the metropolis. 'In London,' remarked
Casanova, 'everything is easy to him who has money and is not
afraid of spending it.'

Londoners certainly devoured eagerly the new opportunities.
No fewer than 12,000 of the culture-hungry paid 2s. 6d. each to
hear a rehearsal of Handel's *Fireworks Music* at Vauxhall. Subscription concerts were pioneered in London, music festivals in the
provinces (the Three Choirs Festival dates from 1724). For
humbler tastes, London had at least sixty-four pleasure-gardens
where, for a small admission fee, one could take the family, have
tea, listen to music, gawp at the strolling macaronis or keep
assignations. Alongside traditional rough-and-tumbles such as
Bartholomew Fair, scores of new diversions were opened to
paying customers in London and elsewhere: prize-rings, masquer-
ades, waxworks, magic-lantern shows, cock-fights, panoramas,
hippodromes, puppet-theatres. And it became increasingly easy
to take some of this culture home, as it were. From 1730 Walsh
was issuing cheap part-music scores in large quantities. Fashion
plates, dolls and magazines such as *The Fashions of London and
Paris* and *The Gallery of Fashion* were produced, enabling people
to have the latest Parisian modes made up for themselves; and
pattern books, such as John Wood's *Series of Plans for Cottages*,
popularized the in-thing in household design. You could ornament your house with ready-made, mass-produced Adam motifs
– fluted fans, plaques, wheat-ear drops, festoons, scrolls. In all such
ways, the idea of the 'public' as the arena of culture was realized.

Opening events in the arts to all who could pay produced a
very mixed company. Admission fees were great levellers. Foreigners were astonished to find the petty bourgeois rubbing shoulders with peers at the ridotto or regatta (pick-pockets had a
jubilee). People actually mixed easily, for John Bull knew he was
as good as his betters, while young bloods enjoyed slumming at
blood sports such as boxing and bull-baiting. All such mixing

took foreigners aback. Louis Simond noted that English stage-coaches were 'crammed with passengers of all sexes, ages, and conditions'. Pastor Moritz asked himself what was so special about St James's Park. 'It is the astonishing medley of people.' César de Saussure wondered the same about cricket, and answered: 'Everyone plays it, the common people and also men of rank.' All sorts went to Ranelagh rotunda – 'You can't set your foot without treading on a Prince of Wales or Duke of Cumberland,' mock-complained Horace Walpole: 'The company is universal: from his Grace of Grafton down to children out of the Foundling Hospital – from my Lady Townshend to the kitten.'

As well as gouty lords, Bath attracted *nouveaux riches* (and *nouveaux pauvres* too, hoping to recoup fortunes), as Smollett listed:

Clerks and factors from the East Indies, loaded with the spoil of plundered provinces; planters, negro-drivers, and hucksters, from our American plantations, enriched they know not how; agents, commissaries, and contractors, who have fattened, in two successive wars, on the blood of the nation; usurers, brokers, and jobbers of every kind; men of low birth, and no breeding, have found themselves suddenly translated into a state of affluence, unknown to former ages.

The rules of etiquette laid down by Beau Nash, the master of ceremonies, ensured that, once arrived there, all ranks had to behave alike. No one was to wear a sword, and all were to minuet in strict rotation, ignoring aristocratic precedence.

As commerce increased its stake in culture, myriad new ventures sprang up, set fair to turn a penny. Some tapped the widening reading public. Foreigners were impressed by the passion for reading and education shown by a wide cross-section of the English. Pastor Moritz ran across a saddler in Derbyshire who struck up a conversation about Homer and Virgil: 'He quoted lines from them moreover, in a way I should have thought possible only in a doctor or a master of arts from Oxford' (Moritz had just visited Oxford). He commented, 'German authors are hardly read [in Germany] outside learned circles except by a few of the middle classes. Yet the common people of England read their English authors. You can tell it, among other things, from the number of editions of their works.'

Slaking this thirst for print, newspapers flooded on to the market. By 1790 there were fourteen London morning papers. In 1788 the first London evening paper appeared; in 1799 the first Sunday paper – 'everyone who reads at all,' exaggerated Southey in 1812, 'reads a Sunday newspaper.'

Up to 1700, all newspapers had been printed in London, being rattled down to the provinces by coach. But a provincial press was soon augmenting the metropolitan. The *Norwich Post* began in 1701, the *Bristol Postboy* in 1702, and before the century was out almost every district got its own paper. 50,000 copies of provincial papers were sold a week in 1700, 200,000 in 1760; sales doubled by 1800. By 1760, thirty-five provincial papers were in business, selling for about 1½d. A successful provincial paper, such as the *Salisbury Journal*, would have a weekly sale running to a few thousand (a flourishing Paris newspaper during the Revolution could not expect to sell more). Its readership was probably five to ten times that number, and many more picked up the contents by word of mouth. Provincial newspapers publicized local events, carried a welter of local commercial advertisements, and conveyed military, political and financial intelligence from London – all important symptoms of the health of trade – to say nothing of the latest fashions. Contemporaries believed that, of all the media, newspapers shaped opinion the most. 'The mass of every people must be barbarous where there is no printing and consequently knowledge is not generally diffused,' remarked Dr Johnson: 'Knowledge is diffused among our people by the news-papers.'

Before the eighteenth century almost no printing presses were licensed in the provinces, where there had been few specialized book stores (Samuel Johnson's father ran one in Lichfield, but it was not a success). By the end of the century, every town had its printer and bookshop.

The output of prints, pamphlets, cartoons and ballads rose and rose, but the market was never saturated. Magazines such as Addison and Steele's *Spectator* created an enduring taste for polite, improving literature, it being Addison' aim to 'bring philosophy out of closets and libraries, Schools and colleges, to dwell in clubs, and assemblies, at tea-tables, and in coffee-houses'. By blending entertainment and instruction, the *Spectator* taught ease and affability to squireens and tradesmen with time on their hands, money in their pockets but little breeding. Magazines had circulations of up to a few thousand copies: the *Spectator* early in the century about 3,000, the *Gentleman's Magazine* from the 1730s up to 10,000. Often appearing monthly and selling at about 6d., they sought to cultivate more specialized readerships. There were soon journals for ladies, for provincials, for fashion; some focused on politics, some were illustrated, many were religious, a few pornographic, some had quizzes, others dress patterns. By 1800, 250 periodicals had seen the light of day, including the *Matrimonial Magazine*, the *Macaroni*, the *Sentimental Magazine*, and the *Westminster*.

Books remained quite dear. A new novel would cost at least 7s. 6d., a work of history or *belles lettres* a guinea. Even so, Henry Fielding's *Joseph Andrews* sold 6,500 copies in 1742. Cheaper pirated editions (the equivalents of paperbacks) could not, however, be suppressed, and second-hand copies could be picked up at auctions or from stalls and peddlers. Enterprising publishers brought out books serially, in parts, at about 6d. a time, to spread the cost (Smollett's *History of England* sold 13,000 in serial form). And the works that really caught the public imagination – political pamphlets, sermons, penny dreadfuls, ballads, etc. – were inexpensive anyway. The innovation of circulating libraries, moreover, made thousands of books available to subscribers for just a guinea or two a year. By 1800 there were 122 circulating libraries in London, 268 in the provinces. Critics condemned them as 'evergreen trees of diabolical knowledge', grumbling that their shelves groaned under sentimental and titillating gothick novels, supposedly devoured by impressionable teenage girls. Others, however, such as the bookseller James Lackington, saw their value as a home university, especially for ladies:

circulating libraries have greatly contributed towards the amusement and cultivation of the other sex; by far the greatest part of ladies now have a taste for books . . . Ladies now in general read, not only novels, although many of that class are excellent productions, and tend to polish both the heart and the head; but they also read the best books in the English language, and may read the best authors in various languages; and there are some thousands of ladies who frequent my shop, and that know as well what books to choose, and are as well acquainted with works of taste and genius as any gentleman in the kingdom, notwithstanding they sneer against novel readers, etc.

For those who could not afford the money or time for literary classics, abridgements were available. Novels were boiled down into chapbooks. John Wesley condensed *Pilgrim's Progress*, pricing it at 4d., alongside his nine-page *Short English Grammar* and his 144-page *Complete English Dictionary*. His *Primitive Physick*, a do-it-yourself guide to health, had gone through twenty-three editions by 1791. 'The sale of books in general,' observed Lackington in 1792,

has increased prodigiously within the last twenty years. According to the best estimation I have been able to make, I suppose that more than four times the number of books are sold now than were sold twenty years since. The poorer sort of farmers, and even the poor country people in general, who before that period spent their evenings in relating stories of witches, ghosts, hobgoblins etc., now shorten the winter nights by hearing their sons and daughters read tales, romances etc., and on entering their houses you may see *Tom Jones*, *Roderick Random*, and other entertaining books stuck up on their bacon racks.

The commercial expansion of the arts was paralleled in other spheres. Village sports continued − such as marbles and cheese-rolling, enjoyed by local communities time out of mind and often linked to calendar festivities − but now 'sport' emerged, in some instances gentrified, and in others organized, with paid performers and a paying audience. Cricket moved from the village green to the estate (Lord Chesterfield instructed his son, 'You will desire to excel all boys of your age at cricket'). As befitted the age of reason, cricket had its rules codified (the leg-before-wicket rule, for example, dates from 1774). The MCC was founded in 1787 at Thomas Lord's ground in Marylebone. Once essentially for participants, cricket (like others) became a spectator sport: 20,000 watched Kent play Hampshire in 1772. By the early nineteenth century, some of the top players were professionals. The sport's enormous popularity lay in its being tailor-made for gambling. Teams themselves competed for high stakes, but thousands of guineas were wagered by spectators betting on the result, leading to gamesmanship and bribery. Bets were also placed on individual innings, and even on particular balls and strokes. Horace Mann thought nothing of staking £1,000 on a match. A later, primmer, age expunged these commercial elements: bookies were banned from Lords in 1825.

Prize-fighting developed in a similar way. Fisticuffs was ancient, but before the eighteenth century there had been no illustrious prize-fighters because boxing was not professional. The reign of George III and the Regency, however, became the golden age of boxing stars such as Jem Belcher, Dutch Sam, Bill Stevens the nailer, Tom Crib and the superstar Daniel Mendoza. They were backed by well-orchestrated publicity (Mendoza mugs, plaques and instruction books were sold; boxers' memoirs became big business). 'The fancy' had its own specialist journalists, who immortalized prize-fighters as Homeric heroes in a patois all their own. Mendoza himself wrote *The Art of Boxing*, opened an academy, and entered a partnership with Philip Astley, the hippodrome proprietor. Tens of thousands of guineas were staked on big bouts. Successful fighters became rich, set up their own gymnasia, and 'gentrified' bruising into the science of pugilism.

It was the same with horse-racing. At the Restoration the turf had been exclusively aristocratic, the sport of kings; Ascot was Queen Anne's own estate. But under the Georges many towns got their race meetings: Norwich held them regularly from 1710, Warwick from 1711, the sport becoming so popular that grandstands had to be built to protect the nobs from the mobs. The turf became big business. The Jockey Club was set up in 1752, the horse-dealers Tattersalls in the 1770s. Professional trainers and jockeys took the initiative. The successes of thoroughbreds such as Eclipse gave rise to blood-stock pedigrees and equine ancestor-worship. 'Classic' races such as the St Leger (from 1778), the Oaks (1779) and the Derby (1780) created the racing calendar. And once again, gambling made the wheels go round.

Even hunting (thanks to the game laws, the most select of sports) became organized and even commercial. Traditionally favourite forms of killing wild animals – hawking, trapping and netting – were fairly solitary; but these gave way to scientific slaughter and a rational approach. Birds were increasingly bred and protected by gamekeepers and flushed out by beaters for the mass shoot, the *battue*. Shooting became competitive, with glory for the biggest 'bags'. Above all, fox-hunting as we know it was a Georgian invention, with horses bred specially for speed and jumping, and packs of hounds for scent. The chase, which in

Stuart times had been more stop-and-start, now went at a gallop. Permanent packs with national reputations, such as the Pytchley, the Belvoir, the Cottesmore, and the Quorn in Leicestershire, date from the 1770s. Although fox-hunting was aristocratic ('the only chase in England worthy of the taste or attention of a high bred sportsman'), hunting clubs with yearly subscriptions became commercial speculations. Whoever could afford the fees – even London plutocrats – could join.

England was gripped by gambling fever. Bets were laid on political events, births and deaths – any future happenings. For a few pounds challengers galloped against the clock, gulped down pints of gin or ate live cats. A common wager consisted of taking out insurance policies on *other* people's lives. When George II led his troops against the French in 1743, you could get four to one against his being killed. Cards were the opium of the polite. Parson Woodforde played all the time: 'Mr and Mrs Custance drank Tea with us in the Afternoon with their eldest Son. After Tea we all got to Loo at which I won o.6.o. Nancy also won at Loo this evening o.6.o.' Gambling itself became nationalized. The state ran a lottery from 1709 to 1824, national institutions from the British Museum to Westminster Bridge being partly funded from the proceeds. But gaming was also the life-blood of London clubs such as Almack's, White's and Boodle's, and astronomical sums flew around. Charles James Fox had lost £140,000 by the age of twenty-five. At White's, Horace Walpole reported, 'Lord Stavordale, not yet one-and-twenty, lost eleven thousand last tuesday, but recovered it by one great hand at hazard: he swore a great oath – "Now, if I had been playing *deep*, I might have won millions".'

Outdoor sports were big attractions, partly because they brought together lords and commons, traditional recreation and profit. Peers – sport's first sponsors – were prepared to share pleasures such as horse-racing with the people, basking thereby in their own supremacy as patrons. Bucks backed bruisers and ran their own cricket teams. Classic races commemorated noble names ('The Oaks' was the name of Lord Derby's Epsom house). Sport was both mimic warfare and a version of pastoral for the Regency toff. The crowd loved the touch of class that lordly presences lent – to say nothing of the trade they created for tapsters, porters and hawkers – and could see peers as men of the people when Lord Sackville batted for a Kent side captained by Rumney, his head gardener. In any case, aristocratic protection was vital for prize-fighting, since technically it was illegal.

The more culture became commercialized, the more box-office appeal shaped taste. Playhouses were springing up everywhere. The Nottingham theatre was built in 1769, the Manchester Theatre Royal opened in 1775, and by the end of the century even small towns such as Wisbech and Bury St Edmunds could boast spacious playhouses, where London stars such as Mrs Siddons would tour. And there were innumerable smaller barns to be stormed by strolling players. But the fare served up was what the customers wanted. Shakespeare was made easy. *A Midsummer Night's Dream* was turned into *The Fairies*; *King Lear* was given a happy ending. Farces, ballads and recitations, pantomimes, tragedies and arias jostled on the same bill: something for everyone. In Birmingham something like the Victorian music-hall was developing. Among the shows of London, freaks, midgets, women gladiators (such as 'Bruising Peg'), contortionists and mathematical pigs were sure-fire money-spinners.

Capitalizing on these commercial opportunities, the culture trade was revolutionized by outstanding entrepreneurs, ready to anticipate, stimulate and satisfy demand. Great actor-managers appeared, such as John Rich, who first staged *The Beggar's Opera*, Colley Cibber and David Garrick, that grand-master of publicity, who floated the Stratford Shakespeare Jubilee in 1769. Philip Astley developed his bare-back stunt riding into a stunning hippodrome spectacle. The printer Edward Cave, proprietor of the *Gentleman's Magazine*, created a readership by pioneering parliamentary reporting. Later in the century, speculators opened galleries in London decked with paintings of scenes from Shakespeare, the Bible and English history. The capital's effervescent musical life was orchestrated by Heidegger, Handel ('composer in ordinary to the Protestant religion') and, later, Salomon. In 1791 Salomon gave Joseph Haydn £50 for each of twenty performances and a £200 benefit on top. Great landscape designers such as William Kent, Lancelot ('Capability') Brown and Humphrey Repton would produce environments to order. Enterprising publishers also seized their chances, quenching the readers' thirst for knowledge, diversion, news, education, sex. John Newbery poured out spelling books, primers, picture books,

chapbooks, joke books and fairy stories, as well as such educational toys as jigsaws. Catherine Hutton remembered reading as
a child

all Mr Newbery's gilt books, as they were called for being covered with
gilt embossed paper. They consisted of *Christmas Box*, *New Year's Gift*,
Goody Two Shoes – nothing delighted me so much as the *Tale of the
Fairies*. I no more doubted their truth than I did my own existence.

Always on the *qui vive* for a new sales opening, publishers hit on
cheap collected editions of British playwrights, poets and essayists;
Elizabeth Cooper put out the first general anthology of English
poetry in her *Muses' Library* (1737). Yet publishers were not
merely mercenary. Some of them – Lintot, Strachan, Millar,
Cadell, Johnson – established cordial terms with leading authors,
selling their works in handsome editions. 'I respect Millar,'
observed Dr Johnson, 'for he has raised the price of literature.'

Scientific lecturers burst on the scene as the Enlightenment's
answer to the itinerant preacher, trading on the new prestige of
Newtonian science and the magic of experiments using dazzling
apparatus (Adam Walker had a 20-foot orrery). Early in the
century James Jurin, William Whiston and others performed in
London (Whiston was also an apocalyptic gospeller, prophesying
the end of the world). Lecturers then went on the road, fanning
out with their apparatus into the provinces. Jurin lectured in
Newcastle in 1710, Whiston in Bristol in 1724. James Ferguson (a
canny Scot who had taken the high road south to London to
become a leading text-book popularizer of science) lectured in
Bath and Bristol in the 1760s and 1770s. By the close of the
century most towns of any size had been milked by science
lecturers offering courses of six or a dozen lectures, as well as
selling their books and instruments, puffing patent medicines,
performing land surveys and giving private tuition. 'Knowledge
is become a fashionable thing,' announced a top lecturer, Benjamin Martin, 'and philosophy is the science à la mode' ('No
man has been more anxious', he flattered himself, 'to make the
rugged paths to knowledge plain and easy and the liberal arts
more generally accessible').

Alongside impresarios of art and science, commercialization
gave birth to the *star*, ablaze with publicity. The Georgian
theatre boasted Garrick (who had tramped to London to seek his

fortune), Macklin, Quin, Mrs Oldfield and Peg Woffington, all of whom became household names. And then there were stranger personalities and publicists – the Black lion-tamer, Macomo, mountebanks such as the self-dramatizing magician, healer and clairvoyant Cagliostro, or the mystic Katterfelto, with his black cats, who delivered lectures on the 'Philosophical, Mathematical, Optical, Magnetical, Electrical, Physical, Chemical, Pneumatic, Hydraulic, Hydrostatic, Proetic, Stenographic, Blaenical, and Caprimantic Arts'. The doctor-cum-sex-therapist James Graham, flanked by near-naked nymphs (one was the future Emma Hamilton), unveiled a Celestial bed in his Temple of Venus at the Adelphi, which he hired out at £50 a night to reinvigorate the impotent, and titillated society with his erotic lectures. Unorthodox healers, such as Mrs Mapp the bone-setter, were nineday wonders in chic society. Samuel Foote the farceur, Henry Angelo, founder of London's premier fencing academy, Cadman, the rope-walker, Grimaldi, the clown – all made a name for themselves, as did 'the amazing Learn'd English Dog', who (according to his tour publicity)

reads, writes, and casts Accompts, by Means of Typographical Cards, in the same Manner that a Printer composes; and, by the same Method, answers various Questions in Ovid's Metamorphosis, Geography, and History; knows the Greek Alphabet, reckons the Number of People present, if not above 30 . . . solves small Questions in the four Rules of Arithmetick, tells by looking on any common Watch of the Company, what is the Hour and Minute.

As well as its impresarios and stars, commercial culture needed its production lines, drudges and managers (Hogarth complained of 'picture-jobbers'). To cope with rising demand, supply was mechanized. 'Grub Street' became the conveyor belt of the printed word, giving employment to hacks, such as 'Sir' John Hill, willing to pen instant copy on any subject for a fee. 'Writing is become a very considerable part of the English commerce,' observed Defoe, who certainly knew by experience. 'The booksellers are the master manufacturers or employers. The several writers, authors, copyers, subwriters, and all other operators with pen and ink are the workmen employed by the said master manufacturers.'

Meeting the demand for pulp reading meant a kind of penal

servitude for many hireling writers (hence the Grub Street joke advertisement: 'An author to be let'). But for many writers, access to a big readership meant freedom, and the chance to be a man of the world. The philosopher and essayist David Hume perceptively commented:

It is with great pleasure I observe, that men of letters in this age have lost in a great measure that shyness and bashfulness of temper, which kept them at a distance from mankind; and, at the same time, that men of the world are proud of borrowing from books their most agreeable topics of conversation.

For many garret scribblers, poverty and anonymity; for the successful, new-found wealth. Whereas Milton's reward for *Paradise Lost* had been £5 down and £5 at the end of the first edition, just half a century later the astute Alexander Pope made £4,000 each out of his *Iliad* and *Odyssey*. With the spread of the reading habit, even journeymen of the Muses such as John Campbell made thousands a year – in his case, out of encyclopaedia compilation, being in Dr Johnson's judgement (a 'harmless drudge' of a lexicographer himself), 'the richest author who ever grazed the commons of literature'. Pot-boiling works of reference were sure-fire commercial speculations, and purveying knowledge became just another trade. As Adam Smith saw it, 'Knowledge was now purchased in the same manner as shoes or stockings, from those whose business it is to make up and prepare for the market that particular species of goods.'

This age in which leisure and letters were gilded with commerce did not see the decline and fall of art, despite the jeremiads of such artists as William Blake ('Where any view of money exists,' he prophesied, 'art cannot be carried on'). Blake believed that commerce killed creativity, that his contemporary artists were traitors to the spirit, and that imagination's prophetic mission had been betrayed. But most writers and artists demurred, thinking it natural that, as in Augustan Rome or Renaissance Italy, commerce should succour culture. The Liverpool banker William Roscoe wrote the life of Lorenzo the Magnificent to highlight the parallels as he saw them between Renaissance Florence and modern Britain.

Imponderables such as genius aside, artistic production and consumption blossomed in the Georgian age. Arts and crafts –

such as cabinet-making in the hands of Chippendale and Sheraton, or interior decoration under the Adam brothers – reached exquisite pinnacles of elegance and delicacy. Elite taste had previously hired foreign painters, but now native talent – Hogarth, Reynolds, Gainsborough, Lawrence, Romney – nosed ahead. Continental skills still excelled in certain arts, but English working conditions and purses lured the maestros across the Channel. In music, Handel and J. C. Bach settled in England (they could do better freelancing then as foreign *Kapellmeister*); Mozart and Haydn did concert tours. Haydn, used to composing to Esterházy Court demands, valued London's artistic freedom: 'How sweet is some degree of liberty! I had a kind prince, but was obliged at times to be dependent on base souls. I often sighed for release and now have it in some measure.'

People clamoured for their place in the sunshine of culture, whether as performers or spectators, idling starers or cognoscenti. In many rural churches, wind bands still struck up the anthem, and tradesmen scraped together to play chamber music or sing glees, catches and bittersweet ballads of seduction. Lancashire textile communities were becoming famous for their choirs, their craftsmen–composers of hymn-tunes, and their fiddle-rounds to dance to. Exhibitions staged by Hogarth, raising money for the Foundling Hospital, drew huge crowds. And in high society, *milord anglais* on his Grand Tour pillaged the Continent for Old Masters (genuine, fake or retouched), took an artist or two in tow, and built and embellished at every opportunity. Frederick Hervey, prelate of Derry and creator of Ickworth, had such an itch for architecture that he was dubbed the 'edifying bishop'. Gentlemen of discernment clubbed together as connoisseurs of antiquities in founding the Society of Dilettanti and lent their patronage when artists sought to raise their profession through bodies such as the Royal Academy. Lords put their personal stamp on the arts. The Earl of Burlington, returning from his Grand Tour, launched the English Palladian movement. In designing the grounds at Stowe, with their temples of Ancient and Modern Virtue and of British Worthies, Viscount Cobham used architectural motifs to construct a Whig pantheon to constitutional freedom. Horace Walpole, who devoted his life and fortune to the arts, was a true experimentalist in taste – in his whimsical gothick home, Strawberry Hill, in his horror novel, *The Castle of Otranto* (1765), and in running his own printing press.

Art was rooted in opulence as in Medici Florence. England had a rich seedbed of skilled craftsmen: plasterers, stuccoists, woodcarvers, statuaries, gilders, etchers, plate-makers and drawing-masters. Some blossomed into creative geniuses – indeed, many leading artists started obscure. Gainsborough was the ninth child of a miller, Constable also a miller's son, Opie a carpenter's son. George Morland lived the life of a gipsy artist. Some got their training and breaks through apprenticeships to goldsmiths, cabinet-makers or engravers. Hogarth, apprenticed to a silver-plate engraver, started as a heraldic painter; Blake was schooled as an engraver. Many writers emerged out of other literary trades – Laurence Sterne (who wrote 'not to be fed but to be famous') was a clergyman, and Samuel Richardson was a master-printer turned author. And though precious connoisseurs liked to parade their exquisite discrimination, in reality there was no sharp divide separating the liberal arts from bread-and-butter craft skills, fine art from commercial. Top novelists such as Defoe and Smollett did not disdain hack-work: they could not afford to. Hogarth ranged from popular moralistic print series, such as *The Rake's Progress* and *Marriage à la Mode*, to noble portraits, as of the philanthropist Captain Coram.

The old Puritan animosity against art dissolved. There were outbursts of High Church rage against the stage (notably from Jeremy Collier), Evangelical thunder, and of course Dissenter scruples, but it was not an age of iconoclasm, nor was philistinism fashionable. Art inveigled itself into the common idiom, and spoke to many on different levels. For some, Hogarth's *Industrious* and *Idle Apprentice* print sequences were simply amusing; for others they probably did serve as wall-poster morality, ideals and warnings. Because visual images and the printed word were ubiquitous, and art was a mirror of life, all the world was a kind of stage. Street life comprised street theatre, for people played out their lives through rhetorical gesture and symbol, and saw real life in fiction. The 'art' in the sashes and colours worn by mobs, the liberty caps, the symbolism of the British lion or the turnip (Jacobite shorthand for George I), were ways of parading people's politics and faith. When theatre-goers heard Macheath in *The Beggar's Opera* exclaim, 'That Jeremy Twitcher should 'peach me, I own surprised me,' they saw mirrored there Lord Sandwich, betraying his former companion-in-rakery, John

Wilkes. They did not just see it, but shouted it out, bringing the performance to a halt, and Sandwich was branded thereafter as 'Jeremy Twitcher'. *The Beggar's Opera*, Hogarth's engravings and political cartoons in general scored such a success precisely because they could be taken at so many different levels by a highly diversified public used to reading between the lines.

The keynote of eighteenth-century art, its alliance with wealth, rang out in various ways. Craft-skill and artistry gave style to the world of things: well-being meant there was more to read, more shows to go and see, more tutors, authors, performers, literati, all depending upon the public for their livelihood. Writers lived less in the pockets of patrons. Patronage's decline was not due to the absolute drying-up of private largesse. Rather, the growth of an audience enabled the resourceful and talented to fare well without it. When learning, taste and wealth became 'general', thought Dr Johnson, 'an author leaves the great, and applies to the multitude'. Hogarth declared his independence from patrons by penning a 'No Dedication' – 'Dedicated to nobody' – for a projected literary work. 'I paint for no lords,' asserted the truculent George Morland.

Better livelihoods were in the offing for those who lived off skills and knowledge. William Herschel, in his pre-astronomical career as a versatile professional musician in Bath in the 1760s, could make a respectable £500 a year out of composing, conducting concerts, and giving lessons. As a successful novelist, Fielding pocketed £800 for *Amelia*. There was money in scholarship too. Dr Johnson received £1,575 for his *Dictionary*, William Robertson £4,500 for his *Charles V*, and Adam Smith £500 for the *Wealth of Nations*. Tobias Smollett became joint editor of a complete edition of Voltaire, panned books for the *Monthly Review*, and then in 1756 launched the *Critical Review*. He helped to prepare a seven-volume anthology of travel essays – his assignment was to write 100 sheets in fifteen months at one and a half guineas a time. He contributed to *A Compendium of Voyages* (at the same rate of pay) and to the *Universal History*, and was involved in a *Complete History of England*, published between 1755 and 1758, for which he wrote a staggering 2,600 quarto pages in fourteen months for £2,000. Similarly, an ultra-fashionable painter such as Reynolds ('this man was hired to depress art,' spat Blake) could receive a hundred guineas for a commission (as much as a small Old Master fetched). Worth over £100,000 when he died, Reynolds was buried in St Paul's with peers for pall-bearers.

Such lions of culture, free of Bohemian fantasy, were unashamed about turning art to monetary advantage. Hogarth had a shrewd business nose, and Pope managed his own literary career superbly, publishing a collected edition of his verse as early as 1717, collected editions of his letters in 1737 and of his prose in 1741, and editing Shakespeare. Even great writers had no compunction about conceiving of authorship as a trade: 'No man but a blockhead,' dogmatized Dr Johnson, 'ever wrote, except for money.' The bid for professional status among painters was marked by the founding of the Royal Academy in 1768.

Of course, only the Olympians of arts and letters got rich, but many got by. A competent professional painter could ask £15 or £20 for a head. Provincial towns such as Norwich and Birmingham began to support sizeable populations of portrait painters, silhouettists, engravers, topographical print-makers, sign-writers, drawing-masters, enamelists, etc. By 1811 Bath had about twenty artists. Industry itself gave openings for artists, Wedgwood employing talented draughtsmen such as Tassie. Top artists – Fuseli, Flaxman, Wright, Stubbs, and Blake himself – turned their hand to commercial and industrial art. Matthew Boulton believed industry's future hinged upon graceful design: without it, manufacturers could not secure luxury markets.

Furthermore, the power of the purse shaped the *content* of art and letters. Many commissions were designed to glorify rank, wealth and status. Paintings of military and naval victories, sycophantic book dedications, heroic statues, funerary monuments, heraldry and monograms were art's tribute to riches (in England, as Blake complained, 'portrait is everything'). The rich wanted their houses and grounds first designed and then immortalized in paint, preferably with rustics sentimentalizing the foreground. The taste, fostered by Capability Brown, for more 'natural' landscaping made Nature herself, when properly improved, seem like the very property of the rich. William Kent's neat device of the ha-ha, the sunken fence running round an estate's perimeter, fostered the illusion that their lands went on for ever.

These were halcyon times for the output of top-quality decorative art targeted at the wealthy – silverware, glass, Delft, porcelain – and good imitations, such as ormolu or plated ware, for those down a peg or two. And the power of money itself stimulated aesthetic innovation. The century had begun with Classical canons entrenched in architecture, verse and drama, largely because aristocratic patrons and their intimate coteries lent their authority to such styles. Austere Augustanism and dignified Palladianism were the languages of noble values. During the century, however, partly as a result of a more varied moneyed clientele emerging, artists and writers became more eclectic.

Classical rules crumbled at the edges; new tastes jostled alongside, making for 'neo-Classical' diversification. In architecture *nouveaux riches* nabobs, planters and plutocrats splashed out on more ostentatious country-house styles. William Beckford, the rich and strange son of a City millionaire, chose to construct (in collaboration with the architect Wyatt) a gothick abbey at Fonthill in Wiltshire, where he lived out his secluded fantasy life. Professional architects such as the Adam brothers, Chambers, and Wyatt himself, began to assert their own individual personalities. Grecian, Italianate, Chinese and Gothic styles, and hybridizations of these, proliferated. 'Decadent' asymmetry came into fashion. Landscaped gardens sprouted grottoes, follies, hermits' caves, and occasionally live hermits (one gave up the job after being pestered by tourists). *Fin-de-siècle* developers speculated in windswept hillside villas ('stareabouts'), mass-christened 'Belvedere', for merchants who wanted to be different. William Cowper noted a clergyman who 'enclosed his gooseberry bushes with a Chinese rail', and Horace Walpole's Strawberry Hill had 'embattled bookcases'. By 1800 more felt free to build their own way.

In painting, regional styles made an impact. Joseph Wright of Derby created the genre of moonlit industrial scenes, East Anglian artists such as John Crome discovered clouds and atmosphere, exploiting the potential of water colours. Local styles sometimes rose to national importance, as in china ware. China manufactories were set up in 1745 at Chelsea, in Worcester and Derby (1751), in Liverpool (1756), in Plymouth (1758) and in Bristol (1771). 'Grassroots' folklore, lays and ballads had their vogue among the elite, Bishop Percy publishing his *Reliques* in 1765. Gothick tales of victims and horror, such as Matthew Lewis's *The Monk*, turned into a craze. In time originality in art and appearance, traditionally condemned as pretentious vanity, found an eager audience. Novelty could even be hallowed as an expression of the English birthright of Liberty, George Mason writing approvingly in 1768 of 'independency . . . in matters of taste, and in religion and government'. Fashions in clothes became wilder. The 1770s saw gargantuan head-pieces for women and macaroni styles for men. The French Revolution produced a complete turnabout, with *citoyen* simplicity and ethnic garb becoming chic; shortly after, the Regency endorsed Beau Brummell's starched and austere dandyism.

As the buying public diversified its tastes, many artists and writers cultivated greater self-expression and individuality (it was a way of being noticed). Under the sway of patronage and the code of Classicism, the writer was expected to be self-effacing, adding his brick to the high cultural edifice of tradition. Time-honoured Classical forms and norms, such as the epic poem and mythological painting, had set the limits. Craft counted more than uniqueness. As late as Dr Johnson's time, it was perfectly acceptable for poets to polish up each other's verses. The rise of a wider, more varied and anonymous readership changed all that, encouraging writers and artists to carve out distinctive niches for themselves. They were freer to experiment, because less commonly working to peer expectation or commission – instead producing in anticipation of demand, even to satisfy their own sense of Creative Truth and personal authenticity. 'With patronage, what flattery! What falsehood!' declaimed Dr Johnson. 'While man is in equilibrio, he throws truth among the multitude, and lets them take it as they please.' For once Blake agreed with Johnson. 'The Enquiry in England,' huffed Blake, 'is not whether a man has talents and genius, but whether he is passive and polite and a virtuous ass and obedient to noblemen's opinions in art and science.' Blake despised toadying, consensus art: 'Without contraries, is no progression.'

This was all very well, but freedom from noble patronage might equally mean debt-bondage to the bookseller. 'That a genius must write for a bookseller, or paint for an alderman!' shuddered Horace Walpole. By the end of the century, some – notably Romantic poets – were hence declaring independence from patrons and public alike, unwilling to bear servility any longer.

Producing for an impersonal, hypothetical audience, writers explored their own sensibilities, dilemmas and imaginations. Some cultivated proud, eye-catching eccentricity – such as Laurence Sterne, spinner of the solipsistic, sentimental, cock-and-bull fantasy-novel *Tristram Shandy*; others, such as the mawkish poet Cowper, found voice in a pre-Romantic introspection. Some began to identify with the poor and dispossessed, as did the impecunious Goldsmith in his anti-enclosure poem, *The Deserted Village*. Others, like the self-appointed artist-reformer Hogarth, strutted as moral missionaries. Yet Hogarth's career reveals the multiple paradoxes of the posturing artist flexing new muscles of independence. Embodiment of the Englishness of English art, Hogarth fumed at patronage and lordly taste, but was not averse to courting it himself. He appealed to the judgement of the public at large, yet despised it when it rejected him. Engraving for the many made him his fortune (*The Harlot's Progress* brought in a staggering £12,000), yet he sulked when connoisseurs found fault with his high art. Though raising burlesque to new heights, his true ambition was to be accepted as a classical painter, master of the grand manner, hating yet envying creatures of the establishment such as William Kent.

For those safely above the poverty trap, the Georgian age was an exhilarating time to be alive. There were more goods and services available than ever before (the colonies and the poor helped to shoulder the cost). Things tended to get cheaper, at least until the last third of the century, when inflation set in. Popular culture's vigour was unflagging. Street life and the public domain remained vigorous and relaxed. New, capitalized forms of culture were growing up alongside, peddling commercialized art to wider audiences; yet these had not yet supplanted or smothered older forms. Folk and elite, popular and patrician cultures were not rigidly stratified. Polite society withdrew somewhat from popular idioms into enclaves of its own, and some, of course, made much of the superior pretensions of the polite. Thus the travelling scientific lecturer Benjamin Martin pandered to better-class audiences by portraying the mob as too dim to understand. 'I remember,' he buttered up his hearers, as my goods were once carrying into my lecture-room, at a certain town, the rabble crouded about the door, to know what it was; and one wiser than the rest immediately cries out, *'Tis a zhow come to town*; and what do we give to zee't? A GUINEA, replies the other. Z—nds, says the fellow, this is the D—l of a *Zhow*; why *Luck-man-zshure*, none but the *gentlevauke* can see this.

It is true that, later in the century especially, magistrates began to throttle certain popular enjoyments. But commercial entertainments were by no means the kiss of death to folk ways and jollifications, and common culture resisted evisceration, having a happy-go-lucky vitality of its own. Ordinary people were able to annexe those features of high art and metropolitan life they valued. When Lancashire artisans sang Handel, it was not a sell-out to an alien cultural mode, for they were actively moulding their own forms of musical life. There was vigorous give-and-take between the popular idiom and the cultural expressions of the polite. In any case, we must never think of oral culture as 'pure', untainted by commerce or high art. Popular singers were as eager as any to have their music printed and sold.

A neo-Puritan sobriety, the work-demon of industrialism, and political panic were eventually to come along and drain the exuberance out of the Georgian cultural legacy, and undermine its social comprehensiveness. But for most of the century these prospects were just clouds on the horizon.

7. Changing Experiences

Keeping your balance on life's tightrope was tricky. For ordinary people, the margins were fine between thriving and faltering, being reputable and being reprobate. Rural labourers and urban journeymen expected to obey superiors, look after themselves and toe the economic and moral line; personal survival and the community demanded it. Misfits and failures could not count on sympathy or second chances, and the Poor Law, with its dependency and surveillance, could feel less like a safety net than a bed of nails. Yet this sturdy independence which was expected was also commonly prized. Working folks had to be self-reliant; but many made a virtue out of necessity and championed individualism, eagerly seizing opportunities in a make-or-break economy which provided scope for initiative, enterprise and enrichment. There were lots of Robinson Crusoes who had made good and Moll Flanders who had married prudently. And, springing from the seedbeds of the Protestant conscience and the Enlightenment, public values saluted the sterling metal of individuality and the rights of men – and of women and children too.

To us, many aspects of Georgian England may seem hard-bitten, smacking more of the mentality of a frontier-post than a bastion of civilization. The powers of the high and mighty were direct, self-defining, only sporadically checked by the state, little answerable to inspection or redress. It seemed a fact of life, as Dr Johnson rued:

> How small, of all that human hearts endure
> That part which laws or kings can cause or cure.

Fine folk were born with silver spoons in their mouths, but he was a foolish common man who thought he had a claim on society for a job, livelihood or education. Owners, however, could expect to have free run of their property, fathers of their children, masters of their servants. The state did not bother itself too much with such ideals as social justice and equality, which figured large in politics from the Victorian age up to the late 1970s – though it did make it its business to protect positive legal rights. Indeed, the offices of central government themselves were cockpits of private faction-fights. Laissez-faire was embedded as practice through much of civil society long before it became the theoretical sacred cow of political economists. 'In England,' wrote Jeremy Bentham, 'abundance of useful things are done by individuals which in all other countries are done either by government or not at all' – for instance fire services, mad-houses, and even certain gaols were privately owned. If rough justice resulted, it was a price which those who ruled the roost were happy for others to pay.

Foreigners found this society robust, often to a fault. Writing in 1725, the Swiss traveller B. L. de Muralt thought the *mot juste* for the English was 'fierce'. It was assumed – if deplored – that public-office holders would be on the fiddle. After all, they had to buy their offices in the first place, and few were properly salaried. The wardenship of the Fleet gaol cost John Huggins £5,000 in 1713: of course he had to milk it aggressively. It shocked no one that gaolers and lock-up keepers maltreated their charges, dunning them with exactions termed 'chummage' and 'garnish': 'pay or strip' greeted new prisoners. Public trustees such as grammar-school or alms-house governors notoriously lined their pockets and promoted their relations. Discovering monstrous misappropriation of funds at a Winchester hospital, John Wesley commented, ''Tis a thing worthy of complaint when public charities designed for the relief of the poor are embezzled and depredated by the rich.' William Jones, vicar of Broxbourne, found his own parish clerk, a tailor, cutting up the parochial records to use the paper for taking measurements.

But little was done to raise the standards of public life. Why? It was partly because would-be reforming movements, such as the Societies for the Reformation of Manners, founded from 1699, failed to win public goodwill. Resented for their busy-bodying, they had declined by the 1740s. Before Evangelicals and Utilitarians gathered strength late in the century, there were few effective pressure-groups for probity, no clean-up-public-life campaigns which achieved true popularity. In any case, everything was against the kind of scruple in public life to which the Victorians aspired. Public servants such as tipstaffs, turnkeys or excise officers were either ill-paid or, like constables, unpaid. In many civil-service departments, the customs for instance, places and promotion went by nepotism and favour. Why should anyone buy a job such as that of gaol-keeper except to feather his own nest? It was left to a few private zealots, such as John Howard, to be scourges of prison and hospital corruption. (The great Howard, noted Sir Samuel Romilly, 'made a visit to every prison and house of correction in England with invincible perseverance and courage'.) True, there were show-trials when enormities became too scandalous – as happened with Thomas Bambridge, warden of Fleet prison in the 1720s, who took bribes to allow wealthy debtors to escape, and perpetrated cruelties. And the fickle public occasionally had fits of self-righteousness, and demanded scapegoats. In 1757, Admiral Byng was court-martialled and shot (*pour encourager les autres*) to assuage public wrath over the loss of Minorca. But few were the curbs on the powerful within their own bailiwicks, especially if they could pull strings in high places.

Respect for rights would not tolerate the sacrilege of 'interference'. A man's office, underlings, apprentices or slaves, a colonel's regiment – all were regarded as his property. Such fetishization of rights, liberty and property often masked naked selfishness and, as Goldsmith noted, could encourage a beggar-my-neighbour, devil-take-the-hindmost nihilism:

> That independence Britons prize too high
> Keeps man from man, and breaks the social tie;
> The self dependent lordlings stand alone,
> All claims that bind and sweeten life unknown.

Yet there was another side to the coin. It was in many ways an extraordinarily free and open society for those not too badly scarred by other people's freedom. English championship of freeborn rights ran deep and rang true. Foreigners were struck. 'I am here in a country which hardly resembles the rest of Europe,' wrote Montesquieu in 1729. 'This nation is passionately fond of liberty . . . every individual is independent.' He pinpointed the vital connection: 'England has progressed the farthest of all peoples of the world in three important things: in piety, in commerce, and in freedom.' French philosophers, frequently debarred from publishing in their own country and occasionally imprisoned, envied English free speech. Pastor Moritz contrasted English towns with Prussian: 'No walls, no gates, no sentries, no garrisons. You pass through town and village as freely and unhindered as through wide-open nature.' Tourists could visit the Tower in London, but not the Bastille in Paris. Günerode observed: 'The Englishman breathes liberty, and anything that even appears to threaten this is an object of hatred to him and capable of driving him to all lengths!'

Law guaranteed Englishmen's freedoms and no one made light of its protection. The Revolutionary Settlement had confirmed parliamentary government, Habeas Corpus and religious toleration. Statutory censorship of books and the press had ended with the lapse of the Licensing Act in 1695 (as late as 1683 Oxford University had made a public bonfire of works by Hobbes, Baxter and Milton). Characteristically, so far as the Government checked the press, it was not by direct censorship but by burdensome taxation following the Stamp Act of 1712. Admittedly in 1737, smarting from blistering satires against his regime, Walpole required that authors submit plays to the Lord Chamberlain for approval and tried to close down all playhouses but Drury Lane and Covent Garden. But his ban was side-stepped – enterprising theatre managers instead staged 'concerts' – with plays as interval-pieces! From 1709 a succession of Copyright Acts guaranteed authors some property in their publications. The practice of parliamentary reporting in the press was pioneered from the 1730s, initially through the subterfuge of reporting on the 'Parliament of Lilliput'. In these and similar ways the individual could secure protection via the machinery of law.

Resistance to executive power was a reflex, localism the English creed. Schemes to extend standing armies and barracks, and centralize police and tax-gathering (for instance, Walpole's Excise Bill) met ferocious and successful opposition: Dr Johnson defined excise as 'a hateful tax levied . . . by wretches'. Foreigners were amazed at the obstreperousness of the common people in the face of their betters. On the highway, they would not melt away before the rich. 'A man in court dress,' reported Casanova, 'cannot walk in the streets of London without being pelted with mud by the mob, while the gentlemen look on and laugh.' A true Prussian, von Archenholz was offended:

The sentiment of liberty, and the ever-active protection of the laws, are the cause why the common people testify but little consideration for persons of quality, and even for persons in office, except they have gained their affection by affable and popular manners. That perfect equality which nature hath at all times established among men, presents itself but too forcibly to the minds of these haughty islanders, and neither dignity nor wealth are capable of effacing it. Even the Majesty of the Throne is often not sufficiently respected. The Englishman considers his sovereign only as the first of the magistrates in his pay.

Foreigners were surprised that the Quality actually paid respect to their inferiors, and in limited but significant ways were prepared to treat them man-to-man. In Madame du Bocage's epigrammatic exaggeration, 'In France we cringe to the great, in England the great cringe to the people.' Or in Madame Roland's view:

The proudest Englishman will converse familiarly with the meanest of his countrymen; he will take part in their rejoicings ... It is true, that persons of higher rank find the common people necessary to realize their ambitious designs, and it is not uncommon, at elections, and those for members of Parliament especially, to see the lowest of citizens receiving letters from the most illustrious candidates, in which, in the most polite terms possible, they solicit the favour of their votes; and when these agree to their request, they are not long in receiving a letter, in which the candidate expresses his gratitude in the warmest terms. Have we not lately seen the Duchess of Devonshire lavishing, on such an occasion, not only gold, but kisses? That great popularity, enjoyed by the nobility which always so much astonishes strangers, is congenial to the constitution of a free state. Is it not the effects of this conduct in the English nobility that makes them the most enlightened of their rank in Europe?

Her account – however tendentious – contains a kernel af truth. The English were passionately attached to their rights, enshrined in the common law, constitution and political settlement. Historians, statesmen and journalists constantly reminded them of the moral virtue of participation in a free commonwealth (even if, with diminishing electoral contests, fewer were actually doing this). 'In some other countries the upper part of the world is free,' commented Bishop Butler, 'but in Great Britain the whole body of the people is free.' Joseph Priestley, who as a Dissenter had a personal stake in the matter, summed up the hymn to English freedom:

A sense of political and civil liberty, though there should be no great occasion to exert it in course of a man's life, gives him a constant feeling of his own power and importance, and is the foundation of his indulging a free, bold and manly turn of thinking, unrestrained by the most distant idea of control.

Moreover, the slogans of the age of reason, filtering down from the literati, fortified these freedoms. Enlightenment thinkers championed liberty and individuality. Liberals, from philosophers such as Locke to popularizers like Addison, mounted a critique of blind traditionalism, rejecting an earlier Calvinist theology of original sin and the depravity of man, while equally despising 'Romish' irrationalism and intellectual surrender to Papal dogmatics. The intelligentsia's liberal and optimistic religion affirmed free-will, salvation for all, the goodness of mankind and its capacity for progress. Each individual, they believed, had the right to moral autonomy and self-realization.

The well-tempered pursuit of happiness in the here-and-now — indeed, the *right* to happiness — became a leading theme of moral essayists. For many (though not for Dissenters) the temper of *Pilgrim's Progress* was a thing of the past. Soame Jenyns summed up a widely-shared new outlook:

Happiness is the only thing of real value in existence: neither riches, nor power, nor wisdom, nor learning, not strength, nor beauty, nor virtue, nor religion, nor even life itself, being of any importance but as they contribute to its production.

Boswell experienced it: 'I felt a completion of happiness,' he wrote in 1772. 'I just sat and hugged myself in my own mind.'

The idea that it was proper to pursue worldly well-being gave the leisured classes a licence to explore their own psyches. In some ways this was, of course, nothing new. From the Catholic confessional to anxious Protestant soul-searchings, Christianity had always required vigilant self-examination, the purging of sinful thoughts and the quest for inner grace. But traditional religious introspection had aimed to lead people out of this mire of egoism on to the straight and narrow path of righteousness under priestly, ecclesiastical or scriptural guidance. When educated Georgian polite society examined itself, however, the tone was more subjective, even narcissistic. Diaries and autobiographies, such as Boswell's, show that people were dwelling more on their own psychological make-up, and often indulging, rather than quelling, their humours and passions. Many of course ended up not with the blueprint for bliss but the rich paradoxes of heightened, introspective sensibility and an alluring but addictive melancholy (often called the 'English malady'). Diary-keeping, silent reading, and perhaps greater privacy (as houses became subdivided into larger numbers of rooms) encouraged introspection.

Georgians believed that it was a social duty to reject gloom and solemnity, and they affirmed the right to personal fulfilment. Public life bears witness to an infectious gaiety and sense of fun of a kind often self-censored in other ages. It was for example the era of humorous gravestones. Samuel Foote, the one-legged comedian, was thus memorialized in Westminster Abbey:

> Here lies one Foote, whose death may thousands save,
> For death has now one foot within the grave.

Perhaps self-defeatingly, a pervasive social etiquette told people to be cheery. Erasmus Darwin the physician set out to combat the 'drunkenness and hypochondriacism' of the idle rich by enjoining good spirits: 'In order to feel cheerful you must appear to be so.' When tedium threatened, activity was the best therapy. 'One must do something . . . otherwise one grows weary of life and becomes a prey to ennui.' As a means of staving off the 'nihility of all things', work, thought Darwin, was 'an inexhaustible source of pleasurable activity'. Among Utilitarian moralists, virtue became reformulated as the 'greatest happiness' principle. Virtue and vice, argued Jeremy Bentham, are but 'the tendency of the action to promote or diminish the general happiness'.

The pursuit of personal gratification found expression in economic individualism, the dictum that each should use his own labour and capital to get on. 'The desire of bettering our condition,' commented the eupeptic Frederick Eden, 'is the predominant principle that animates the world,' which, 'expanded into action, gives birth to every social virtue'. The economy was pictured as a hurly-burly of restless, ambitious men, sights trained upon gain. 'The wants of the mind are infinite,' argued Nicholas Barbon in 1690:

Man naturally aspires & his mind is elevated, his senses grow more refined & more capable of delight. His desires are enlarged, & his wants increase with his wishes, which is for everything which is rare, qualify his senses, adorn his body & promote ease, pleasure & pomp of life.

There was nothing new about seeing people as grasping and go-getting. What was new was treating egoism, and even greed, not as sinful and anti-social, but as natural and even admirable. Adam Smith, convinced of 'the uniform, constant & uninter-rupted effort of every man to better his condition', believed that, providentially, by a hidden hand, unrestricted economic sel-fishness benefited the commonwealth. 'Private vices, public virtues': though Bernard de Mandeville's formula scandalized many by its audacity, it was the golden rule by which many lived.

The long-standing Christian and Classical sense of the de-pravity or limitations of human nature melted into something more optimistic. Many Georgians cocked a snook at killjoy denunciations of the pleasures of the flesh, finding them morbid, envious or splenetic. Puritans became Aunt Sallys in plays and novels; figures such as Joseph Surface in Sheridan's *School for Scandal* were seen not merely as ridiculous but as arrant hypocrites. Contemporary diaries and letters suggest that, for many, living in Enlightenment England afforded a relaxed, emotionally frank breathing space after the strait-laced patriarchal solemnities of the world of their parents or grandparents – a brief interlude, perhaps, before the doubt, anxiety and muscular stridency characteristic of the probity-conscious Victorians.

Most took their pleasures in decent, measured ways: in the quiet delights of a clay pipe or plum pudding, browsing through a sermon, tickling a trout, strolling with the family or paying calls on a Sunday, practising self-improvement, singing in a catch-club, patronizing charity concerts, or cultivating one's garden. There was also a tolerated hedonistic fringe. Shandyesque outlandishness had a free run. 'Surely our nation produces more originals than any other,' pondered Sir Horace Mann, aware of the pride English eccentrics took in riding their hobby-horses. Major Peter Labelière, dying in 1800, wanted to be buried head down, because the world itself had always been upside down. Edward Wortley Montagu contracted two bigamous marriages, then turned Papist and Muslim (his father disinherited him). The transsexual Chevalier d'Eon was a welcome guest in polite homes. The rich built architectural follies and revived Druid cults.

There was an easy-going indifference to punctilio about English manners, which foreigners found odd but attractive. Addison recommended an 'agreeable negligence' in matters of form (the Spectator Club was his parable, showing how men of diverse humours could rub along together). Later in the century Thomas Gisborne remarked how 'the stiffness, the proud and artificial reserve, which in former ages infected even the intercourse of private life, are happily discarded'. The German Moritz noted how, when mixing in society, officers 'do not go in uniform but dress as civilians'. Dress etiquette grew less rigid. In the House of Lords, Lord Effingham had the appearance, according to Samuel Curwen, 'both in his person and dress of a Common Country Farmer, a great coat with brass buttons, frock fashion, his hair short, strait, and to appearance uncombed, his face rough, vulgar and brown, as also his hands'.

Relaxation of strict protocols gave greater breathing space to personal relations. 'Formality counts for nothing', observed La Rochefoucauld:

and for the greater part of the time one pays no attention to it. Thus, judged by French standards, the English, and especially the women, seem lacking in polite behaviour. All the young people whom I have met in society in Bury [St Edmunds] gave the impression of being what we should call badly brought up: they hum under their breath, they whistle, they sit down in a large armchair and put their feet on another, they sit on any table in the room and do a thousand other things which would be ridiculous in France, but are done quite naturally in England.

Such informality was reinforced by the metropolis's anonymity. 'There is no place in the world,' thought Pastor Wendeborn, 'where a man may lie more according to his own mind, or even his whim, than in London.' Hanoverian London grew ever more cosmopolitan, its migrant communities – Sephardic Jews, Huguenot refugees, Germans, Swiss – all finding their niche.

Among the affluent and leisured, there was more open

expression and exploration of sexuality.* The libido was liberated, and erotic gratification increasingly dissociated from sin and shame. Sex, in the opinion of Dr Erasmus Darwin, was the 'chef d'oeuvre, the masterpiece of nature', 'the purest source of human felicity, the cordial drop in the otherwise vapid cup of life'. John Wilkes's doggerel,

> Life can little else supply
> But a few good fucks and then we die

found its gloss in Boswell's observation that there was no 'higher felicity on earth enjoyed by man than the participation of genuine reciprocal amorous affections with an amiable woman'. He practised what he preached, with gusto. While a young man-about-town in 1763 he performed many sexual feats, among others 'solacing his existence ... with a strong, plump, good-humoured girl called Nanny Baker' in St James's Park, and taking a whore (wearing a condom, for safe sex) on the recently opened Westminster Bridge:

At the bottom of the Haymarket I picked up a strong, jolly young damsel, and taking her under the arm I conducted her to Westminster Bridge, and then in armour complete did I engage her upon this noble edifice. The whim of doing it there with the Thames rolling below us amused me very much.

But sacrificing to Venus led to dosing with mercury, for Boswell contracted 'Signor Gonorrhoea' a score of times. Nevertheless, sexual activity was positively prescribed on medical and psychological grounds, for retention of semen was believed harmful, and ageing spinsters were proverbially thought frustrated and ill-tempered. 'I was afraid I was going to have an attack of gout the other day,' wrote Lord Carlisle. 'I believe I live too chaste. It is not a common fault with me.' Bagnios – high-class bath-houses-cum-brothels – may have had the beneficial side-effect of getting wenching men to bathe.

Sex was on public view, being regarded with an earthy matter-of-factness, quite alien from the common Romantic and Victorian idealization of love. The vicarious eroticism of bawdy songs and pornographic prints formed part of the landscape, and

---

* There is much less evidence for lower-class attitudes towards sexuality, as distinct from lower-class patterns of procreation and family formation.

raised few eyebrows. Francis Place recorded the lewd songs
common in his youth (though he thought these were disappearing
by the early nineteenth century):

> One night as I came from the play
> I met a fair maid by the way;
> She had rosy cheeks and a dimpled chin
> And a hole to put poor Robin in.

The master-cartoonist Rowlandson engraved pornographic
prints, some for the Prince Regent (Gillray drew obscene cartoons *of* the Prince). Politicians suffered scatological satire without respite, Pitt the Younger being lampooned as the Bottomless
Pitt ('stiff to everyone but a lady'), Walpole and George II
pictured with breeches down, farting and defecating. The leading
feature of female fashion was a very conspicuous *décolletage*.
Erotic literature multiplied almost unchecked, from John Cleland's *Fanny Hill* (which netted the publisher, Ralph Griffiths,
£10,000) to sentimental tales of titillation, such as *The Innocent
Adultress, Venus in the Cloister* or *Cuckoldom Triumphant*, and salty
accounts of adultery trials. Newspaper advertisements peddled
sexual services from gigolos to aphrodisiacs, VD cures to abortifacients, and window-shopping gallants could buy prostitutes'
directories, such as Jack Harris's *The Whoremonger's Guide to
London*. Sexual prowess was a matter of public pride. The
orgiastic demoniacs of the Hell-Fire Club, or Medmenham
Abbey, who included Lord Sandwich and the Revd John Kidgell,
chaplain to the Earl of March, did not lose caste. 'Wilkes and
libertinism' was as popular as 'Wilkes and liberty'. A Whitby
collier of the 1760s was named *The Free Love*.

Gallantry was, of course, a man's world. Yet, at least in racy
London society, ladies were assumed to possess strong sexual
appetites and the right to their gratification. They were not kept
prudishly innocent or ignorant, as perhaps in Victorian times, for
sex manuals, such as *Aristotle's Masterpiece*, seem to have circulated
widely among women (and maybe even youngsters: Francis
Place read it while a schoolboy). London waxworks mounted
'educational' displays of female reproductive organs. And the
Nottingham Weekly Courant of 26 November 1717 carried an
advertisement informing readers that:

Any able young Man, strong in the Back, and endow'd with a good

Carnal Weapon, with all the Appurtenances thereunto belonging in good Repair, may have Half A Crown per Night, a Pair of clean Sheets, and other Necessaries, to perform Nocturnal Services on one Sarah Y——tes, whose Husband having for these 9 Months past lost the Use of his Peace-Maker, the unhappy Woman is thereby driven to the last Extremity.

Whether spoof or genuine, Georgian frankness is unmatched.

In this more relaxed atmosphere, sexual jealousies were held in check. High-society *ménages à trois* were quite common, wives and mistresses, lovers and wittols often maintaining studiously polite terms (a wife anxious not to conceive again might welcome her husband taking a mistress). The Duke of Devonshire had three children by the Duchess and two by Lady Elizabeth Foster, who lived under the same roof; for her part the Duchess had a child by Lord Grey. A man of the world did not automatically challenge his wife's lover to a duel, but he expected acceptance from others. 'I often dined with him,' wrote Horace Walpole of Archbishop Blackburne:

his mistress, Mrs Cruwys, sat at the head of the table, and Hayter, his natural son by another woman, and very much like him, at the bottom, as chaplain. Hayter was afterwards Bishop of London. I have heard, but do not affirm it, that Mrs Blackburne, before she died, complained of Mrs Cruwys being brought under the same roof.

One story I recollect, which showed how much he was a man of this world, and which the Queen herself repeated to my father. On the King's last journey to Hanover, before Lady Yarmouth came over, the Archbishop being with her Majesty, said to her: 'Madam, I have been with your minister Walpole, and he tells me that you are a wise woman, and so do not mind your husband's having a mistress.'

Polite society loved scandal but was sufficiently worldly-wise to be blasé about its dangers.

Certain forms of sexual permissiveness were taken as the order of things. It was taken for granted that maid-servants were fair game for philanderers; the gentlemen were thought gallants so long as they made arrangements for resulting bastards. Though women were clearly victims of harassment, many seem to have been compliant or active. Young William Hickey was first seduced at the age of ten by a maid, Nanny Harris. One of his early memories was of waking one morning to find himself between Nanny's legs, 'with one of my hands upon the seat of love where I have no doubt she had placed it'. Men such as Hickey and Boswell found no difficulty in getting partners among respectable women, quite apart from prostitutes. Actresses and dancers were assumed to be sexually easy, and many women obviously felt better off being kept as mistresses by gentlemen than being servants or wives. Classy demi-mondaines and courtesans, such as Grace Dalrymple and Fanny Murray, won fame and respect, becoming much-prized models for leading painters. Women of easy virtue were not automatically treated as pariahs. In the 1780s Francis Place's master was a London leather-breeches-maker, Mr France, who had three daughters.

His eldest daughter was and had been for several years a common prostitute. His youngest daughter, who was about seventeen years of age, had genteel lodgings where she was visited by gentlemen; and the second daughter ... was kept by a captain of an East India ship, in whose absence she used to amuse herself as such women generally do.

Evidently neither Place, nor France, nor the women themselves, were embarrassed by this situation. Public men commonly kept mistresses and walked out in public with them, as the Duke of Grafton did with Nancy Parsons. Despite Hogarth's print sequence, not all harlots' progresses were tragic: Mrs Hayes, the society brothel keeper, retired reputedly worth £20,000. Great men sometimes even married their mistresses. The Earl of Coventry married Mary Gunning, and the Duke of Hamilton her sister, Elizabeth. The reverse even happened, though rarely. Lady Henrietta Wentworth, Lord Rockingham's sister, wed her footman.

Though bastardy still carried a stigma, bearing children out of wedlock could be winked at in smart society. 'I deplore the unpopularity of the married state,' fumed Lady Mary Wortley Montagu,

which is scorned by our young girls nowadays, as once by the young men. Both sexes have discovered its inconveniences, and many feminine libertines may be found amongst young women of rank. No one is shocked to hear that 'Miss So and So, Maid of Honour, has got nicely over her confinement.'

Bastards were often brought up alongside legitimate children, publicly acknowledged by their fathers. The son for whom Lord

Chesterfield wrote his *Letters* was a bastard. Dr Erasmus Darwin set up his two illegitimate daughters as the governesses of a school, noting that natural children often had happier (because less pretentious) upbringings than legitimate. The pious Joseph Addison sired a child on the Countess of Warwick, and Lady Harley reputedly had children by so many lovers that her brood ✓ was known as the 'Harleian Miscellany'. For his part, the tenth Earl of Pembroke fathered children on two mistresses. His illegitimate son became intimate friends with his heir and with the Countess (who however insisted that the bastards should not take the family name of Herbert). Bastards might even marry well. The illegitimate daughter of Sir Edward Walpole married Lord Waldegrave, and, on his death, George III's brother, the Duke of Gloucester.

When profligacy was discreet and genteel, a blind eye was turned. Mrs Theresa Berkeley ran a flagellants' brothel in Charlotte Street, and there was at least one female flagellants' club in late-century London. Though buggery remained a capital offence, it was no secret that London harboured sodomites' clubs and brothels ('molly houses'), and well-connected male homosexual activity ran little risk of prosecution. Some notorious homosexuals, however, such as William Beckford, found it prudent to go abroad or to retire to rural privacy, and plebeian homosexuals, especially in the armed forces, risked being savagely punished.

Masked balls, such as those staged in Soho by Casanova's one-time lover Mrs Cornelys, were well-known fronts for pick-ups — 'the whole Design of the libidinous Assembly seems to terminate in Assignations and intrigues'. London teemed with brothels and other pleasure domes such as Mrs Hayes's serail in Pall Mall, whose floor-show included a Tahitian 'Love Feast' between twelve nymphs and twelve youths, and naked dancing. Roués could get a street-walker for 6d., though Casanova thought that a night with a high-class courtesan at a bagnio cost 6 guineas. London had in excess of 10,000 prostitutes, openly plying their trade at the theatre and on the street. 'Women of the town,' wrote John Macky,

seem to give the magistrates of London very little trouble. Yet they are more numerous than at Paris, and have more liberty and effrontery than at Rome itself. About nightfall they range themselves in a file in the foot-paths of all the great streets, in companies of five or six, most of them dressed very genteelly. The low-taverns serve them as a retreat, to receive their gallants in: in those houses there is always a room set apart for this purpose. Whole rows of them accost passengers in the broad day-light; and above all, foreigners. This business is so far from being considered as unlawful, that the list of those who are any way eminent is publicly cried about the streets: this list, which is very numerous, points out their places of abode.

Although disgruntled clients sometimes avenged themselves on pilloried bawds, attempts by Societies for the Reformation of Manners to hound whores off the streets got no general backing.

In this relaxed — or lax — atmosphere, in which neither state, Church nor opinion was hyper-vigilant in policing the morals of the urban and the moneyed, it was affluent males who enjoyed greatest latitude. But other people's claims to a place in the sun — registered in such slogans as the birth-right of the freeborn Englishman, the rights of man, and, as Mary Wollstonecraft, protested, of *woman*, and the greatest happiness of the greatest number — were also being acknowledged. Opinion-leaders liked to see themselves as humane and sympathetic, sensitive to the claims and feelings of others. Much breast-beating went on about the plight of underlings such as servants, and unfortunates such as abandoned mothers. Where once malefactors had been unconditionally execrated, now reformers put them under the microscope (*what*, they asked, made such people go to the bad?). Novelist and magistrate Henry Fielding argued that mere moralism was pointless, for pauper boys become 'thieves from necessity', and 'their sisters are whores from the same cause . . . Who can say these poor children had been prostitutes through viciousness? No. They are young, unprotected and of the female sex, therefore they become the prey of the bawd and the debauchee.' Following Rousseau, many vented disgust — some sincerely, some modishly — at the gilded vacuities of smart society. The blessings of Nature, artlessness and simplicity could be displayed as counter-attractions — endorsing the common 'primitivist' view that the labouring classes were 'natural' souls, backs bowed under an artificial, corrupt civilization. Even the *Gentleman's Magazine* pondered in 1782:

The collier, the clothier, the painter, the gilder, the miner, the makers of glass, the workers in iron, tin, lead, copper, while they minister to our necessities or please our tastes and fancies, are impairing their health, and shortening their days.

Views such as these smoothed the path for philanthropists such as Jonas Hanway, campaigning on behalf of society's victims, who contended that 'we ought no more to suffer a child to die for the want of the common necessaries of life, though he is born to labour, than one who is the heir to a dukedom.'

Yet caution is needed. Tears for the exploited, the unfortunate and the afflicted flowed freely, but sympathy cost little, and was only occasionally translated into action. Pity demonstrated the superior sensibilities of the tender-hearted and assuaged the conscience. In an age of lax collective devotional practice, humanitarian gestures could be spiritual securities. Some were impressed: 'Religion in England,' wrote Prévost, 'in towns, and even in the smallest villages finds its expression in hospitals for the sick, homes of refuge for the poor and aged of both sexes, schools for the education of the children.' Yet many thought such tenderheartedness was but humbug. 'We live in an age when humanity is in fashion,' sneered Sir John Hawkins in 1787. But though contemporaries were not slow to indict the poverty of humanitarianism, attitudes and practices were in fact changing.

Children – the largest captive audience – were notably affected. Hitherto children had attracted little attention, despite, or perhaps because of, their vast numbers: about a quarter of the population was under ten. Childhood was traditionally a stage of life passed over without much notice. Calvinism had reckoned souls sinful from birth, needing to be beaten into obedience and reason. Not being civilized or rational, they were no company for adults. But this all changed. From Locke to Rousseau (whose educational writings received much lip-service) liberal religion and Enlightenment pedagogy argued for the natural innocence of children and hence their potential for rational thought and civilized behaviour. In polite society at least, children's feelings, cuteness and wishes came to command interest and even respect. In a model of childhood giving new prominence to nurture over nature, education grew in importance and the psychology of parent–child and teacher–child relations received attention. Most significantly of all, affluent parents began taking conspicuous pride in their offspring. For instance, child portraits became suddenly popular (Reynolds could charge up to £150). Couples became more child-oriented. 'If there could be found a fault in the conduct of my mother towards her children,' wrote 'Perdita' Reynolds, 'it was that of too unstinted indulgence, a too tender care.' Richard Steele boasted of his son, 'We are most intimate play-fellows.' Travellers such as Henri Misson found the new attention to children in polite society quite remarkable:

They have an extraordinary Regard in *England* for young Children, always flattering, always caressing, always applauding what they do; at least it seems so to us *French* Folks, who correct our Children as soon as they are capable of reasoning, being of the Opinion, that to keep them in Awe is the best Way to give them a good Turn in their Youth.

Though groups such as the Wesleyans kept faith with flogging, enlightened parents laid off the rod, trying reason, coaxing and kindness instead. Infants were hugged and petted more. Affection tempered authority. 'Parents here in general,' noted Pastor Moritz, 'nay, even those of the lower classes, seem to be kind and indulgent to their children; and do not, like our common people, break their spirits too much by blows and sharp language.' When Henry Fox was unhappy at his son's long hair, he was reduced to pleading, in a form of address unthinkable a century earlier, 'You gave me hopes that if I desired it, you would cut it . . . I will, dear Ste, be much obliged if you will.' But Fox was notoriously liberal in his attitudes. When his younger son, Charles James, went to hurl his watch on the floor, 'If you must, I suppose you must' was the father's highly Rousseauesque response. Lord Chesterfield opened his letters to his son with the egalitarian and respectful 'Dear Friend'. As a mark of childhood's new privileged state, children came to be dressed less as miniature grown-ups, being allowed to wear looser, less formal clothes. Gentlefolks started to nickname their little ones as Sukey, Jackee or Dickee (though first-born were less likely to be given pet names). At her birth in 1775, Jane Austen's father wrote, 'she is to be Jenny . . . as like Henry or Cassy is to Neddy.'

Children even became foci of consumption, the toy market in particular increasing by leaps and bounds. Books, playthings and educational aids poured onto the market. Old games such as hoops, trap-ball and barley-break were being replaced by instructional toys such as Wallis's *Educational Cards for the Amusement of Youth* (1785), stuffed with improving morals such as:

> The rocking horse pursues the course
> Directed by your hand.
> Children should thus their friends obey
> And do what they command.

The new attention to children defies easy evaluation. Polite society 'discovered' childhood, but it was adults who did the discovering (what did children make of it?). In some ways the 'discovery of childhood' amounted to little more than fresh opportunities for pampering in newly intensified domestic settings. The ideas of childhood innocence developed ('where ignorance is bliss,' wrote Thomas Gray, ''tis folly to be wise'), but in its own way it could be no less pernicious than the myth of the child as originally sinful. New outlooks made children childish and adults serious. Children, previously kept at arm's length by their parents, now perhaps had their lives invaded with intrusive grown-up ideas of what was good for them, such as Mrs Barbauld's prim learning books, crammed with 'geography and natural history', which – so Charles Lamb complained – 'have banished all the old classics of the nursery'.

From the eighteenth century, children have become focal points of attention, their differentness, autonomy and rights acknowledged. The same is true for other groups. As the plight of the destitute worsened, pioneer social investigators, such as Frederick Morton Eden, studied them more and expressed greater concern. Mocking the mad and the deformed became offensive: they were not for laughter, but for pity and treatment. Sophie von la Roche noted that whereas in Paris, Damiens, the would-be assassin of Louis XV, was tortured to death, George III's attempted assassins were pronounced insane and stuck in Bethlem. The cult of the noble savage gained ground, especially when South Sea voyagers such as Captain Cook returned with such handsome prize specimens as Omai the Tahitian and reports of an Edenic Polynesia. Crude white ethnocentrism was jolted by awareness of majestic civilizations such as the Chinese or Indian, subscribing to different socio-ethical values. A campaign was

launched against the slave trade, bearing fruit in 1807. Wedgwood struck a medallion with the legend, over a chained black-
amoor slave, 'Am I not a man and brother?' And the English,
though already doting on their pets (one thinks of Hogarth's
pug, of Gray's cat Selena, and of Dr Johnson feeding his cat with
oysters), at last began to question their heartless treatment of
animals. In 1751 Hogarth produced a print sequence exposing
cruelty to animals, about which he wrote:

The Four Stages of Cruelty were done in hopes of preventing in some
degree that cruel treatment of poor animals which makes the streets of
London more disagreeable to the human mind than anything whatever,
the very describing of which gives pain . . . It gratifies me highly and
there is no part of my works of which I am so proud, and in which I
feel so happy as in the series of the Four Stages of Cruelty, because I
believe the publication of them has checked the diabolical spirit of
barbarity which I am sorry was once so prevalent in this country.

Other barbaric prejudices were softening. Jew-baiting probably
declined. Francis Place reported in the 1790s how Jews who
within his memory had been 'hooted, hunted, cuffed, pulled by
the beard and spat upon', now were 'safe', believing that 'the
few who would be disposed to insult them merely because they
are Jews would be in danger of chastisement from the passer-by
and of punishment from the police'.

Yet evaluating this growing humanitarianism itself requires
sensitivity. It seems probable that society's victims wrung heightened pity and guilt precisely because they were being more
savagely exploited than heretofore. Work-beasts were being
driven harder and the slave trade became an ever greater abomination. In transit, sick slaves would sometimes be thrown overboard
alive *en masse* for the insurance. Mere callousness caused quite
needless suffering. Other nations cleaned chimney flues with
brushes; England with climbing boys. Unguarded machinery in
new factories reaped a grim harvest of young limbs. Moreover,
as defenders of the status quo remarked, those campaigning
righteously against abuses were not always the best placed to
cast the first stone. Opponents of the slave trade in the colonies
were often 'slave-driving' manufacturers at home, many of them
Quakers.

Sympathies were selective. The labouring classes and the poor *en bloc* received little relief, though charities were directed to improve the lot of harmless sub-groups and token 'unfortunates', such as orphans, child prostitutes or disabled servicemen, who posed no threats. Moreover, apart from certain laws safeguarding debtors, practically no *legislation* was passed to protect the weak. And, while professing to dignify objects of pity, charity could easily demean them. Personal slaves were sometimes freed with a flourish, but they usually ended up as personal servants, trapped within condescending nicknames such as Zeno, Socrates or Pompey. Care of unfortunates often meant surveillance, and humanitarianism could often serve as a way of extending control.

Over time, the English became more aware they were living through and participating in momentous and accelerating changes. Most were proud of what they saw – and seeing such changes, they wanted them recorded: demand surged for prints of landscapes and townscapes, houses, prize bulls and pedigree families. 'In travelling thro' England,' wrote the admiring Defoe in the 1720s,

a luxuriance of subjects presents itself to our view. Wherever we come, and which way soever we look, we see something new, something significant, something well worth the traveller's stay and the writer's care . . .

(And as Christopher Hill has commented, with Defoe, 'We are already in the modern world, the world of banks and cheques, budgets, the stock exchange, the periodical press, coffee-houses, clubs, coffins, microscopes, shorthand, actresses and umbrellas.')

Times were changing. Harking back to Defoe, the *Gentleman's Magazine* noted in 1754: 'Were the same persons who made a full tour of England 30 years ago, to make a fresh one now they would find themselves in a land of enchantment. England is no more like to what England was than it resembles Borneo or Madagascar.' The nation lost its martial front: public sword-wearing became less common, and largely decorative. The gates of London – Cripplegate, Ludgate, Aldgate, Moorgate, Newgate – were demolished in the 1760s and 1770s to accommodate the flood tide of traffic. Man conquered the air for the first time. In 1785 Horace Walpole nonchalantly observed, 'Three more balloons sail today' – it was the year of the first cross-channel flight, and soon express coaches were nicknamed 'balloon coaches'. Like everything else, ballooning was instantly commercialized, with admission fees charged for watching ascents. Needing to be up-to-the-minute, people became newsmongers. Ephemeral reading-matter – newspapers, pamphlets, periodicals – challenged classics such as the Bible, Horace and *Foxe's Book of Martyrs*.

Improvement was going on all around. In 1754 getting from Newcastle to London had taken six days; by 1783 it took just three. The four and a half days needed to travel from Manchester to London in 1754 had been slashed to twenty-eight hours by 1788. And the future came to occupy people's thoughts – in many cases with eager expectancy, in some with foreboding. In the 1790s Frederick Morton Eden thus saluted technological change:

With regard to mechanical knowledge, it is probable that we are still in our infancy, and when it is considered that, fifty years ago, many inventions for abridging the operations of industry, which are now in common use, were utterly unknown, it is not absurd to conjecture that, fifty years hence, some new contrivance may be thought of in comparison with which the steam engine and spinning jennies, however wonderful they appear to us at present, will be considered as slight and insignificant discoveries.

The English prided themselves upon being practical and down-to-earth. 'Our business here,' Locke had taught, 'is not to know all things, but those which concern our conduct.' Inventions were introduced to simplify labour, speed production and by-pass bottlenecks. Fertile minds such as Erasmus Darwin and Richard Lovell Edgeworth invented as readily as others doodled: carriages, oil-lamps, agricultural tools and canal locks poured from their brains. Early in the century Charles Povey conceived of a newspaper totally dependent on advertisements, a salvage corps, a water-bomb for putting out fires, and a typewriter. After 1750, technological changes came thick and fast. In textiles there was the flying shuttle, the spinning jenny, the water frame, Crompton's mule and Cartwright's power loom. Newcomen's sturdy steam pump drained mines, while Watt's steam engine, with its separate condenser, economized on fuel and, in its rotary form, was adapted to provide power for driving machinery.

Smelting iron with coke enabled abundant fossil fuels to replace scarce timber. Water-wheel engineering became a model of experimental efficiency, and John Smeaton perfected lighthouse design. In 1758 the 'Improved Birmingham Coach' had blazoned on its side 'FRICTION ANNIHILATED'. By 1801, Richard Trevithick had put a steam carriage on the road. Strides were also made in scientific instruments. Most spectacularly of all, John Harrison's marine chronometer solved the age-old navigational problem of gauging longitude.

Innovativeness became all the rage. 'Almost every Master & Manufacturer,' wrote Dean Tucker of Birmingham in 1757, 'hath a new invention of his own, & is daily improving on those of others.' 'The English are great in practical mechanics,' congratulated Louis Simond at the beginning of the nineteenth century, 'In no country in the world are there, perhaps, so many applications of that science, I might say, of that instinct of the human species.' In his role as seer, however, William Blake distrusted the machine as all too emblematic of the evils of modernity: 'it is destructive of humanity and of art: the word Machination.'

The most prophetic inventions were those multiplying power. In 1783 James Watt coined 'horse power' as a measure for his steam engines (significantly the horse was still the index of power), and his partner, Matthew Boulton, bragged to Boswell, 'I sell Sir what all the world desires: POWER.' 'The people in London, Manchester and Birmingham are all steam mill mad,' Boulton claimed in 1781. 1788 saw Symington's first workable steamship. Erasmus Darwin prophesied:

> Soon shall thy arm, UNCONQUER'D STEAM! afar
> Drag the slow barge, or drive the rapid car;
> Or on wide-waving wings expanded bear
> The flying-chariot through the fields of air.
> – Fair crews triumphant, leaning from above,
> Shall wave their flattering kerchiefs as they move,
> Or warrior-band alarm the gaping crowd,
> And armies shrink beneath the shadowy cloud.

Scores of *domestic* gadgets also came into use, or at least into mind; lucifer matches, umbrellas, the modern tooth-brush (designed by William Addis), stoves and chimneys built not to smoke, patent kitchen ranges, alarm clocks which automatically lit candles, bell-pulls, dumb-waiters, ventilators, the argand oil-lamp (a French invention), clockwork cradles, Pears soap, Friar's Balsam, Mr Schweppe's mineral waters – all found their way into the home. Tom Paine, later political revolutionary, experimented with smokeless candles and iron suspension bridges. Prototypes of fountain pens, telescopic candlesticks, roller skates and patent exercisers appeared. Condoms were new to England. The heavy, dangerous, overhead London street signs were dismantled. From the 1770s, the numbering of houses began, and was mandatory in London streets from 1805. In 1778 Joseph Bramah patented his superior ball-cock WC and had marketed 6,000 by 1797. In Nelson's house at Merton, each of the five bedrooms had a WC fitted in the adjoining dressing-room, together with a washstand and bowl, lead tank and tap, and a bath filled by servants.

The wealthy festooned their houses and grounds with the latest exotica – pet monkeys, parrots and goldfish, fuchsias, acacias and pineapples; veronicas from the Falkland Islands, camellias from Japan and jade ornaments from the Orient. Imperial expansion led to great experimentation with clothes and building styles. Foreigners tasted delicacies unknown in England before, from sardines and kippers to Stilton cheese. The father of all convenience foods, the sandwich, appeared. 'The slices of bread and butter given you at tea are thin as poppy leaves,' simpered Pastor Moritz, in his most Anglophile tone, 'but there is a way of roasting slices of buttered bread before the fire which is incomparable. One slice after another is taken and held to the fire with a fork till the butter soaks through the whole pile of slices. This is called *toast*.'

In 1751 England introduced – at long last – the Gregorian Calendar. Old London Bridge was pulled down in 1760. Street lighting and sanitation improved. The world's first iron bridge spanning a river was erected at Coalbrookdale in 1776. The first national medical register appeared in 1774. The Ordnance Survey was founded in 1791. English increasingly replaced Latin as the language of administration. From early in the century London had its own local penny post, and other towns followed. Ralph Allen pioneered a scheme of crossroads to guarantee that all parts of the country were well covered by the post. Later John Palmer replaced post-boys with mail-coaches to ensure greater safety and punctuality. Change, in short, was everywhere.

This crescendo of inventions and improvements produced a collective desire for advance — rational, technical, scientific and industrial — which captivated the public imagination. Man's conquest of Nature was widely trumpeted. Josiah Wedgwood the potter captured the faith in scientific method: 'Everything yields to experiment.' His friend Joseph Priestley stressed science's practical side: 'Knowledge, as Lord Bacon observes, being power, the human powers will in fact be enlarged; nature, including both its materials and its laws, will be more at our command.' Groups such as the Society of Arts (founded in 1754) sought to activate improvements. This voluntary society, financed by the fashionable, gave rewards to inventors on condition they did not patent their inventions. Prizes were offered mainly for improvements in agriculture, the liberal arts and handicrafts: not until the last decades of the century did the prospects of transforming heavy industry seem so inviting. Agricultural improvement societies sprouted — there were about fifty by 1800, awarding prizes for improved tools, good management and trusty labourers; some published their own journals. Itinerant lecturers spread the taste for scientific knowledge.

In the last third of the century, the Royal Society of London was joined by new provincial scientific societies, such as the informal Lunar Society of Birmingham and the Manchester Literary and Philosophical Society (founded 1781), providing a local forum for knowledge and culture, drumming up interest in science, and advancing manufacturers. Their (all male) members — the Lunar Society included James Keir the glass manufacturer and William Withering the doctor — united amateur love of science with involvement in practical improvements in manufactures, husbandry and medicine, all under the banner of a humanitarian ethos, which they saw best served by the spread of capitalist industry. Although the Royal Society lacked energy, up and down the country thousands of spare-time devotees made observations, collected and experimented. In 1798 Malthus could celebrate

the great and unlooked for discoveries that have taken place of late years in natural philosophy, the increasing diffusion of general knowledge from the extension of the art of printing, the ardent and unshackled spirit of inquiry that prevails in the lettered and even unlettered world.

The eyes of earlier generations had been trained on the past – seeking visions of arcadian innocence, or authorities and precedents in the truths of the Apostolic Church or the prescriptions of the British Constitution. The eighteenth century focused its gaze far more upon the present – and then forward into the future. Optimism instilled faith in progress and human perfectibility, and made people eager to try new ways, from infant care to crop rotations, and sometimes novelty for its own sake. Even the fastidious Gibbon deigned to 'acquiesce in the pleasing conclusion that every age of the world has increased and still increases the real wealth, the happiness and knowledge and perhaps the virtue of the human race'.

Of course change had its diehard critics, who thought newfangled ways were so much flam. 'The age is running mad after innovation,' fumed Dr Johnson over the abolition of public executions at Tyburn in 1783. 'All the business of the world is to be done in a new way. Tyburn itself is not safe from the fury of innovation.' (Public hangings there had to be ended because Tyburn Tree adjoined newly smart residential Mayfair, and swarming riff-raff lowered the tone.) And, of course, much didn't change at all, traditional habits retaining their vigour. Customs and folkways, magic and pagan practices remained deep-rooted. Belief in fate, evil spirits, spells and omens made sense, particularly of countryfolks' lives, for the sophistries of polite culture still had little to offer gnarled husbandmen (Wesley's hellfire meant more). Suicides continued to be buried at crossroads, stakes driven through the heart. The Blundell family, Lancashire gentry though they were, still cut their hair at full moon. Babies' cauls, used as protective charms, fetched high prices.

Though social statistics and political arithmetic made headway, tabulating information on diet, income and population, this was no guarantee against credulity. In 1771 a newspaper reported a seventy-five-year-old gander in Worcester. In any case self-congratulating 'modernity' was often only skin-deep. Sophisticated London panicked when minor earth tremors struck in 1750 and 1755. Thousands fled the metropolis, momentarily giving up their vices to placate the angry God. George II called a public fast, and Bishop Sherlock's *Pastoral Letter*, proving the quakes were divine punishment of London's fleshpots, sold 100,000 copies.

In the absence of dramatic medical breakthroughs, old wives' herbal medical wisdom survived – dung tea, crabs' eyes, vipers' flesh, stewed owl, pike eye as a specific for toothache. 'To Cuire t^e Aguie,' scrawled James Brindley in his pocket book, 'Drink your own Youren whan warm.' 'I drank snails' tea for breakfast,' recorded the Hon. John Byng, 'for my chest is very sore.' When Parson Woodforde had a stye on his eye, he heard

that the eyelid being rubbed by the tail of a black cat would do it much good, if not entirely cure it, & having a black cat a little before dinner I make a trial of it, & very soon after dinner I feel my eyelid much abated of the swelling.

(The cat had to be black because of residual witchcraft associations.)

And, of course, there was no reason why the new should supersede the old. Traditional female midwives were challenged by the fancy new male *accoucheur*, armed with forceps. But whether such 'man midwives' truly made deliveries safer remains open to question. Certainly dirty forceps could easily harbour infection and thus do more harm than good. Not everything 'new' was new anyway. Physicians 'discovered' digitalis for treating heart conditions: in the form of foxglove, it was an old folk remedy. Doctors took up cod-liver oil, but it had long been used by Lancashire fishermen to combat rheumatism. Many folk cures worked: dung *is* an effective poultice. Where traditional and new, popular and polite, cultures confronted each other, there was often objectively little to choose between them. Some people refused to accept the Gregorian Calendar when it replaced the Julian in 1751, afraid that 'losing' eleven days would rob them of their wages. After the calendar switch, the *Salisbury Journal* reported:

Yesterday being Old Christmas Day, the same was obstinately observed by our Country People in general, so that it being Market Day (according to the order of our magistrates) there were but few at market, who combined the opportunity of raising their Butter to ninepence or tenpence a pound.

In need of personal guidance, the lower classes still sought out 'wise women' or consulted almanacs which contained horoscopes, prophecies and proverbial advice: *Old Moore's* sold over 100,000 copies a year. The fashionable, for their part, began writing to the 'agony columns' of magazines (such as John Dunton's *Athenian Mercury*, founded in 1689) for solutions to their intimate problems. Similarly, when sick, the wealthy often called the physician, but also tried folk or quack remedies. Sir Robert Walpole ate soap by the pound for his stomach complaints. Patent medicine panaceas such as 'Daffy's Elixir' (for biliousness) and 'Dr James's Powder' (for fevers) sold to people high and low.

The elite liked to think of themselves as pioneering more rational, liberal and humane values. They condemned folklore as silly, cruel and vulgar, and pooh-poohed traditional proverbial wisdom, preferring tags from the Classics. Unlike the French Bourbons, Hanoverian monarchs no longer 'touched for the King's Evil' (the plebs retaliated by clutching at the bodies of executed criminals, trusting to their thaumaturgical powers). The intelligentsia smiled at vulgar belief in a literal Hell and eternal punishment, in the Devil, guardian angels, hobgoblins and ghosts. Sensitive parents stopped frightening their children with threats of the bogey man – Maria Edgeworth, the immensely popular children's writer, asked 'Why should the mind be filled with fantastic visions instead of useful knowledge?' Sarah Trimmer was one of many superior children's writers who objected to fairy stories: they were both untrue and common. 'The histories of little Jack Horner, Cinderella, Fortunatus and other tales which were in fashion half a century ago,' she frowned, 'are full of romantic nonsense,' suggesting that solid factual works such as natural history be substituted to combat such 'pernicious' rubbish. Fairy tales after all contained magic (which science had disproved) and prejudiced children against wolves and step-mothers, and stories such as Dick Whittington gave them dangerous ideas about social climbing.

The debonair contrasted their own rationality with the wild passions of the herd, envisaging the civilizing process as a progress from 'rudeness' to 'refinement', from gut prejudice to reason. True taste, manners and morals, they emphasized, were matters of rational, even scientific, judgement rather than mere instinct or preference. The well-bred looked down on yokels, with their quaint speech and irrational folklore. As Henry Bourne reflected about folkways, 'though some of them have been of national and others perhaps of universal observance, yet at present they would have little or no being if not observed among the vulgar.' The elite gave the withering away of folk customs a helping hand (though considerately recording them, somewhat expurgated, for posterity). The maypole in the Strand was felled in 1717.

Above all, polite society finally ceased to believe in the reality of witchcraft, to the wrath of scriptural fundamentalists (for John Wesley, 'the giving up of witchcraft is in effect giving up the Bible'). From the late seventeenth century, the torchbearers of Enlightenment argued that so-called witches were just lonely, isolated, deluded old women. 'When an old woman begins to doat,' argued Joseph Addison in the *Spectator*:

and grow chargeable to a parish, she is generally turned into a witch, and fills the whole country with extravagant fancies, imaginary distempers, and terrifying dreams. In the meantime, the poor wretch that is the innocent occasion of so many evils, begins to be frighted at herself, and sometimes confesses secret commerces and familiarities that her imagination forms in a delirious old age. This frequently cuts off charity from the greatest objects of compassion, and inspires people with a malevolence towards those poor decrepit parts of our species, in whom human nature is defaced by infirmity and dotage.

Magistrates became unwilling to sustain witchcraft allegations. After the 1680s no witch purge occurred, and in 1737 the witch laws were repealed, though throughout the century panicking villagers continued to take punishment into their own hands, meting out vicious and sometimes fatal lynch-law to suspected witches. Even then, gentlemen could intervene as guardians of the helpless: 'A few days ago,' the *Public Advertiser* reported in 1761,

one Sarah Jellicoat of this town [Wilton] escaped undergoing the whole discipline usually inflicted by the unmerciful & unthinking vulgar on witches, under pretence that she had bewitched a farmer's servant & a tallow chandler's soap, which failed in the operation, only by the favourable interposition of some humane gentlemen & the vigilance of a discreet magistrate, who stopped the proceedings before the violence thereof had gone to a great pitch.

'Spirits are lawful, but not ghosts,' punned the indignant

Blake: 'especially Royal Gin is lawful spirit.' But how far did the elite onslaught on popular superstitions, on mystery and the spirit world go? Should we see it as the thin end of a secularizing wedge leading to atheism? Certainly many 'rational' Christians no longer viewed the daily course of their lives as a succession of divine fingerposts. 'The doctrine of a particular providence,' lamented John Wesley in 1761, 'is absolutely out of fashion in England' (for many being 'provident' seemed more to the point). 'The influence of religion is more and more wearing out of the minds of men,' bewailed Joseph Butler, Bishop of Durham, in 1736. 'The number of those who call themselves unbelievers increases, and with their number, their zeal. The deplorable distinction of our age is an avowed scorn of religion in some and a growing disregard of it in the generality.' Religion seemed a shadow of its former self. John Wesley in fact rated it a most profane age:

Ungodliness is our universal, our constant, our peculiar character . . . a total ignorance of God is almost universal among us — High & low, cobblers, tinkers, hackney coachmen, men and maid servants, soldiers, tradesmen of all rank, lawyers, physicians, gentlemen, lords are as ignorant of the Creator of the World as Mohametans & Pagans.

And it was said of Birmingham folk in 1788 that 'the great mass of the people give themselves very little concern about religious matters, seldom if ever going to church . . . What religion there is . . . is to be found amongst the Dissenters.'

Secularizing views were certainly supplanting Christian in many spheres. In the seventeenth century suicides were still religiously condemned as guilty of wilful and mortal sin: men of the Enlightenment looked on them, by contrast, as sick people who had acted while their mind was disturbed. The rise of insurance (accompanied by probabilistic thinking) silently challenged belief in Providence. In time, popular almanacs contained fewer religious, and more patriotic, prophecies. Secular and Classical practices edged in where Christianity once had a monopoly. Plenty of Christians still saw the grave as the gateway to salvation, but others faced dying in new ways. For instance, the *Gentleman's Magazine* recorded in 1733 the funeral of Mr John Underwood of Whittlesea:

At his Burial, when the Service was over, an Arch was turn'd over the Coffin, in which was placed a small piece of white Marble, with this

Inscription, *Non omnis moriar*, 1733. Then the 6 Gentlemen who follow'd him to the Grave sung the last Stanza of the 20th Ode of the 2nd Book of *Horace*. No Bell was toll'd, no one invited but the 6 Gentlemen, and no Relation follow'd his Corpse; the Coffin was painted Green, and he laid in it with all his Cloaths on; under his Head was placed Sanadon's *Horace*, at his feet *Bentley's* Milton; in his Right Hand a small Greek Testament . . . After the Ceremony was over they went back to his House, where his Sister had provided a cold Supper; the Cloth being taken away the Gentlemen sung the 31st Ode of the 1st Book of *Horace*, drank a chearful Glass, and went Home about Eight. He left near 6000L. to his Sister, on Condition of her observing this Will, order'd her to give each of the Gentlemen ten Guineas, and desir'd they would not come in black Cloaths; the Will ends thus – *Which done I would have them take a chearful Glass and think no more of* John Underwood.

Gravestones and funeral tablets shed their macabre skulls and charnel-house carvings, and sprouted solacing urns and laurels. Yet this does not at all amount to atheism. What many Georgians wanted was a basically secular life with the comforts of religion superadded. Sacerdotalism was certainly out. Benefit of clergy was curtailed, Convocation prorogued, ecclesiastical courts reduced to a husk, the transcendental and mysterious elements of faith minimized. And this was the way even the Anglican hierarchy wanted it, for many of the clergy did not aim to be priestly at all, but to merge into county society, hobnobbing with the gentry. 'The English clergy,' remarked Pastor Moritz, 'and I fear still more particularly those who live in London, are noticeably and lamentably conspicuous by a very free, secular and irregular way of life.' Louis Simond dubbed them 'free and easy'. Not untypical of this breed was the Revd Henry Bate: a prebendary of Ely Cathedral, he was a journalist, dramatist, formidable pugilist, art critic and greyhound-breeder. His duels while editing the *Morning Post* earned him the nickname of 'the fighting parson', and in his seventies he led a troop of volunteers against rioters in the village of Littleport in Cambridgeshire. John Wesley was appalled by the worldiness of many of the clergy he met. In 1743 he wrote of one of his sermons:

While I was speaking, a gentleman rode up very drunk, and after many unseemly and bitter words, laboured much to ride over some of the people. I was surprised to hear he was a neighbouring clergyman. And this too is a man zealous for the Church! Ah, poor Church! if it stood in need of such defenders!

Just a fortnight earlier he had written:

At our inn I found a good-natured man, sitting and drinking in the chimney corner; with whom I began a discourse, suspecting nothing less than that he was the minister of the parish. Before we parted I spoke exceedingly plainly. And he received it in love; begging he might see me when I came that way again.

Of course, many defended a low religious profile as the truly civilized posture. Zeal would be vulgar, inflammatory, and smack of 'enthusiasm' (defined by Dr Johnson as 'a vain confidence of divine favour or communication'). Only a fully rational faith could command intellectual and scientific respect and, by encompassing free inquiry and scholarly method, be tested and proven true.

Endorsement of 'philosophical' religion, and of moderate behaviour in general, was one way the educated and propertied justified their own lifestyle against the 'vulgar'. What the elite considered rational they often backed with power: exposing the 'irrational' and 'traditional' sometimes led to banning them. Thus various calendar festivities were abolished, ostensibly because they were relics of paganism or popery which had outlived their usefulness. And behind these rationalizations lay desires to re-order society. It was indeed humane to end witch-prosecutions, yet this step looks puny alongside the intensifying 'witch-hunts' against poachers, squatters, vagrants and combining workers. The triumph of 'rationality' also meant rewriting the ground-rules in favour of the powerful, for the concept of reason that prevailed was theirs.

Many matters, traditionally ruled by custom, left to chance or held sacred, were gradually being brought under rational control. As the economy became more complex and investments rose, so the need correspondingly grew to make life more regular and predictable. Weights and measures were standardized somewhat between regions, fighting men were put into uniform. Price tags – pioneered by the Quaker fair-price ethic – appeared in shops. The introduction of coach schedules and the royal mail led to the standardization of the time of day across the country. From the 1780s Cary's cheap road atlases helped people find their way.

Following an Act of 1773, more mileposts and signposts were erected. Teach-yourself books told people the correct way to do things, for example, *The Country Housewife's family Companion or Profitable Directions for whatever relates to the Management and good Economy of the Domestic Concerns of a Country Life. According to the Present Practice of the Country Gentleman's, the Yeoman's, the farmers and Wives in the Counties of Hertford, Bucks and other parts of England, shewing How great Savings may be made in Housekeeping* (1750).

Rising sales of calendars, diaries, ledgers and account books suggest a desire to keep tabs on life. The political and market information in newspapers helped the commercial classes to cope with uncertainty and plan ahead. Dictionaries slowly led to more uniform spelling – yet what became standard written English was not the speaking voice, but rather elite orthography. Thus, though everybody said 'landskip' and traditionally spelt it thus, that spelling bowed out to 'landscape' – first in writing and then in speech. Yet even as late as mid-century a gentleman such as Henry Purefoy could still, within one letter, spell 'periwig' in three different ways (all wrong to us!).

The hurly-burly of life was taken under control in new attempts to stabilize the environment, predict the future and protect investments. Entrepreneurs imposed factory discipline upon their workers, Wedgwood hoping to make 'such machines of men as cannot err'. Task-orientation tended to give way to time-orientation, and factory time was introduced with bells and clocking-on (Wedgwood's friend, John Whitehurst, designed special timepieces for the purpose). Keeping good time mattered more – 'Everybody has a watch,' observed Misson in 1719 – for 'in a commercial country,' as Dr Johnson reflected, 'time becomes precious.' Sir John Barnard gave homely advice: 'Above all things learn to put a due value *on Time &* husband every moment as if it were to be your last; in Time is comprehended all we possess, enjoy, or wish for; & in losing that we lose them all.' Even the leisured classes did not escape. 'There is nothing which I more wish that you should know and which fewer people do know,' Lord Chesterfield advised his son:

than the true use and value of Time . . . I knew a gentleman, who was so good a manager of his time, that he would not even lose that small portion of it which the calls of nature obliged him to pass in the necessary house, but gradually went through all the Latin poets in those moments. He bought, for example, a common edition of Horace, of which he tore off gradually a couple of pages, carried them with him to that necessary place, read them first and then sent them down as a sacrifice to Cloacina; that was so much time fairly gained, and I recommend you to follow his example . . . it will make any book which you shall read in that manner very present in your mind.

The most systematic plan for the rational reorganization and policing of life was Jeremy Bentham's Utilitarian philosophy, in which all activity was to be remoulded on the basis of quantified calculations of costs and benefits, pains and pleasures. Bentham described his panacea for all social ills, the Panopticon, a total surveillance institution or 'a machine for grinding rogues honest'.

The desire to extend control was implemented in many walks of life. Landscape gardening exemplified dominion over Nature on a bijou scale. Landowners could redesign corners of creation, making it 'picturesque', like a picture. Urban amenities and utilities were improved, parks laid out, marshy ground drained. In London, the Thames was embanked, the Fleet Ditch covered (in 1747) and sewerage improved:

Beneath the pavements are vast subterraneous sewers arched over to convey away the waste water which in other cities is so noisome above ground, and at a less depth are buried wooden pipes that supply every house plentifully with water, conducted by leaden pipes into kitchens or cellars, three times a week for the trifling expence of three shillings per quarter . . . The intelligent foreigner cannot fail to take notice of these useful particulars which are almost peculiar to London.

Westminster Bridge was built in 1750, followed by Blackfriars in 1756.

Many embraced the Promethean myth that man could, should, and must command his own destiny. There were admittedly few spectacular advances in medicine, though smallpox inoculation and subsequently vaccination were successful, and Cook showed how diet and hygiene could keep scurvy and other diseases at bay on trans-oceanic voyages. Yet doctors grew more confident that disease was a foe medical science could vanquish, Dr Erasmus Darwin loving 'to make war upon a pox or a fever'. Moreover, medicine assumed more public roles. Physicians had traditionally treated patients individually, concentrating on the bedside role. But now increasing numbers of them, such as Sir John Pringle, looked to social and preventive medicine – the health of the armed forces, or improved hygiene in industrial communities. The relations between epidemics and environment were explored, and a case argued for better public health provisions and legislation.

Illness was subject to this gradual secularization, being seen less as visitation, trial or punishment, and death less as fate or divine retribution. Increasingly, doctors hoped to cure, not just to relieve. Erasmus Darwin speculated on 'means of preventing old age', and James Graham, partly quack, partly popularizer, promised to reveal 'the whole art of enjoying health & vigour of body & mind, & of preserving & exalting personal honour & loveliness or in other words of living with health, honour, & happiness in the world for at least a hundred years'.

'Humane Societies' were founded to teach artificial respiration and reduce deaths from drowning (a matter of extreme importance in the canal age). New optimism about coping with disease led to a mighty wave of hospital foundation. Traditionally, hospitals had been 'hospices', places of 'hospitality' for the needy. Now they became centres of care and treatment for the sick poor (the rich were nursed at home). Five great new London hospitals were founded through bequests and private philanthropy: the Westminster (1720), Guy's (1724), St George's (1733), the London (1740) and the Middlesex (1745). Provincial foundations followed. The first outside London was the Edinburgh Royal Infirmary in 1729, followed by Bristol (1735), Winchester (1736), York (1740), Exeter (1741), Bath (1742), Northampton (1743) and many others. Specialist hospitals, such as the Foundling Hospital for abandoned babies, lying-in hospitals, and 'lock' hospitals for venereal diseases, were also set up. New dispensaries diagnosed illnesses and provided drugs for out-patients. By 1800 London dispensaries were treating 50,000 people a year. Like hospitals, these were supported philanthropically, with the needy as patients and the wealthy as subscribers.

Of course, hospitals and dispensaries provided valuable medical treatment for the common people, but at the same time they served the interests of their masters. Trainee physicians and surgeons got the bodies of the patients to practise on. The poor were meant to show gratitude, and, while hospitalized, would be less of a health risk to their betters (vital when so many of them were in-living servants). There they also formed a captive audience for discipline and sermons – the Exeter Hospital advertised itself as being 'of the greatest consequence not only for the health & welfare, but also to the religion & morals of the laborious poor'. The Revd Alured Clarke, founder of the Winchester Hospital, regarded his mission as being to 'instruct the sick and reclaim the bad'. The London Hospital gave discharge certificates only to those patients who had attended chapel to give thanks for their recovery. Hospitals were thus charity prudently dispensed.

Precisely how much hospitals achieved by way of healing the sick has been much debated. Most enforced the perfectly sensible policy of refusing chronic or highly infectious cases – nothing could usefully be done for these. Hospitals wrought no spectacular cures, particularly as in the age of agony before antiseptics and anaesthetics, internal surgery was out of the question. Surgery was limited to simple, quick or desperate operations, such as amputations, removing bladder-stones and setting fractures, and to a host of useful, but rarely life-saving, items of patching-up. Nevertheless, the old view that hospitals were 'gateways to death' is probably exaggerated.

Changes in therapies for lunatics affords a spectacular barometer of rising optimism – and its ironies. Before the eighteenth century, madness was commonly seen as spiritual derangement (in some cases, demonic possession), or as a kind of regression to animality. There were almost no institutions for the insane, with the exception of London's Bethlem Hospital (Bedlam), where frequent abuses led to inmates being chained up and neglected, and the old-fashioned therapeutics of blood-lettings and emetics long remained the staple treatment. Till the 1770s, Bethlem was open to sightseers, and patients were subjected to gawping visitors.

All this began to change. Enlightened physicians dismissed notions of demonic possession and emphasized that madness was a disease – believed at first to be of the body, and then, progressives argued, of the mind. Hence the mad were neither brutes nor possessed by devils, but were sick and therefore

amenable to treatment and cure. But the right environment
would be needed – preferably asylums in rural surroundings, set
apart from hubbub and anxiety. Privately run madhouses were
founded for those who could afford it (increasingly parishes also
paid for the mad poor to be sent there too). Towards the end of
the century, the traditional recourse to heavy sedative medication,
mechanical restraint or physical punishment was yielding to
novel notions of psychological management. 'Kindness' became
the magic word for a new 'moral therapy', in which patients
were to be treated with reason, calmness and example. Early in
the nineteenth century, Louis Simond, visiting the prestigious
York Retreat, found humanity the keynote:

There is near York a retreat for lunatics, which appears admirably
managed, and almost entirely by *reason* and kindness: it was instituted
by Quakers. Most of the patients move about at liberty, without noise
and disorder, and by their demure and grave deportment shew they
have not quite forgotten to what sect they belong.

Even so, the optimism induced by the new asylums sowed its
own problems. Some were abused as lock-ups for troublesome
relatives; confinement of a wife or a child as insane could be the
first step to laying hands on a fortune. Once confined, patients
had little legal protection or redress. The growing use of mad-
houses perhaps also indicates a decline in general tolerance towards misfits and simpletons around the household and in the
community.

   Similar tales could be told about many walks of life. Reason
and control brought order and care, but also more segregation,
more social engineering and greater expectations of conformity.
In polite society, greater attention towards the young perhaps led
to over-protective parental anxiety. Parenting became preoccupied with toilet-training, building up moral backbone by cold
baths, and psychological conditioning. Protectiveness demanded
that childhood sexuality be stamped out. Moralists began to
expose adolescent masturbation as an evil, books such as *Onania,
or the Heinous Sin of Self-Pollution* 'proving' that it led to physical
and psychological damage, even madness. James Graham prophesied that it would cause:

debility of body and of mind, – infecundity, – epilepsy, – loss of memory, – sight, and hearing, – distortions of the eyes, mouth and face, – feeble, harsh and squeaking voice, – pale, sallow and blueish black complexion, – wasting and tottering of the limbs, – idiotism, – horrors, – innumerable complaints – extreme wretchedness – and even death itself.

Hence doctors set about preventing and eradicating it by medical, physical and moral treatments.

Belief in achieving improvement through organization, system and surveillance was making inroads elsewhere. Educating squads of children in charity schools with few masters created logistic problems analogous to those of factory discipline. In answer, Andrew Bell and Joseph Lancaster mapped out factory methods of teaching, in a schooling system to be dubbed 'the steam engine of the moral world'. By division of labour, student monitors were to funnel instruction down from a single teacher to the pupils. 'Such is the intellectual organ,' wrote Bell in 1797,

which puts the whole scholastic machine in motion; such ... the principle on which every *schoolroom*, *factory*, *workhouse*, *poorhouse*, prison *house*, the *administration* of the poor laws, and every public or even private institution of any magnitude should be conducted.

Lawbreakers felt the winds of change most keenly. Traditionally felons were executed, transported or whipped to satisfy community wrath. Except for debtors, prisons had chiefly been transit places, where the accused awaited trial. Long gaol sentences had been very rare. Even in the early 1770s, only 2–3 per cent of judges' verdicts at the Old Bailey were for gaol sentences, and then the terms were short. Internally, as John Howard's visits revealed, gaols had been open-plan dens of disorder, drunkenness, corruption and disease. But in the last third of the century, reformers – both secular, such as the Utilitarians, and religious, such as Quakers – cast doubt upon essentially physical retribution, deeming it both cruel and inefficacious: thus branding was abolished in 1779. In the new penology, vengeance yielded to correction. Reformers developed alternative schemes of minutely controlled and supervised punishment centred on prison, aimed at deterring and (a new emphasis) reforming. The anarchic self-governing gaol with its own robust subculture was on the way out. The new penitentiaries, it was hoped, would become 'total institutions' under public scrutiny, with clear chains of expert command organized from above. Courts had traditionally sought to empty prisons: now the answer was to fill them. Purpose-built gaols would commit prisoners to regimes of discipline and hard labour. Prisoners were for the first time cooped in solitary confinement in cells, where they would repent and learn how to lead useful lives.

Such were the schemes. From the 1780s several such prisons were actually constructed (though most remained as before). Gloucester got a new gaol in 1792 at a cost of £40,000 (instantly and inevitably dubbed 'The Gloucester Bastille'). Fanny Burney was impressed:

This jail is admirably constructed for its proper purposes – confinement and punishment. Every culprit is to have a separate cell; every cell is clean, neat and small, looking towards a wide expanse of country, and (far more fitted to his speculation) a wide expanse of the heavens. Air, cleanliness and health are all considered, but no other indulgence. A total seclusion of all commerce from accident, and an absolute impossibility of all intercourse among themselves, must needs render the captive secure from all temptation to further guilt, and all stimulus to hardihood in past crimes, and makes the solitude become so desperate that it not only seems to leave no opening for any comfort save in repentance, but to make that almost unavoidable.

The reforming impulse was humane, with its faith in improved hygiene and healthy exercise, and its clampdown on intimidation. Yet 'humanitarianism' tightened the screw – and designedly so. 'I am not of the number of those,' the Gloucestershire philanthropist Sir George Onesiphorous Paul insisted, 'who from a misplaced tenderness of heart would unbind the just terrors of the law. I am far from thinking that prisons should be places of comfort . . . they should be places of real terror.' Now felons were to be gaoled for longer terms and psychologically racked. The new prison was a harbinger of a new species of planned punitiveness: long-term institutional control, using new disciplines and drills and technological tortures such as the treadmill – all in specially designed buildings. Jeremy Bentham planned a custodial institution, the Panopticon, which maximized surveillance by means of a central omniscient gaze. It was simplicity itself:

Morals reformed – health preserved – industry invigorated – instruction diffused – public burthens lightened – economy seated as it were upon a rock – the gordian knot of the Poor Laws not cut but untied – all by a simple idea in Architecture.

The perils of neglect were thus to be superseded by the pains of attention.

The pioneer new institutions did not, however, fulfil expectations. There was never enough money, they became overcrowded; prison labour, like workhouse toil, never paid its way, and dedication was not a strong-point of Georgian warders. And they failed to reform. When they didn't solve the problems the response was to set up more, giving a further twist to the spiral of institutionalization. The age was just dawning when, alongside new wealth, new freedoms and new powers, labour was being subordinated to machine time, and society's misfits (paupers, the mad, the ill and the criminal) were being set apart, drilled to conform under the management of 'experts'. The eighteenth century, however, saw only the beginnings. The central state did little. New hospitals and prisons were built on local and private initiatives; Bentham's Panopticon was not constructed. Yet the ball had been set rolling. The modern, the rational, the humanitarian, had its more sombre face; the Enlightened mind forged its own manacles.

The complexion of power in Georgian society was personal, rough-and-ready; *sauve qui peut* was the bottom line. Authority was backed up by physical terrors, from the gamekeeper's blunderbuss to the gallows. Yet these were not sure *deterrents* against riot and crime: at best they offered sporadic, angry, clumsy retribution. In village England where social discipline was strong, the Poor Law served as a powerful agent of stabilization. But the central state possessed few of the grinders of control available in other countries: censorship, the Inquisition, judicial torture, a centralized bureaucracy, administrative justice, education in the hands of religious orders, a secret police. Hence, to maintain public order, the English ruling class had to bank heavily upon inertia and the restraining forces of traditional society: scarcity, paternal discipline, community opinion, dependency, hostility to strangers and foreigners, and so forth.

Growing fears were expressed that these time-honoured bands of repression were beginning to fray. Labour shortage and rising real wages in the first half of the century sparked incessant employers' complaints about truculence and the erosion of work discipline. In growth industries, commercial expansion was giving labour bargaining power. 'When we strike, the masters cannot help themselves,' boasted an Old Bailey witness in 1765. Faced with such ominous threats, industry began to look to creating a well-drilled workforce.

Authorities are forever haunted by the spectre of the masses answering back. This danger was now felt especially acutely because the national Church could not awe them, and (unlike later) central government could command little direct local police power. To fill this void, voluntary initiatives were launched to coax and cajole the people into quietness. In floating such schemes, urban moneyed interests were particularly prominent. Westminster did little; Parliament passed fresh hanging statutes, but these were ineffective if not counter-productive. Nor could the Anglican Church corporately act (Convocation was prorogued); in any case, it was weakest where the risks of disorder were worst, in the boom towns and newly industrializing regions. Grandees for their part could afford to be a bit nonchalant. Dependency still bound rural labourers to the soil. They also had a shrewd confidence in the rock-solid stability of landed society, a faith in horse-whipping and a steady nerve. In any case aristocrats had no desire for a regulated, bureaucratic society: their ascendancy was encapsulated in personal power. As politicians, grandees learned to ride occasional disturbances, since they often made capital through agitation out-of-doors themselves.

Those eager and anxious to clean up society were rather the affluent, uneasy and assertive substantial bourgeoisie: men such as John Bellers, the Quaker London cloth merchant, or Thomas Guy, the London bookseller (who gave £220,000 from his Bible-printing monopoly to found his hospital) near the beginning of the century, or, at its end, William Wilberforce, scion of a Hull trading family, or Robert Raikes, a Gloucester printer, newspaper proprietor and pioneer of Sunday schools. For such moneyed men, everything was at stake. Their aim was to establish a personal ascendancy above the herd as right-minded, responsible and successful citizens, and at the same time to impress their worth upon their social betters, including God. In the last decades of the century above all, prosperous moneyed men were striving for a collective voice, a more cohesive sense of identity. Lacking direct power at Westminster, the vocal bourgeois chose not to challenge the aristocratic political machine, but rather to consolidate their own parallel *moral* authority, to cower their inferiors and impress their betters. *The World* magazine thus reflected on the claims of such activists to moral superiority:

There are certain vices which the vulgar call 'fun' and the people of fashion 'gallantry' but the middle rank, and those of the gentry who continue to go to church still stigmatize them by the opprobrious names of fornication and adultery.

Prominent among those leading with their moral fists were Dissenters, so conspicuous in movements to discipline and improve the masses. In contempt of the profligate heathenish eminences who excluded them from their rightful stake in the state, they made a parade of their own superior piety. Women such as Hannah More and Elizabeth Fry were also conspicuous among reformers and philanthropists. In a society which barred women's managerial energies from professional life, charity offered one eligible outlet for them to exercise their talents.

Far more than the great on their estates, the bourgeoisie were daily confronted with urban crime, drunkenness, ale-house brawls and prostitution. As employers, their profits were threatened by absentee, feckless and pilfering workers; and as vexed ratepayers they bore the brunt of poor relief and of service in unpaid local office. In the programme of reforming the manners of the poor, duty and advantage converged, and the appeal to personal self-interest was never far from the surface. 'If compassion cannot move you,' preached William Sharp in 1755,

let considerations of interest prevail with you. For neglect this poor man's numerous family, leave them to follow their own imagination and to make what wretched shift they can, and experience the sad consequence. They will soon grow up to public nuisances, infect your families with their idle disorderly behaviour, fill your streets with vice and violence; break in upon your comfort and your security: take the same persons under your patronage, teach them what is right and hear how you will be repaid. They will be serviceable to you in many ways by themselves, and by their examples, Industry, Sobriety, Good Order and Good Manners will get ground among you. Your city will be stocked with honest laborious ingenious artisans, some of the most useful members of a community; wealth will increase.

Sharp said it all.

There is no reason to doubt the sincerity of high-minded reformers of manners (though we might agree that Blake saw through such employer-philanthropists: 'They reduce the man to want and then give with pomp and ceremony'). Men such as Jonas Hanway and John Howard devoted their lives and fortunes to such improving labours, and the moral supervision of the poor was a prime duty to earnest men of condition. 'God has distributed men into these different ranks,' Bishop Butler noted,

and has formally put the poor under the superintendency & patronage of the rich. The rich then are charged by natural providence as much as by revealed appointment with the care of the poor.

The Nonconformist Liverpool physician James Currie agreed: 'The labouring poor,' he explained,

demand our constant attention. To inform their minds, to repress their vices, to assist their labours, to invigorate their activity, and to improve their comforts: – these are the noblest offices of enlightened minds in superior stations.

Many were moved to moral reformism out of disgust for the luxurious, money-crazed, self-seeking, indifferent society festering around them. Young Elizabeth Gurney (later Fry), brought up within a relaxed ('gay') Quaker household, turned idealistic and puritanical, rejected her easy-going family and purified her soul with philanthropy. Above all, Christian humanitarians were aghast that the poor were allowed to vegetate in pagan ignorance of Scripture.

Moral reformers wanted to improve life, but to do so in line with their own blueprints, and on their own terms, for they were absolute against indiscriminate charity and thoughtless philanthropy. They had no brief for the transformation of the social structure, but sought rather the alleviation of personal distress among the deserving and the universal conquest of vice. They wanted to make the poor neither equal nor affluent, but virtuous and, above all, God-fearing. 'Children fed by charity,' wrote the improving writer Sarah Trimmer, unctuous as ever, 'ought in a more special manner to be clothed in humility.'

Most philanthropists were sworn enemies of political radicalism, and those alive in the 1790s were to detest the spirit of the French Revolution. 'Who can forbear observing and regretting,' asked the bluestocking Hannah More,

that not only sons, but daughters, have adopted something of that spirit of independence and disdain of control, which characterizes the times? The rights of man have been discussed, till we are somewhat wearied with the discussion. To these have been opposed ... the rights of women. It follows that the world will next have – grave descants on the rights of youth – the rights of children – the rights of babies!

Rather, moralists looked to charity as a prophylactic against, or an antidote to, mutinous stirrings from the grassroots. As the Quaker John Bellers delicately hinted, 'It is the interest of the rich to take care of the poor.'

The campaign to moralize the poor was organized through voluntary associations, to which individuals subscribed sums which conferred upon them shares in the management. The turn of the eighteenth century saw 'joint stock religion' in bodies such as the Societies for the Reformation of Manners (founded from the 1690s), comprising eminent merchants and full-time philanthropists, all headed by a halo of higher clergy. Such movements were Protestant but inter-denominational: combating irreligion and disciplining the poor were more urgent than scrupulous attention to dogmatic niceties. They channelled deep-seated puritan impulses into social and legal expression, in many respects supplementing the declining church courts by laying prosecutions before the civil courts for vice offences, above all swearing, drunkenness, gaming, sabbath profanation, blasphemy, keeping unlicensed ale-houses, pornography, prostitution and homosexuality. Their vigilante smut-hounds brought many thousands of cases in the first third of the century – about 1,400 a year – before they underwent decline, having brought upon themselves widespread ridicule and hatred in the process.

At a later stage, their activities were taken up by the Proclamation Society (1787), and then the Society for the Suppressing of Vice (1802), patronized by wealthy businessmen and a sprinkling of peers. Rather unfortunately known as the Vice Society, it was dubbed by the Revd Sydney Smith 'a corporation of informers supported by large contributions bent on suppressing not the vices of the rich but the pleasures of the poor': an unsympathetic but not inaccurate summary, for, as Smith wrote apropos of the moral vision – or rather blinkers – of its members,

A man of £10,000 a year may worry a fox as much as he pleases, encourage the breed of a mischievous animal on purpose to worry it: & a poor labourer is carried before a magistrate for paying a sixpence to see an exhibition of courage between a dog and a bear.

Smith indeed thought the Vice Society misnamed: better by far had it been called a 'Society for Suppressing the Vices of Persons whose income does not exceed £500 per annum'.

Vice societies of this kind and private prosecutions sought to stifle popular culture in various ways. Popular sports, church ales and fairs – the saturnalian solaces of common people – were assailed, for such wanton mirth wasted money and led to idleness, while drunkenness and folk festivities, judged high-minded reformers, resulted in barbarities, such as killing cocks. Not least, they disrupted work rhythms, encouraged insubordination and challenged deference. 'Should publicans be allowed' (it was asked in 1764),

to promote and even advertise such ridiculous diversions as horse, foot, or ass races, or any similar pastime for the populace, on the view of profit to themselves by the promotion of idleness & drinking: such proceeding I must consider as unlawful in their nature – How often do we see the whole inhabitants of a country village drawn from their harvest work, to see cudgel playing, or a cricket match?

Especially in the last third of the century, popular recreations were suppressed in an increasing tide, abetted by the enclosure movement, which, by abolishing the commons, often took the very ground away from under a fair or sports. In 1745 cock-throwing was banned in Worcester, in 1750 in Bewdley and Kidderminster, in Liverpool in the late 1770s. The Revd William Grimshaw put a stop to football and horse-racing at Haworth in the 1740s. In 1778 'the Minister, Church-wardens and principal inhabitants' of Pebmarch prohibited the Midsummer Fair, directing the constables to forbid merriments. Even the harmless ceremony of the Dunmow Flitch – a competition to find the most happily married couple in the village – was suppressed. In 1772 the claimant of the prize was turned away by the Lord of the Manor, and future attempts to revive the custom were foiled.

In London, May Fair was abolished as early as 1709 (Mayfair was getting fashionable), and by 1803 the Vice Society was recommending that all fairs whatsoever be suppressed. In 1780 London magistrates closed skittle grounds outside taverns.

Looking back in 1801, the Revd Richard Warner was pleased to report some overall success. It was rather a disgrace that

the sports which sufficiently satisfied our ancestors of the sixteenth and seventeenth centuries had been the pranks of mountebanks, the feats of jugglers, tumblers and dancers, the jests of itinerant *mimes* or mummers, and the dangerous amusement of the quintane, diversified occasionally by the pageant and the masque, or the *elegant* pastimes of bullbaiting, cock-fighting, cock-scaling, pig-racing, bowling, football, grinning through a horse-collar, and swallowing scalding hot frumenty . . .

Things, however, were on the mend. 'As national manners gradually refined,' he reported with some complacency, 'the ideas of elegance were proportionally enlarged, and public amusements insensibly approximated to the taste and splendour which they at present exhibit; balls, plays, and cards, usurping the place of those rude athletick sports, or gross sensual amusements, to which the hours of vacancy had before been devoted.'

Philanthropists came up with bans, but they also offered bait. They showered working people with sermons and pamphlets, charities such as the Society for the Promotion of Christian Knowledge (1699) and the Society for Distributing Religious Tracts among the Poor (1782) pouring out tracts of Christian truth. The SPCK issued 5,000 copies of the *Soldier's Monitor* to Marlborough's army. Societies for the Reformation of Manners distributed *Kind Cautions against Swearing* to hackney-carriage drivers, mindful, doubtless, of the delicate ears of the passengers. Sermons and admonitions were supplemented by the edifying doggerel and uplifting tales penned by such do-gooders as Hannah More in her series of cheap *Repository Tracts*. Worldly and heavenly reward – thus ran their moral – would in time repay labouring families who were meek and did what they were told. For the rest there was *The Story of Sinful Sally*, the sad tale of how obstreperous folk, who drank and cursed their lot, went to the bad. Falling in a steady drizzle all through the century, such tracts became a deluge in the years immediately following the French Revolution.

School complemented Church as a means for indoctrinating the masses' children. Charity and Sunday schools were set up by the dozen. Some were staffed by lady bountifuls. 'At Windsor,' wrote Robert Raikes, 'the ladies of fashion pass their Sundays in teaching the poorest children.' But lesser mortals – blacksmiths and tradesmen – taught as well. Manchester Sunday schools boasted 5,000 pupils in 1788. By 1797 there were 1,086 Sunday schools across the country with 69,000 pupils, some of them adults. They taught reading (though less frequently writing: 'Reading will help the people's morals,' Jonas Hanway had written, 'but writing is not necessary'), Scripture, piety, drill, and elementary manual skills. Catechizing was the key activity. Mrs Sarah Trimmer wrote edifying dialogues designed to be read out in their classes. One went:

Instructor: There is one kind of dishonesty which is often practised without thought by workmen, and that is wasting the time for which they are paid and the materials belonging to the Trade or Manufacture they work at. Of the same nature with this is the crime of many household servants who take every opportunity of being idle and who make no scruple of wasting provisions or giving them away without leave . . .
Question: Is it honest for workmen to waste and destroy the materials and implements which they make use of?
Answer: No.
Question: Who do these things belong to?
Answer: Their Master.
Question: Whose eyes see you when your master is not by?
Answer: God's.

Sunday schools were clever inventions because they ensured that children who worked from Monday to Saturday received instruction on their day off. 'By this wise expedient,' beamed the Bishop of Chester.

that most desirable *union*, which has been so often wished for in Charity Schools, but which it has been generally found so difficult to introduce, is at length accomplished, the union of *manual labour* and *spiritual instruction*. These are by means of the Sunday schools both carried on together and the interests both of this life and the next so consulted, as not to interfere with or obstruct each other.

Better still, the schooling was cheap: 'The whole expence of instructing twenty children,' the reassuring bishop added, 'including books, rewards, and every other charge, will not amount to five pounds a year; a sum so trifling and so easy to be raised that it cannot create the smallest difficulty.'

The dream of colleges of industry (work-schools) for poor children had a lustre no set-backs could tarnish. Their original promoter, Quaker John Bellers, had spelt out their rationale at the close of the seventeenth century: 'therein is 3 things I aim at: first Profit to the Rich (which will be life to the rest); Secondly a plentiful living for the poor, without difficulty; Thirdly a good education for youth, that may tend to prepare their souls.' As Bellers stressed, investing in colleges of industry promised to yield better returns than mere alms-giving. He was confident that the privatization of institutions for the poor must be more efficient than the public Poor Law.

Alongside schools, however, many other bodies were set up to help out, or buy off, the troublesome classes. Refuges such as the Magdalen Hospital were founded to rescue penitent prostitutes. The Marine Society for Educating Poor Destitute Boys to the Sea took waifs off the streets to turn them into sailors, each boy receiving his copy of *Christian Knowledge Made Easy*. The Foundling Hospital (opened in 1741) aimed to save the lives of abandoned babies (most were bastards). The National Truss Society and the Society for the Ruptured Poor were to help men whose physiques had been broken by heavy labour to keep in employment. The Philanthropic Society, dating from 1788, was to reform criminal children. Spiralling inflation from the 1780s led to the Society for Bettering the Condition and Increasing the Comfort of the Poor (1790), teaching them to go and drink soup, and publishing recipes showing how their present diet was wasteful, and that they could feed more nutritiously with reduced outlays. Local dearth and disasters usually led to relief subscriptions and soup kitchens.

As pauperism worsened, new charities were founded: ten were launched in London from 1771 to 1780, eighteen from 1781 to 1790, and thirty from 1791 to 1800. Two goals were always paramount. First, the desire to make the lower orders God-fearing and deferential. They had to be habituated to hardship. 'Scarcity has been permitted,' pontificated the ever Panglossian Hannah More, 'by an all wise & gracious Providence to unite all ranks of people together, to show the poor how immediately they are dependent upon the rich, & to show both rich & poor that they are all dependent on Himself.'

And, second, there was the aim of encouraging in the labouring poor the petty-bourgeois ethic of dedication to industry, thrift, sobriety and self-help. The tireless philanthropist Jonas Hanway appealed in these terms to the poor:

> though you are born to a humble estate in this world, let your AMBITION rise as high as heaven itself: there direct your hopes – But you can hardly be honest unless you are industrious – & would you be a good man, you must add to industry & religion good nature or a happy temper. Thus you will insure happiness.

Backing the Poor Law and the courts, philanthropic gestures thus multiplied to reform the lives of the lower orders. Yet it is not easy to gauge the impact of this encroachment upon plebeian life from above. Sermonizers and snoopers met with catcalls, hecklers and stones, doles were mistrusted, and self-styled tribunes of the people such as the journalist William Cobbett were suspicious – 'Nothing is taught,' ran Cobbett's verdict on village schools, 'but the rudiments of servility, pauperism and slavery.' Property, he judged, would have done more real good than all the propaganda in the world: 'A couple of flitches of bacon are worth 50,000 methodist sermons and religious tracts.'

Yet children flocked to charity and Sunday schools. Was this because uniforms and meals were often free? Or because of moral bullying? This certainly happened; one set of ordinances for founding a Sunday school in 1786 states: 'Those parents who . . . obstinately refuse to send their children to the Sunday School shall be deemed improper objects to receive any Charity that shall in future be distributed to the parish of Curry Rivel.' And it is at least possible that such schools proved a Pandora's box. Without philanthropic schools, where would Paine have got his hundreds of thousands of readers? Even Bible-reading was doubled-edged, for, as Thomas Laqueur has observed, 'working-class politics was largely the creation of people steeped in religion and the Bible.'

And yet, up to the end of the century, there had been no grand, united repudiation of hierarchy and capitalism; the mills of the industrial revolution and the regiments of Britannia's armies *were* manned. Had the lower orders absorbed the values with which they had been bombarded? Had they undergone embourgeoisement? It is hard to say. Many observers certainly believed that the industrious poor were becoming more tractable. 'In the last century,' wrote Matthew Boulton,

Birmingham was as remarkable for good forgers and filers as for their bad taste in all their works. Their diversions were bull baiting, cock fightings, boxing matches and abominable drunkenness with all its train. But now the scene is changed. The people are more polite and civilized, and the taste of their manufactures greatly improved.

But Boulton attributed this transformation not to twopenny tracts but to trade.

Perhaps the cream of the lower classes was being skimmed off. Certainly there were able, articulate and ambitious working men – Francis Place would be an obvious example – who could see virtue in the values beckoning from above. Place rejected the beery, brutal ne'er-do-wells with whom he grew up in late-eighteenth-century London – men who tyrannized over their families and squandered their wealth and health. Place advocated self-help, sobriety, education, getting-on. He got on himself, beginning as an apprentice cutter and becoming one of the largest tailors in the metropolis, with thirty-two journeymen under him, and making £3,000 a year. 'I never lost a minute of time,' claimed this forerunner of Samuel Smiles,

was never on any occasion diverted from the steady pursuit of my business, never spent a shilling, never once entertained any company. The only thing I bought were books, and not many of them. I adhered steadily to the practice I had adopted, and read for two or three hours every night after the business of the day was closed.

Place was a radical, an atheist, a birth-controller, a Painite; yet he also believed in self-advancement out of the immorality, the coarseness, the obscenity, drunkenness, dirt and depravity of the 'middling and even of a large portion of the better sort of tradesmen, the artisans, & the journeymen tradesmen of London in the days of my youth':

I cannot, like many other men, go to a tavern. I have attained my position *solely* by my own exertions. I left off everything which could in any way tend to impede my future progress in the world, or was in any way calculated to bring deserved reproach upon me or was likely to compel me on a close review of my conduct to reproach myself with injustice towards any one, or with having on any occasion acted meanly.

Offering opportunities for the leaders perhaps did more for stability than all the attempts to convert the masses.

Moreover, the pervasive propaganda conditioning had its effect on the masses too. Certainly there were village atheists and 'republican' agitators. Yet patriotism and xenophobia were etched on to the brain, and droves would indeed cheer for Church and king – it could be one way of getting back at the lofty Dissenting tradesmen to whom they were in debt. There were working people of all complexions. Some lived absolutely on their own terms. Frederick Eden thus paid tribute to the lives of two Surrey farm-workers, James Strudwick and his wife Anne:

He worked more than threescore years on one farm; and his wages, summer and winter, were regularly a shilling a day. He never asked more: nor was he ever offered less. Strudwick continued to work till within seven weeks of the day of his death; and at the age of fourscore, in 1787, he closed, in peace, a not inglorious life; for, to the day of his death, he never received a farthing in the way of parochial aid. His wife survived him about seven years; and though bent with age and infirmities, and little able to work, excepting as a weeder in a gentleman's garden, she also was too proud either to ask or receive any relief from her parish. For six or seven of the last years of her life, she received twenty shillings a year from the person who favoured me with this account, which he drew up from her own mouth.

With all her virtue, and all her merit, she yet was not much liked in her neighbourhood; people in affluence thought her haughty, and the paupers of the parish, seeing, as they could not help seeing, that her life was a reproach to theirs, aggravated all her little failings.

Even this paragon, however, ultimately proved a disappointment to her betters. Eden reported:

A more serious charge against her was, that, living to a great age, and but little able to work, she grew to be seriously afraid that, at last, she might become chargeable to the parish (the heaviest, in her estimation, of all human calamities); and that thus alarmed, she did suffer herself more than once, during the exacerbations of a fit of distempered despondency, peevishly (and, perhaps, petulantly) to exclaim that God Almighty, by suffering her to remain so long upon earth, seemed actually to have forgotten her.

What we surely see here are two working people who stubbornly refuse to conform to any of the radical or reactionary stereotypes.

Whatever the impact of philanthropy upon its recipients, it served the benefactors well. Merchants and manufacturers in particular were often uncomfortable about their own station and *mœurs*. Situated beneath the swells and holding themselves above the *canaille*, they needed to achieve self-respect. Though it was Dissenters who were most directly debarred from public life, many other solid bourgeois remained disqualified from voting until 1832. Their own course of life, in business, shepherding and investing their own capital, trying to establish a family line, bred insecurity and demanded prudence. Tradesmen and dealers needed respect. They put trust in their own virtues, their 'credit'. Philanthropy enlisted the ambitious bourgeois in a moral mission, a vindication of their own superior worth – a mentality which finds unctuous expression in Hannah More's verdict on the Mendip colliery villagers: 'they have nothing human to look to but us.' In any case, as Bishop Horne pointed out, charity was 'the most exquisite luxury'.

But moral seriousness was not exclusive to the commercial classes. Many propertied families emerged shell-shocked from the Stuart 'century of revolution'. Political extremism – from Stuart tyranny to regicides – had been mirrored by religious bigotry, from Fifth Monarchists to Papist traitors. One king had been executed, another deposed. Public morals had swung from the Zeal-of-the-land busy-ness of Cromwellian saints and major-generals to the libertines of Charles II's Court (where not having a mistress was reputedly a stumbling block to advancement). Neither was readily stomached by the 'silent majority' of men of substance who thought themselves the backbone of the nation. With parties and sects still at each other's throats, and families divided among themselves, the danger was real that if men remained so factionalized, hot-tempered and dogmatic, civil society would cannibalize itself. Furthermore, strains upon the lifestyle of propertied society were intensifying as a result of alluring new prospects for enrichment, speculation and high living (punctuated by nightmares of overreaching, of bankruptcy). *Nouveaux riches*, whose egoism had known no manners, needed to win acceptance. Beset by bewildering change, temptations and anxieties, many substantial citizens sought anchorage by putting their own houses in order. Moderation, decorum and accommodation were needed. 'Romping, struggling, throwing things at one another's head,' Lord Chesterfield advised his exasperating son, 'are the becoming pleasantries of the mob, but degrade a gentleman.' The *dolce vita* was to be enjoyed, but only through behaviour which was liberal, polite and genteel. Given that so many of the propertied had indeed been splenetic boors, bigots, braggarts and drunkards, and their sons profligates, the Spectatorial call to gentility was not foppish tinsel, but crucial to personal and social adjustment, the best resource for ensuring respect for the propertied and for securing the world for their enjoyment. Restraint, control and propriety were vital if society was not to explode in their face.

After his drinking bouts, the Sussex grocer Thomas Turner was all Boswellian remorse: 'Oh! with what horrors does it fill my heart, to think I should be guilty of doing so, & on a Sunday too!' Some thought it wiser to refrain from hard liquor altogether. 'I drink only water,' boasted Erasmus Darwin, 'and am always well.' Though there was no total abstinence movement, there were a few staunch teetotallers, such as the prison reformer John Howard – also a vegetarian, severe in dress and austere in morals. Cliques such as the bluestockings tried to wean their friends on to tea evenings, and William Cowper penned his own poetic tribute to 'the cups That cheer but not inebriate'. Bluestockings also tried to cut card-playing ('that hun, whist'), encouraging conversation instead.

Sectors of affluent society (though less so the aristocracy) were indeed becoming starchy as the age of Jane Austen approached. Joseph Farington noted, from about 1770,

a change in the manners and the habits of the people of this country was beginning to take place. Public taste was improving. The coarse familiarity so common in personal intercourse was laid aside, and respectful attention and civility in address gradually gave a new and better aspect to society. The profane habit of using oaths in conversation no longer offended the ear, and bacchanalian intemperance at the dinner-table was succeeded by rational cheerfulness and sober forbearance.

For many, propriety meant the long retreat from 'coarseness'. Addison and Steele had themselves deplored the vulgarity of their times, but – if Jane Austen's *Northanger Abbey* is any guide – even their writings caused blushes a century later. Grandfather's everyday colloquialisms became obscenities. 'Piss' was a vulgarism from about the the 1700s, and the four-letter words were kept out of blunt Dr Johnson's *Dictionary*. Terms such as 'stink' and 'sick' began to offend polite ears. Bob Acres in Sheridan's *The Rivals* (1775) explained that nowadays one had to go in for 'sentimental swearing': 'Damns have had their day.' Leigh Hunt, born in 1784, recalled that his mother instilled in him a blind horror of swearing. Etiquette also received attention. Greater use was made of table napkins and clean sheets, helped by the replacement of expensive linens by cheap cottons. Eating with one's hands and spitting were condemned as boorish.

Accompanying self-restraint, greater value was laid upon *sociability*, the ability to mix, and so sink party, religious and family differences in common company. The arts of conversation and the tea-table graces were spruced up. Good manners, in Swift's definition, were 'the art of making those people easy with whom we converse'. Upbringings were oriented to groom the young for society (and Enlightenment educationists believed that, because the mind was originally like a lump of wax, it was malleable enough to be moulded to society's requirements). Locke and his followers stressed that education should be geared towards living, not just learning, and Lord Chesterfield, in his instructions to his son, preached the cardinal importance of being agreeable. 'Pleasing in company is the only way of being pleased in it yourself.' Politeness and good breeding would open life's doors. 'By the art of good breeding,' Fielding wrote, 'I mean the art of pleasing, or contributing as much as possible to the care & happiness of those with whom you converse.' In a world intimate enough for personal power still to count, yet fluid enough to be increasingly anonymous, form and address were crucial visas. The finesses of etiquette helped to secure entrée and advancement in a world of social niceties. Life was a stage on which good

actors would shine: courtesy books, dancing masters and elocu-
tionists abounded to teach the parts. Not too much of the inner
self was to be exposed.

Politics, religion and a thousand and one material interests
divided men: culture, it was hoped, might re-unite them. And so
the Town devoted itself to cultivating *taste*. 'The Graces, the
Graces, remember the Graces!' Chesterfield urged his son. The
pure breath of Olympian culture would invigorate the elite
mountain above the plebs, booby squires and mere moneybags
(yet taste could also baptize wealth). True taste in the arts, people
began to stress, should not be flash or racy, but modest and
decent, congruent with goodness. Addison and Steele thus sought
to end 'the long divorce of wit from virtue' which had tarnished
cynical Restoration culture. 'I shall endeavour,' Addison wrote,
'to enliven morality with wit, and to temper wit with morality,
that my readers may, if possible, both ways find their account in
the speculation of the day.'

Refinement would polish a person's true mettle, for art, after
all, was nature refined, just as the civilized man was the natural
man burnished. The *Spectator* advertised itself as a 'work which
endeavours to cultivate and polish human life', aiming 'to establish
among us a taste of polite writing'. 'Polish or perish' became the
watchword, attractive to top people who wished to be *le dernier
cri*, to fustian squires aiming to impress, and to parvenu farmers
and tradesmen who sought to gentrify themselves. Not least, it
was the chorus of everyone in the booming culture business.
Encouraging Manchester manufacturers to join its Literary and
Philosophical Society, the secretary, Thomas Henry, argued 'a
taste for polite literature, and the works of nature and art, is
essentially necessary to form the gentleman,' quoting Addison's
view that learning gave a gentleman 'a kind of property in everything he sees'.

In a parallel way, Lord Chesterfield urged his son to refine his
sexual tastes. Polite sex had real advantages, being more erotic
and also less risky to health. He recommended him to win his
sexual spurs with a genteel Parisian lady rather than with a
streetwalker because it was more educative:

Un arrangement, which is, in plain English, a gallantry is in Paris as
necessary a part of a woman of fashion's establishment as her house . . .

A young fellow must therefore be a very awkward one to be reduced to, or of a very singular taste to prefer, drabs and danger to a commerce (in the course of the world not disgraceful) with a woman of health, education and rank.

Alongside manners and taste, morals needed attention. Georgian essayists, tutors and parents were long-winded on the need to cultivate virtue precisely because the old sheet anchors of morality – the Christian commandments and the absolute authority of tradition – had had their cables cut. In Georgian polite society virtue came to have two particular resonances. First, a disposition of *benevolence* towards self and others, leading to actions productive of happiness. In the amused and ironical worldly atmosphere of affluent society, traditional moral precepts enjoining hair-shirt self-denial were beside the point. People wanted to do good but also to do well. Few were as nakedly pragmatic as Archdeacon Paley, whose touchstone was that 'whatever is expedient is right', or as Jeremy Bentham, for whom the only test of good or evil was the greatest happiness of the greatest number. But in blander form, similar sentiments about the marriage of virtue and happiness echoed down the corridors of society.

Second, there was a growing emphasis on the culture of the heart, on sensibility, and on private moral judgement. In this more liberal milieu, where the Church no longer gave commandments and authority was toned down, the shrine of morality migrated within the self. For those, women especially, rich enough to enjoy the luxury of a conscience, goodness became a more introspective, and even aesthetic, matter, involving cultivating and exercising finer, more sensitive feelings. 'Delicacy in pleasures,' wrote Steele, 'is the first step people of condition take in reformation from vice.' The quiet sociable virtues – friendship, forbearance, loyalty, cheerfulness – moved centre stage. Tenderheartedness towards the suffering and the unfortunate became a barometer of sensibility, sometimes collapsing into mawkishness, melancholia, and perhaps *anorexia nervosa*.* Thus on the death of her father, Abigail Gawthern, a prosperous Nottingham widow, reflected in her diary on her outward mourning and inner grief:

* 'We Hypochondriacks,' wrote Boswell, 'may console ourselves in the hour of gloomy distress, by thinking that our sufferings make our superiority.'

That the sable trappings of woe too often cover the heart divested of every *exquisite feeling* is certain, but the truly delicate and sensible mind depends not upon the mere semblance of affliction. The dingy shade of a garment can neither add to or diminish the sensations of *dear and unfading regret*; heartfelt and unaffected grief turns with disgust from the hackneyed display of ostentatious sorrow whilst it enjoys a *secret luxury* which the hardened and unfeeling mind can *never experience*.

In the latter part of the century virtues of a more private and domestic nature were championed, especially among the middling people, spurred by the example of the faithful, frugal, home-loving George III, who reputedly made toast by the fire while Queen Charlotte fried the sprats. Some repudiated the *beau monde*, cultivating a pre-Romantic preference for peace and quiet and cosy retreat. 'I often think that those people are happiest,' mused Mrs Montagu, queen of the bluestockings, 'who know nothing at all of the world & sitting in the little empire of the fireside, where there is no contention or cabal, think we are in a golden age of existence.' Hannah More agreed. 'As to London,' she wrote in 1790, 'I shall be glad to get rid of it; the old, little parties are not to be had; everything is great and vast and late and magnificent and dull.' The Dissenting moralist Mrs Barbauld wrote a work characteristically entitled *Evenings at Home*.

Especially towards the close of the century moral rearmament became a clarion call for certain groups. In the conscious pursuit of virtue lay one way whereby the swelling ranks of the self-made and the moneyed could come to terms with the temptations and paradoxes of their own success. New wealth needed to be consecrated by goodness. Bankers and dealers well knew that secure financial well-being rested upon their good name and credit. Being 'good' took on greater importance with young ladies. Having an impeccable reputation helped them to secure some space and leverage against family pressures, now that many were claiming greater personal choice in the business of marriage. For other women, introspection and delicate concern with purity of heart helped them to cope with their lack of external control over lives lived under oppressive parents or husbands. In households where the religion of the heart and soul took hold, these effects were intensified. Women became guardians of morality.

Moral eagerness made itself felt especially among certain professional and business strata and at the strident, alienated margins of the intelligentsia: there was no lack of corruption and materialism from which to feel alienated. In real life no less than in maudlin novels, refined ladies and sentimental gentlemen suffered agonies of heartache and became tearful over thwarted love, the death of children, cruelty to dumb animals. Sincerity and simplicity became badges of personal identity and integrity. Missions overseas and purity campaigns at home were launched. For some, sabbath-keeping became a touchstone. George III abolished Sunday Court dinners, and the Sunday Observance Society was founded in 1775.

Such people were also anxious to remove 'indecency' (sex) from public life. Delicacy (desexualization) became a matter of moment, especially to protect women. As John Bennett wrote in 1789: 'Delicacy is a very general and *comprehensive* quality. It extends to everything where woman is concerned. Conversation, books, pictures, attitude, gesture, pronunciation should all come under its salutary restraints.'

Sparing the blushes of the innocent knew no bounds for those who saw lasciviousness and smut everywhere. Codpiece Row (next to Breeches Yard in London) thus had to be renamed Coppice Row. Some would no longer call a bitch a bitch, but rather a 'mother mastiff'. No longer were women 'big with child' but 'pregnant'. 'Bellies' became 'stomachs', and 'smocks' and 'shifts' became 'chemises' (yet poetic diction had long been full of similar euphemisms). To meet changing taste, Reynolds draped his statues with togas. Protests – as yet hardly effectual – grew against nude bathing. Thomas Bowdler's castrated Shakespeare was first published in 1802 (Doll Tearsheet exited from *Henry IV*).

Of the many manifestations of the flesh, sexuality was the most sinister, sinful and insidious. Bowdlerism, Grundyism, prudery, repression, anxiety and shame were all summoned to button up Eros. Sensuality came to be the antonym of respectability. By association, cleanliness became a cardinal virtue. For Wesley it was next to godliness, yet Hannah More rated it a higher priority, at least for the poor: 'The necessity of going to church in procession with us on the anniversary, raised an honest ambition to get something decent to wear, and the churches on Sunday are now filled with very clean looking women.' All in all, 'Victorianism' was already casting its long shadows in the age of Victoria's grandparents. 'By the beginning of the nineteenth century,' wrote G. M. Young, 'virtue was advancing on a broad, invincible front.'

The vanguard of this drive for self-esteem through self-censorship, largely occurring in moneyed society, was specifically Christian, the Evangelical Movement within the Church of England. The Evangelical Revival had multiple sources – for example Charles Simeon in Cambridge, or John Newton, the reformed slave-trader – but it was galvanized above all by a plutocratic elite in London, the so-called Clapham sect, headed by merchants and bankers such as William Wilberforce, Zachary Macaulay, and John Thornton and his sons. The 'Saints' rejected Latitudinarian religion, renouncing reason for faith and easiness for the conquest of sin by muscular, crusading struggle; the call to seriousness repudiated what Wilberforce called 'the universal corruption and profligacy of the times, which taking its rise amongst the rich and luxurious has now extended its baneful influence and spread its destructive poison, through the whole body of the people'. The 'Spiritual Barometer' (opposite), printed in the *Evangelical Magazine* in 1800, tabulated the columns of sin and salvation, showing the urgency of exorcising Satan from society.

As can be seen from the barometer, almost all the cultural developments of the Georgian century, from Vauxhall to novels, were beneath contempt and salvation. 'Novels,' thundered the *Evangelical Magazine* in 1793, 'generally speaking are instruments of abomination and ruin. A fond attachment to them is an irrefragable evidence of a mind contaminated, and totally unfitted for the serious pursuits of study, or the delightful exercises and enjoyments of religion.'

Wilberforce's aim was to promote practical, crusading religion: 'God has set before me as my object the reformation of manners.' The 'Saints' set out to re-Christianize the great, fitting them for their duty of leadership. Starting with the home, and thus setting the pattern for nineteenth-century family life, they were not much concerned to work through legislation, preferring voluntary action. Thus the Grays, a York Evangelical family, were prominent in setting up spinning schools, Sunday schools, friendly societies and charity schools. They drew up cheap diets for the poor and helped the campaign against the slave trade.

In the tense world of self-made riches surrounded by growling

70 —	Glory: dismission from the body.
60 —	Desiring to depart to be with Christ; patience in tribulation; glorying in the cross.
50 —	Ardent love to the souls of men; followed hard after God: Deadness to the world by the cross of Christ.
40 —	Love of God, shed abroad in the heart; frequent approach to the Lord's Table; meeting for prayer and experience.
30 —	Delight in the people of God; looking to Jesus.
20 —	Love of God's house and word; daily perusal of the Bible with prayer; vain company wholly dropped.
10 —	Evangelical light; retirement for prayer and meditation; concern for the soul; alarm.
0 —	Indifference; family worship only on Sunday evenings; private prayer frequently omitted; family religion wholly declined.
10 —	Levity in conversations; fashions, however expensive or indecent, adopted.
20 —	Luxurious entertainment; free association with carnal company.
30 —	The theatre; Vauxhall; Ranelagh, etc.; frequent parties of pleasure; home of God forsaken; much wine, spirits, etc.
40 —	Love of novels, etc.; scepticism; private prayer totally neglected; deistical company prized.
50 —	Parties of pleasure on the Lord's day; masquerades; drunkenness; adultery; profaneness; lewd songs.
60 —	Infidelity; jesting at religion; sitting down in the chair of the scoffer.
70 —	Death; perdition.

The Spiritual Barometer (from the *Evangelical Magazine*, 1800)

disaffection, Evangelicalism offered what many patriarchs and their families needed – a stern, steely clear-cut, personal creed to stabilize and energize the demanding calls of business, minimize insecurity and win respect. Each man took paternalistic responsibility for himself and his family, aiming to build characters that were reliable, hard-working, sober, accustomed to deferring gratification. Evangelicalism gave respect to parvenu manufacturers such as Peel as Methodism did to artisans, and renewed the moral authority of peers such as the Earl of Hardwicke. Respectability – a word first used in 1785 – was beginning its meteoric career.

★

The Georgian age gave plenty of scope to those living comfortably above the breadline to explore new lifestyles. The low profiles of Church and state, continued internal peace and security, the generally relaxed moral atmosphere, economic opportunities and optimism about the future – all these spurred worldliness, individualism and pluralism. This freedom, however, also threw back burdens upon the personality. Success or failure hinged upon dexterity in negotiating and manipulating complex codes of conduct and social rituals. Great premium came to be placed upon self-management and presentation. In the bewildering clamour of individualism, many struggling souls looked for beacons of clearer religious and moral ideals to guide, illuminate and inspire their lives – and others'. Within a more intricate economy, and where social disturbances arose, certain groups and occasionally the state were beginning to press for reform or greater control. This was rarely due to industrialization as such; indeed where industrialization was precocious, reforming movements were less urgent. But capitalism was generating substantial material wealth for large sectors of the population who, indulging in a more refined lifestyle, felt increasingly threatened by the *hoi polloi*. Property-owners had more to preserve – more to lose – and a greater stake in order, in finding ways to make the world safe for capital and self-advancement. Moreover, secular outlooks, the rationalism and pragmatism of the Enlightenment, the vision of human educability, improvement and new technological wizardry – all were fuelling a Promethean myth which argued that regulated change was necessary, possible and desirable. Ambition, power and control were the brood of the Georgians.

8. Towards Industrial Society

In the last quarter of the century, economic activity and population surged forward strikingly. 'After 1782,' wrote T. S. Ashton,

almost every available statistical series of industrial output reveals a sharp upward turn. More than half the growth in the shipments of coal and the mining of copper, more than three-quarters of the increase of broadcloths, four-fifths of that of printed cloth and nine-tenths of the exports of cotton goods were concentrated in the last eighteen years of the century.

Real national output, growing at about 1 per cent per annum between 1749 and 1780, was increasing by about 1.8 per cent between 1780 and 1800. From 1780, pig-iron output doubled every eight years. Whereas the years from 1660 to 1760 had seen 210 patents for inventions, between 1760 and 1789, 976 new patents were taken out. The expansion in economic activity and the rise in population went hand-in-glove. For, despite certain labour-saving machinery, rising manufactures needed more hands, yet without rising output (not least of food) more mouths would have created subsistence crises, similar to those in nineteenth-century Ireland. Because both kept roughly in step, neither was checked, and the result was that massive transformation we call the Industrial Revolution and the birth of industrial society. After centuries of the precarious balancing of food supply, family size and employment opportunities within an agriculture-based cottage-industrial economy, a watershed was passed.

Some historians have questioned the value of terms such as 'industrial revolution'. But the idea seems valuable provided that we keep in mind that what was revolutionary was not an initial cataclysm but rather the magnitude of the consequences, and so long as we see it not as a 'programme' engineered by factory owners but rather as the cumulative outcome of millions of individual actions throughout the system. Towards the end of the century, more of these were involving bets upon a buoyant future. Entrepreneurs were risking heavier investment in plant, anticipating new markets. As grain prices and profits reached dizzy heights, farmers put hill-slopes under the plough. Canal mania set in. In industrializing areas people were adapting to conditions, marrying younger and having larger families (in line with Arthur Young's advice: 'Away! my boys; get children; they are worth more than ever they were'). Not all risks came off. Many canals yielded scant profit, and competition caused cotton-spinners to crash. But the gambles on expansion paid off often enough – despite trade-cycle troughs, multiple bankruptcies, inflation, mounting social distress and pauperism – to cause momentum to gather. The astute and the serendipitous made fat killings: a big textile factory could spin profits of 100 per cent or more. The entrepreneurial whales of the Industrial Revolution, such as the Arkwrights and the Peels, became rich beyond the dreams of cautious industrialists a couple of generations earlier, such as the Darbys of Coalbrookdale. Furthermore, however disruptive its consequences and unevenly distributed its rewards, industrialization meant that a much larger aggregate national work-force could actually be supported.

England was the original soil of the Industrial Revolution. How far was this – the fact that England staged such a revolution at all, and was the first nation to do so – due to the particular quality of its society? Naturally, rapid industrialization did not have just one single cause; it depended on the felicitous chemistry of many disposing elements, some only obliquely connected with social features. Conveniently sited and easily extractable natural resources were indispensable. Coal and iron ore were often cheek-by-jowl, as in South Yorkshire or the Black Country. Cornish copper and tin could speedily be shipped for smelting with South Wales coal. The abundant streams of Pennine and Peak provided washing-water and water-power for textiles. Through the war years (1793–1815) and even during Napoleon's blockade the Royal Navy enabled island England to slip out of an absolute stranglehold on the import of vital raw materials from overseas, above all the increasingly crucial raw cotton.

Growing export outlets to foreign markets were also indispen-able. Averaging about £9 million a year in 1780, exports had shot up to £22 million by the end of the century. Iron and steel shipments, running at 16,770 tons in 1765–74, almost doubled to 30,717 in 1795–1804. Over the same period, export of woollens went up from £4,356,000 to £6,323,000, and of cottons from £236,000 to £5,371,000. During Napoleon's Continental blockade manufacturers' ability to sell to the colonies and to create markets in areas such as Latin America kept the imperilled English economy afloat. How far it was limitless export horizons that impelled industrial expansion remains controversial. Certainly some two thirds of the output of the fastest-growing industry, cotton, was shipped abroad.

Many of these advantages were 'natural', 'fortuitous' or 'external'. Yet the capacity to *exploit* them was enhanced by favourable developments in the socio-economic infrastructure. Thus the new web of navigable waterways and canals was greatly easing and cheapening carriage of bulky natural resources such as minerals, explaining why it was in the late eighteenth century and not before that many timeless 'natural' advantages could be utilized.

In certain industries, the vast late-eighteenth-century surge in output was achieved thanks largely to technological breakthrough. In cottons, inventions such as Arkwright's water frame (1769) and Crompton's mule (1779) dramatically boosted productivity per operative, proportionately slashing unit costs. In cotton-yarn spinning, new machinery led cost elements to shift as follows:

	1779	1784	1799	1812
Raw cotton	2s.	2s.	3s. 4d.	1s. 6d.
Capital and labour	14s.	8s. 11d.	4s. 2d.	1s.
Total	16s.	10s. 11d.	7s. 6d.	2s. 6d.

This cheapening was largely because technology expedited operations. To process 100 lb. of cotton, an Indian hand-spinner took 50,000 operative manhours, a Crompton mule (1780) took 2,000, a 100-spindle mule (1790) took 1,000, a power-assisted mule (1795) took 300, and by 1825 Roberts's automatic mule took just 135 manhours.

In the metal industries, widespread adoption of smelting cast-iron by coke ended the stricture created by the growing shortage and rising price of charcoal. Henry Cort's reverberatory furnace and the process of purifying iron by 'puddling' made mass use of wrought-iron a practical proposition. Not least, by the end of the century, rotary steam engines were just beginning to become attractive as power sources for driving mills – flour mills in London, cotton mills in Lancashire, Derbyshire and Nottinghamshire. Steam power enabled spinning factories (once confined to out-of-the-way up-country river valleys) to migrate to town centres such as Manchester. By vastly increasing productivity, technological change cheapened products, and thereby multiplied markets.

England led in technological application not because she had the most scientific inventors. Advanced textile machinery and canal technology had been available much earlier in Italy, and, in certain fields such as warship design, France continued to excel. Certainly France boasted more scientifically trained professional engineers than England. England scored rather in transforming the germs of inventions into industrial application. Central bureaucratic control of industrial processes and standards, linked to the effect of guild powers, probably stifled the innovative drive on the Continent. State patronage in France, Austria and Russia lured scientists and engineers away from manufacturing industry towards teaching, administration and military service. In England the very lack of state support for science and engineering ironically encouraged, by default, the close working-partnerships between scientific, technical and entrepreneurial talents that were found, for instance, in the coteries of the Lunar Society of Birmingham. As legal regulation of industry withered, there were no outside impediments to technological change. The patent laws perhaps encouraged inventors such as James Watt to invest heavily in improvements in design – although, as Watt's case suggests, they may subsequently have retarded the wide and rapid diffusion of their inventions.

Alongside technological explanations, narrowly economic accounts have sometimes been put forward to account for England's industrial surge. For instance, it was once argued that industrialization shot ahead when capital formation or investment levels crossed certain critical thresholds. Others have claimed that the exponential growth of cotton acted as a 'leading sector', boosting the rest of the economy by a multiplier effect. These views, however, are hardly supported by the evidence. Capital investment in manufactures did not rise very significantly. It did not need to. Because plant remained generally small-scale, fixed capital requirements were not huge. Credit, loans, partnerships, and a certain sleight of hand, saw entrepreneurs through. Though many individual capitalists failed, English industry at large was never parched by a capital drought. Requirements could be raised privately; there was no need for an industrial stock exchange. The sum total in any case was modest. By 1815, £20 million had gone into canals, but governments raised fifty times as much to finance the Napoleonic wars. Nor is it true that cotton galvanized the rest of the economy. In 1800 that industry was still largely using wooden machinery and water-power. Unlike the iron industry's products, those of the cotton industry were not the plant and hardware required for tooling further basic industries and thus producing huge knock-on effects.

The character of English society was critical to industrialization. Trends in society at large provided the potential for industrialization, particular features of it facilitating rapid economic expansion, and one group proving exceptionally influential. Without an expanding population capable of being drilled into a supple labour force, rapid industrialization would soon have faltered. For even the introduction of spectacular labour-saving machinery in certain processes, notably cotton-spinning, created the need for more operatives in others, such as weaving. Stocking-knitting, the metal trades, transport, building, and all the processing, distributive and service industries required more hands. Fresh employment opportunities sustained the steep climb of the population: from 5.7 million in 1750 to 8.6 million in 1800 and 11.5 million in 1820. Migration into industrial areas quickened. Most of it, such as the move from the Pennines and the Lake District into lowland Lancashire, was creeping, though Irish and Scots flocked into the cotton towns. The fact that many of these extra hands were themselves skilled operatives bringing children with them eased their absorption into the workforce.

Admittedly, technological innovation sometimes met powerful labour resistance. In March 1792 there was an attack on Grimshaw's factory in Manchester, the first to use Cartwright's power loom. Only two years after its opening, the factory was burnt down by hand-loom weavers, and its destruction inhibited power-loom weaving in the area for several years. Even so, the scale of physical opposition to mechanization was trivial in comparison to the scale of the transformations taking place. With the exception of old craft areas where guilds remained strong, technical innovation proceeded without sustained disruption. This was partly because English workers were already thoroughly inured to wage labour. Many had been brought up from infancy in industrial by-employments, which could easily become full-time. Women and children had long been working at carding and spinning within cottage industry. Migrating to mill towns, they were readily integrated into the new textile factories (unlike, it is said, dispossessed Scottish highlanders, who kicked against factory discipline).

Furthermore, English artisans were able to adapt to and even promote rapid change in crafts such as the wheelwright's, because they were the inheritors of proud and proven traditions of resourceful workmanship – a fact which had impressed foreign observers such as Abbé le Blanc. ''Tis not in great works alone that the English excel,' he reflected,

the most common trades here seem to partake of the perfection of arts ... With regard to the neatness and solidity of work of all kinds they succeed better in the least towns of England, than in the most considerable cities of France. I have seen here, in country places, common hands work and put together the several parts of a piece of joiner's work with a degree of exactness and propriety which the best master-joiners of Paris would find it difficult to come near.

The English artisan has the quality, extremely commendable, and peculiar to him, which is, never to swerve from the degree of perfection in his trade which he is master of: whatever he undertakes, he always does as well as he can. The French workman is far from deserving this commendation.

However exaggerated, this view carries some plausibility because so many other commentators thought likewise. Though industrialization created a swelling residuum (largely of women and children) in de-skilled, machine-minding jobs, in a range of other trades high-skill and well-paid jobs multiplied, such as puddling iron, fitting machine parts, pottery painting, and many sectors of Black Country metal manufactures.

Vital, of course, was agriculture's capacity to feed the booming population. This it did, partly through greater unit productivity and partly by the continuing enclosure of common and waste (involving ploughing up downland, chiefly in the South, and converting pasture to arable). Corn output rose from 17,353,000 quarters in 1770 to 21,102,000 in 1800. Greater demand, bad harvests, runaway inflation, and wartime conditions meant that grain and bread prices shot through the roof in the 1790s. A quartern loaf, traditionally costing about 7d., had reached 1s. 2d. by 1796. Newly converted to laissez-faire, governments did little to peg prices, for it was precisely rocketing prices and mushroom profits which made it worth farmers' while to keep boosting output (poorer consumers, utterly dependent on bread, footed the bill of rapid agrarian change).

As well as possessing a tractable labour force swelling to meet the demands of industry, England boasted a socio-economic infrastructure ripe to support the enterprise of manufacturers. Systems of credit, bill-broking and banking permitted growth in scale; road, river and sea links and haulage services sped distribution. Chains of wholesalers, middlemen and shops hooked up supply to demand. Turnpikes and canals, often originally built to serve local interests (for conveying agricultural produce to market, for instance), could be commandeered by industrialists moving merchandise long distances. Similarly in many districts banking facilities had originally been developed largely to serve property-owners investing savings in the Funds; their facilities could later be taken over by entrepreneurs who capitalized on their credit and bill-redemption services. Manufacturers were beneficiaries of the fact that great landed proprietors had long behaved as capitalists, deploying surplus wealth in profitable ways; the magnates formed an elite who themselves gained vastly from industrialization. Neither High Society nor the state put serious obstacles in the way of industrialization. England's industrial revolution generated its own steam without the need for economic bellows from Westminster. Yet it must not be forgotten that high tariff walls had long given home industry a breathing space. Both liquid capital and profits escaped direct taxation; capital could be freely deployed.

A broad distribution of affluence among the swelling middling ranks of society created healthy demand for increased commodity output. As many observed, there were more comfortable master-craftsmen, petty bourgeois and farmers, and spinsters and widows living off invested income to be found in England than elsewhere.

Their capacity to fuel consumer demand was critical to sustained expansion. 'The English,' noted Josiah Tucker,

have better conveniences in their houses, & affect to have more in quantity of clean, neat furniture, & a greater variety such as carpets, screens, window curtains, chamber bells, polished brass locks, fenders, etc. – things hardly known abroad among persons of such a rank – than are to be found in any other country in Europe, Holland excepted.

Thus, he clinched his point about home demand, 'the people of Great Britain may be considered as the customers to or the manufacturers for each other.' The 'average family', it has been suggested, was buying £10 worth a year of British-made goods in 1688, £25 worth in 1750, and £40 worth in 1811.

Consumer demand, for instance, stimulated the rise of the pottery towns, as earthenware and china replaced pewter. Similarly, much of the late-eighteenth-century expansion in the iron and metal trades did not depend (unlike later) upon heavy capital goods – plant, urban utilities, ships, pipes, girders, bridges, track, engines, etc. Machinery, even water-wheels and steam engines, was still made largely of wood. Rather the demand was for agricultural implements, horses' harnesses, and the vast proliferation of domestic hardware: locks, pots and pans, fenders, fireplaces, carriage and household fittings, and ornaments.

Without such *nationwide* elements of economic 'fitness' as profitable agriculture, an energetic distributive system and a broadening consumer market, there could have been no quickening of industrialization. Yet it was in only a small number of regions that concentrations of heavy industry and factory employment had clustered by the close of the century. Highly localized, new manufactures were extremely unevenly distributed. The metropolis and most country market towns were essentially unaffected, and across most of the country the landscape bore no scars of industrialism until the coming of railways under Victoria. A countryman such as William Cobbett could stand without incongruity as the mouthpiece of working people during the Regency before ever visiting an inferno of new industrialism.

Not only was primitive industrialization geographically particularized, but its locations were far flung and in traditional 'dark corners' of the land. Peninsular Cornwall had an abnormally highly industrialized workforce because of its key importance in tin, copper and lead extraction and quarrying china clay. Coal-mining and smelting were booming in the narrow valleys of South Wales, in Ebbw Vale and around Merthyr Tydfil, where the Dowlais iron-works were situated. Tinplate-works developed at Pontypool, copper at Neath. The massive chemical and iron plant of the Carron works sprouted by the Firth of Forth. Lead-works clustered in lonely settlements high in the Pennines, such as Wharfedale, High Teesdale and Alston Moor. The Parys 'copper mountain' brought prosperity to Anglesey – Thomas Williams, the 'Copper King', employed up to 1,500 workers there. Coal-pits expanded on England's distant perimeter in Cumbria, beyond the Lakes. All this was dictated by the topo-graphy of raw materials – ore, coal, water – for the critical first phase of industrialization lay in maximizing primitive extraction. To some degree entrepreneurs planted factories – rather like slave plantations – where labour was unregulated and rivalry least. This sudden, highly localized and uneven development was what shocked visitors who found belching industrial works poised like giant military encampments deep amidst sylvan scenery (most saw them as sublime, rather than as blots upon the landscape). Early industrialization involved the ultra-rapid trans-formation of hitherto relatively under-developed areas, above all Lancashire, South Wales and Clydeside, rather than the steady expansion of regions such as Devon, Gloucestershire or London, where regulated trades and workshop industry had been rooted for centuries.

Though the race for riches was open, the industrialization had its sprinters, the entrepreneurs. Challenged to organize staggering new concentrations of production, they were a remarkable breed. Most were essentially self-made, starting small. A high proportion – for example the Peels, Wedgwoods and John Kay (one of twenty-two children) came from the yeomanry or had begun as petty tradesmen, like Arkwright, a barber and wig-dresser who shrewdly quit when wigs went out of fashion. William Radcliffe described his own rise into the ranks of the manufacturers:

Availing myself of the improvements that came out while I was in my teens, by the time I was married [aged twenty-four, in 1785], with my little savings, and a practical knowledge of every process from the cotton-bag to the piece of cloth, such as carding by hand or by the engine, spinning by the hand-wheel or Jenny, winding, warping, sizing, looming the web, and weaving either by hand or fly-shuttle, I was ready to commence business for myself; and by the year 1789 I was well established, and employed many hands both in spinning and weaving, as a master manufacturer.

By 1801 he had command of over a thousand weavers.

Successful iron-masters generally rose through expanding small workshops: Aaron Walker began as a nailer, William Hawks of Newcastle and John Parker of Staffordshire both as blacksmiths; George Newton of Thorncliffe was a spade-maker; Benjamin Huntsman came to steel from clock-making. Samuel Garbett began life as a brass-worker; John Roebuck's father was a maker of small wares in Sheffield, William Reynolds the son of a Bristol iron-trader. Great brewers, such as Courage and Strong, began as inn-keepers. Industrialization was largely launched with small master skills on small master capital.

From these acorn beginnings they came to run capitals, plant and workforces on a scale hitherto unknown in British industry, exercising local power as great as any noble proprietor's. They innovated spectacularly in work organization, labour discipline, management and merchandising (the scale of their operations, expanding to anticipate markets, demanded constant innovation). Like Korea or Taiwan today, they banked upon selling basic goods in vast quantities to new markets at low unit costs, risking slim profit margins.

Entrepreneurs did not, of course, God-like, create the Industrial Revolution on their own, out of nothing. Yet they were forgers of a new world, and their personal innovating role often proved decisive. Whereas City merchant princes played for fortunes within the well-plotted practices of the Exchange, entrepreneurs were ploughing virgin fields, having to excel as capitalist, financier, technocrat, works manager, engineer, merchant and salesman all in one. Only in England did entrepreneurs become so prominent so early. On the Continent ambitious *bourgeois gentilhommes* continued to seek office, professional or rentier status.

Max Weber suggested long ago that entrepreneurs such as these emerged out of the crucible of Calvinism, justifying themselves to God by industry, frugality and sober living, their secret being not to dissipate profits but to plough them back. There were indeed many entrepreneurs who were Dissenters, such as John Wilkinson and the Quaker Darbys (though few were strictly Calvinists). But many others, such as the Peels and Arkwrights, were Anglicans, and some like Robert Owen, were no friends of orthodox Christianity at all. Nonconformists *were* prominent as entrepreneurs, though not because of their creed, but because (like the Jewish community) they formed a tight-knit, 'marginal' group spared the fashionable world of dissipation – Quakers in particular shut themselves off from landed High Society. They aimed to dignify the world left open to them, business, with success.

The early years of rapid industrialization should not be seen as marking a sharp break with the past. Expansion quickened within a familiar economic framework, though at accelerating rates. Production even of goods made by time-honoured processes soared: between 1785 and 1800 commodity output in such trades increased as follows:

small beer 30%	soap 41%	spirits 73%
strong beer 33%	tobacco 58%	tea 97%
tallow candles 33%		

Moreover, what became the great firms of the early industrial revolution were not vast combines, floated on landed, City or finance capital, under the eye of established merchant princes, but small enterprises which made the best of opportunities to keep growing. And a small works could get going almost for a song. Workshops were to be had at low rates: 'Suitable for a beginner in Trade in the sailcloth manufacture and other branches in Linen and Cotton', announced an advertisement from Prescot:

Shops for 8 or 10 Hacklers, two Rooms for laying up Hemp, Flax, etc., one Shop with 8 Sail Cloth Looms, one ditto for six Starching Frames, one ditto for Warping, counting Yarn, etc., the Mill ready fix'd, a large Boukhouse, with plenty of good Water, and a Croft of a proper Size adjoining, the present rent of the whole only £16 per Annum.

Even a steam engine could be purchased for a couple of hundred pounds. Used machinery was easily purchased. In 1792 a second-hand 'forty-spindle jenny of the best sort' could be had for £6; a large scribbling or carding machine would fetch £50. A small factory would cost no more than £2,000. In 1741 Abraham Walker set up his Sheffield iron foundry on £600 – by

1801 the business was worth £235,000. In 1793 Jedediah Strutt's mill at Belper, one of the giants, cost a modest £5,000 for the building, £5,000 for the machinery, and £5,000 for the materials; William Marshall's first flax-spinning mill in Leeds cost about the same (a stately home, by contrast, could swallow up to £100,000).

Capital was raised privately (bankers were not eager to make long-term loans to industry for plant, preferring to lend 'short'), and capital burdens were typically pooled between partners in an infant firm. Thus, early in the century, Abraham Darby had joined three others to set up the Vale Royal Furnace in Cheshire, each contributing materials, skills and money. Every Monday the pig-iron produced at the works was shared out between the four in proportions dictated by the partnership agreement. In 1759 the Dowlais iron-works in South Wales was built on £4,000 put up by eight partners. Sometimes labyrinthine sub-contracting and sub-letting arrangements had to be devised to share out the capital load. When Robert Owen set up his first factory, financial stringency forced him to sub-let almost the whole of it.

Furthermore, because most of the money needed to set up in business was not fixed but circulating capital, it might be largely 'illusory', floated chiefly by credit (that is, in effect footed by other people). The ratio of fixed to working capital was often in the region of 1:4. By 1800 no more than £2 million in fixed capital had gone into the cotton industry (little more than the cost of rebuilding Bath). In short, in the early days of the Industrial Revolution it was relatively easy for a modest man, indeed a beginner, to start up a business of enormous expansive potential without having to own much capital. He whose father had rested content with a workshed, might now be king of a factory.

Establishing a business was relatively simple, because most thrived on machinery that remained cheap, simple and traditional. All through the century, steam power remained exceptional in manufacturing industry. The bulk of steam engines were used for draining mines not driving wheels. Even in textiles, the shift from stream-power to steam power came slowly, for water-wheels were cheap, durable and highly efficient, albeit vulnerable to drought and ice. Not till 1785 was steam harnessed to a cotton mill (at Popplewick in Nottinghamshire). By 1800 there were only 490 Watt steam engines (the meticulous Boulton and Watt assembled about a dozen a year); and the horses in London and Middlesex alone still outnumbered all the steam 'horsepower' in England and Wales. Steam's chief advantage lay in affording a geographical mobility which water-power lacked. It allowed heavy industry eventually to move back into the cities.

Setting up in industry was easy. Yet it was never secure. Fierce competition, technological transformation, frontierism in the market, and financial panics all combined to bankrupt many, even big guns, including Lancashire spinners such as Horrocks or McConnels. Whereas aristocrats by blood could strut through chronic indebtedness, when the magnates of manufacturing were caught short for want of funds it was serious indeed; they had no lands to mortgage. Even Matthew Boulton was perennially cadging from his friends to tide him over bad times, and he dragged his heels about repaying (maybe that is what explains his success).

Industrialization could involve a revolution in relations of production. The concentrated workplace, employing several hundred men, women and children, ceased to be a freak, characteristic chiefly of dockyards, and became an integral feature of employment. Not all large works were multi-storey factories housing serried ranks of identical machines fed from a single belt or power shaft. Some were highly organized chains of distinct workshops engaged on multifarious processes. In Birmingham, the Soho foundry of Matthew Boulton was an interlocking system of workshops, each serially engaged on its own particular segment of the metal processes – casting, assembly, stamping, burnishing, etc. Boulton spatially located each operation in a flow-line so as to minimize movement, time-wastage and transport. He maximized the division of labour, endorsing in his practice Adam Smith's dictum that 'the greatest improvement in the productive powers of labour and the greater part of the skill, dexterity & judgment with which it is anywhere directed, or applied, seem to have been the effects of the division of labour'.

But the centrally powered factory was the true herald of the future. Though the first modern English factory was the silk mill set up in 1719 by Thomas Lombe in Derby (its six storeys housed 300 workers, the machinery driven by a central water-wheel), cotton-spinning was the sector in which factories paid dividends. Kay's flying shuttle (1733) and Hargreaves's spinning jenny (1767) had been cheap and compact enough for use in cottage industry. But once Arkwright developed the water frame (1769), efficient spinning machinery was too costly to be owned by individual out-workers, too bulky to be housed at home, and increasingly needed to be harnessed to mechanical power-sources. Arkwright furthermore stipulated that his frame must be deployed in 1,000-spindle units, to pre-empt evasions of his patent. The new factories which housed such technology were purpose-built. Industrialists experimented with fire-proof cast-iron frames, steam-heating, and, later, gas-lighting to facilitate capital-efficient, round-the-clock shift-work.

For centuries, putting-out and sub-contracting had made excellent sense for capitalists as appropriate modes of industrial organization. Through them they escaped heavy investment in central plant or even tools; workers could be instantly laid off, and maintenance of the workplace, labour discipline and collecting and delivering materials were the workers' problems. It was a flexible system, minimizing employers' responsibilities. Now, with artificial power and labour-saving technology promising sky-rocketing output in such fields as cotton, the prospect of concentrating the workforce all in one works came to have the edge. Behind the walls and under the roof of a factory, it was easier for a manufacturer to safeguard advanced and secret machinery from industrial espionage, a trauma haunting the most technologically sophisticated entrepreneurs (who nevertheless also appreciated the selling power of visibility, and were pleased to show visitors over public parts of their works). One of Boulton's aims in dividing up his premises into separate workshops was to prevent information leakage among the workforce, craftsmen being banned from all shops except those where their trade lay. Employers threatened no quarter to workers who spilt trade secrets. Inside a factory it was in any case easier to ensure that hands worked the maximum number of hours a week, like clockwork, every hour, every workday, every week. Moreover, in the factory, it was easier for employers to reduce pilfering.

Factories employing platoons of workers required new labour relations. In the first place, owners needed to create a workforce. Workers were wooed by newspaper advertisements – as, for instance, this one placed by Strutt and Arkwright in the *Derby Mercury*:

Cotton Mill, Cromford, 10th Dec. 1771
Wanted immediately, two journeymen clock-makers, or others that understand tooth and pinion well. Also a smith that can forge and file. Likewise two wood turners, that have been accustomed to wheelmaking spoke-turning, etc. Weavers residing at the mill, may have good work. There is employment at the above place for women, children etc. and good wages.

Adults were lured into factories by prospects of secure work and higher wages, but until 1816 many manufacturers conscripted their child labour by contracting with parish authorities to take infant paupers off their hands as apprentices. 'It is a very common practice,' noted Samuel Romilly,

with the great populous parishes in London to bind children in large numbers to the proprietors of cotton-mills in Lancashire and Yorkshire, at a distance of 200 miles. The children, who are sent off by wagon loads at a time, are as much lost forever to their parents as if they were shipped off for the West Indies.

Romilly's observation was borne out in practice. Between 1786 and 1805, Cuckney Mill in Nottinghamshire secured juvenile workers as follows:

from 24 parishes in Notts. and the adjacent parts of Derbyshire and Yorkshire	63
from 26 parishes in London and the adjacent parts of Middlesex and Essex	498
from 4 other parishes	44
Total sent by parishes	605
from 3 philanthropic organizations	98
from parents, relatives and private individuals	77
	780

Child and female labour was prized by new masters, being more tractable and less militantly organized, and commanding lower wages than men. In 1793, almost a fifth of Robert Owen's workforce was under nine years old.

This new labour force needed to be tamed and trained. Out-workers had been used to pacing their own work by the piece, not by the clock, chatting, drinking and larking on the job. Punctuality, regularity and accuracy, by contrast, were demanded by the metronomic tempo of the new factory. Ambrose Crowley had already faced the problem of resistance to labour discipline early in the century. 'Some have pretended,' he complained,

a sort of right to loyter, thinking of their readiness and ability to do sufficient in less time than others. Others have been so foolish to think bare attendance without being imployed in business is sufficient ... Others so impudent as to glory in their villany and upbrade others for their diligence ...

The problem was endemic. As the hosier Isaac Cookson put it in 1806:

I find the utmost distaste on the part of the men, to any regular hours or regular habits ... The men themselves were consistently dissatisfied because they could not go in & out as they had been used to do; & were subject during after hours, to the ill-natured observations of other work-men to such an extent as to completely disgust them with the whole system.

This was partly because entrepreneurs were seeking to impose longer hours. Crowley had stipulated,

To the end that sloath and villany should be detected and the just and diligent rewarded, I have thought meet to create an account of time by a Monitor, and do order and it is hereby ordered and declared from 5 to 8 and from 7 to 10 is fifteen hours, out of which take 1 for breakfast, dinner, etc. There will then be thirteen hours and a half neat service ...

This service, Crowley insisted, must be calculated 'after all deductions for being at taverns, alehouses, coffee houses, break-fast, dinner, playing, sleeping, smoking, singing, reading of news history, quarrelling, contention, disputes or anything foreign to my business, any way loytering'. Cotton operatives were regularly having a thirteen- or fourteen-hour day thrust upon them. Adults kicked against the discipline. Many left, or were dismissed (plenty were queuing at the gates to replace them). McConnel and Kennedy in Manchester had a workforce turnover of 100 per cent a year.

Employees hankered after traditional holidays. 'Our men will go to the Wakes if they were sure to go to the D . . . l next,' fumed Josiah Wedgwood in 1772, 'I have not spared them in threats & I would have thrashed them right heartily if I could.' His success in handling this 'leisure preference' was but partial. Four years later he complained, 'Our men have been at play 4 days this week, it being Burslem Wakes. I have rough'd and smooth'd them over & promised them a long Xmass, but I know it is all in vain, for Wakes must be observed though the world was to end with them.' He wanted to end such atavism and make craftsmen go like clockwork. Southey commented in 1806: 'In commerce, even more than in war, both men and beasts are considered merely as machines, and sacrificed with even less compunction.'

Various attempts were made to inject labour discipline. Supervision was tightened – for Boulton workmen must be 'under our eyes & immediate management – everyday & almost every hour'. Many entrepreneurs set up schools to break in the very young. Wedgwood tried yoking workers within long-term contracts. Swingeing fines punished malefactors – those who were late or out of position, who dozed, talked or slacked. The iron-master William Reynolds drew up 'Rules for the Preservation of good order in the works of William Reynolds and Co.'. Wedgwood's rule-book stipulated:

Any workman striking & likewise abusing an overlooker, to lose his place. Any workman conveying ales or liquor into the manufactory in working hours, forfeit 2/-.

And – the carrot – exemplary workers were rewarded: with bonuses, special clothes, promotion. Wedgwood, John Christian Curwen and other employers set up compulsory, contributory sickness benefit and pension schemes for their workers, to give them a lasting interest in the firm. Matthew Boulton founded the Soho Society, to which workers contributed between ½d. and 4d. a week, receiving up to 80 per cent of their earnings in compensation when sick. Contemporaries believed attention to labour discipline and personnel management paid off, one remarking about Soho:

The rules of this Manufactory have certainly been productive of the most laudable and salutary effects, and besides the great attention paid to cleanliness and wholesome air etc., this Manufactory has always been distinguished for its order and good behaviour and particularly during the great riots at Birmingham.

Entrepreneurs had to be titans and tyrants, because of the sheer scale of their operations. By 1793, Reynolds' iron-works were valued at £138,000. In 1770 Boulton had some 700 workers at Soho, and by 1795 Peel was employing a workforce of 15,000. Their sights rose and rose. 'I shall ASTONISH THE WORLD ALL AT ONCE,' wrote Wedgwood to his partner Thomas Bentley, 'for I hate piddling you know.' Becoming 'vase-maker general to the universe', he died worth £½ million. By way of appropriate self-commemoration, John Wilkinson the iron-founder stipulated burial in an iron coffin (prudent protection also against body-snatchers).

The labours involved in the relentless enterprise of nursing large-scale industry from the cradle were Herculean. Some – like Wedgwood – saw scientific management as the philosopher's stone: understanding cash-flow better, promoting time-and-motion efficiency, and making accountancy more rigorous. John Marshall, the Leeds flax-spinner, trusted to the nitpicking business of enforcing exact order:

In Marshall's every man chases his business . . . the hands have very particularly printed instructions set before them which are as particularly attended to . . . so strict are the instructions that if an overseer of a room be found talking to any person in the mill during working hours he is dismissed immediately – two or more overseers are employed in each room, if one be found a yard out of his own ground, he is discharged. No overseer is allowed to touch a tool or shift a pinion with his own hands, on pain of dismissal – everyone, managers, overseers, mechanics, oilers, spreaders, spinners and reelers, have their particular duty pointed out to them, and if they transgress, they are instantly turned off as unfit for their situation.

Marketing policy was also crucial. Wedgwood, aided by his faithful merchant partner, Bentley, shrewdly banked on psychological snobbery, pioneering up-market brand names and showrooms. For Matthew Boulton, it was of paramount importance to reach the broadest markets:

Though you speak contemptuously of Hawkers, Pedlars, and those who supply *Petty Shops*, yet we must own that we think they will do more towards supporting a great Manufactory, than all the Lords in the Nation. We think it of far more consequence to supply the people than the nobility only.

Each had his own special strength. Richard Arkwright's entrepreneurial successes were achieved by bulldozing. Though his interest in technological innovation waned, his opportunism remained acute. Still others, like the Strutts, kept up religiously with every minuscule technical wrinkle. The great entrepreneurs kept tabs on their empires, monarchs of all they surveyed, down to the last petty operation. Wedgwood strode around his works smashing 'rejects' with his wooden leg. If the owner didn't bother, no one else would, for there were no boards of directors, and trusty middle-managers were rare as rubies. Rather like a king, a proprietor would pray for an heir to inherit the family business (though sons as often as not became absentees and prodigals).

Entrepreneurs were the frontiersmen of the new industrial world, colonizing virgin corners of the land. Their factories straddled the fast-flowing streams of rural Derbyshire, Lancashire and Yorkshire. Arkwright set up his works at obscure Cromford, Belper, Milford, Birkacre and Holywell, far from the old cities and guilds. Hence they needed not just to drill labour *inside* their own factories but also to create total community environments from scratch. They ran up terraces of cottages, lodging houses, shops, roads, bridges, weirs, chapels, drains and schools. Youths working for Strutt and Arkwright had to attend school for four hours on Saturday afternoons and Sundays to 'keep them out of mischief'. Angling for loyalty, the bluff Arkwright built an inn at Cromford, whereas the sober Strutts set grounds aside for kitchen gardens. John Farey praised 'the vast numbers of neat and comfortable cottages . . . erected by the late Sir Richard and by the present Mr Richard Arkwright, by Messrs Strutts, Mr Samuel Oldknow and numerous others of the cotton spinners and manufacturers'.

Where parish aid was rudimentary they established benefit clubs and health schemes (they had first created industrial disease and accidents). Aping paternalist grandees, bosses organized sports and feasts, inventing works loyalties and traditions (as in Japanese industry nowadays, ballads were sung toasting success to the works). When Matthew Boulton's son came of age, he staged a jamboree for 700 workers. Works bands and choirs soon followed. Thus captains of industry had to create willy-nilly a new environment. With the exception perhaps of colonial governors, they had unequalled scope to dictate the shape of things to come, and some had shining new views of society, the most remarkable embodiment being the New Lanark Mills, where Robert Owen was to attempt by paternalism to establish a cooperative utopia.

Owen himself epitomizes the new world of the manufacturers. Son of a Welsh saddler, he tramped to London at the age of ten with forty shillings in his pocket, later working behind a haberdasher's counter for £25 a year. At eighteen, by borrowing £100 from his brother, he set up in business in Manchester, manufacturing spinning-mules. His first year's profit was £300. At twenty-eight he married into the Dales, a wealthy Scottish textile family, finally buying up his father-in-law's mills for £60,000. Once rich, his attention turned from making money to making utopian socialism, for, having created an environment for his own workforce, he came to believe that people were wholly creatures of environment. Social perfection was therefore a matter of social engineering. Industrialization, within a socio-economy of cooperation and communism, would conquer poverty and end the curse of labour.

Certain industries – iron, for example – spurted ahead in the last part of the century. Iron had not hitherto been the key English metal trade (brass, tin and copper were more prominent, and much iron had been imported from Sweden). But the introduction of the new technology of coke-smelting, the puddling process for wrought-iron (it boiled off the harmful sulphur) and rolling-and-slitting mills relieved bottlenecks. No charcoal furnace was built after 1775. Output shot up from 17,350 tons in 1740 to 68,300 in 1790 and 125,019 in 1796. Iron was beginning to replace wood for machine parts, tools and screws. Iron pillars, beams and girders were being tried in buildings (including Wesleyan chapels): they were admirably fire-proof. John Wilkinson developed precision boring for cannon and steam-engine cylinders. The first iron bridge, over the Severn, was constructed in 1779, the first iron ship in 1787. More durable than wood, iron was preferable where wear and tear were heavy (for instance for gears, for the rails within pit workings, and the waggonways on which colliery trucks ran down to canals and quays). From 1793 war gave a blank cheque to the metal trades. Whereas in 1770 charcoal furnaces had been small and sited in the rural woodlands (the Weald in Sussex, for instance) because of the availability of firing, by the end of the century blast furnaces were complex and costly, many needing steam engines to provide the jet of air. Close on 90 per cent of iron production was by then centred on the coalfields, confirming Arthur Young's observation that 'All the activity & industry of this land is fast concentrating where there are coal pits.'

The same thing happened in the cotton industry. Up to mid-century, cottons had been rather insignificant (total sales amounting to perhaps £600,000 a year in 1760). They were not cheap, the price of raw cotton being higher than that of wool. Indian calicoes and muslins were better in quality. Most English 'cottons' were linen mixtures: and when fine fabric was required, linen, though expensive, was preferred.

Output of English cottons began to pick up from the 1760s, largely through breaking into and expanding continental and colonial markets. Imports of cotton wool, at 2.8 million lb. in 1750, shot up to 14.8 million in 1780 and 59.5 million in 1800. Paul's carding machine and Kay's flying shuttle increased the speed of carding and weaving so dramatically that by the 1760s numerous spinners were required to supply a weaver (Arthur Young claimed as late as 1780 that 'they reckon twenty spinners and two or three other hands to every weaver'). The spinning jam was solved by Hargreaves's jenny (developed 1767, patented 1770), which began with about sixteen spindles but, by the end of the century, was taking up to a hundred, and then by Arkwright's water frame (1769), which produced a yarn strong enough to be used as both warp and weft, inaugurating English pure cotton fabrics. Once Arkwright's patents had been cancelled in 1785, the way was open for the general introduction of huge factory steam-spinning. By the early nineteenth century, one spinner was as productive as 200 had been seventy years earlier. In the words of the manufacturer William Radcliffe, 'Cotton,

cotton, cotton has become the almost universal material for employment.'

Between 1780 and 1800, imports of raw cotton went up eightfold. Handicraft weaving ceased to be largely a winter fall-back by-employment, becoming a lucrative and quickly learnt full-time occupation. The industry which had rated barely a mention in Adam Smith's *Wealth of Nations* (1776) was accounting for some 7–8 per cent of Britain's national income by the early nineteenth century, employing about 100,000 spinners. The twenty spinning factories of 1770 had increased to 150 by 1790. By 1788 there were forty cotton mills in South Lancashire alone, and spinning was busying some quarter of a million weavers in cottage and workshop industry up and down the country. There seemed no limit to demand, not least because prices tumbled all the time.

Other industries shared in the rapid late-century expansion, chemicals assuming particular importance. The wealth-multiplying consequences of expansion produced euphoria: 'It is impossible,' wrote Patrick Colquhoun just after the turn of the century,

to contemplate the progress of manufactures in Great Britain within the last thirty years without wonder and astonishment. Its rapidity, particularly since the commencement of the French revolutionary war, exceeds all credibility. The improvement of the steam engines, but above all the facilities afforded to the great branches of the woollen and cotton manufactories by ingenious machinery, invigorated by capital and skill, are beyond all calculation; and as these machines are rendered applicable to silk, linen, hosiery and various other branches, the increased produce, assisted by human labour, is so extensive that it does more than counter-balance the difference between the price of labour in this, and other countries – the latter cannot enjoy the same facilities without those extensive capitals, skill, and experience which the British manufacturers have acquired, and which cannot be transferred to foreign nations without those requisites (capital and skill) which they will probably not possess for a long series of years, and which very few of them can ever hope to enjoy.

What, however, was the wider social impact? Industrialization had drastic *long-term* consequences, which those living through it knew very well: sooty Coketowns made up of barrack-like back-to-backs; grime, fog, sulphureous smoke, choking chemical wastes; the Great Exhibition in the Crystal Palace; the horrors of factory accidents and industrial diseases, cholera, the triumphs of the railways, cheap cottons, cheap books, cheap travel, Marx's vision of class conflict, a revolutionary bourgeoisie facing an alienated proletariat; a world of affluence and effluents. As the economy industrialized, individual capitalists and operatives alike felt that control over their own destinies was waning, and that they were becoming the puppets of market forces and the trade cycle. Even the greatest might go to the wall. But what had industrialization changed by 1800?

Romantics were already assailing stony materialism and waste-land blight, the scandal of child labour, the tyranny of lucre, the robot system in which 'getting and spending we lay waste our power'. Yet such criticisms of commercialism and alienated labour had been expressed throughout the eighteenth century, indeed since Biblical times. Equally we must stress that many sectors of the economy – even many manufacturing trades – had been hardly touched by new industrial technology, and that by no means all rapid change was due to transformations in the manufacturing system. 'London is, I am certain, much fuller than ever I saw it,' observed Horace Walpole in 1791: 'I have twice been going to stop my coach in Piccadilly [to inquire what was the matter] thinking there was a mob, and it was only nymphs and swains, sauntering and trudging.' London expanded, but not because of what is known as the Industrial Revolution.

Until the end of the century, the face of industrialization was found more impressive than horrifying (though John Byng thought it 'destroyed the course and beauty of nature'). Forges and chimneys belching flame into the night had their own sublime majesty, qualities picked out by artists such as Joseph Wright of Derby, more endearing to tourists than to choking residents. Iron bridges and canal viaducts (with barges sailing through the air) were new wonders of the world. Industrial towns appeared businesslike, thronging with activity. Productive labour was a heart-warming sight. The worst of the desolate lunar landscapes of mineral slag, abandoned workings and chemi-cal pollution in Lancashire, the Black Country and South York-shire were largely things of the future. The most appalling slums were not in new centres of dense industrialization, but in over-crowded traditional cottage-industry villages, in ports, and in ancient cities such as Bristol. Before the turn of the century, however, overburdened sanitation was breeding decimating waves of feverous diseases in Manchester,* Bury, Bolton, Ashton and other parts of industrial Lancashire, and tuberculosis and rickets worsened.

What had industrialization done for the people up to 1800? It certainly hadn't produced a uniform improvement in living standards among the working population. Industrializing trades, of course, needed to offer attractive wages. Whereas in 1700 wage-rates in under-developed Lancashire had been below those of the rural South (between 8d. and 1s. a day as compared with about 1s. 2d.), they outran them as industrialization proceeded. But the replacement of male labour by female and child labour in textile factories took its toll on family incomes (women's pay was about two thirds that of men). And as inflation took off, even rising wages failed to keep pace with the rocketing cost of food, particularly during the 1790s. The pressure of demand, exacerbated by harvest crises in 1783, 1792–3, 1795–6 and 1799–1800, pushed bread to staggering prices. Wheat cost 48s. a quarter in 1760, 36s. in 1770, 54s. in 1780, 75s. in 1790, and a record 113s. a quarter in 1800. The cost of living almost doubled between 1770 and 1795, and went up by as much again by 1800.

There were, however, rich pickings in certain trades. With unlimited demand for cloth, and enormous expansion in the output of spun yarn, hand-loom weavers shot up in numbers, and were enjoying a spectacular Indian summer before their catastrophic demise in the teeth of power-weaving from the 1820s. A Lancashire or Derbyshire hand-weaver could command £3 a week or more at the turn of the century (an agricultural labourer was probably on less than ten shillings). Up to the end of the century, no general crisis of technological obsolescence faced out-workers. Even businesses with large turnovers such as West Riding worsteds long continued on strictly traditional small-master lines. In some areas, however, staple industries (Devon worsteds for example) had been hit by competition.

Had industrialization already spelt a revolution in the conditions of life? Generalization is hazardous and, of course, the bulk

---

* Manchester failed to cope with a rising population of 27,000 in 1773, 39,000 in 1780, and 75,000 in 1801.

of the labour force had been barely touched. (The number of nailers, for instance, trebled between 1770 and 1810, but they were all domestic or workshop workers.) In many trades, industrialization had certainly eroded independence. Mechanization diminished workers' bargaining power over production processes and introduced new health dangers. Steam pumps allowed deeper coal-mining, resulting in more explosions (the introduction of the Davy 'safety' lamp from 1815 further multiplied hazards, since it encouraged the reopening of abandoned 'unsafe' pits). The damp atmosphere of factories contributed to the appalling rise of tuberculosis. Dry-grinding in the cutlery trades, paint-making, and the use of lead glazes in the potteries were often lethal. Josiah Wedgwood proved stubborn even when informed of the dangers — to consumers and workers alike — of lead in his glazes. Unguarded machinery in textile factories, into which exhausted children had to crawl to pick up broken threads, made mutilations commonplace. Factory labour was extremely long, often over twelve or thirteen hours a day, six days a week. Factories were stifling, machine-minding was dead-end, soul-destroying work (though also comparatively light, all-the-year-round, and fairly secure).

Above all, factories drastically reduced operatives' control over their work — as Robert Owen frankly put it, under this system, 'to support life you must be tyrant or slave'. In the family-oriented, work-where-you-live economy typical among craftsmen and out-workers, the group (whether barge crew or family workshop) customarily regulated its own work practices, though obviously within the wider constraints of necessity. This option was dramatically curtailed within the martinet discipline of the factory, where even talking was suppressed. Yet family life adjusted rapidly to the widespread migration and new patterns of work involved in factory towns. Many migrants moved to districts where they already had friends and kin; grandparents and aunts minded children while mothers were out at work (though most female factory hands were unmarried), and strong neighbourly support-systems cared for the sick and out-of-work. Migrants in new manufacturing communities re-established old roots or put down new ones through ale-houses, friendly societies, parades, union activities and chapels; the works themselves became foci of loyalty.

By contrast, labour sometimes united to resist the installation of new machinery. Arkwright's carding factory at Birkacre in Lancashire was attacked in 1776 when

a most riotous and outrageous Mob assembled in the Neighbourhood, armed in a warlike Manner, and after breaking down the Doors of the Buildings, they entered the Rooms, destroyed most of the Machinery, and afterwards set fire to and consumed the whole Buildings, and every Thing therein contained.

Responses to new conditions of production differed, however, from place to place. In 1787 the attempt to apply Arkwright's roller principle to worsted-spinning in Leicester led to riots, the death of the mayor, and the smashing of the machinery; but the process was accepted in Nottingham. In Coventry there was such successful resistance to the mechanization of ribbon-weaving that the trade became uncompetitive and died off.

For the individual worker, industrialization involved a complex profit-and-loss account. What industrialization was doing as a whole, however, was multiplying toil (seemingly a paradox given the growth of 'labour-saving' technology). Artisans in traditional manufactures may not have received larger wages, and many trades had been – and remained – sweated. But artisans had been accustomed to flexible work hours, to fringe benefits, and to time off for fairs, holidays or anniversaries. Where industrialization occurred, it spelt the iron cage of working six days a week, every week. Holidays and leisure were squeezed; fatigue stared out from unsmiling faces. As Godwin pointed out, mechanization, which should have made machines the servants of men, freeing them to enjoy new commodities, was actually making men the slaves of work – the slaves of machines – more than ever before.

Many claimed that in industrializing districts the faces of Nature and of society were becoming more opulent, sprucer and more civilized. 'The general diffusion of manufactures throughout a country,' thought Robert Owen, 'generates a new character in the inhabitants.' Visiting Stoke in 1781, John Wesley commented on the beneficial effects of the rise of the Potteries:

How the whole face of the country has changed in about 20 years, since which inhabitants have continually flowed in from every side – the wilderness is literally become a fruitful field. Houses, villages, towns have sprung up; & the country is not more improved than the people.

Josiah Wedgwood likewise invited his young workers to consider the benefits industry had brought:

ask your parents for a description of the country we inhabit when they first knew it; and they will tell you that the inhabitants bore all the marks of poverty to a much greater degree than they do now. Their houses were miserable huts, the land poorly cultivated and yielded little of value for the food of man or beast, and these disadvantages, with roads almost impassable, might be said to have cut off our part of the country from the rest of the world, besides rendering it not very comfortable to ourselves. Compare this picture, which I know to be a true one, with the present state of the same country, the workmen earning near double their former wages, their houses mostly new and comfortable, and the lands, roads, and every other circumstance bearing evident marks of the most pleasing and rapid improvements . . . Industry has been the parent of this happy change.

Against this, however, there were costs to the quality of life. 'The poor are crowded in offensive, dark, damp, and incommodious habitations, a too fertile source of disease!' commented John Aikin in 1795 on the festering mill town of Manchester:

In some parts of the town, cellars are so damp as to be unfit for habitations . . . The poor often suffer from the shattered state of cellar windows. This is a trifling circumstance in appearance, but the consequences to the inhabitants are of the most serious kind. Fevers are among the most usual effects; and I have often known consumptions which could be traced to this cause. Inveterate rheumatic complaints, which disable the sufferer from every kind of employment, are often produced in the same manner . . . I have often observed, that fevers prevail most in houses exposed to the effluvia of dunghills in such situations.

It is hardly surprising that workers were nostalgic for rusticity, and remained so throughout the coming century. Yet no new laws of settlement were needed to corral the proletariat within the mill towns. Labouring men colluded in the creation of the new economy. Overall, what the Hammonds called 'the curse of Midas' was double-sided. Now cheap cotton garments were easier to clean and more hygienic – but smoky atmospheres dirtied them faster (and lungs can't be washed). Factories paid good wages but denied labourers the small perks and pleasures gleaned by country-dwellers. Above all no one took overall responsibility for the new worlds that captains of industry were creating. Though entrepreneurs were kings in their own bailiwick, they lacked a collective voice and social vision, and competition among them was cutthroat. After the swift demise of the General Chamber of Manufactures (1785), no parliamentary lobby spoke for them as a whole.

Already by the end of the eighteenth century, industrialization was lending its weight to a new tilting of the economy (though it was tilting quite slowly). Distribution of Gross National Product shifted towards the town and the manufacturing sector:

	1700 (% GNP)	*1800*
Agriculture	40	33
Industry	20	24
Services	35	44
Urban population as percentage of total	*c.* 22	*c.* 30

Economic change, however, had wrought during the century an unparalleled transformation of social *geography*. In 1700 the major centres of population, wealth and industry had lain within a southern triangle of which Bristol, London and Norwich were the points. By 1800 the triangle had rotated north-west to become contained by Bristol, Hull and Preston. Many of the conurbations of modern England – Birmingham, Manchester, Bradford, Huddersfield, Preston, etc. – had merely been sprawling villages in 1700, but had grown into great towns by 1800, the change being due largely to industrial developments. The classic mill towns were shooting up before the end of the century. By 1801 Wigan had a population of 10,989, Bury 7,072, Oldham 12,024, Blackburn 11,980, Bolton 12,549, Preston 11,887 and Stockport 14,850. These totals are about as high as those of any town (London, Norwich and Bristol excepted) in 1700. Areas of England lightly peopled in 1700 were fast becoming densely populated industrial regions, the West Riding of Yorkshire and Lancashire in particular:

Estimated population per square mile

	1700	*1750*	*1801*
Lancashire	127	179	253
Yorks, West Riding	91	122	212
Worcestershire	141	139	189
Cheshire	92	105	174
Staffordshire	111	133	210
Warwickshire	112	152	236

In 1700 Norfolk, Somerset and Lancashire all had comparable populations (242,000, 214,000 and 238,000 respectively). The first two had climbed steadily by 1800 (to about 282,000 each). Lancashire, by contrast, had shot up to 694,000.

The destiny of this new geography of industrialization still lay unresolved in 1800. The burgeoning new mill towns of Lancashire, Cheshire, Derbyshire and the West Riding, as well as the mining and foundry centres dotted about the country, still lay on the fringes of established society – that older nation of parliamentary boroughs, grandees' seats, assize towns, cathedral cities, public schools – and above all the metropolis. Almost none had a corporation. They lacked churches, hospitals and other civic amenities. Sparseness of local gentry meant that there were few active JPs on the spot, a crucial factor in responses to radical disturbances from the 1790s. How these 'gold-rush towns' would eventually relate to the traditional nation – its political interests and representation, its social elevators, its sources of power and prestige, its ecology of local communities – was still entirely open-ended. And, in any case, two thirds of the population still lived in the countryside, more people worked on the land than in any other form of employment, and domestic service was absorbing an ever-growing fraction. Yet the proportion of the Gross National Product attributable to industry and commerce was steadily rising; Britain was indeed becoming the workshop of the world.

9. Conclusion

This book has highlighted three main aspects of eighteenth-century English society. First, the fundamental strength and resilience of its social hierarchy. It was presided over by a super-confident proprietorial oligarchy, swimming with the tide, with no obvious Achilles' heel; an order whose dominion was consolidated early in the century and never – at least not till the 1790s – seriously challenged, let alone jeopardized. The grip of magnates upon power – capital, economic leverage, office, local influence, pervasive manipulation of patronage in state, Church and armed forces – was tightening. Crown and nobility saw more eye-to-eye, and the no-holds-barred sectarian and party antagonisms among the officers that at many points in the Stuart age had threatened to capsize the ship of state were tamed, to become civilized, ritual infighting. The English ruling class knitted itself together.

National stability could be maintained – despite endemic pockets of local disorder – because the economy worked well enough to profit the rich, to keep practically everyone alive, to prevent sudden subsistence crises, and to give prospects of individual improvement. The parochial Poor Law muffled acute distress. There was no nationwide politics of famine or panic, nor were hedgerows infested with beggars and bandits. Crucially, Albion was uniquely successful in war, conquest and colonization; eupeptic patriotism and profit became heads and tails of Britannia's golden guinea. Moreover, the growing practice of financing government by borrowing meant that the tax burdens of empire-building were not utterly crippling, and debt finance secured the loyalty of the widening circles of fund-holders. Many layers of society became modestly more affluent, and none which could topple the oligarchs was suddenly or chronically disrupted. (Religious Dissenters, the Stuart century's crusading saints, fought among themselves, becoming introspective.) The traditional disciplines of family and workplace, prudential morality, natural beliefs and religious taboos continued to guide regular reproduction of the generations and renewal of the cyclical rhythms of the workaday world. Even rapid industrial change, or the abrupt disruption to ingrained patterns of rural life that enclosure could create, did not produce Jacqueries or *la grande peur*. Labour steadily became more completely absorbed within the wage nexus.

In its socio-political stability England was (superficially at least) characteristic of most contemporary European nations. Before the cataclysm of the French Revolution, *ancien régime* society appeared more secure than in the destabilized preceding centuries of Reformation, Counter-Reformation, the great inflation, the Thirty Years' War and the so-called 'general crisis'. On the Continent peasant share-cropping, serf-labour, seigneurial exactions and privilege all went on with the seed-time and the harvest. Yet, in the event, the English hierarchy was uniquely tough. In France the bones of the old order's skeleton, after all, proved brittle and broke, and the Netherlands, Italy and many German principalities succumbed to French invasion and the enforced 'rationalization' of their regimes. By contrast, menaced by the contagion of the French Revolution and the upheavals of the Continental wars, the English body politic held up, despite the prophecies of Painite radicals that the walls of power and privilege would tumble before the trumpet-blasts of Reason and Liberty. Not only that, but English industrialization romped ahead despite the shackles of blockade and war.

My second theme has been this: though the social hierarchy was inegalitarian and oozing privilege (some of it hereditary), it was neither rigid nor brittle. There was continual adaptiveness to challenge and individual mobility, up, down and sideways. More than in other nations, money was a passport through social frontiers. English society was not frozen into immobilized, distended and archaic forms by the mortmain of law, courts of heralds, nobiliary protocol or the pantomime pageantry of absolutist courts. Men could not be parted from their property, capital was allowed to take root and sprout where it would, and new riches could be manicured into respectability. Private gain was expected to lead, thanks to the magic of the invisible hand, to public benefit. For those with their chins safely above the poverty line, goods, services and opportunities multiplied. The consuming public – the nation of shopkeepers – broadened and made its stake in prosperity felt. Peace and well-being allowed some relaxation of punitive authoritarianism and religious terrors, or at least their displacement into substitute bogeys, such as Francophobia. Compared with most contemporary nations, and with its own recent past, Georgian England was an unintrusive, relaxed society in which ordinary toes were relatively infrequently stamped upon by central officials and priests. Many congratulated themselves that prosperity, freedom, confidence, knowledge and happiness were marching on together, arms linked. Looking back in 1800 on the dying century, the *Annual Review* reflected:

On a general recollection or review of the state of society or human nature in the eighteenth century, the ideas that recur oftenest, and remain uppermost in the mind, are the three following: the intercourses of man were more extensive than at any former period with which we are acquainted; the progression of knowledge was more rapid, and the discoveries of philosophy were applied more than they had been before to practical purposes ... This present age may be called an age of humanity.

For this editor, as indeed later for Marx, the dynamo of the market was the secret of this transformation:

Whence this happy change? Not from the progressive effects of moral disquisitions and lectures; not even from the progressive effects of preaching, trimmed up by the artifices of composition taught by professors of rhetoric; but from the progressive intercourses of men with men, minds with minds, of navigations, commerce, arts and sciences.

But at what price? For many feared that in this market society, where money was the *lingua franca* and everyone had his price, social cohesion, public virtue, justice, authority, respect and compassion would drown in a maelstrom of greed and envy. In this Mandevillian world – moralists worried – public well-being was being corroded by private ambition, statesmen seduced and suborned by executive graft. Yeomen were abandoning native hearths for the fleshpots of London, and servants had become choosy about their masters. Profit, not fair prices, ruled exchange. The Church was feeding itself, not its sheep. Disturbances and violent crime, knaves and thieves, were rampant. Incensed preachers and sentimental novelists warned the rich that through their reckless greed and neglect of duty they were digging their own graves:

Noblemen and gentlemen have almost abandoned the country, so amongst the first great people now residing there may be reckoned the innkeepers, the tax gatherers and the stewards of great estates who with the lawyers rule the country ... the poor must plunder because not provided for ... corporations are venal; trade and manufactories are overstrained; banks and bankruptcies in and over every town; laws, from being multiplied beyond comprehension, cannot be enforced ... and as that increasingly when the metropolis must be fed the body will gradually decay why then there will come a distress, a famine and an insurrection; which the praetorian guards, or the whole army cannot quell; or even the parliament pacify; the latter because they have connived at the (now general) alarm, from having been continually employed in struggles for power; and regardless of the peace and interior happiness of their country!

Thus prophesied the Hon. John Byng on the very eve of the French Revolution, but the country he wrote about was England. Recent historians have agreed with Byng that the ruling classes wanted to have their cake and eat it. 'A fundamental contradiction lay at the heart of English agrarian society in the period of the Industrial Revolution,' argue Hobsbawm and Rudé:

Its rulers wanted it to be both capitalist and traditionalist and hierarchical. In other words, they wanted to be governed by the universal free market of the liberal economists (which was inevitably a market for land and men as well as for goods) but only to the extent that suited nobles, squires and farmers; they advocated an economy which implied mutually antagonistic classes, but did not want it to disrupt a society of 'ordered ranks'.

Many warned that English society was corrupt and rushing lemming-like to the precipice. And meanwhile, from below rose the wail of the oppressed, Blake's 'marks of weakness, marks of woe' in London's chartered streets.

The ruling order was, however, alert to the problems of maintaining order within the fluid and to some extent polarizing society they presided over, recognizing that they had to find ways to continue cracking the whip of capitalism without the workhorses rearing up. Hence the third main focus of this book has lain on their attempts to secure consensus within this acquisitive, restless society. Resort to brute force could succeed only in a local, specific and sporadic way. Sailors were routinely lashed, but (children apart) labouring men were not slaves to be frog-marched into the fields or factories. Feuding private, sectarian interests, particularism, and gentry heel-digging against the executive, meant that military might was generally neither on tap nor politically acceptable as a solution. Towards the close of the century, schemes were being mooted to renew social discipline through exemplary institutions such as purpose-designed prisons deploying solitary confinement. Thus, between 1776 and 1800 boom-town Liverpool built a new lunatic asylum, bridewell and gaol. Such were the ominous harbingers of a more therapeutic, surveying, controlling state, but before the nineteenth century they remained but prototypes. The Georgian battle, rather, was mainly for the mind. The hope was to win acquiescence and endorsement by influence and persuasion – bluster, grandeur, liberality, promises, show and swank, the open door held just ajar. Those in power and their mouthpieces in newspapers and the pulpit dangled before people's eyes ambition, self-respect, new enjoyments, polite values and fashionable lifestyles. Certain of these goals, such as education, Methodism or New Dissent, with their gratifications of inner-light, self-improvement and a Heaven in prospect, were spiritual. Jesus would save, even if the labouring poor could scarce afford to. Other prospects, such as promotion and prosperity through toil and sobriety, leading to larger shares in material well-being and gentility, were worldly. In the distant prospects of self-betterment (through 'Bibles, religious tracts, gospel shops, itinerant tub-men and national schools', as Cobbett sardonically dubbed them) lay the aim of creating the English dream a divided people could share.

Society did not polarize into bristling camps. The bloody internecine wars of religious truth of Stuart times slowly subsided into pamphlet polemics, vituperative though these remained. Anglicans and Dissenters established coexistence. It wasn't only Voltaire who observed how business overrode confessional fences. The political spoils-system and the civil list encouraged men on the make to fall in line with Crown and ministry. The swelling, prosperous middle ranks of brokers, shippers, wholesalers, hauliers and dealers – and all the other masses of retailers, petty manufacturers and superior craftsmen – gave society a stout midriff and prevented simple class dichotomization. In any case much of society was still encased in small face-to-face communities. In 1800, fewer than one person in five lived in towns of more than 20,000 inhabitants.

In the last third of the century seismic rumblings gave notice of growing social tension. Spurred by fiercer spokesmen such as Richard Price and Joseph Priestley, Protestant Dissenters flexed their muscles and reactivated campaigns against the civil disabilities of the Test and Corporation Acts ('So long as we continue Dissenters,' declared Priestley, 'it is hardly possible that we should be other than friends to civil liberty'). Government 'tyranny' in waging war against the Thirteen Colonies, and its incompetence in losing it, gave opposition sitting targets and strengthened agitation, especially among the trading classes, for efficiency and retrenchment. The War of American Independence proved a watershed, acutely dividing the political nation on a constitutional issue, and inciting many City merchants and tradesmen to side with His Majesty's enemies.

Americans' demands for representation were echoed by voteless taxpayers at home, and fears that executive and Court machinations were undermining the Constitution were rekindled. From the 1760s political grievances fanned into flame – though fitfully – out of doors: groups such as the Society of the Supporters of the Bill of Rights (1769) began assailing the citadels of power, seeking to 'restore the constitution'. John Wilkes made an eye-catching anti-ministerial hero and martyr. Redistribution of seats to restore due weight to stout county opinion was demanded by Christopher Wyvill's Yorkshire Association (1779) and the Society for Constitutional Information (1780). Agitation mounted for the relief of Irish Catholics. The swelling ranks of middling men voiced ever more scathing criticisms of privilege, corruption and aristocratic hauteur.

All this led to soul-searching in well-bred breasts. The Evangelical movement within the Church, gathering from the 1770s, sought to purge profligacy and debauchery from the hearts of high-livers. Liberals questioned subscription to the Thirty-Nine Articles, and a few noble spirits such as John Jebb in Cambridge proposed university reform. Jeremy Bentham embarked upon his lifelong, single-handed, Utilitarian labour of cleansing the Augean stables of the law and redesigning the machinery of administration head-to-foot. Even Establishment figures such as

Archdeacon William Paley ventured to doubt whether the distribution of wealth and power brought the greatest possible happiness. Within Westminister itself in the 1780s, Lord Shelburne and Pitt the Younger were prepared to tinker with reforms (though the effect of this was actually to split the radicals). Radical and Dissenting journalists frothed against corruption, imperialism and arbitrary power, and a new wave of preachy novelists, such as Mrs Inchbald and Robert Bage, prescribed the knife for the cancers of pride, privilege and superciliousness which infected high society. Lord George Gordon, fearing subversion of true reformed faith, founded the Protestant Association, and William Blake began to prophesy Doom. For Blake and others the bugbears all around gave the lie to the diabolical house the Georgians had built: hunger stalking in the midst of the smarmy self-congratulators who mouthed pieties and doled out philanthropic halfpennies, while denying life, love, joy and hope to God's innocents.

As growing criticism lashed corruption, strains in the social and administrative fabric became more visible. The surge of industry and population outran local government and left the distribution of parliamentary seats increasingly grotesque. Cornwall had twenty-one boroughs, Lancashire six. With an electorate of barely 250,000, the enfranchised proportion of the population (about 3 per cent) had dwindled to lower than it had been since before the Civil War. The provinces were showing signs of an autonomous counter-life and problems of their own, a second nation erupting in the midst of the old. 'Polite society', R. E. Schofield has written,

> by state and custom established, might still be concerned with land and title, they might still spend their time disputing in an unrepresentative Parliament, discussing literature and the arts in London coffee shops, and drinking and gambling at White's; but the world they knew was a shadow. Another society, in which position was determined by an ungenteel success, was creating a different world more to its liking.

Further social rifts were indeed widening. Polite society, growing increasingly fastidious, was distancing itself from the dirty, pungent, and sometimes dangerous world of the *hoi polloi*, withdrawing from village and community activities, and emasculating the culture of its inferiors.

And yet, until the dawn of the French Revolution, these portents of trouble were but straws in the wind. The Wilkite movement was a spectacle of stage thunder and lightning, a gala performance for the greater glory of John Wilkes himself. With its preoccupation with the defence of individual legal rights, but indifference to social change, the movement left an ambiguous legacy. Wilkes – soon to describe himself as 'an extinct volcano' – later became alderman and mayor, siding with the City authorities against the Gordon Riots, and living to be a friend of Dr Johnson and a foe to the French Revolution. The Gordon Riots of 1780 persuaded parlour liberals that those who brandished the torches of popular agitation got their fingers burnt. The disastrous American war over, Wyvill's parliamentary reform movement had dwindled to shadow-boxing by 1784. In the countryside, enclosure awards sparked no château-burning, and the building of the first great factories of the Industrial Revolution produced no concerted defiance.

Whether or not to be young was very heaven, the 1790s were certainly a new dawn. The tocsin of *Liberté*, *Egalité*, and *Fraternité* gave fresh heart to normally insular radicals and liberals this side of the Channel. Apocalyptic visions of a clean slate swam before the eyes of sober parliamentary reformers such as Horne Tooke, Godwin (with his wish for the 'true euthanasia of government'), and Blake:

> The fields from Islington to Marybone
> To Primrose Hill and St John's Wood
> Were builded over with pillars of gold
> And there Jerusalem's pillars stood.

Just outside Jerusalem, in Westminster, events in France had the sympathy of patrician radicals and vanguard Whigs, at least until the execution of Louis XVI in 1792. Artisan radicals harangued meetings and set up reform societies, hoping, especially after Tom Paine's *Rights of Man* (1791), to plant the liberty tree. 'Frenchmen, you are already free,' declared the London Corresponding Society in 1792, 'but the Britons are preparing to be so.' From 1793 war against revolutionary France – with crippling taxes, inflation, press-gangs, trade disruption, anti-war protests and (in 1797) naval mutinies and the counteracting waves of loyalist bullying – created unparalleled antagonisms within

English society. About a third of the century's strikes occurred in this decade.

Through the 1790s the margin of success enjoyed by Government, magistrates and loyalists in battening down the hatches against the seething waters of unrest was often slim. It was not just hawks and paranoid squires who dreaded that Anarchy stalked the land. Republican whisperings grew more audible, and for the first time since the Civil War, plebeian radicals were organizing their own independent political programmes. Corresponding Societies now linked agitation from town to town and planned their own shadow government, the Convention. In retaliation, Pitt, during his 'white terror', suspended constitutional freedoms, such as Habeas Corpus (1794, 1798), passed the Treason and Sedition Act (1795), the Unlawful Oaths Act (1797), and the Corresponding Societies Act (1799), banned public meetings, and recruited gaggles of spies and informers. Radical leaders like Thomas Hardy, secretary of the London Corresponding Society, had their premises raided, suffered arrest and were put on trial. The administration bought up newspapers and posted troops through the country in specially constructed barracks.

The prospect of civil strife and even bloody revolution in the 1790s was sudden and traumatic. It was obviously made *possible* by a long-term build-up of stress-points, such as the concentration of disaffected and literate artisans in northern and Midland towns which were weak links in the chain of local government. But it was not *precipitated* by these developments. It was, rather, a sudden conflagration, sparked from outside. 'Rights of Man' radicalism, republican toasts, dark mutterings about peers and priests being strung up – all, of course, tapped a libertarian rage that had flowed largely underground since the collapse of the Puritan revolution. Yet without the example, success and wild-fire spread of revolution abroad, their explosive expression would have been unthinkable. The refrain of most eighteenth-century English plebeian protest had, after all, been local, piecemeal and traditional, drawing on ideals of community within the validating framework of custom, common law and Constitution. The working man's cry had traditionally been to call his betters to their duties. Tom Paine – seasoned American, and subsequently French, revolutionary – had quite another song: 'The present age will hereafter merit to be called the Age of Reason,' he proclaimed, 'and will appear to the future as the Advent of a new World.'

Yet though the *ideology* was new, Painites could build upon foundations laid earlier. Working men had got used to running their own micro-republican friendly societies and combinations. Debating societies, such as London's Robin Hood Club, had given tub-thumpers practice in para-political invective. Methodism and popular Dissent had loosened fiery tongues which easily switched from religious to political scores. The spread of printing presses, brave publishers, literacy and reading habits made it remarkably easy to gobble up radical pamphlets and the ideas of Tom Paine (hundreds of thousands of copies were sold). Newspapers had attuned the provinces to the political key of the capital.

Political radicalism spread in the regions alongside economic disturbances, the two often being mutually reinforcing, though never ultimately losing their separate identities. Grain riots worsened as prices rocketed in the mid 1790s. Unemployment worsened, and antagonism between rich and poor grew more menacing. 'It is from neglect and despair,' argued John Byng,

that Democracy, that Anarchy, spring: . . . while the unaided paupers of the country will look at a dog kennel with envy, and the starvers of the town are to peer down without hope upon the blazing displays of cookery – I will say, 'something is rotten in the State of Denmark'.

Furthermore, initially at least, the impact of the French Revolution was to split the Establishment. The Revolution won ringing plaudits among Whigs and Dissenters (though only one bishop supported it). 'How much the greatest event that has ever happened in the world,' exclaimed Charles James Fox at the fall of the Bastille. Erasmus Darwin, the Midlands physician, thought it 'the dawn of universal liberty'; Theophilus Lindsey, aspiring reformer of the Church of England, pronounced, 'The Revolution in France is a wonderful work of Providence in our days, and we trust it will prosper and go on and be the speedy means of putting an end to tyranny everywhere.' Most Dissenters supported it, as did strata of professional and commercial opinion eager for reform at home, and above all the intelligentsia. Even staid burghers walked around on air for a while, addressing each other as 'citizen'. Joseph Priestley caught this mood in urging men to snatch the hour:

While so favourable a wind is abroad, let every young mind expand itself, catch the rising gale, and partake of the glorious enthusiasm, the great subjects of which are the flourishing state of science, arts, manufactures, commerce ... the abolishing of all useless distinctions which were the offspring of a barbarous age (producing an absurd haughtiness in some and a base servility in others), and a general release from all such taxes, and burdens of every kind, as the public good does require. In short, to make government as beneficial, and as little expensive and burdensome, as possible.

In the event, the talk about liberty, natural rights and a new order did not engender a new order of things. The 1790s produced reform societies, a blizzard of pamphlets and boisterous agitation. Revolutionary enthusiasms and Romantic ideals left scars on the hearts and minds of a generation of poets, artists and thinkers. Many magistrates were paralysed with fear. But there were no large-scale assaults on the hierarchy, spontaneous or organized, in England (though this is not true for Scotland and Ireland, and less true of English radicalism between 1802 and 1820, which produced insurrections, assassinations and conspiracies). No one stormed stately homes or cathedrals, or burnt Whitehall, St James's or Newgate. No heads rolled. Most violence flared out of sudden impromptu flashpoints, such as the activities of press-gangs; most agitation focused on practical issues:

> Peace and large bread
> Or a king without a head.

Certainly everyone saw with sobering clarity the people ranged against the privileged, and the possibility that the people might have Justice on their side. But there was not yet a mass proletarian consciousness (most popular agitation came from craftsmen), and the ideology of English Jacobinism remained individualistic. Even so, E. P. Thompson is right to see the 1790s as critical in the process of the formation of the English working class, for until then the wrath of injustice had been masked behind shows of deference and subordination. Now the lower orders were beginning to erupt onto the political scene as an articulate, disruptive, obdurate, avenging force, powerful in their own right. Sectors of them were to become truly menacing in the first decades of the next century. Moreover, it was to take a couple of generations of failure, repression and discipline in the school of industrialism, and the articulation of gradualist political ambitions for them *within* the system, to ease them back again, by mid-century, into a stunned quiescence.

Yet there is no denying that the authorities, pummelled on the ropes, held up; Louis Simond was to observe, with astonishment and admiration, in the early years of the new century:

There is not another government in Europe who could long withstand the attacks to which this is continually exposed. The things published here would set on fire any other hearts in the world, but either from insensibility, reason, or habit, they make but little impression.

The old order battled through partly by unabashed repression. Civil liberties which were the toast of the Constitution – such as Habeas Corpus and freedom of association – were suspended by 'gagging bills'. Hundreds were arrested. Show trials were held of the 'seditious' (though in England, unlike Scotland, most were acquitted). Disturbances, in which national and local grievances reinforced each other, were quelled with unwonted violence. The toll-bridge riots in Bristol in 1793 left eleven protesters dead. In the Birmingham riots of 1791, 'Church and King' loyalist mobs, encouraged by magistrates, destroyed the property of Dissenters, Unitarians and radicals. 'I cannot but feel better pleased,' wrote George III to Henry Dundas, 'that Priestley is the sufferer for the doctrines he and his party have instilled.' The political nation saved its skin only by jettisoning much-vaunted moderation and constitutional guarantees: its soul was bared.

The oligarchy held up, partly because of splits among its opponents. Faced by the execution of Louis XVI and the Terror, Whigs soon splintered into pro- and anti-Revolution factions and, once divided, ceased to provide a serious political challenge to the Government. Standard-bearers of revolution, such as Paine and Thomas Spence, sanguinely believed it would come about not by force of arms but by spontaneous rational Enlightenment. Radical intellectuals speechified and scribbled, but it was all sound and fury, for few had the stomach for killing, and all feared mob extremism from below. Many, such as William

Frend (stripped of his Cambridge fellowship for radicalism), campaigned for liberty, but did not see it in terms of direct *political* goals or bloody rebellion. Like the anarchist philosopher William Godwin (who was, according to Hazlitt's devastating thumb-nail sketch, the 'metaphysician engrafted on the Dissenting Minister') and many others, Frend chiefly desired the cultivation of individuality, wanting reason and freedom to have full play. Moral integrity meant more than democracy. In any case, prosperous craftsmen radicals in Norwich and Sheffield did not see eye-to-eye with scarecrow proletarians, and insurrectionary artisans in the City did not agree with eloquent demagogues such as Major Cartwright and John Thelwall, of whose type Arnold Harvey has written:

The Westminster reformers were upwardly mobile, confident, resilient: they had no need to seek consolation in millenarian fantasies. In Lancashire and the North Midlands, by contrast, where less sophisticated workers were more seriously affected by the economic crisis of the war years, religious enthusiasm and half-baked conspiracy seem to have taken a rather firmer hold.

But the *status quo* held up for other reasons too. Appeals to national defence split the opposition. Under invasion threat, patriotism was more popular than Paine. Cartoonists such as Gillray ridiculed the 'French disease' and native radicalism alike. War proved the ultimate rivet of the nation, restoring the virility of a ruling caste licking its wounds after the War of American Independence. The war years proved good for businessmen, farmers, speculators and rentiers too, and for commission-hungry younger sons seeking paths to glory in the forces.

Furthermore, the propertied closed ranks. There had never been much love lost between the squirearchy and City money-manipulators; paternalist magistrates had not always stood four-square behind middlemen against grain rioters; parvenu manufacturers were often despised by landowners (they competed for labour, raising its price). The Gordon Riots and the loss of the American colonies eroded the trading classes' confidence in Parliament's fitness to safeguard their vital interests. But the propertied were eager to sink their differences in the 1790s over the cardinal issues of the defence of property, the law and the Constitution. The loyal toasts of the militia, yeomanry and Volunteers brought

squires' and merchants' sons together, tenantry mingling with
'employers on horseback'. Certain historians, such as E. P. Thompson, have suggested that without the lucky accident or contrivance of war, aristocratic dominion would shortly have been
assailed head-on by bourgeois challenge. This, however, is to
take too catastrophic a view: the propertied always knew on
which side their bread was buttered. Great manufacturers such as
the Peels, Boultons, Arkwrights and Strutts were already giving
their vote of confidence to the old order by buying up estates.
Matthew Boulton purchased the illustrious estate of Great Tew,
and Richard Arkwright was knighted and appointed High Sheriff
of Derbyshire in 1787, in 1789 becoming Lord of the Manor of
Cromford. For their part, shopkeepers and stock-holders formed
loyalist groups and Associations for the Defence of Property.
Agitation for parliamentary reform among middling men throt-
tled back for a decade or two, while ministries and magistrates
exorcised the spectre of plebeian anarchy. As society closed
ranks, radicalism's sting was drawn. The Dissenter scientist
Joseph Priestley might gravely warn that 'The English hierarchy
. . . has equal reason to tremble at an air pump or an electrical
machine.' Yet he was wrong, for science (like Romanticism and
religion) could equally serve reaction. It was fashionable society
that flocked to the Royal Institution, founded in 1799. Its wizard
experimentalist, Humphry Davy, a poor Cornish lad made good,
assured his glittering audience that science proved 'society
was necessarily and rightly grounded on property and inequality'.

Indeed, many of the propertied saw the light, and recanted
erstwhile liberal and Enlightenment credos, the 1790s producing
more turncoats than any decade since the 1650s. Former Romantic utopians such as Wordsworth, Southey and Coleridge, aghast
at the Terror, turned Tory. The execution of Louis XVI and the
French declaration of war on England turned reaction into style,
Samuel Romilly believing that their consequence was 'among
the higher orders . . . a horror of every kind of innovation'.
Liberal sentiments, humanitarianism, optimism about human
nature, sympathy for the aspirations of the weak, the have-nots
and the oppressed, all bowed to hard-bitten realism. Patriarchal
attitudes were back, and in religion original sin was resurrected.
'Man is an apostate creature,' declared Wilberforce. 'It is a

fundamental error,' echoed Hannah More, burying the Enlightenment commonplace, 'to consider children as innocent . . . rather than as beings who bring into the world a corrupt nature and evil dispositions.' Other nostrums from the Enlightenment 'new deal', such as belief in inevitable progress, were tossed upon the flames.

It became urgent to reassert to the lower orders the politics not of consensus but of hierarchy and subordination. Burke dismissed them as the 'swinish multitude', the Bishop of London could hardly believe 'the extreme depravity and licentiousness which prevails . . . amongst the lowest orders of the people'. Didn't the poor know how lucky they were? Archdeacon Paley proved it, showing that 'frugality itself is a pleasure'. Bishop Horsley applied casuistry to deprivation: 'Poverty . . . can be nothing more than an imaginary evil of which the modest will never complain.' Yet, he claimed, the 'evil of poverty' was also 'a public good'. In any case, the poor needed to be told what was what. Two-penny repository tracts ('Burke for beginners') deluged from the presses, 300,000 copies being printed in 1795 alone. Hannah More wrote a pamphlet for labouring people subtitled *Half a Loaf Is Better Than No Bread*, telling the heroic tale of one pleased to go without:

> And though I've no money, and tho' I've no lands
> I've a head on my shoulders and pair of good hands.
> So I'll work the whole day, and on Sundays I'll seek
> At Church how to bear all the wants of the week.
> The gentlefolks too will afford us supplies
> They'll subscribe – and they'll give up their puddings and pies.

Outrage against the grumbling lower orders grew more shrill. Bishop Watson, renegade liberal, called country labourers 'perverse, stupid, and illiterate' and town artisans 'debauched, ill-mannered'. In 1795 in soup-kitchen mood, *The Times* gave the poor more mealy-mouthed (and anti-canine) advice:

THE WAY TO PEACE AND PLENTY

Rules of the Poor
1. Keep steadily to your work, and never change masters, if you can help it.
2. Go to no gin-shops, or alehouse: but lay out all your earnings in

food, and clothes, for yourself, and your family: and try to lay up a little for rent and rainy days.

3. Avoid bad company.
4. Keep no dogs: for they rob your children, and your neighbours.
5. Go constantly to church, and carry your wives, and children with you, and God will bless you.
6. Be civil to your superiors, and they will be kind to you.
7. Learn to make broth, milk pottage, rice-pudding, etc. One pound of meat, in broth, will go further than two pounds boiled or roasted.
8. Be quiet, and contented, and never steal, or swear, or you will never thrive.

For their part, the Quality would do their bit.

Rules for the Rich
1. Abolish gravy soups, and second courses.
2. Buy no starch when wheat is dear.
3. Destroy all useless dogs.
4. Give no dog, or other animal, the smallest bit of bread or meat.
5. Save all your skim-milk carefully, and give it all to the poor, or sell it at a cheap rate.
6. Make broth, rice-puddings, etc., for the poor, and teach them to make such things.
7. Go to church yourselves, and take care your servants go constantly.
8. Look into the management of your own families, and visit your poor neighbours.
9. Prefer those poor who keep steadily to their work, and go constantly to church, and give nothing to those who are idle, are riotous, or keep useless dogs.
10. Buy no weighing meat, or gravy beef: if the rich would buy only the prime pieces, the poor could get the others cheap.

The rich would thus considerately buy only the best cuts of meat and oversee the poor to keep them good. Smiling Old Leisure had become poker-faced. Cobbett noted this new mood soon afterwards:

Never did we, until these days, hear of millions of 'Tracts, Moral and Religious' for the purpose of keeping the poor from cutting the throats of the rich. The parson's sermon, once a week or a fortnight, used to be quite sufficient for the religion and morals of a village. Now we had a busy creature or two in every village, dancing about with 'Tracts' for the benefit of the souls of the labourers and their families. The gist of the whole of the 'Tracts' was to inculcate content in a state of misery!

To teach people to starve without making a noise! What did all this
show? Why, a consciousness on the part of the rich, that the poor had
not fair play; and that the former wished to obtain security against the
latter by coaxing.

Eminent Georgians preserved themselves. They did so by
pinching the lower orders, many of whom were pauperized or
pressed into the army or navy. A few were transported or
gaoled. The elite maintained itself at the price of putting its more
conciliatory, accommodating principles or poses on ice. The
Enlightenment dream that there was indeed a hidden hand,
which without human effort united 'selflove and social', creating
a natural identity of economic interests, faded with the new
century's dismal Malthusian and Ricardian visions of ineradicable
class antagonism, population explosion, the iron-law of starvation
wages, and crises of over-production. For many, optimism about
rational progress was now pie in the sky, for society seemed
gripped by forces – international trade cycles, internal strife,
inflation, demographic pressure, Continental war – beyond the
power of individuals or governments to regulate. Certain of
these forces, however – the laws of political economy – did
require the canonization of private property, for the one freedom
not called in doubt but endlessly endorsed was that of capital. As
a Commons Committee put it in 1806:

The right of every man to employ the capital he inherits, or has
acquired, according to his own discretion, without molestation or
obstruction, so long as he does not infringe on the rights or property of
others, is one of those privileges which the free and happy Constitution
of this Country has long accustomed every Briton to consider as his birth-
right.

The same fate met the easy-going morals of the Georgians.
Though still paraded by real swells, these now appeared scandalous and inflammatory to the more tight-lipped spokesmen of the
insecure respectable classes. Stricter family discipline, paternal
authority and sexual propriety were all urgently needed. 'Do not
luxury, corruption, adultery, gaming, pride, vanity, idleness,
extravagance and dissipation prevail too generally?' thumped the
outraged Thomas Bowdler. 'Every man,' reflected Lady Frances
Shelley, 'felt the need recently for putting his house in order.'

Underwriting all these came a grand-scale religious revival. 'The churches were well attended, and sometimes even crowded,' reflected the *Annual Review* just after the outbreak of the French Revolution:

It was a wonder to the lower classes, throughout all parts of England, to see the avenues to the churches filled with carriages. This novel appearance prompted the simple country-people to inquire what was the matter.

Evangelicalism won converts, even among old roués such as the Duke of Grafton. 'Vital religion' would spiritualize crumbling social relations. Religion's political message was not lost: it was 'to the decline of religion and morality,' wrote Wilberforce,

that our national difficulties must both directly and indirectly be chiefly ascribed ... my only solid hopes for the well-being of my country depend not so much on her fleet and armies, not so much on the wisdom of her rulers, or on the spirit of her people, as on the persuasion that she still contains many who in a degenerate age love and obey the Gospel of Christ; on the humble trust that the intercession of these may still be prevalent, that for the sake of these Heaven may still look upon us with an eye of favour.

Arthur Young largely agreed. 'The true Christian,' he insisted, 'will never be a Leveller and will never listen to French politics or to French philosophy.' Cobbett replied that Evangelicalism was a bid 'to keep the poor from cutting the throats of the rich, to starve without making a noise'. As Lucy Aikin remarked, 'the precepts of Christianity have been pressed into the service of a base submission to all established power.' The light of 'Reason' was too glaring. Canning jingled in the *Anti-Jacobin Review*:

> Reason, Philosophy, 'fiddledum, diddledum'
> Peace and Fraternity, higgledy, piggledy
> Higgledy piggledy, 'fiddledum, diddledum'.

'Instead of casting away our prejudices, we cherish them,' boasted Burke. 'From liberty, equality and the rights of man,' sighed Hannah More, 'Good Lord deliver *us*.'

He did. English society nosed into the nineteenth century immensely richer than in 1700, every day generating new wealth. 'The rapid and prodigious increase of late years in the

Manufactures and Commerce of this Country,' boasted a parliamentary report in 1806,

is universally known, as well as the effects of that increase on our Revenue and National Strength; and in considering the immediate causes of that Augmentation, it is principally to be ascribed to the general spirit of enterprise and industry among a free and enlightened People, left to the unrestrained exercise of their talents in the employment of a vast capital.

Yet, as John Burnett has noted, that wealth was 'being built upon a sub-structure of poverty more extensive than it has been for centuries past'. Those standing on the shoulders of the poor, however, were set fair to do very well. At the top, the Bedfords, Bridgewaters, Devonshires and Northumberlands were all netting more than £50,000 a year by 1800.

   This increase in wealth and the prospect of its acceleration had become a kind of master-key, the ideological open-sesame of society. The view from above was that nothing ought to stand in the way of the triumphal progress. Viewed from below, it was profit and credit that ground the faces of the poor. 'England had long groaned,' Cobbett complained, 'under a commercial system which is the most oppressive of all possible systems, and it is, too, a quiet, silent and smothering oppression that it produces which is more hateful than all others.' It was British finance that had won her wars and proved her imperial destiny, and the fundamental political ideology (as Marx was to recognize) was becoming political economy. Even the 'paternalist' Burke thought government could do nothing to relieve the poverty which the laws of nature decreed. 'The laws of commerce,' he argued, 'are the laws of nature, and consequently the laws of God.' Sectors of the politically excluded (including many bourgeois) could console themselves with the thought that wealth gave them local influence, understudying for some future national stage.

   Political and economic opportunism tided the ruling classes over into the nineteenth century intact, and buoyed the rest of the propertied with them. Landed incomes and peers' rent-rolls were shooting up especially fast (many rents doubled during the war years), and aristocrats were not just richer than ever, but even more secure in the driving seat of power. In 1800, no fewer than six out of twenty-six bishops were peers' sons, and whereas in 1734 there had been seventy-five peers' sons in the Commons, by 1812, 143 had blue blood (the peerage itself had, admittedly, expanded). In the 1790s some ninety MPs were returned effectively at the nomination of peers, and another 120 thanks to their influence. Pitt's wartime ministry was entirely composed of peers and their sons. The cynicism of the Regency was soon to see grandees, headed by George III's own sons, pursuing luxury and vice more nakedly, more grossly, than ever. Cruikshank's satire 'The Court of Love' starred the Duke of York (boasting 'I am proud to say that the greater part of my life has been passed in the commission of adultery') and the Duke of Clarence ('I have lived in adultery with an actress for 25 years and have a pretty number of illegitimate children'). The age of Crockfords, Harriet Wilson, Brighton pavilion and Beau Brummell's dandyism was about to dawn. And down the road from Piccadilly many others were getting a lick of the jampot: 'The people are better dressed, better fed, cleanlier, better educated in each class respectively, much more frugal, and much happier' judged the radical tailor Francis Place, early in the nineteenth century:

Money which would have been spent at the tavern, the brothel, the tea-garden, the skittle yard, the hurly burly and the numerous other low-lived and degrading pursuits, is now expended in comfort and conveniences, or saved for some useful purpose.

The THING – as Cobbett dubbed the monstrous nerve centre of establishment power, patronage, clientage, wealth, machination and corruption – had survived. A smaller percentage of the people held the franchise than in 1700, and, because grandees were still able to forestall hustings contests, even they were able to exercise their rights less frequently. Aristocratic dominion had come under fire, and the offices, sinecures and rake-offs of state had been slightly slimmed down in the cold sweat induced by radicalism. But privilege was still alive and flourishing. In his *Political Justice* (1793) William Godwin demanded *Götterdämmerung*: an end to kings, lords, priests, taxes and governments. Yet his anarchism was a flailing response to the fact that all of these were more securely entrenched than ever. Central government, spending £3.2 million in 1700, handled £51 million in 1800, its debts having risen from £14.2 million to £456.1 million (yet debts were its strength). It is remarkable how, even under pressure, so few reforms had been needed. Up to the beginning of the nineteenth century, no sweeping changes had been passed to modernize the state, so as to cope with the new scale of population, wealth and power. There was still no central police, no modernization of local government, no new mandarin bureaucracy appointed on talent. Generals and admirals retained great freedom of command (Sandhurst was a nineteenth-century invention). There was no English *levée en masse*. Men of property prized 'independence' above all else. So late as 1811, John William Ward could write:

They have an admirable police at Paris, but they pay for it dear enough. I had rather half-a-dozen people's throats to be cut in Radcliffe Highway every 3 or 4 years, than be subject to domiciliary visits, spies, and all the rest of Fouché's contrivances.

Derek Jarrett is, of course, right to state that 'by making themselves the richest nation on earth the English created in their own country problems which could no longer be solved by the old easy-going methods of local management' – hence 'the age of neglect gave way to the age of supervision'. But only in the longer run: in the short term, the English, precisely by making themselves the richest nation on earth, were able to *avoid* confronting the obsolescence of the devolved, traditional methods. Ingrained inequalities, self-help, high hopes, work discipline, twopenny tracts and a whiff of grapeshot saw the propertied through. The Georgians created vast problems they left for others to solve.

And landed society, with its entourage of plutocrats and fundholders, pamphleteers, preachers and flunkeys, was still in undivided possession of the THING. England stood on the threshold of the nineteenth century successfully – without paradox – as the foremost capitalist society in Europe, yet the one most resistant to pressure for violent change. It was business as usual.

Statistical Tables

Table 1: Populations of England

Year	Total (millions)	% growth per decade
1681	4.930	− 1.06
1691	4.931	0.02
1701	5.058	2.58
1711	5.230	3.40
1721	5.350	2.29
1731	5.263	− 1.63
1741	5.576	5.95
1751	5.772	3.52
1761	6.147	6.50
1771	6.448	4.90
1781	7.042	9.21
1791	7.740	9.91
1801	8.664	11.94
1811	9.886	14.10

Reproduced with permission from E. A. Wrigley and R. Schofield, *The Population History of England 1541–1871: A Reconstruction* (Edward Arnold, London, 1981).

Table 2: Population Distribution in 1801

County Population

Yorkshire	858,892	Durham	160,861
Middlesex	818,129	Sussex	159,311
Lancashire	672,731	Northumberland	157,101
Devon	343,001	Nottingham	140,350
Kent	307,624	Worcester	139,333
Somerset	273,750	Northampton	131,757
Norfolk	273,371	Leicester	130,081
Surrey	269,049	Cumberland	117,230
Gloucester	250,803	Dorset	115,319
Stafford	239,153	Oxford	109,620
Essex	226,437	Berkshire	109,215
Hampshire	219,656	Buckingham	107,444
Suffolk	210,431	Hertford	97,577
Lincoln	208,557	Cambridge	89,346
Warwick	208,190	Hereford	89,191
Shropshire	197,639	Bedford	63,393
Cheshire	191,751	Monmouth	45,582
Cornwall	188,269	Westmorland	41,617
Wiltshire	185,107	Huntingdon	37,568
Derby	161,142	Rutland	16,356

Chief Provincial Towns in 1801

Over 50,000		10,000–20,000 (contd)	
Manchester/Salford	84,000	Stockport	15,000
Liverpool	78,000	Shrewsbury	15,000
Birmingham	74,000	Wolverhampton	13,000
Bristol	64,000	Bolton	13,000
Leeds	53,000	Sunderland	12,000
		Oldham	12,000
20,000–50,000		Blackburn	12,000
Plymouth	43,000	Preston	12,000
Norwich	37,000	Oxford	12,000
Bath	32,000	Colchester	12,000
Portsmouth/Portsea	32,000	Worcester	11,000
Sheffield	31,000	Ipswich	11,000
Hull	30,000	Wigan	11,000
Nottingham	29,000	Derby	11,000
Newcastle upon Tyne	28,000	Huddersfield	11,000
		Quick	11,000
10,000–20,000		Warrington	11,000
Exeter	17,000	Chatham	11,000
Leicester	17,000	Carlisle	10,000
York	16,000	Dudley	10,000
Coventry	16,000	King's Lynn	10,000
Chester	15,000	Cambridge	10,000
Dover	15,000	Reading	10,000
Great Yarmouth	15,000		

Table 3: Distribution of Population in 1801

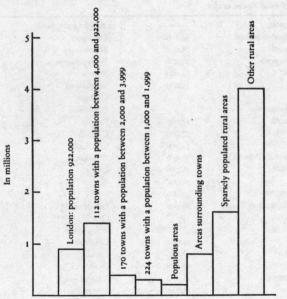

Reproduced with permission from D. Marshall, *Industrial England 1776-1851* (Routledge and Kegan Paul, London, 1973).

Table 4: Indicators of Economic Growth

Year	Retained imports of raw cotton (m. lb.)	Raw and thrown silk Imports (000 lb.)	Raw and thrown silk Retained imports (000 lb.)	Flax (rough) imports (000 cwt.)	Linen yarn (raw) imports (m. lb.)	Scottish linen stamped for sale (m. yards)	Bar-iron imports (000 tons)	London coal imports (000 London chaldrons)	Cornish copper ore production (000 tons)	Cornish tin production (tons)	Tin retained for home use (tons)	Strongbeer production (000 barrels)	Wood imports (£000)
1695–1704	1.14	525	—	34	2.1	—	16.4	327	—	1,323	232	3,446	114
1700–1709	1.15	499	—	34	2.1	—	16.0	339	—	1,426	308	3,673	114
1705–14	1.00	482	—	34	2.1	—	16.3	355	—	1,476	174	3,387	112
1710–19	1.35	557	—	42	2.8	—	17.3	389	—	1,453	194	3,483	115
1715–24	1.68	629	—	44	3.1	—	19.0	433	—	1,396	326	3,744	135
1720–29	1.55	675	—	48	2.7	—	19.7	468	—	1,482	333	3,669	146
1725–34	1.44	685	—	66	2.7	3.87	21.5	475	6.6	1,632	345	3,588	143
1730–39	1.72	645	—	80	2.7	4.53	25.5	475	7.7	1,667	278	3,606	138
1735–44	1.79	563	—	74	2.8	4.81	24.2	484	7.4	1,691	290	3,512	136
1740–49	2.06	552	—	79	3.1	5.68	22.5	480	6.3	1,744	251	3,536	140
1745–54	2.83	607	—	98	3.6	7.50	26.6	492	9.1	2,159	474	3,679	153
1750–59	2.81	670	—	113	4.2	9.04	29.3	508	13.8	2,658	937	3,777	168
1755–64	2.57	777	—	119	4.9	10.82	33.0	527	16.7	2,669	1,023	3,818	176
1760–69	3.53	906	—	127	5.2	12.42	39.7	582	19.5	2,728	913	3,775	203
1765–74	4.03	946	—	129	6.5	12.58	44.9	634	25.2	2,851	990	3,744	239
1770–79	4.80	950	—	131	8.4	12.84	44.5	653	28.8	2,751	1,089	3,957	248
1775–84	7.36	1,083	—	125	9.1	14.68	43.0	666	29.7	2,657	808	4,220	249
1780–89	15.51	1,132	—	132	9.0	17.49	44.1	709	33.3	2,958	918	4,329	275
1785–94	24.45	1,177	1,093	—	—	19.38	—	771	37.1	3,327	945	4,690	—
1790–99	28.64	1,181	1,094	242	8.7	20.89	49.9	825	46.7	3,245	822	5,278	489
1795–1804	42.92	1,128	1,041	317	8.8	21.42	43.0	875	52.9	2,881	861	5,407	558

Reproduced with permission from P. Deane and W. A. Cole, *British Economic Growth 1688–1959* (Cambridge University Press, 1967).

Table 5: Gregory King's 'Scheme of the income and expense of the several families of England ... for 1688' compared with Joseph Massie's 'Estimate of the social structure and income, 1759–1760'

KING				MASSIE	
Number of families	Heads per family	Number of persons	Classification	Number of families	Annual income or expenses
					(£)
160	40	6,400	Temporal lords		
26	20	520	Spiritual lords		
800	16	12,800	Baronets		
600	13	7,800	Knights		
3,000	10	30,000	Esquires		
12,000	8	96,000	Gentlemen		
			(Massie does not	10	20,000
			distinguish the top	20	10,000
			ranks by status,	40	8,000
			but by financial	80	6,000
			turnover per	160	4,000
			family per annum)	320	2,000
				640	1,000
				800	800
				1,600	600
				3,200	400
				4,800	300
				6,400	200
5,000	8	40,000	Persons in greater offices and places		
5,000	6	30,000	Persons in lesser offices and places		
			Civil officers	16,000	60
2,000	8	16,000	Eminent merchants		
8,000	6	48,000	Lesser merchants		
			Merchants	1,000	600
			,,	2,000	400
			,,	10,000	200
			Master manufacturers	2,500	200
			,, ,,	5,000	100
			,, ,,	10,000	70
			,, ,,	62,500	40
10,000	7	70,000	Persons in the law	12,000	100
2,000	6	12,000	Eminent clergymen	2,000	100
8,000	5	40,000	Lesser clergymen	9,000	50
40,000	7	280,000	Freeholders, better sort		
120,000	5½	660,000	,, lesser sort		
			,,	30,000	100
			,,	60,000	50
			,,	120,000	25

Number of families	Heads per family	Number of persons	Classification	Number of families	Annual income or expenses
	KING			MASSIE	
150,000	5	750,000	Farmers	5,000	150
			,,	10,000	100
			,,	20,000	70
			,,	120,000	40
15,000	5	75,000	Persons in liberal arts and sciences	18,000	60
50,000	4½	225,000	Shopkeepers and tradesmen		
			Tradesmen	2,500	400
			,,	5,000	200
			,,	10,000	100
			,,	20,000	70
			,,	125,000	40
60,000	4	240,000	Artisans and handicrafts		
			Manufacturers of wood, iron etc. Country		
			9s. per week	100,000	22.5
			London 12s.	14,000	30
			Manufacturers of wool, silk etc.		
			Country 7s. 6d.	100,000	18.75
			London 10s. 6d.	14,000	26.25
5,000	4	20,000	Naval officers	6,000	80
4,000	4	16,000	Military officers	2,000	100
50,000	3	150,000	Common seamen		
			Seamen and fishermen	60,000	20
364,000	3½	1,275,000	Labouring people and outservants		
			Husbandmen (6s. per week)	200,000	15
			Labourers, country 5s.	200,000	12.5
			Labourers, London 9s.	20,000	22.5
			Innkeepers, alesellers	2,000	100
			Alesellers, cottagers	20,000	40
			,, ,,	20,000	20
400,000	3¼	1,300,000	Cottagers and paupers		
35,000	2	70,000	Common soldiers	18,000	14
		30,000	Vagrants, as gipsies, thieves, beggars, etc.		
Total		5,500,520			

Reproduced with permission from W. Speck, *Stability and Strife* (Edward Arnold, London, 1977).

Table 6: Social Structure: P. Colquhoun's Estimates Based on the Census Returns of 1801 and the Pauper Returns of 1803

No. of heads of families		Persons in each family	Aggregate of persons	Yearly income per family averaged	Aggregate income of each rank
				£	£
287	Temporal peers and peeresses, including princes of the blood	25	7,175	8,000	2,296,000
26	Bishops	15	390	4,000	104,000
540	Baronets	15	8,100	3,000	1,620,000
350	Knights	10	3,500	1,500	525,000
6,000	Esquires	10	60,000	1,500	9,000,000
20,000	Gentlemen and ladies living on incomes	8	160,000	700	14,000,000
2,000	Persons in higher civil offices (state and revenue)	7	14,000	800	1,600,000
10,500	Persons in lesser civil offices (state and revenue)	5	52,500	200	2,100,000
2,000	Eminent merchants, bankers, etc.	10	20,000	2,600	5,200,000
13,000	Lesser merchants trading by sea	7	91,000	800	10,400,000
11,000	Persons of the Law (judges, barristers, attorneys, clerks etc.)	5	55,000	350	3,850,000
1,000	Eminent clergymen	6	6,000	500	500,000
10,000	Lesser clergymen	5	50,000	120	1,200,000
40,000	Freeholders of the better sort	5½	220,000	200	8,000,000
120,000	Lesser freeholders	5	600,000	90	10,800,000
160,000	Farmers	6	960,000	120	19,200,000
16,300	Liberal arts and sciences (medical, literary, and fine arts)	5	81,500	260	4,238,000
74,500	Shopkeepers and tradesmen	5	372,500	150	11,175,000
445,726	Artisans, handicrafts, and labourers employed in manufactures, building, and works of every kind	4½	2,005,767	55	24,514.930

PERSONS NOT INCLUDED IN GREGORY KING'S ESTIMATE

No. of heads of families		Persons in each family	Aggregate of persons	Yearly income per family averaged	Aggregate income
				£	£
1	The Sovereign, household, etc.	50	50	200,000	200,000
5,000	Shipowners, letting ships for freights only	5	25,000	500	2,500,000
25,000	Manufacturers employing capital in all branches, wool, cotton . . .	6	150,000	800	20,000,000
500	Principal warehousemen selling by wholesale	6	3,000	800	400,000
300	Persons employing capital in building and repairing ships and crafts, etc.	6	1,800	700	210,000
25,000	Persons employing capital as tailors, mantua-makers, milliners, etc., including army clothiers	5	125,000	150	3,750,000
5,000	Persons employing professional skill and capital as engineers, surveyors, master-builders of houses	5	25,000	200	1,000,000
30,000	Clerks and shopmen to merchants, manufacturers, shopkeepers, etc., etc.	5	150,000	75	6,750,000
2,500	Clergymen regularly ordained, dissenting from the established Church	5	12,500	120	300,000
500	Persons educating youth in universities and chief schools	4	2,000	600	300,000
20,000	Persons employed in the education of youth of both sexes and generally employing some capital	6	120,000	150	3,000,000

Table 7: Index Numbers of Real Output (1700 = 100)

Year	Export industries (18)	Home industries (12)	Total industry and commerce (30)	Agriculture (43)	Rent and services (20)	Government and defence (7)	Total real output (100)	Average real output
1700	100	100	100	100	100	100	100	100
1710	108	98	104	104	103	165	108	105
1720	125	108	118	105	103	91	108	105
1730	142	105	127	103	102	98	110	108
1740	148	105	131	104	102	148	115	113
1750	176	107	148	111	105	172	125	119
1760	222	114	179	115	113	310	147	130
1770	256	114	199	117	121	146	144	119
1780	246	123	197	126	129	400	167	129
1790	383	137	285	135	142	253	190	134
1800	544	152	387	143	157	667	251	160

Reproduced with permission from P. Deane and W. A. Cole, *British Economic Growth 1688–1959* (Cambridge University Press, 1967).

Table 8: National Wealth and State Expenditure

Year	National debt (cumulative) £m.	Total debt charges £m.	%	Military expenditure £m.	%	Civil government £m.	%	(Eduction) £m.	%	Total £m.	%
1700–1709	19.1	1.3	21	4.0	66	0.7	12	—	—	6.1	100
1710–19	41.6	2.7	35	4.2	55	0.8	10	—	—	7.7	100
1720–29	52.1	2.8	47	2.1	36	1.0	17	—	—	5.9	100
1730–39	46.9	2.1	39	2.3	43	0.9	17	—	—	5.4	100
1740–49	77.8	2.4	25	6.2	65	0.9	9	—	—	9.5	100
1750–59	91.3	2.9	33	4.9	55	1.1	12	—	—	8.9	100
1760–69	130.3	4.5	33	8.1	59	1.1	8	—	—	13.7	100
1770–79	153.4	4.8	38	6.3	49	1.2	9	—	—	12.8	100
1780–89	244.3	8.4	39	11.5	53	1.4	7	—	—	21.6	100
1790–99	426.6	11.6	35	19.4	58	1.9	6	—	—	33.4	100
1800–1809	599.0	20.0	33	35.3	59	4.6	6	(0.1)	0	60.6	100

Reproduced with permission from P. Mathias, *The First Industrial Nation* (Methuen, London, 1969).

Table 9: Prices

Year	Consumers' goods	Consumers' goods other than cereals	Producers' goods	Wheat prices (shillings per quarter)	Bread prices: London (pence per 4 lb. loaf)
1700–1704	101	101	102	29.80	4.8
1705–9	95	92	98	38.02	5.7
1710–14	112	105	100	40.21	5.7
1715–19	98	97	90	34.64	4.9
1720–24	95	94	89	30.05	4.8
1725–9	100	94	93	37.29	5.7
1730–34	89	88	91	25.68	4.5
1735–9	90	86	83	29.79	5.3
1740–44	97	91	94	26.81	4.6
1745–9	92	92	88	27.32	4.9
1750–54	92	87	85	31.25	5.1
1755–9	100	92	96	36.54	5.6
1760–64	98	93	102	32.95	4.9
1765–9	106	94	97	43.43	6.6
1770–74	112	99	97	50.20	6.8
1775–9	113	101	103	42.80	6.3
1780–84	119	108	114	47.32	6.7
1785–9	119	108	110	44.92	6.1
1790–94	126	114	114	49.57	6.6
1795–9	151	134	132	65.67	8.8
1800–1804	186	156	153	84.85	11.7

index 1701 = 100

Reproduced with permission from P. Mathias, *The First Industrial Nation* (Methuen, London, 1969).

Further Reading

The following lists give an indication of the works which have influenced me most in writing this book and which can be recommended for follow-up reading. I confine myself here almost wholly to *books* (whose publication place is London unless otherwise indicated). Lists of periodical articles, and more extensive reading suggestions, can be found in the bibliographies of many of the books below. The standard, if very dated, bibliography of the period is S. Pargellis and D. J. Medley, *Bibliography of British History: The Eighteenth Century 1714–1789* (Oxford, 1951). Copious listings of new works in socio-economic history are published annually in the *Economic History Review*, and reviews are published in such journals as *Social History*. Helpful reference works and source books include two volumes in the *English Historical Documents* series, ed. David C. Douglas: VIII (1660–1714), ed. Andrew Browning (1953), and IX (1714–1783), ed. D. B. Horn and Mary Ransome (1957); E. N. Williams, *The Eighteenth Century Constitution 1688–1815* (Cambridge, 1960); and C. Cook and J. Stevenson, *British Historical Facts 1760–1830* (1980).

General

Excellent general chronological overviews of the period are offered by J. H. Plumb, *England in the Eighteenth Century* (1950), J. Carswell, *From Revolution to Revolution: England 1688–1776* (1973), D. Jarrett, *Britain 1688–1815* (1965), D. Marshall, *Eighteenth Century England* (1962), J. B. Owen, *The Eighteenth Century 1714–1815* (1974), R. B. Jones, *A Political, Social, and Economic History of Britain, 1760–1914: The Challenge of Greatness* (1987), I. R. Christie, *Wars and Revolutions: England 1760–1815* (1982) and P. Langford, *A Polite and Commercial People: England 1727–1783* (Oxford, 1989), which is especially strong on the rise of the middle classes and middle-class culture; and M. Reed, *The Georgian Triumph (1700–1830)* (1983) emphasizes change. J. Kenyon, *Stuart England* (1978), is an important revision of the Stuart background.

More thematic interpretations of society are Christopher Hill, *Reformation to Industrial Revolution* (1969), D. Jarrett, *England in the Age of Hogarth* (1974), W. Speck, *Stability and Strife, England 1714–1760* (1977),

E. N. Williams, *Life in Georgian England* (1962), G. M. Trevelyan, *English Social History* (rep. 1977), P. Earle, *The World of Defoe* (1976), and M. D. George, *England in Transition* (1931, 1953, 1978). The first chapters of J. H. Plumb's *Sir Robert Walpole*, Vol. 1 (1956), offer a succinct and penetrating introduction to early-eighteenth-century society. First-rate and up-to-date surveys of society are provided by K. Wrightson, *English Society, 1580–1680* (New Brunswick, N.J., 1982), J. A. Sharpe, *Early Modern England: A Social History 1550–1760* (1987), M. Falkus, *Britain Transformed: An Economic and Social History, 1700–1914* (Ormskirk, 1987), and Trevor May, *An Economic and Social History of Britain 1760–1970* (1987). For broad cultural and literary perspectives see A. R. Humphreys, *The Augustan World* (1955), B. Willey, *The Eighteenth Century Background* (1950), A. S. Turberville (ed.), *Johnson's England* (2 vols., Oxford, 1933), J. L. Clifford (ed.), *Man Versus Society in Eighteenth Century Britain* (Cambridge, 1968), and P. Rogers, *The Augustan Vision* (1974).

Anthologies etc.

Useful collections of extracts from contemporary material include M. D. George, *England in Johnson's Day* (1928) (as is her *Hogarth to Cruikshank: Social Change in Graphic Satire* (1967)), J. Hampden, *An Eighteenth Century Journal. Being a Record of the Years 1774–1776* (1940), A. Briggs, *How They Lived, 1700–1815* (Oxford, 1969), A. F. Scott, *Every One a Witness: The Georgian Age* (1970) and his *The Early Hanoverian Age 1714–1760* (1980), E. R. Pike, *Human Documents of Adam Smith's Time* (1974) and *Human Documents of the Industrial Revolution* (1966), and C. Morsley (ed.), *News from the English Countryside 1750–1850* (1979).

Contemporary Foreign Writings about England

Foreigners' views have been discussed in M. Letts, *As a Foreigner Saw Us* (1935), and F. M. Wilson, *Strange Island: Britain Through Foreign Eyes* (1955). Writers frequently referred to in the present book include J. von Archenholtz, *A Picture of England* (Dublin, 1791), Casanova, *Memoirs* (8 vols., 1940), P. Kalm, *Account of a Visit to England*, trs. J. Lucas (New York, 1892), M. L. Mare and W. H. Quarrell, *Lichtenberg's Visits to England* (Oxford, 1938), H. Misson, *Memoirs* (1719), C. P. Moritz, *Journeys of a German through England in 1782*, ed. R. Nettel (1965), F. de La Rochefoucauld, *A Frenchman in England, 1784*, trs. S. C. Roberts (Cambridge, 1933), L. Simond, *An American in Regency England*, ed. C. Hibbert (1968), C. de Saussure, *A Foreign View of England in the Reigns of George I and George II*, trs. and ed. Mme van Muyden (1902), F. M. Voltaire, *Letters Concerning the English Nation* (1733), and Pastor Wendeborn, *A View of England* (2 vols., Dublin, 1791).

Contemporary English Writings

The tone of English social life is best captured by contemporary letters, diaries and fiction. Ones I have most relied upon include T. Bewick, *A Memoir*, ed. E. Blunden (1961), J. Boswell, *Life of Dr Johnson*, ed. G. B. Hill (6 vols., Oxford, 1934), *The Yale Edition of the Private Papers of James Boswell*, ed. F. A. Pottle and others (1950–), F. Burney, *Diary and Letters*, ed. C. Barrett (1905), J. Byng, *The Torrington Diaries*, ed. C. B. Andrews (4 vols., 1934–8), W. Cobbett, *Rural Rides* (1912), *The Autobiography of William Cobbett*, ed. W. Reitzel (1933), *The Essential Writings of Erasmus Darwin*, ed. D. King Hele (1968), D. Defoe, *Tour through the Whole Island of Great Britain*, ed. G. D. H. Cole (1962), *Selected Writings of Daniel Defoe*, ed. J. Boulton (Cambridge, 1975), E. Gibbon, *Autobiography*, ed. M. M. Reese (1970), W. Hickey, *Memoirs*, ed. A. Spencer (4 vols., 1948), F. Macky, *A Journey through England* (1714), *Priestley's Writings*, ed. J. Passmore (1965), *The Purefoy Letters*, ed. G. Eland (2 vols., 1931), R. Southey, *Letters from England*, ed. J. Simmons (1951), J. Tucker, *A Collection of his Economic and Political Writings*, ed. R. L. Schuyler (New York, 1931), T. Turner, *The Diary of Thomas Turner 1754–65*, ed. D. Vaisey (1984), H. Walpole, *The Yale Edition of Horace Walpole's Correspondence*, ed. W. S. Lewis (39 vols., New Haven, Conn., 1937–83), J. Wesley, *Journal* (4 vols., 1904), and James Woodforde, *The Diary of a Country Parson 1758–1802*, ed. J. Beresford (5 vols., Oxford, 1924–31). See also *The Diary of Abigail Gawthern of Nottingham 1751–1810*, ed. A. Henstock (Nottingham, 1980). Invaluable insights are offered by publications such as the *Spectator* and the *Gentleman's Magazine*. Roger Lonsdale (ed.), *The New Oxford Book of Eighteenth Century English Verse* (Oxford, 1984) affords a fresh look at social and cultural concerns through poetry, and Michael Duffy (ed.), *The English Satirical Print, 1600–1832* (7 vols., Cambridge, 1986) is a collection of caricatures as mirrors upon society.

1. *Contrasts*

The situation and changing position of women within the family have been most recently discussed in L. Stone, *The Family, Sex and Marriage in England 1500–1800* (1977), R. Trumbach, *The Rise of the Egalitarian Family* (New York, 1978), S. Amussen, *An Ordered Society: Class and Gender in Early Modern England* (Oxford, 1988), and Mary Prior (ed.), *Women in English Society, 1500–1800* (1985). Jane Rendall, *The Origins of Modern Feminism: Women in Britain, France and the United States, 1780–1860* (1985), and K. M. Rogers, *Feminism in Eighteenth-Century England* (Chicago, 1982) are helpful on women's consciousness. For blue-stockings see M. A. Hopkins, *Hannah More and Her Circle* (New York, 1947). C. Tomalin's *The Life and Death of Mary Wollstonecraft* (1974) is an illuminating biography. For women's work see Alice Clark, *Working Life of Women in the Seventeenth Century* (1968), I. Pinchbeck, *Women Workers and the Industrial Revolution* (1969), Lindsey Charles and Lorna Duffin (eds.), *Women and Work in Pre-Industrial England* (1985), E. Richards, 'Women in the British Economy since about 1700: An Interpretation', *History*, 59 (1974), 337–57, and Bridget Hill, *Women, Work and Sexual Politics in Eighteenth-Century England* (Oxford, 1989). Excellent bibliography is contained in B. Kanner (ed.), *The Women of England* (1980). On childbirth and women's diseases see Judith S. Lewis, *In the Family Way: Childbearing in the British Aristocracy 1760–1860* (New Brunswick, N.J., 1986), and E. Shorter, *A History of Women's Bodies* (1983). On wife-sales, see S. P. Menafee, *Wives for Sale* (Oxford, 1981), and on women's oppression see Anna Clark, *Women's Silence, Men's Violence: Sexual Assault in England, 1770–1845* (1987). For individual women discussed in the text see *Letters from Lady Mary Wortley Montagu*, ed. R. Brimley Johnson (1906), The Duchess of Northumberland, *Diaries of a Duchess*, ed. J. Grieg (1926), and D. Monaghan (ed.), *Jane Austen in a Social Context* (1981).

Among discussions of minority groups, David Dabydeen, *Hogarth's Blacks: Images of Blacks in Eighteenth Century English Art* (1985), is extremely lively, and I. Scoutland (ed.), *Huguenots in Britain and their French Background, 1550–1800* (Basingstoke, 1987) is highly informative.

The socio-economy of England in 1700 is well covered in H. C. Darby (ed.), *A New Historical Geography of England* (1973), W. G. Hoskins, *The Making of the English Landscape* (1970), L. A. Clarkson, *The Pre-Industrial Economy in England 1500–1750* (1971), D. C. Coleman, *The Economy of England 1450–1750* (1977), C. Clay, *Economic Expansion and Social Change in England, 1500–1700*, (2 vols., Cambridge, 1984), and B. A. Holderness, *Pre-Industrial England: Economy and Society 1500–1750* (1976). For its cultural implications see R. Williams, *The Country and the City* (1973). Provincial life is explored in E. Hughes, *North Country Life in the Eighteenth Century* (2 vols., Oxford, 1952–65), E. Moir, *The Discovery of England* (1964), D. Read, *The English Provinces c. 1760–1960* (1964), and W. G. Hoskins, *Provincial England* (1963). Provincial towns are discussed in C. W. Chalklin, *The Provincial Towns of Georgian England 1740–1820* (1974), P. J. Corfield, *The Impact of English Towns 1700–1800* (Oxford, 1982), M. Daunton, 'Towns and Economic Growth in Eighteenth Century England', in P. Abrams and E. A. Wrigley (eds.), *Towns in Societies* (Cambridge, 1978), J. Walvin, *English Urban Life, 1776–1851* (1984), and P. Borsay, *The English Urban Renaissance: Culture and Society in the Provincial Town 1660–1770* (Oxford, 1989). For London see M. D. George, *London Life in the Eighteenth Century* (1925), and J. Lindsay, *The Monster City: Defoe's London 1688–1730* (1978). A first-rate regional study is John K. Walton, *Lancashire: A Social History, 1558–1939*

(Manchester, 1987) For Scotland, see H. G. Graham, *A Social Life of Scotland in the Eighteenth Century* (Edinburgh, 1901), and J. Rendall, *The Origins of the Scottish Enlightenment 1707–1776* (1976); for Ireland, C. Maxwell, *Dublin under the Georges* (1956); and for Wales, D. Moore (ed.), *Wales in the Eighteenth Century* (Swansea, 1976), and P. Jenkins, *The Making of a Ruling Class: The Glamorgan Gentry, 1640–1790* (Cambridge, 1983). For imperial expansion in general see A. Calder, *Revolutionary Empire* (1981). The definitive discussion of English demography, from which all the population figures in this book are taken, is now E. A. Wrigley and R. Schofield, *The Population History of England 1541–1871: A Reconstruction* (1981). Contemporary evaluations of the social structure by Gregory King and Joseph Massie etc., are discussed in P. Mathias, *The Transformation of England* (1979).

Keith Thomas, *Man and the Natural World: A History of Modern Sensibility* (New York, 1983) offers a fascinating view of man and his environment in this period.

J. C. D. Clark, *English Society, 1688–1832: Ideology, Social Structure and Political Practice During the Ancien Regime* (Cambridge, 1985), and his *Revolution and Rebellion: State and Society in England in the Seventeenth and Eighteenth Centuries* (Cambridge, 1986) presents a revisionist and alternative reading of Georgian social history, minimizing change and elements working for change. His interpretation is evaluated in Jeremy Black, '"England's Ancien Regime"?', *History Today* 38 (1988), 43–51, J. Innes, 'Jonathan Clark, Social History, and England's Ancien Regime', *Past and Present* 115 (1987), 165–200, and Roy Porter, 'English Society in the Eighteenth Century Revisited', in Jeremy Black (ed.), *British Politics and Society from Walpole to Pitt* (1990).

2. The Social Order

Important discussions of social structure and its interpretation are to be found in D. Marshall, *English People in the Eighteenth Century* (1956), H. Perkin, *The Origins of Modern English Society* (1969), and E. P. Thompson, 'Patrician Society, Plebeian Culture', *Journal of Social History* (Summer 1974), 382–405, and his 'Eighteenth Century English Society: Class Struggle Without Class?', *Social History* (1978), 133–65. Thompson's work is extensively reviewed in R. S. Neale, *Class in English History 1680–1850* (Oxford, 1981). For recent discussion see Peter H. Lindert, 'English Occupations, 1670–1811', *Journal of Economic History*, xl (1980), 701–7, and Peter H. Lindert and Jeffrey G. Williamson, 'Revising England's Social Tables, 1688–1812', *Explorations in Economic History*, xix (1982), 385–408; xx (1983), 94–109.

The best treatments of the world of the landowners are J. V. Beckett, *The Aristocracy in England, 1660–1914* (Oxford, 1986), M. L. Bush, *The English Aristocracy: A Comparative Synthesis* (Manchester, 1984), John

Cannon, *Aristocratic Century: The Peerage of Eighteenth-Century England* (Cambridge, 1984), Lawrence Stone and Jeanne C. Fawtier Stone, *An Open Elite? England 1540–1880* (Oxford, 1984). Still valuable are G. E. Mingay, *English Landed Society in the Eighteenth Century* (1963), and his *The Gentry* (1976); H. Habakkuk's essay in A. Goodwin (ed.), *The European Nobility in the Eighteenth Century* (1953), and M. Girouard, *Life in the English Country House* (1979). See also R. Bayne-Powell, *English Country Life in the Eighteenth Century* (1937), and E. W. Bovill, *English Country Life 1780–1830* (1962).

On middling men, there is much of interest in W. Prest (ed.), *The Professions in Early Modern England* (Beckenham, 1987), M. J. Reader, *Professional Men* (1966), R. B. Westerfield, *Middlemen in English Business 1600–1760* (1915), T. S. Willan, *An Eighteenth Century Shopkeeper: Abraham Dent of Kirkby-Stephen* (Manchester, 1970), and R. G. Wilson, *Gentlemen Merchants: The Merchant Community in Leeds 1700–1830* (Manchester, 1971). Geoffrey Holmes, *Augustan England: Professions, State and Society 1680–1730* (1982), and Peter Earle, *The Making of the English Middle Class: Business, Society and Family Life in London, 1660–1730* (1989) have argued that the early years of the eighteenth century were of cardinal importance in the advance of the professional classes. *The Autobiography of Francis Place*, ed. M. Thale (Cambridge, 1972), *The Life of William Hutton*, ed. L. Jewitt (1869), and J. Lackington, *Memoirs* (13th edn, 1810), make fascinating reading on self-made men late in the century. The late-Georgian bourgeoisie is interpreted in Leonore Davidoff and Catherine Hall, *Family Fortunes: Men and Women of the English Middle Class, 1780–1850* (1987).

On the lower orders see W. Hasbach, *A History of the English Agricultural Labourer* (1908), J. L. and B. Hammond, *The Town Labourer, 1760–1832* (1917), *The Village Labourer 1760–1832*, (1919) and *The Skilled Labourer 1760–1832* (1919), and J. J. Hecht, *The Domestic Servant Class in Eighteenth Century England* (1956). For work and the working man see J. Rule, *The Experience of Labour in Eighteenth Century Industry* (1980), C. R. Dobson, *Masters and Journeymen* (1980), and R. W. Malcolmson, *Life and Labour in England, 1760–1780* (1981). For the poor see D. Marshall, *The English Poor in the Eighteenth Century* (1926), and J. R. Poynter, *Society and Pauperism* (1969). See also the works of Snell and Kussmaul listed below (under Chapter 5).

An unrivalled profile of the structure of a village community at the beginning of our period is Richard Gough's *History of Myddle*, written in 1700, now edited by D. Hey (1981). See also P. Horn, *A Georgian Parson and His Village: The Story of David Davies (1742–1819)* (Abingdon, 1981).

3. *Power, Politics and the Law*

The role of public violence in English society is discussed in G. Rudé,

The Crowd in History (1964), his *Paris and London in the Eighteenth Century* (1952) and his *Wilkes and Liberty* (1962); and in J. Brewer and J. Styles (eds.), *An Ungovernable People* (1980), E. P. Thompson, 'The Moral Economy of the English Crowd in the Eighteenth Century', *Past and Present*, 50 (1971), and J. Stevenson, *Popular Disturbances in England, 1700–1870* (1979). For a specific study see J. Castro, *The Gordon Riots* (1926). P. Slack (ed.), *Rebellion, Popular Protest and Social Change in Early Modern England* (Cambridge, 1984) is a valuable collection of essays.

For power, politics, the state, and the grip of oligarchy see J. H. Plumb, *The Growth of Political Stability in England* (1967) and his *Sir Robert Walpole*, 2 vols. to date (1956–60), W. A. Speck, *Tory and Whig 1701–1715* (1970), G. S. Holmes, *British Politics in the Age of Anne* (1967) and his *Britain after the Glorious Revolution 1689–1714* (1969), L. Namier, *The Structure of Politics at the Accession of George III* (rev. edn, 1957) and his *England in the Age of the American Revolution* (1930), B. Kemp, *King and Commons 1660–1832* (1959), and R. Pares, *George III and the Politicians* (1954); and for constitutional beliefs and political debate see J. Brewer, *Party Ideology and Popular Politics at the Accession of George III* (1976). Commentary on these is to be found in J. Cannon (ed.), *The Whig Ascendancy* (1981). On financing government see P. G. M. Dickson, *The Financial Revolution in England 1688–1756* (1967), J. Brewer, *The Sinews of Power* (1989), Peter Mathias, 'Taxation and Industrialization in Britain, 1700–1870', in *The Transformation of England* (1979). For monarchy see J. H. Plumb, *The First Four Georges* (1956), J. M. Beattie, *The English Court in the Reign of George I* (1967), and R. Hatton, *George I* (1979).

The most thorough works on local government remain S. and B. Webb, *English Local Government from the Revolution to the Municipal Corporation Act* (2 vols., 1906–8) and their *English Poor Law History* (1927–9). These should be supplemented with J. D. Marshall, *The Old Poor Law 1795–1834* (1968), M. E. Rose, *The English Poor Law 1780–1930* (Newton Abbot, 1971), G. Taylor, *The Problem of Poverty, 1660–1834* (1969), U. Henriques, *Before the Welfare State* (1979), and B. Keith Lucas, *The Unreformed Local Government System* (1980). For London local government see G. Rudé, *Hanoverian London* (1971). An eye-opening contemporary survey is F. M. Eden, *The State of the Poor* (1974).

The fundamental discussion of the criminal law remains L. Radzinowicz, *A History of English Criminal Law* (1948–   ). Discussion of the law in its social context may be found in Brewer and Styles and S. and B. Webb, both listed above, and also in E. P. Thompson, *Whigs and Hunters* (1975), D. Hay and others (ed.), *Albion's Fatal Tree* (1975), and J. S. Cockburn (ed.), *Crime in England 1550–1800* (1977). J. A. Sharpe, *Crime in Early Modern England 1550–1750* (1984) is an excellent up-to-date survey. A. Macfarlane, *The Justice and the Mare's Ale* (Oxford, 1981), is a case-history of one crime in Westmorland in 1680. J. Innes and J. Styles, 'The Crime Wave: Recent Writing on Crime and Criminal Justice in Eighteenth Century England', *Journal of British Studies*, 25 (1986), 380–435, and John Styles, 'The Criminal Past: Crime in Eighteenth-Century England', *History Today*, xxxviii (1988), 36–42, review questions of the social interpretation of crime.

4. *Keeping Life Going*

The leading discussions of population and family life are E. A. Wrigley, *Population and History* (1969), E. A. Wrigley (ed.), *An Introduction to English Historial Demography* (1966), P. Laslett, *The World We Have Lost* (rev. edn, 1971) – now to be supplemented with P. Laslett, *The World We have Lost, Further Explored*, 3rd edn (1983). See also his *Family Life and Illicit Love in Earlier Generations* (1978), and P. Laslett, K. Oosterveen and R. M. Smith, *Bastardy and Its Comparative History* (1980), and, for a brilliant discussion of rival interpretations of family history, M. Anderson, *Approaches to the History of the Western Family 1500–1914* (1980). J. Gillis, *For Better, For Worse: British Marriages, 1600 to the Present* (Oxford, 1985) is good on plebeian marriages, and Alan Macfarlane, *Marriage and Love in England: Modes of Reproduction, 1300–1840* (Oxford, 1986) argues vigorously the interplay of matrimony and economic considerations – as do D. Levine, *Family Formation in an Age of Nascent Capitalism* (1977) and his *Reproducing Families: The Political Economy of English Population History* (Cambridge, 1984) from a more Marxist perspective. For divorce, see Roderick Phillips, *Putting Asunder: A History of Divorce in Western Society* (Cambridge, 1989). Bold overviews are afforded by E. Shorter, *The Making of the Modern Family* (1976), and by Stone and Trumbach, cited above. *Bamford's Passages in the Life of a Radical* and *Samuel Bamford, Early Days,* ed. by Henry Dunkley (1893) are interesting on lower-class family life. A fine anthology is Ralph Houlbrooke, *English Family Life, 1576–1716: An Anthology from Diaries,* (Oxford, 1989). For the calendar and its customs, see David Cressy, *Bonfires and Bells* (1989).

The best broad survey of education is Rosemary O'Day *Education and Society, 1500–1800: The Social Foundations of Education in Early Modern England* (1982). Well worth reading is J. Lawson and H. Silver, *A Social History of Education in England* (1973). For universities see L. Stone (ed.), *The University in Society* (2 vols., Princeton, N.J., 1975), John Gascoigne, *Cambridge in the Age of Enlightenment: Science, Religion and Politics from the Restoration to the French Revolution* (Cambridge, 1989), L. S. Sutherland and L. G. Mitchell (eds.), *The History of the University of Oxford, Vol. 5: The Eighteenth Century* (Oxford, 1986), and W. R. Ward, *Georgian Oxford* (Oxford, 1958); for grammar schools, R. S. Tompson, *Classics or Charity? The Dilemma of the Eighteenth Century Grammar Schools* (Manchester, 1971), and W. A. L. Vincent, *The Grammar Schools*

1660–1714 (1969). For dissenting education see H. McLachlan, *English Education under the Test Acts: The History of Non-conformist Academies 1662–1820* (Manchester, 1931). For discussion of popular education see N. Hans, *New Trends in Education in the Eighteenth Century* (1951), V. E. Neuburg, *Popular Education in Eighteenth Century England* (1972), M. G. Jones, *The Charity School Movement* (Cambridge, 1938), and B. Simon, *Studies in the History of Education* (1960). Immensely revealing about ideals of culture and the gentleman is C. Strachey (ed.), *The Letters of the Earl of Chesterfield to his Son* (2 vols., 1932). On education and children, see Linda Pollock, *Forgotten Children: Parent–Child Relations from 1500 to 1900* (Cambridge, 1983) and her *A Lasting Relationship: Parents and Children over Three Centuries* (1987).

Surveys of religious developments include A. D. Gilbert, *Religion and Society in Industrial England* (1978), N. Sykes, *Church and State in the Eighteenth Century* (Cambridge, 1934), and S. C. Carpenter, *Eighteenth Century Church and People* (1959). Trends in religious thought are covered in R. N. Stromberg, *Religious Liberalism in Eighteenth Century England* (1954), and G. R. Cragg, *Reason and Authority in the Eighteenth Century* (Cambridge, 1964). The history of Nonconformist sects is handled in M. R. Watts, *The Dissenters* (Oxford, 1978), and their social significance in I. Grubb, *Quakerism and Industry before 1800* (1930), R. Vann, *The Social Development of English Quakerism 1655–1750* (Cambridge, Mass., 1969), E. D. Bebb, *Nonconformity and Social and Economic Life 1660–1800* (1935), and A. Raistrick, *Quakers in Science and Industry* (1950). On the radicalization of Nonconformity, see A. Lincoln, *Some Political and Social Ideas of English Dissent, 1763–1800* (Cambridge, 1938). Amid the vast literature on Methodism see M. Edwards, *John Wesley and the Eighteenth Century* (1955), and R. F. Wearmouth, *Methodism and the Common People of the Eighteenth Century* (1945). For Catholics, J. Bossy, *The English Catholic Community* (Cambridge, 1975), for sectaries see J. F. C. Harrison, *The Second Coming* (1979), and for hostility to such movements, R. Knox, *Enthusiasm* (1950).

5. Getting and Spending

Mainstream interpretations of the relations between wealth, economic growth and population are offered in C. H. Wilson, *England's Apprenticeship 1603–1763* (Cambridge, 1965), Peter Mathias, *The Transformation of England* (New York, 1979), T. S. Ashton, *Economic Fluctuations in England 1700–1800* (Oxford, 1959) and his *An Economic History of England: The Eighteenth Century* (1961), P. Deane and W. A. Cole, *British Economic Growth 1688–1959* (1967), and J. D. Chambers, *Population, Economy and Society in Pre-Industrial England* (1972). For agriculture see E. L. Jones and G. E. Mingay (eds.), *Land, Labour and Population in the Industrial Revolution* (1967), E. Kerridge, *The Agricultural Revolution* (1967), E. L.

Jones, *Agriculture and the Industrial Revolution* (Oxford, 1974), E. L. Jones (ed.), *Agriculture and Economic Growth in England 1600–1815* (1967), P. Horn, *The Rural World 1780–1850* (1980), and J. D. Chambers and G. E. Mingay, *The Agricultural Revolution 1750–1880* (1966). For enclosure see M. Turner, *English Parliamentary Enclosure* (1980) and his *Enclosures in Britain, 1750–1830* (1984), and also J. M. Yelling, *Common Field and Enclosure in England 1450–1850* (1977). A local study is W. G. Hoskins, *The Midland Peasant* (1957). Ann Kussmaul, *Servants in Husbandry in Early Modern England* (Cambridge, 1981), R. Malcolmson, *Life and Labour in England, 1700–1780* (1981), Keith Snell, *Annals of the Labouring Poor: Social Change in Agrarian England, 1660–1900* (Cambridge, 1985) all tell us a great deal about rural labour in the age of enclosures. For the dynamic interplay of population, nutrition and wealth, see John Walter and Roger Schofield (eds.), *Famine, Disease and the Social Order in Early Modern Society* (Cambridge, 1989).

For communications see E. C. R. Hadfield, *British Canals* (1966), W. Albert, *The Turnpike Road System of England 1663–1840* (1972), E. Pawson, *Transport and the Economy: The Turnpike Roads of Britain* (1977), and D. Hey, *Packmen, Carriers and Packhorse Roads* (Leicester, 1980). For finance see P. G. M. Dickson, *The Financial Revolution in England 1688–1756* (1967), and L. S. Pressnell, *Country Banking in the Industrial Revolution* (Oxford, 1956). Among the various histories of particular industries see P. Mathias, *The Brewing Industry in England 1700–1830* (Cambridge, 1959), M. W. Flinn, *Men of Iron: The Crowleys in the Early Iron Industry* (Edinburgh, 1962), T. S. Ashton, *Iron and Steel in the Industrial Revolution* (Manchester, 1924), W. H. B. Court, *The Rise of the Midland Industries 1600–1838* (Oxford, 1938), H. Heaton, *The Yorkshire Woollen Worsted Industries* (Oxford, 1920), and A. P. Wadsworth and J. de L. Mann, *The Cotton Trade and Industrial Lancashire 1600–1780* (Manchester, 1965). C. MacLeod, *Inventing the Industrial Revolution* (Cambridge, 1988) is admirable on patenting. For a stress on the importance of distribution see E. Pawson, *The Early Industrial Revolution* (1979), while J. D. Chambers, *The Vale of Trent 1660–1800* (Economic History Review Supplement no. 3, 1957), remains a masterly regional study. National wealth is assessed in S. Pollard and D. Crossley, *The Wealth of Britain* (1968). The question of how precisely to interpret what came before the Industrial Revolution is raised in Leslie Clarkson, *Proto-industrialization: The First Phase of Industrialization* (1985). Roderick Floud and Donald McCloskey (eds.), *The Economic History of Britain since 1700* (2 vols., 1981) offers by far the most detailed quantification of the eighteenth-century economy available.

6. *Having and Enjoying*

What ordinary Georgians actually possessed is now excellently surveyed in Lorna Weatherill, *Consumer Behaviour and Material Culture, 1660–1760* (1988). Some indication of basic styles and standards of living can be got from J. C. Burnett, *The History of the Cost of Living* (1969), J. Drummond and A. Wilbraham, *The Englishman's Food* (1957), D. Davis, *A History of Shopping* (1966), A. Adburgham, *Shops and Shopping, 1800–1914* (1964), Hoh-cheung and L. Mui, *Shops and Shopkeeping in Eighteenth-Century England* (1987), C. W. Chalklin, *The Provincial Towns of Georgian England 1740–1820* (1974), and J. H. Plumb, *Georgian Delights* (1980). For clothes see A. Buck, *Dress in Eighteenth Century England* (1979). N. McKendrick, John Brewer and J. H. Plumb, *The Birth of a Consumer Society: The Commercialization of Eighteenth-Century England* (1982), N. McKendrick, 'Home Demand and Economic Growth: A New View of the Role of Women and Children in the Industrial Revolution', in N. McKendrick (ed.), *Historical Perspectives: Studies in English Thought and Society* (1974), and E. J. Jones 'The Fashion Manipulators. Consumer Tastes and British Industries, 1660–1800', in L. P. Cain and P. J. Uselding (eds.), *Business Enterprise and Economic Change* (Kent State, Ohio, 1973) have much to say about the rise of 'consumerism'.

For the spread of commercial culture and its relations to the popular idiom see J. H. Plumb, *The Commercialization of Leisure in Eighteenth Century England* (Reading, 1973), Peter Clark, *The English Alehouse: A Social History, 1200–1830* (1983), R. Malcolmson, *Popular Recreations in English Society 1700–1850* (Cambridge, 1975), R. Elbourne, *Music and Tradition in Early Industrial Lancashire 1780–1840* (Woodbridge, Suffolk, 1980), H. Cunningham, *Leisure in the Industrial Revolution* (1980), R. Paulson, *Popular and Polite Art in the Age of Hogarth and Fielding* (1979), and, more broadly, Peter Burke, *Popular Culture in Early Modern Europe* (1978). For the provinces see J. Money, *Experience and Identity: Birmingham and the West Midlands 1760–1800* (Manchester, 1977), G. Jackson, *Hull in the Eighteenth Century* (1972), A. Barbeau, *Life and Letters at Bath in the XVIII century* (1904), and R. S. Neale, *Bath: A Social History 1680–1850* (1981). The press is explored in G. A. Cranfield, *The Development of the Provincial Newspaper 1700–1760* (Oxford, 1962), Jeremy Black, *The English Press in the Eighteenth Century* (1986), while reading is examined in Isabel Rivers (ed.), *Books and Their Readers in Eighteenth Century England* (Leicester, 1982). For London, W. Boulton, *The Amusements of Old London* (1900), and R. D. Altick, *The Shows of London* (1978) are mines of information. For particular artistic, cultural and sporting forms see I. Watt, *The Rise of the Novel* (1957), A. Nicoll, *A History of Eighteenth Century Drama 1700–1750* (Cambridge, 1925), *1750–1800* (Cambridge, 1927), J. Ashton, *The History of Gambling in England* (1898), R. Longrigg, *The English Squire and his Sport* (1977), A. Ellis, *The Penny Universities: A History of the Coffee Houses* (1956), Margaret Spufford, *Small Books and Pleasant Histories* (Athens, Ga, 1981), J. A. R. Pimlott,

The Englishman's Holiday (1947), and E. D. Mackerness, *A Social History of English Music* (Toronto, 1964).

For the position of artists and performers see, John Barrell, *English Literature in History, 1730–80: An Equal, Wide Survey* (1983), W. A. Speck, *Society and Literature, 1700–1760* (Dublin, 1983), A. S. Collins, *Authorship in the Days of Johnson* (1927), J. Saunders, *The Profession of English Letters* (Toronto, 1964), P. Rogers, *Grub Street* (1972), M. Foss, *The Age of Patronage: The Arts in Society 1660–1750* (1972), D. Jarrett, *The Ingenious Mr Hogarth* (1976), and Ian Pears, *The Discovery of Painting: The Growth of Interest in the Arts in England 1680–1768* (New Haven, 1988). M. McKeon, *The Origins of the English Novel 1600–1740* (Baltimore, Md., 1987), Jane Spencer, *The Rise of the Woman Novelist, From Aphra Behn to Jane Austen* (Oxford, 1986), and Dale Spender, *Mothers of the Novel: 100 Good Women Novelists Before Jane Austen* (1986) all survey the significance of the rise of the novel. For changing artistic styles see T. Fawcett, *The Rise of English Provincial Art* (Oxford, 1974), F. D. Klingender, *Art and the Industrial Revolution* (1947), K. Clark, *The Gothic Revival* (1928), B. Sprague Allen, *Tides of British Taste 1619–1800* (Cambridge, Mass., 1937), Sir J. Summerson, *Georgian London* (1945), and N. Pevsner, *The Englishness of English Art* (1956). For reading, see John Feather, *The Provincial Book Trade in Eighteenth-Century England* (Cambridge, 1985). The tensions between art and society are examined in J. Barrell, *The Dark Side of the Landscape* (Cambridge, 1980), and J. Bronowski, *William Blake and the Age of Revolution* (1972); see also W. Blake, *Complete Writings*, ed. G. Keynes (1972).

7. *Changing Experiences*

The fundamental, and arguably growing, individualism of eighteenth-century English society has been brought out in very different ways by D. Jarrett, *England in the Age of Hogarth* (1974), A. Macfarlane, *The Origins of English Individualism* (Oxford, 1978), and L. Stone, *The Family, Sex and Marriage in England 1500–1800* (1977). The Enlightenment dimensions of such ideas are stressed in Roy Porter, 'The English Enlightenment', in Roy Porter and M. Teich (eds.), *The Enlightenment in National Context* (Cambridge, 1981); for other perspectives on the Enlightenment in England see E. Halévy, *The Growth of Political Radicalism* (1928), J. Redwood, *Reason, Ridicule and Religion* (1976), and L. Stephen, *A History of English Thought in the Eighteenth Century* (1876). Political aspects of freedom are treated in G. Rudé, *Wilkes and Liberty* (1962). For the growth of philanthropy see D. Owen, *English Philanthropy 1660–1960* (Cambridge, Mass., 1965), B. Rodgers, *Cloak of Charity: Studies in Eighteenth Century Philanthropy* (1949), and F. J. Klingberg, *The Anti-Slavery Movement in England* (New Haven, Conn., 1926). See also J. H. Hutchins, *Jonas Hanway, 1712–86* (1940). For changing attitudes towards children see J. H. Plumb, 'The New World of the Children in Eighteenth Century England', *Past and Present*, 67 (1975), 65–95, and I. Pinchbeck and M. Hewitt, *Children and English Society* (2 vols., 1969–73). For surveys of sexual attitudes see P. G. Boucé (ed.), *Sexuality in Eighteenth Century Britain* (Manchester, 1982), G. S. Rousseau and Roy Porter (eds.), *Sexual Underworlds of the Enlightenment* (Manchester, 1987), Terry Castle, *Masquerade and Civilization: The Carnivalesque in Eighteenth-Century English Culture and Fiction* (Cambridge, 1986), and Peter Wagner, *Eros Revised: Erotica of the Enlightenment in England and America* (1988).

Various aspects of change, modernization, rationalization and secularization are covered in K. Thomas, *Religion and the Decline of Magic* (1971), A. Briggs, *The Age of Improvement* (1959), J. Roach, *Social Reform in England 1780–1880* (1978), B. Capp, *Astrology and the Popular Press: English Almanacs 1500–1800* (1979), Patrick Curry (ed.), *Astrology, Science and Society: Historical Essays* (Woodbridge, Suffolk, 1987), and Michael MacDonald, 'The Secularization of Suicide in England, 1660–1800', *Past and Present*, 111 (1986). Science and technology are discussed by R. E. Schofield, *The Lunar Society of Birmingham* (Oxford, 1963), A. E. Musson and E. Robinson, *Science and Technology in the Industrial Revolution* (Manchester, 1969), and G. S. Rousseau, 'Science', in P. Rogers (ed.), *The Context of English Literature: The Eighteenth Century* (1978). D. King-Hele's *Doctor of Revolution: The Life and Genius of Erasmus Darwin* (1977), and M. MacNeil, *Under the Banner of Science* (Manchester, 1987) are contrasting biographies of a leading scientist-doctor. Particular fields of 'rational' change are analysed in M. Ignatieff, *A Just Measure of Pain* (1978), Margaret Delacy, *Prison Reform in Lancashire, 1700–1850* (Manchester, 1986), and R. Evans, *The Fabrication of Virtue: English Prison Architecture 1750–1840* (Cambridge, 1982); A. Scull, *Museums of Madness* (1979), W. Ll. Parry-Jones, *The Trade in Lunacy* (1972), and Roy Porter, *Mind Forg'd Manacles: A History of Madness from the Restoration to the Regency* (1987) cover treatment of lunacy. J. Woodward, *To Do the Sick No Harm* (1974), G. Williams, *The Age of Agony: The Art of Healing c. 1700–1800* (1975), Roy Porter, *Health for sale: Quackery in England 1660–1850* (Manchester, 1989), Dorothy Porter and Roy Porter, *Patient's Progress: The Dialectics of Doctoring in 18th Century England* (Cambridge, 1989), Roy Porter and Dorothy Porter, *In Sickness and In Health: The British Experience 1650–1850* (1988), Irvine Loudon, *Medical Care and the General Practitioner 1750–1850* (Oxford, 1986), and L. Granshaw and Roy Porter (eds.), *Hospitals in History* (1989) all examine health and medical care. For death see C. Gittings, *Death, Burial and the Individual in Early Modern England* (1984).

Movements in the second half of the century to police popular culture more effectively, refine patrician culture and introduce respectability are dealt with in J. M. Golby and A. W. Purdue, *The Civilization of the Crowd: Popular Culture in England, 1750–1900* (1984), R. W. Malcolmson, *Popular Recreations in English Society 1700–1850* (Cambridge, 1973), E. J. Bristow, *Vice, and Vigilance: Purity Movements in Britain since 1700* (Dublin, 1977), T. C. Curtis and W. A. Speck, 'The Societies for the Reformation of Manners: A Case Study in the Theory and Practice of Moral Reform', *Literature and History*, 3 (1979), 45–64, T. Laqueur, *Religion and Respectability: Sunday Schools and Working Class Culture 1780–1850* (1976), and Stanley Nash, 'Prostitution and Charity: The Magdalen Hospital, A Case Study', *Journal of Social History*, 17 (1984), 617–28. For evangelicalism see F. K. Brown, *Fathers of the Victorians: The Age of Wilberforce* (Cambridge, 1961), G. Rattray Taylor, *The Angel Makers: A Study of the Psychological Origins of Historical Change* (1973), M. J. Quinlan, *Victorian Prelude* (New York, 1941), M. Jaeger, *Before Victoria* (1956), and P. Fryer, *Mrs Grundy* (1963). Insights upon individuals are afforded by R. Brimley Johnson, *The Letters of Hannah More* (1925), and O. Warner, *William Wilberforce and His Times* (1962). Leonore Davidoff and Catherine Hall, *Family Fortunes: Men and Women of the English Middle Class 1780–1850* (London, 1987) contains a major discussion of the 'moralization' movement, while N. Elias, *The Civilizing Process* (Oxford, 1983) remains indispensable for understanding the drive towards culture.

8. *Towards Industrial Society*

General surveys of the early Industrial Revolution include P. Deane, *The First Industrial Revolution* (Cambridge, 1965), E. Hobsbawm, *Industry and Empire* (1968), P. Mathias, *The First Industrial Nation* (1969) and his collection of essays, *The Transformation of England* (1979), T. S. Ashton, *The Industrial Revolution 1760–1830* (1948), D. Landes, *The Unbound Prometheus* (Cambridge, 1969), P. Mantoux, *The Industrial Revolution: The Eighteenth Century* (1928), and D. Marshall, *Industrial England 1776–1851* (1973). Its historiography is discussed in David Cannadine, 'The Present and the Past in the English Industrial Revolution, 1880–1980', *Past and Present*, 103 (1984), 131–72, R. M. Hartwell, *The Industrial Revolution and Economic Growth* (1971), and M. W. Flinn, *The Origins of the Industrial Revolution* (1966). Maxine Berg convincingly contends, in her *The Age of Manufactures, 1700–1820* (1985), that concentration upon factories misleadingly distracts attention from smaller scale but more characteristic economic organization. An important regional study is W. Rowe, *Cornwall in the Age of the Industrial Revolution* (Liverpool, 1953), and studies of particular groups of workers include D. Bythell, *The Handloom Weavers* (Cambridge, 1969), and M. Thomis, *The Town Labourer and the Industrial Revolution* (1974). For debates about industrialization's effect on the standard of living and the quality of life see E. Gilboy, *Wages in Eighteenth Century England* (1934), M. Thomis, *Responses to Industrialization* (Newton Abbot, 1976), A. J. Taylor (ed.), *The Standard of Living in Britain in the Industrial Revolution* (1975), and R. Glen, *Urban Workers in the Early Industrial Revolution* (London, 1984). For studies of entrepreneurship see Eric Robinson, 'Eighteenth Century Commerce and Fashion: Matthew Boulton's Marketing Techniques', *Economic History Review*, 16 (1963–4), R. S. Fitton and A. P. Wadsworth, *The Strutts and the Arkwrights* (Manchester, 1958), H. W. E. Dickinson, *Matthew Boulton* (Cambridge, 1937), W. G. Rimmer, *Marshalls of Leeds* (Cambridge, 1960), and E. Roll, *An Early Experiment in Industrial Organization: A History of the Firm of Boulton and Watt, 1775–1805* (2nd edn, 1968). For an entrepreneur in his social context see B. and H. Wedgwood, *The Wedgwood Circle 1730–1897* (1980). See also J. T. Ward, *The Factory System* (2 vols., Newton Abbot, 1970).

For the latest discussions of what essentially constituted the 'secret' of British industrialization see N. F. C. Crafts, 'Industrial Revolution in England and France: Some Thoughts on the Question, "Why was England first?"', *Economic History Review*, 30 (1977), and his *British Economic Growth during the Industrial Revolution* (Oxford, 1985), C. Harley, 'British Industrialization before 1841: Evidence of Slower Growth During the Industrial Revolution', *Journal of Economic History*, 42 (1982), 267–90, Julian Hoppit, 'Understanding the Industrial Revolution', *Historical Journal*, 30 (1987), and Patrick O'Brien and Caglar Keyder, *Economic Growth in Britain and France, 1780–1914: Two Paths to the Twentieth Century* (1978). The crucial role of urbanization is stressed in E. A. Wrigley, *Continuity, Chance and Change: The Character of the Industrial Revolution in England* (Cambridge, 1988). E. Evans, *The Forging of the Modern State: Early Industrial Britain, 1783–1870* (1983) admirably situates industrialization in its social and political contexts.

9. Conclusion

Developments in the 1790s and early into the nineteenth century may be studied in C. Emsley, *British Society and the French Wars 1793–1815* (1979), and A. D. Harvey, *Britain in the Early Nineteenth Century* (1978). Ian Christie, *Stress and Stability in Late Eighteenth-Century Britain: Reflections on the British Avoidance of Revolution* (Oxford, 1984) rightly emphasizes the sheer strength of late-Georgian society. The roots of radicalism are discussed in G. S. Veitch, *The Genesis of Parliamentary Reform* (1913), and J. Cannon, *Parliamentary Reform 1640–1832* (Cambridge, 1973), radicalism itself in A. Goodwin, *The Friends of Liberty* (Manchester, 1979), and Iain McCalman, *Radical Underworld: Prophets, Revolutionaries and Pornographers in London 1795–1840* (Cambridge, 1988). Pre-Romantic disaffection is brought to life in J. Bronowski, *William Blake* and the *Age of Revolution* (1972). R. Soloway, *Prelates and People 1783–1852* (1969), charts growing religious rejection of the Georgian century, and D. Cannadine, in *Lords and Landlords* (Leicester, 1980), indicates magnate strength and wealth. The ideological struggles of the period are illuminated in S. Deane, *The French Revolution and Enlightenment in England 1789–1832* (Cambridge, Mass., 1989). The issues of what kind of social structure the eighteenth century bequeathed to the nineteenth are discussed by R. J. Morris, *Class and Class Consciousness in the Industrial Revolution 1780–1850* (1979), E. P. Thompson, *The Making of the English Working Class* (1963), H. Perkin, *The Origins of Modern English Society* (1969), and E. Halévy, *A History of the English People in the Nineteenth Century:* Vol. 1: *England in 1815* (1964). See also E. Hobsbawm and G. Rudé, *Captain Swing* (1969). There are valuable discussions of the rise of 'patriotism' in Linda Colley, 'Whose Nation? Class and National Consciousness in England, 1750–1850', *Past and Present*, 113 (1986), 96–117, her 'The Apothesis of George III: Loyalty, Royalty and the English Nation', *Past and Present*, cii (1984), 94–129, and Gerald Newman, *The Rise of English Nationalism: A Cultural History, 1740–1830* (New York, 1987).

Index

Discover more about our forthcoming books through Penguin's FREE newspaper...

Penguin

Quarterly

It's packed with:

- exciting features
- author interviews
- previews & reviews
- books from your favourite films & TV series
- exclusive competitions & much, much more...

Write off for your free copy today to:
Dept JC
Penguin Books Ltd
FREEPOST
West Drayton
Middlesex
UB7 0BR
NO STAMP REQUIRED

READ MORE IN PENGUIN

In every corner of the world, on every subject under the sun, Penguin represents quality and variety – the very best in publishing today.

For complete information about books available from Penguin – including Puffins, Penguin Classics and Arkana – and how to order them, write to us at the appropriate address below. Please note that for copyright reasons the selection of books varies from country to country.

In the United Kingdom: Please write to *Dept. JC, Penguin Books Ltd, FREEPOST, West Drayton, Middlesex UB7 0BR*

If you have any difficulty in obtaining a title, please send your order with the correct money, plus ten per cent for postage and packaging, to *PO Box No. 11, West Drayton, Middlesex UB7 0BR*

In the United States: Please write to *Penguin USA Inc., 375 Hudson Street, New York, NY 10014*

In Canada: Please write to *Penguin Books Canada Ltd, 10 Alcorn Avenue, Suite 300, Toronto, Ontario M4V 3B2*

In Australia: Please write to *Penguin Books Australia Ltd, 487 Maroondah Highway, Ringwood, Victoria 3134*

In New Zealand: Please write to *Penguin Books (NZ) Ltd, 182–190 Wairau Road, Private Bag, Takapuna, Auckland 9*

In India: Please write to *Penguin Books India Pvt Ltd, 706 Eros Apartments, 56 Nehru Place, New Delhi 110 019*

In the Netherlands: Please write to *Penguin Books Netherlands B.V., Keizersgracht 231 NL–1016 DV Amsterdam*

In Germany: Please write to *Penguin Books Deutschland GmbH, Friedrichstrasse 10–12, W–6000 Frankfurt/Main 1*

In Spain: Please write to *Penguin Books S. A., C. San Bernardo 117–6° E–28015 Madrid*

In Italy: Please write to *Penguin Italia s.r.l., Via Felice Casati 20, I–20124 Milano*

In France: Please write to *Penguin France S. A., 17 rue Lejeune, F–31000 Toulouse*

In Japan: Please write to *Penguin Books Japan, Ishikiribashi Building, 2–5–4, Suido, Bunkyo-ku, Tokyo 112*

In Greece: Please write to *Penguin Hellas Ltd, Dimocritou 3, GR–106 71 Athens*

In South Africa: Please write to *Longman Penguin Southern Africa (Pty) Ltd, Private Bag X08, Bertsham 2013*

READ MORE IN PENGUIN

THE PENGUIN SOCIAL HISTORY OF BRITAIN

General Editor: J. H. Plumb

English Society in the Later Middle Ages   Maurice Keen

In 1350, the traditional idea of the 'three estates' – priests, knights and labourers – offered an idealized but essentially accurate picture of society. By 1500, a far more complex structure based on landowning wealth, the city commercial élite and 'bastard feudal' relations was in place. Maurice Keen traces this great transformation to give us a subtle and three-dimensional portrait of England during a major watershed in our history.

Sixteenth-Century England   Joyce Youings

The Tudor period is generally considered to have been a time of great enterprise, a 'golden age' in the history of civilization. Here Joyce Youings exposes a darker side and reveals how inflation, poverty and the population explosion, changes in domestic affairs and the collapse of the traditional church affected the ordinary people. Her richly detailed account provides an illuminating backcloth to the times.

Private Lives, Public Spirit: Britain 1870–1914   Jose Harris

'An original and brilliant overview, decisively bringing to the foreground subjects of recent historiographical debate' – *Independent on Sunday*

'Provides the most convincing – and demanding – synthesis yet available of these crowded and tumultuous years' – David Cannadine in the *Observer* Books of the Year

and

British Society 1914–45   John Stevenson
British Society since 1945   Arthur Marwick
Second Edition

READ MORE IN PENGUIN

POLITICS AND SOCIAL SCIENCES

National Identity Anthony D. Smith

In this stimulating new book, Anthony D. Smith asks why the first modern nation states developed in the West. He considers how ethnic origins, religion, language and shared symbols can provide a sense of nation and illuminates his argument with a wealth of detailed examples.

The Feminine Mystique Betty Friedan

'A brilliantly researched, passionately argued book – a time-bomb flung into the Mom-and-Apple-Pie image … Out of the debris of that shattered ideal, the Women's Liberation Movement was born' – Ann Leslie

Peacemaking Among Primates Frans de Waal

'A vitally fresh analysis of the biology of aggression which deserves the serious attention of all those concerned with the nature of conflict, whether in humans or non-human animals … De Waal delivers forcibly and clearly his interpretation of the significance of his findings … Lucidly written' – *The Times Higher Educational Supplement*

Political Ideas David Thomson (ed.)

From Machiavelli to Marx – a stimulating and informative introduction to the last 500 years of European political thinkers and political thought.

The Raw and the Cooked Claude Lévi-Strauss

Deliberately, brilliantly and inimitably challenging, Lévi-Strauss's seminal work of structural anthropology cuts wide and deep into the mind of mankind, as he finds in the myths of the South American Indians a comprehensible psychological pattern.

The Social Construction of Reality
Peter Berger and Thomas Luckmann

The Social Construction of Reality is concerned with the sociology of 'everything that passes for knowledge in society', and particularly with that 'common-sense knowledge' that constitutes the reality of everyday life for the ordinary member of society.

READ MORE IN PENGUIN

HISTORY

The World Since 1945   T. E. Vadney
New edition

From the origins of the post-war world to the collapse of the Soviet Bloc in the late 1980s, this masterly book offers an authoritative yet highly readable one-volume account.

Ecstasies   Carlo Ginzburg

This dazzling work of historical detection excavates the essential truth about the witches' Sabbath. 'Ginzburg's learning is prodigious and his journey through two thousand years of Eurasian folklore a *tour de force*' – *Observer*

The Nuremberg Raid   Martin Middlebrook

'The best book, whether documentary or fictional, yet written about Bomber Command' – *Economist*. 'Martin Middlebrook's skill at description and reporting lift this book above the many memories that were written shortly after the war' – *The Times*

A History of Christianity   Paul Johnson

'Masterly ... It is a huge and crowded canvas – a tremendous theme running through twenty centuries of history – a cosmic soap opera involving kings and beggars, philosophers and crackpots, scholars and illiterate exaltés, popes and pilgrims and wild anchorites in the wilderness'– Malcolm Muggeridge

The Penguin History of Greece   A. R. Burn

Readable, erudite, enthusiastic and balanced, this one-volume history of Hellas sweeps the reader along from the days of Mycenae and the splendours of Athens to the conquests of Alexander and the final dark decades.

Modern Ireland 1600–1972   R. F. Foster

'Takes its place with the finest historical writing of the twentieth century, whether about Ireland or anywhere else' – Conor Cruise O'Brien in the *Sunday Times*

READ MORE IN PENGUIN

HISTORY

The Guillotine and the Terror   Daniel Arasse

'A brilliant and imaginative account of the punitive mentality of the revolution that restores to its cultural history its most forbidding and powerful symbol' – Simon Schama.

The Second World War   A J P Taylor

A brilliant and detailed illustrated history, enlivened by all Professor Taylor's customary iconoclasm and wit.

Daily Life in Ancient Rome   Jerome Carcopino

This classic study, which includes a bibliography and notes by Professor Rowell, describes the streets, houses and multi-storeyed apartments of the city of over a million inhabitants, the social classes from senators to slaves, and the Roman family and the position of women, causing *The Times Literary Supplement* to hail it as a 'thorough, lively and readable book'.

The Anglo-Saxons   Edited by James Campbell

'For anyone who wishes to understand the broad sweep of English history, Anglo-Saxon society is an important and fascinating subject. And Campbell's is an important and fascinating book. It is also a finely produced and, at times, a very beautiful book' – *London Review of Books*

The Making of the English Working Class   E. P. Thompson

Probably the most imaginative – and the most famous – post-war work of English social history. 'A magnificent, lucid, angry historian ... E. P. Thompson has performed a revolution of historical perspective' – *The Times*

The Habsburg Monarchy 1809–1918   A J P Taylor

Dissolved in 1918, the Habsburg Empire 'had a unique character, out of time and out of place'. Scholarly and vividly accessible, this 'very good book indeed' (*Spectator*) elucidates the problems always inherent in the attempt to give peace, stability and a common loyalty to a heterogeneous population.

READ MORE IN PENGUIN

HISTORY

Citizens Simon Schama

The award-winning chronicle of the French Revolution. 'The most marvellous book I have read about the French Revolution in the last fifty years' – Richard Cobb in *The Times*

To the Finland Station Edmund Wilson

In this authoritative work Edmund Wilson, considered by many to be America's greatest twentieth-century critic, turns his attention to Europe's revolutionary traditions, tracing the roots of nationalism, socialism and Marxism as these movements spread across the Continent creating unrest, revolt and widespread social change.

Jasmin's Witch Emmanuel Le Roy Ladurie

An investigation into witchcraft and magic in south-west France during the seventeenth century – a masterpiece of historical detective work by the bestselling author of Montaillou.

Stalin Isaac Deutscher

'The Greatest Genius in History' and the 'Life-Giving Force of socialism'? Or a despot more ruthless than Ivan the Terrrible and a revolutionary whose policies facilitated the rise of Nazism? An outstanding biographical study of a revolutionary despot by a great historian.

Aspects of Antiquity M. I. Finley

Profesor M. I. Finley was one of the century's greatest ancient historians; he was also a master of the brief, provocative essay on classical themes. 'He writes with the unmistakable enthusiasm of a man who genuinely wants to communicate his own excitement' – Philip Toynbee in the *Observer*

British Society 1914–1945 John Stevenson

'A major contribution to the *Penguin Social History of Britain*, which will undoubtedly be the standard work for students of modern Britain for many years to come' – *The Times Educational Supplement*

BY THE SAME AUTHOR

Winner of the Leo Gershoy Prize for 1988

Mind-Forg'd Manacles

A History of Madness in England from the Restoration to the Regency.

In this pioneering study Dr Porter examines the rise of psychiatry and the asylum system, elucidates the variety of approaches to madness, both barbarous and humane, and looks at the particular treatment of deranged women. Powerful and often disturbing writings by people who were themselves insane – or *believed* to be insane – offer us the authentic 'voice of the mad', while the author's subtle analysis throws new light on the 'complex relationships between lunacy, literature and the law, between mad people, madhouses and mad doctors, between attitudes and action, society and psychiatry' that preceded the reforms of the nineteenth century.

'A major achievement' – *The Times Higher Education Supplement*

'One of the factors which makes Roy Porter's scholarly and riveting book such a goldmine of instruction is his ability to put himself into the mental climate in which the seventeenth and eighteenth centuries addressed "madness" – the other is the number of humiliating comparisons it invites with what has happened since' – Alex Comfort in the *Guardian*